PATERNOSTER BIBLICAL AND T

CW00970729

The Priesthood of Some Believers

Developments from the General to the Special Priesthood in the
Christian Literature of the First Three Centuries

PATERNOSTER BIBLICAL AND THEOLOGICAL MONOGRAPHS

A full listing of all titles in this series will be found at the close of this book.

PATERNOSTER BIBLICAL AND THEOLOGICAL MONOGRAPHS

The Priesthood of Some Believers

Developments from the General to the Special Priesthood in the Christian Literature of the First Three Centuries

Colin J. Bulley

Foreword by David F. Wright

PATERNOSTER PRESS

Copyright © Colin Bulley, 2000

First published 2000 by Paternoster Press

Paternoster Press is an imprint of Paternoster Publishing,
P.O. Box 300, Carlisle, Cumbria, CA3 0QS, U.K.
and
P.O. Box 1047, Waynesboro, GA 30830-2047, U.S.A.

03 02 01 00   7 6 5 4 3 2 1

British Library Cataloguing in Publication Data
A catalogue record for this book is available from the British Library

ISBN 1-84227-034-6

Typeset by Nottingham Alpha Graphics
and printed and bound in Great Britain by
Nottingham Alpha Graphics

I dedicate this book to my wife, Carol, without whom it would not have been written.

Contents

FOREWORD

At the beginning of the third millennium of the history of Christanity, churches of different traditions are endeavouring with sharper seriousness to foster patterns of ministry and leadership less reliant on ordained priests and pastors. This has entailed reconsideration of the general priesthood of all Christian people and the notion of a special priesthood of the ordained alone. It is to this continuing enquiry that Dr Colin Bulley's work is a major contribution of front-rank significance.

That the New Testament never calls any of the leaders of the earliest Christian congregations 'priest', despite the Jewish background, is a remarkable fact which is well enough known and still too often minimized or evaded. What Dr Bulley has done is not only to trace the emergence and growth of ideas of a restricted priesthood in the first centuries of the Christian church, with a comprehensiveness not previously attained, but also to track the accompanying downward slide in the strength and prevalence of the common priesthood in Christian thought and life. Dr Bulley has searched the range of source material with commendable persistence, to make this the most thorough study so far of a highly significant development in the structural theology of patristic Christianity.

Church traditions accustomed for centuries to use the language of priesthood (or for that matter, of ministry too – but that is another story) solely of the ordained professional will not easily promote an ecclesial consciousness of being a royal priesthood in Christ without confronting the tale Dr Bulley has to tell. If general priesthood is to increase, special priesthood must decrease. Here is solid scholarly evidence that, like the proverbial cuckoo in the nest, the two will not comfortably co-habit.

I warmly commend this book, the fruit of dedicated, careful research, to all who wish to know how, from the signal absence of priestly clergy in the apostolic communities, the church came to be so dependent on its exclusive priesthood. With sound learning of this kind, remedial action cannot be beyond hope.

David F. Wright, *Edinburgh, March 2000*

x

PREFACE

This study was first submitted to Edinburgh University at the end of 1993 as a PhD thesis and I am grateful to Paternoster Press that it now appears in book form.

In preparing it for publication I have not judged it necessary to note all the works that have appeared connected with priesthood since 1993. This is mainly because the modern discussion of priesthood provides only a backdrop to my main study. I have, however, taken note of R.R. Noll's very fine work entitled *Christian Ministerial Priesthood: A Search for Its Beginnings In the Primary Documents Of the Apostolic Fathers*, published in 1993. I have also taken some note of A. Brent's *Hippolytus and the Roman Church in the Third Century*, published in 1995. I have taken very limited note of this because its conclusions do not alter significantly the dating of the materials appearing in this thesis under the name of Hippolytus and because its conclusions, albeit in the nature of the case, and buttressed with an impressive array of arguments, are very speculative.

This may be the place to note that I have used good English translations of documents written in Greek and Latin in the early church wherever possible. Where such translations do not exist, I have translated texts into English myself, using editions of the original Greek or Latin and translations into other modern languages, almost always French, where they exist. My first degree studies in French and, regarding the secondary literature consulted, German, have at last come in useful!

I have not included an index in this book because it would have very limited usefulness. The main reason is that the book's arrangement is such as to make clear where and when subjects and ancient authors are covered.

I have had a long-standing interest in church leadership and ministry from both theoretical and practical points of view, in both the U.K. and Nigeria. I remain convinced that, if the church is to be effective in winning and retaining converts and in ministering to people's needs, there needs to be a return to the type of communal ministry that can be glimpsed in the earliest NT documents. I also remain convinced that the setting apart of certain individuals as priests, and the allocation to them of what have been considered the most important aspects of ministry, has militated against the recognition that all Christian believers are priests and against their effective involvement in ministry. I offer this study to show that this proposition is supported by the literature from the first three hundred years of the church's history and it is high time that we learnt from it.

I would like to express my heartfelt appreciation to Dr. David Wright, who supervised my studies in this area effectively and supportively, and to my former and present colleagues at Northumbria Bible College and Redcliffe College for their encouragement and support. I am especially grateful to Dr Rob Cook for suggesting the title. Finally, I dedicate this book to my wife, without whom it would never have been written.

Redcliffe College, Gloucester
January, 2000

CHAPTER 1

Introduction

1.1 Aim and outline

As its title indicates, the main aim of this thesis is to examine the evidence of the Christian literature of the first three centuries AD concerning the general priesthood of the church and the special priesthood of the ordained clergy, showing that there was a movement away from the former and towards the latter. In order to relate this evidence to the present day, it will begin with an examination of some recent discussion concerning these priesthoods. This will show the need of, and pose some important questions for, an investigation of the early church's understanding of these priesthoods. A study of the NT's evidence on the subject of priesthood will then set the scene for the examination of the developments which ensued in the rest of the first three centuries. Material touching on the relationship between the laity and the ordained will also be studied, since, as we shall see, this relationship was intimately connected with the aforementioned priesthoods. A summary and conclusion will relate the results of this study to the questions posed by the modern literature on the subject.

The first three centuries have been chosen as the main subject for this study both because they form a convenient length of time for a thesis of this kind and because they span the most significant time in the church's history for the development of that understanding of the priesthood of the ordained which came to dominate thereafter. As will be shown, the NT marks a significant departure from Jewish views of priesthood, whilst the third century marks something of a return to the ancient Jewish view.

1.2 Some remarks on terminology

The current meaning of 'priest' and related words will be derived from
the documents examined, but two things need to be made clear from the
outset with regard to the terminology employed in this thesis. The first
is that every attempt will be made to use consistently the English word
'priest' to mean and translate what was meant by the Greek *hiereus* and
the Latin *sacerdos*, whilst 'presbyter' or 'elder' will be used to mean
and translate what was meant by *presbyteros* and *presbyter*. This is not
done in all modern literature, 'priest' often being used for both. Usually
justified on the basis that in English 'priest' is a contraction of
'presbyter', this procedure had some validity when 'presbyter' was not
used at all in English, but results only in confusion today when it is.[1]

Second, the terms 'the general priesthood', 'the priesthood of all the
faithful', 'the common priesthood', 'the priesthood of the church', and
various combinations of these will be used to describe that priesthood in
which all Christians share; and the terms 'the hierarchical priesthood',
'the priesthood of the clergy', 'the special priesthood', 'the priesthood
of the ordained', and combinations thereof will be used to describe that
priesthood in which only the ordained have been considered to share.

---

[1] On this subject see Wright, D.F., 'Ministry and Priesthood: Further Reflections', *Anvil* 3
(1986), 195-6.

CHAPTER 2

Modern Discussion of Priesthood

This examination of some modern discussion of priesthood is intended only to demonstrate the reasons why a study of the evidence of the first three centuries on the subject is important, and to adduce the kinds of questions which need to be asked of that early evidence if the modern discussion is to be furthered to the church's benefit. It is not intended to be exhaustive, nor to give a balanced representation of the whole of this discussion. It does, however, represent some of the discussion and present some of the most important issues.

Nearly all of the literature referred to comes from the past 50 years,[1] and deals mainly with the priesthoods of the ordained and of the church in general. Since these are related to the larger subjects of the church's ministry and the role of the laity, some works on these have been consulted. Attempts have been made to look at both works by individual Christian theologians and documents produced by larger groups of Christians which are likely to have more general influence in the churches.

2.1 Reasons why study of this subject is important today

There are three main reasons given in the literature to explain why this subject is especially important today.

2.1.1 A shortage of clergy

Several scholars present the desire to cope with and reverse the reduction in the numbers offering themselves for ordination and the

---

[1] The sole exception to this is Moberly, R.C., *Ministerial Priesthood* (London, 1897). This was used because of its reissue in 1969 and continuing influence on Anglicanism and the ecumenical movement in the past 50 years. On this see Wright, 'Ministry and Priesthood', *Anvil* 3 (1986), 198-202 and Card, T., *Priesthood and Ministry in Crisis* (London, 1988), 35-47. No attempt has been made to update this discussion beyond what had been published at the end of the 1980s.

increase in the numbers leaving the clergy as a reason for the considerable amount of writing on the ordained ministry in the past twenty to thirty years in particular.[2] A major reason for both these developments is given as a 'crisis of identity' for both ordinands and the ordained.[3] A second reason is identified as the Roman Catholic Church's demand for the celibacy of the ordained,[4] whilst a third is the unwillingness of many churches to ordain women.[5]

2.1.2 A rediscovery of the role of the laity

Scholars have discerned the following factors as contributing to a rediscovery of the laity's role in the church: first, the relative paucity of the ordained noted above which has resulted in 'the development of the phenomenon of small congregations thrown back on their own resources';[6] second, a desire to rediscover the personal aspect of life through relationships within community;[7] third, the longing to bring about social and economic liberation and justice often linked with the keenness to bear witness to the insights given in Christianity;[8] fourth, the return to liturgical sources, at least within the Roman Catholic Church, resulting in the rediscovery of the laity's active role in the church's worship;[9] and fifth, new biblical and theological insights in the church on this subject,[10] the ecumenical movement and the World

---

2 So Küng, H., *Why Priests?* (London, 1972), 9; Harvey, A.E., *Priest or President?* (London, 1975), 1; Kerkhofs, J. 'From Frustration to Liberation?' in Grollenberg, L., et al., *Minister? Pastor? Prophet? Grass-roots leadership in the churches* (London, 1980), 6-12; Schillebeeckx, E., *The Church with a Human Face* (London, 1985), 1; and Card, 14-7.

3 So Küng, 13-4; Harvey, *Priest or President?*, 1; Cooke, B., *Ministry to Word and Sacraments* (Philadelphia, 1976), 1; Card, 21-4; and especially O'Neill, D.P., *The Priest in Crisis* (London, 1968). The very titles of *The Priest in Crisis* and *Priest or President?* emphasize this point.

4 So Kerkhofs, 'From Frustration to Liberation?' in Grollenberg et al., *Minister? Pastor? Prophet?*, 17-20; and Card, 19-20.

5 So Kerkhofs, 'From Frustration to Liberation?' in Grollenberg et al., *Minister? Pastor? Prophet?*, 16-7; and Card, 17-9.

6 Card, 25. See too Kraemer, H., *A Theology of the Laity* (London, 1958), 33-4.

7 So Card, 25-6.

8 So ibid., 26; on the rediscovery of the evangelistic or missionary responsibility by the laity see Congar, Y.M.-J., *Lay People in the Church* (London, 1957), xxiv and Kraemer, 12-3 and 28-30; on the role of the laity in the nineteenth century in responding to the process of secularisation, see Kraemer, 29.

9 So Congar, *Lay People*, xxiv.

10 So Congar, *Lay People*, xxiv; Kraemer, 10; and Cooke, 9-10. As examples of theological and biblical reflection concerning the nature and role of the laity, see, in addition to Congar and Kraemer, Torrance, T.F., *Royal Priesthood* (Edinburgh and London, 1955) and Manson, T.W., *Ministry and Priesthood: Christ's and Ours* (London, 1958).

Council of Churches contributing significantly.[11]

This greater emphasis on the laity's role in the church's life has inevitably increased the pressures to redefine that role in comparison with that of the ordained.[12] So has the perception that it has not yet been as fully articulated and realized as it should be.[13]

2.1.3 The desire to reunite the churches

A number of the documents and books to which reference will be made later in this section were prepared in connection with attempts to reunite the churches. The focus in these attempts on the issues of ministry and the sacraments, with which the question of priesthood is so closely bound up, has been necessitated by the fact that the non-recognition of the validity of other churches' ministries and so of their sacraments has been one of the most significant hindrances to reunion. This has resulted in both documents which have been produced as a result of inter-church discussions aimed at producing greater mutual understanding and agreement, and documents which have aimed at contributing to these discussions.[14]

Each of these three factors, then, has played a highly significant role in raising and keeping the issue of the correct understanding and function of the ordained and the laity within the churches near the top of the theological agenda. The priesthoods of the ordained and the laity have formed a vital aspect of this because of the importance the category of priesthood has assumed in the past in understanding the nature and role of the ordained.

---

[11] So Torrance, vii and Kraemer, 43-5.

[12] So Cooke, 6.

[13] So Kraemer, 13-4 and 17-8; and O'Neill, 187.

[14] As examples of the former, see Anglican-Roman Catholic International Commission (abbreviated to ARCIC below), *The Final Report* (London, 1982), Faith and Order Commission of the World Council of Churches, *Baptism, Eucharist and Ministry* (Geneva, 1982, abbreviated to *BEM* below), and Anglican-Reformed International Commission (ARIC below), *God's Reign and Our Unity* (London, 1984). As examples of the latter, see Torrance, Hanson, R.P.C., *Groundwork for Unity* (London, 1971), Tillard, J.M.R., *What Priesthood has the Ministry?* (Bramcote, 1973) and Faith and Order Advisory Group (FOAG below) of the Board for Mission and Unity of the General Synod of the Church of England, *The Priesthood of the Ordained Ministry* (London, 1986).

2.2 Non-priestly issues raised

2.2.1 The importance of the evidence of the first three centuries

There has been a great deal of recognition of the importance of the NT's evidence concerning both the role of the laity and that of the church's ministry. Houtepen, for example, writes of 'convergence in exegetical and historical investigations' and, like so many others, feels it important to return to study of the NT evidence in order to provide better understanding of the church's ministry.[15] He views the declarations of agreement produced within the church on this subject as made 'above all on the basis of the exegetical rediscoveries which have been made in recent years.'[16] Evidence of this can be seen in the way in which the modern literature on the subject returns repeatedly to the NT in order to discover its teaching on ministry and how that can be related to today's situation and problems.[17]

The need has also been perceived to examine the evidence of the Christian literature from post-NT times in order to establish that the view of the ministry which has dominated at least parts, and, arguably, the whole of the church down to the present,[18] was or was not in line with that in the NT itself.[19]

2.2.2 The distinction between clergy and laity

Although the distinction between leaders and led is generally accepted as divinely ordained and present from the beginning of the church,[20] there has been some questioning of the nature of the later distinction

---

[15] In Grollenberg et al., 27-37.

[16] In ibid., 37-40.

[17] So, e.g., Hanson, A.T., *The Pioneer Ministry* (London, 1961), 14-107 and 155-171; Brown, R.E., *Priest and Bishop – Biblical Reflections* (London, 1971), 2 and 13-86; Tillard, 8-19 and 26-28; Harvey, *Priest or President?*, 1-16; Hanson, R.P.C., *Christian Priesthood Examined* (London, 1979), 7-27; Houtepen in Grollenberg et al., 27-40; ARCIC; Schillebeeckx, 40-123; FOAG, 5-7, 12 and 17-27. Note too Galot, J., *Theology of the Priesthood* (San Francisco, 1984), 17-27 for his discussion of 'Inadequate Criteria' for defining ministerial priesthood and his promotion of Christ and his teaching as its source and model.

[18] Mackey, J.P., 'Another Test Case: Church Ministry (1) A View from Systematic Theology' in Dunn, J.D.G. and Mackey, J.P., *New Testament Theology in Dialogue* (London, 1987), 115, argues that a 'priestly' understanding of the ordained dominates the view of ministry even in churches which do not use the name 'priest' for the ordained.

[19] So, e.g., Hanson, A.T., *The Pioneer Ministry*, 108-118; Tillard, 20-25; Harvey, *Priest or President?*, 16-26; Hanson, R.P.C., *Christian Priesthood Examined*, 27-58; Schillebeeckx in Grollenberg et al., 60-65; Schillebeeckx, 124-160; and FOAG, 31-4.

[20] So Moberly, 89 and 91; ARCIC, section 6; and ARIC, 47-8.

between the clergy and the laity. Whilst some would continue to discern this as an ontological distinction brought about through the sacrament of orders,[21] others would see it as no more than a functional distinction,[22] whilst still others would view it as unnecessary and a deviation from the ideal.[23] Card argues that the disagreement between ontological and functional is largely due to 'two diametrically opposed views of life and of faith', the one being 'essentialist' and the other 'existentialist.'[24] Since the former emphasizes the separation of the holy, the image of the priest has appealed to it a great deal and is central to its understanding of ministry. This is certainly so in the Roman Catholic tradition, as was brought out in the documents of Vatican II.[25]

On the other side, the lack of a distinction between clergy and laity in the NT has been noted, together with its otherwise early emergence. There has also been considerable concern over its eventual results in the devaluation of the laity and their demotion to a largely passive role in the church's life.[26] Even within the Roman Catholic communion, voices have been raised welcoming the loss of men from the ranks of the clergy as 'a clear sign of its [sc. the clergy's] irrelevance' and advocating 'that priests should ... seek ... to move right out into the secular world, renouncing the privileges and securities of the clerical group.'[27] O'Neill views as relevant to the present and future situation the fact that 'priesthood, in the Judaeo-Christian tradition, is a community function exercised by all who are called together by God to be his witnessing people',[28] rightly seeing the intimate link between the clergy-laity divide and the issue of the nature of the priesthood.

To a considerable extent, then, as will become even clearer below, the issue of the right understanding of the priesthoods of the ordained and of the whole church is an important, even a central, part of the issue of the right understanding of the relationship between the clergy and the laity.

---

[21] As noted by Schillebeeckx, 218-9 and exemplified by Galot, 207-9.

[22] So Schillebeeckx in Grollenberg et al., 75 and in Schillebeeckx, 233-4.

[23] So Cooke, 197.

[24] Card, 95-100.

[25] On this see Mackey, 'Another Test Case' in Dunn and Mackey, *New Testament Theology in Dialogue*, 103-117.

[26] So Kraemer, 48-58; Cooke, 197 and 398; Houtepen in Grollenberg et al., 22-4; and Wingren, 'Der Begriff "Laie"' in Schröder, H. and Müller, G., *Vom Amt des Laien in Kirche und Theologie* (Berlin, 1982), 3-16.

[27] O'Neill, 184, quoting from and referring to I. Illich, 'The Vanishing Clergyman,' in *The Critic*, June-July 1967, 18-27.

[28] O'Neill, 186. See too Houtepen in Grollenberg et al., 23-4, on the relevance of the teaching in the NT and early church on the role of the non-leaders of the church and its connection with the NT's teaching on the general priesthood.

2.3 Issues regarding the priesthood of the ordained

For one thing, scholars have disagreed whether priesthood is a central and defining category for understanding and expressing the life and role of the ordained, and over what the correct understanding of that priesthood is. This disagreement is usually related to the correct understanding of the ordained's priesthood and the relationship between that priesthood and the priesthood of the whole church. Because of the importance of the NT and post-NT developments noted in section 2.2.1 above, these discussions have, in most cases, included treatments of the relevant NT and post-NT evidence, usually seeking to give an account of why priestly terminology was not used of the ordained in the NT and how and why it came to be so used later. Explicitly or implicitly, justifications have been presented for the continuing application of priestly ideas to the ordained.

2.3.1 The part priesthood plays in the understanding of the ordained

On one side there are those developing the traditional Roman Catholic view, for whom priesthood is the central and defining category by which the ordained ministry is to be understood and described. This can be seen from *The Documents of Vatican II*, in which the two main decrees on the ordained ministry are entitled 'Decree on Priestly Formation' and 'Decree on the Ministry and Life of Priests.' The same is true for such as Brown, Congar and Galot. This can be seen in the way in which Brown views the four main NT roles or ministries (disciple, apostle, presbyter-bishop and the one who presided at the eucharist) as funnelling into the priesthood of the ordained.[29] Similarly, Congar views the essence of the church as residing in its hierarchical structure which represents Christ and generates the church and so is chronologically and logically prior to it.[30] Galot has entitled his book *Theology of the Priesthood*, and it is the ordained to whom he is referring.

There is a second group of scholars, mainly, but not only, from the Anglican tradition, who wish to retain the category of 'priesthood' in their understanding of the ordained, but are uneasy with the traditional Roman Catholic emphasis on it and find 'ministry', 'pastoring' or 'oversight' summing up their view of the ordained better. This can be illustrated from Moberly and the Hanson brothers, from the Roman Catholic Tillard, and from the ecumenical documents on the subject.

Moberly entitled his work *Ministerial Priesthood* and defends the

---

[29] Brown, *Priest and Bishop*, 21-45.
[30] Congar, *Lay People*, 249-250.

importance of the priestly understanding of the ordained, particularly with respect to the offering of the eucharist.[31] However, after considering some NT passages, he concludes that the dominant idea in them

> is something far more general, and more inclusive of all vital activities and meaning .... It is the unreserved offering, the total self-dedication, of what is ... wise oversight, anxious forethought and rule, an unwearied guidance, preaching, teaching, discipline .... It is the care of an utterly loving pastor, ...[32]

R.P.C. Hanson, with explicitly ecumenical motives,[33] defends a concept of priesthood which involves 'a ministry of men or women who stand for God to their fellow-men and represent their fellow-men to God.' On the other hand, he rejects a 'sacerdotal' understanding of priesthood centred on the eucharistic cult and continues to use 'ministry', as he had in an earlier work, as his normal way of describing the activity of the ordained.[34] Tillard's paper, commissioned by the Anglican-Roman Catholic International Commission, argues that 'priest' is an appropriate title for a Christian minister, but 'not only does the gospel "ministry" appear broader than the "sacerdotal" function, but what the scripture says does not explicitly concern the latter.'[35]

Understandably, this same kind of view is to be found in ecumenical documents, particularly those emanating from discussions between Anglicans and Roman Catholics.[36]

A third group of scholars, mainly liberal Roman Catholic and both liberal and conservative Protestant, find leadership to be what distinguishes the ordained from other Christians. Some of these feel that priesthood should play little or no part in the understanding of the clergy. For example, Küng argues, on the basis of NT evidence, that the whole church is to serve and minister to the Christian community, so

---

[31] See, for example, Moberly, 266-8.

[32] Ibid., 284-5. Archbishop Carey endorsed Moberly's view in 'Reflections upon the Nature of Ministry and Priesthood in the Light of the Lima Report', *Anvil* 3 (1986), 27-9.

[33] He entitles his concluding subsection 'Ecumenical Priesthood' in *Christian Priesthood Examined*, 115-7.

[34] Ibid., 99-100. Ministry is even more clearly the main way he understands the ordained in *Groundwork for Unity*, see especially 26 and 46-48. See too Hanson, A.T. and Hanson, R.P.C., *The Identity of the Church* (London, 1987), 132 and 151, cf. 189.

[35] Tillard, 27-8. Cooke is another Roman Catholic who makes 'ministry' central to his understanding of the clergy, whilst even Galot, for whom 'priesthood' is otherwise normative, as can be seen from his chapter headings, unites the functions of the ordained under the idea of 'shepherd': see Galot, 135-142.

[36] See ARCIC, 29-45; *BEM*, 20-27; and ARIC, 46-65.

that, whilst service or ministry is central to the function of the ordained, it is a particular form of service which differentiates them from the rest of the community. This form is leadership or presidency, which is the most appropriate general term to be used for the functions of the ordained. For Küng, 'the term "priestly ministry" applied not to all Christians, but only to those entrusted with a specific church service, misrepresents the situation recorded in the New Testament' and so should be dispensed with.[37] Harvey, Schillebeeckx and Card follow Küng in this view, although they do not dismiss completely the use of priestly ideas to apply to the ordained.[38]

There are also those who view ministry and/or leadership as the dominant understanding of the ordained and share Küng's reluctance to use priestly terminology of them. For example, Wright argues that 'if we have regard to the balance of New Testament guidance, we will not give our ministers the title of "priest", even though we may conclude that their ministry includes a priestly element.' This element, however, is no different from that enjoyed by the rest of the Christian community except in that ministers 'may be thought of as leading or focusing' that.[39] Mackey and O'Neill take a very similar view.[40]

2.3.2 The understanding and derivation of this priesthood

It will already be apparent that different understandings of the priesthood of the ordained are involved in the above views.

For the first view noted above, as indicated by the documents of Vatican II, the priesthood of the ordained is different from that of the whole church 'in essence and not only in degree.' This essential difference is defined in terms of a 'sacred power' to bring about the eucharistic sacrifice and rule God's people.[41] As Mackey comments, 'this sacred power is ... what makes a priest a priest.'[42] It is regarded as

---

[37] Küng, 28-30.

[38] Harvey, *Priest or President?*, especially 71; Schillebeeckx in Grollenberg, 56-84; on the use of priestly language, see 75; see too Schillebeeckx; on the use of priestly language, see 144 and Card, 119-124.

[39] Wright, 'Ministry and Priesthood', *Anvil* 3 (1986), 204-7.

[40] Mackey, 'Another Test Case' in Dunn and Mackey, *New Testament Theology in Dialogue*, 114-8. See too O'Neill, 182-7 and 214-220 and ARIC, 50.

[41] 'Lumen Gentium', n.10 in Abbott, W.M. (ed.), *The Documents of Vatican II* (London, 1966), 27.

[42] Mackey, 'Another Test Case' in Dunn and Mackey, *New Testament Theology in Dialogue*, 104-6. See also 'Presbyterorum ordinis', n.2 in Abbott, 533-6; and Galot, 27, where he writes of 'the power immanent in the priesthood itself' and goes on to link this with the Eucharist in particular.

being conveyed to the priest during and through the sacrament of orders when a new priestly 'character' is mystically engraved in the person. Whilst Galot maintains that this event involves a deepening of, not an addition to, the mark already made on the person in baptism and confirmation, he still views it as entailing 'a new creation', fashioning 'a new being' and effecting an 'ontological transformation.' He considers this as expressed in 'the capacity to make the Lord present' and to be '"another Christ" in a special way .... The priest's identification with Christ culminates in the words of consecration, "This is my body" and "This is my blood".'[43]

The consequences of this identification for the church are enormous. For one thing, the priest receives

> the capacity to so lead the community in the name of Christ that it will be led more and more by the Lord himself ... to speak in the name of Christ, to proclaim the Word of God, and to expound with authority the gospel message ... to represent Christ in worship and in the sacraments, to let grace spring forth and be shared through the performance of perceptible signs, to speak in his name the words that impart forgiveness of sins, and to offer the Eucharist.[44]

He is thus 'a mediator, but on the strength of a participation in Christ's own mediation, ...'[45]

For another, 'there will never be a time when lay men and women are not on their knees before the altar and sitting before the pulpit, ... lay people will always be a subordinate order in the Church ....'[46] Finally, for the priest himself, 'the character impressed on the soul by the priestly ordination bespeaks a new being which in turn calls for a way of life to be the expression of it. ... For Jesus ... it included the renunciation of a secular profession, abstention from political involvement, and voluntary celibacy', and so it should for the priest too.[47]

As has already been noted, this view of the ordained priesthood involves more disjunction than continuity between it and the general priesthood. Congar works this out mainly in terms of different, though related, sacrifices, the general priesthood involving Christians' self-

---

[43] Ibid., 201-8. It is only fair to add that Galot strives to avoid 'a theory of priesthood marked by an excessive cultic bias that exerts a regrettable influence on the teaching on character' and broadens the view of the ministerial priesthood considerably. Congar, Y.M.-J., 'Structure du sacerdoce chrétien', *La Maison-Dieu* 27 (1951), 51-6, represents the earlier, narrower Roman Catholic understanding of priesthood mainly in terms of sacrifice.

[44] Galot, 208-9.

[45] Ibid., 143. See also Congar, 'Structure', *La Maison-Dieu* 27 (1951), 64-77.

[46] Congar, *Lay People*, xxiii.

[47] Galot, 219.

sacrifice and self-giving to God, and the ordained priesthood the
representation of Christ's self-sacrifice on the cross. They are linked via
the Eucharist, the one giving and the other receiving Christ's life.[48] This
view further presents the ordained priesthood as deriving directly from
Christ and his priesthood and not from the church and its priesthood.[49]

The second and third groups noted in the previous section adopt a
basically functionalist, as opposed to ontological, understanding of the
priesthood of the ordained, but they are divided, to some extent, over
whether this priesthood is derived from Christ directly or via the
Christian community and its priesthood.

Amongst Anglicans at least Moberly has influenced a number
towards the former view. He opposes strenuously the view that there is
any essential difference between the minister and the laity, maintaining
that the difference is that of function and not kind, and that the priest is
not closer to God nor holier nor working for God vicariously for all,
making the layman right with God. He is, rather, the representative of
the Christian body, the priestly 'character' involving 'a status, ...
capacities, duties, responsibilities of ministerial life, yet separable from,
and, in a sense, external to the secret character of the personal self.'
Priests are, 'by ordination, specialized and empowered to exercise
ministerially and organically the prerogatives of the whole.'[50]

Nonetheless, Moberly equally vigorously opposes the view that the
minister receives authority solely by delegation from the church.
Priesthood is not 'conferred by the voice of the Body simply, without
authorizing or enabling empowerment of directly and distinctly Divine
ordaining.' Ministers, whilst not 'intermediaries between the Body and
its life ... are organs of the Body, through which the life, inherent in the
total Body, expresses itself in particular functions of detail.'[51] They
therefore derive their priesthood both from participation in the church's
and from divine empowerment which enables them, and them alone, to
exercise the church's priesthood ministerially for the benefit of the
community. Küng takes a very similar view to Moberly,[52] except that, as
noted above, he sees no need for priestly understandings of the
ordained.

It is difficult to decide whether to assign the modern ecumenical
statements on the ministry to the group which takes an ontological view

[48] Congar, 'Structure', *La Maison-Dieu* 27 (1951), 66-7 and *Lay People*, 159-180 and Abbott, 27.
[49] See Congar, *Lay People*, 162 and Galot, 26.
[50] Moberly, 91-8 and 258-262.
[51] Ibid., 72-3 and 68.
[52] See especially Küng, 60 and 72-3.

of the ministry or to that which takes a functional view. Those studied all maintain that, while ministers

> are - particularly in presiding at the eucharist - representative of the whole Church in the fulfilment of its priestly vocation of self-offering to God as a living sacrifice ... their ministry is not an extension of the common Christian priesthood but belongs to another realm of the gifts of the Spirit. It exists to help the Church to be "a royal priesthood, ...".[53]

Nothing that is said in these statements rules out an ontological view of the priesthood of the ordained, but nothing definitely indicates it either. Most of what is said could be readily understood of a functional view and there is nothing that clearly contradicts it. The nearest that any of these texts comes to being decisive on this subject is perhaps in the Anglican-Roman Catholic International Commission's characterisation of ordination as a 'sacramental act',[54] although this is capable of interpretation in either an ontological or a functional way. This ambiguity is to be expected in documents which seek to unite those who hold opposing views on the subject.

Finally, others take the functionalist view of the nature of the priesthood of the ordained and view that priesthood as derived solely from the church's and its participation in Christ's. As A. Hanson expresses it: 'the priesthood of the ministry is mediated through the priesthood of the Church; both are derived from Christ's priesthood.' He also maintains that 'the ministry must not be represented as doing anything that the Church cannot, or should not, do ... it is the Church that ordains, or rather Christ in the Church.'[55] R.P.C. Hanson agrees, describing the priesthood of the ordained as 'a priesthood which concentrates and expresses within the Church the priestly functions which the whole Church corporately possesses because it is united with Christ, the High Priest par excellence.'[56]

A central area of disagreement concerning the priesthood of the ordained, then, concerns whether this priesthood involves an ontological or essential difference between the ordained and the laity or only a

---

[53] ARIC, 36, quoted with approval in FOAG, 83; see also FOAG, 97 and 99 and ARIC, 51. *BEM*, 23, is similar.

[54] ARIC, 36 and 42.

[55] Hanson, A.T., *The Pioneer Ministry*, 166 and 155-6. He also argues that 'if Moberly had taken his admirable doctrine of representative priesthood seriously, he too would have arrived at this conclusion.'

[56] Hanson, R.P.C., *Groundwork*, 47. See also Hanson, R.P.C., *Christian Priesthood Examined*, 28 and 100-101, and Hanson, A.T. and R.P.C, *The Identity of the Church*, 153. Wright, 'Ministry and Priesthood', *Anvil* 3 (1986), 206-7, reaches much the same conclusion.

functional one. Another concerns its derivation: does it derive directly from Christ in a way different from that of the Christian community, or does it derive only indirectly from Christ, representing and focusing his priesthood as it is enjoyed by the Christian community? These areas of disagreement are further related to different ways of justifying the application of priestly ideas to the ordained.

2.3.3 Justifications of priestly understandings of the ordained

It is the nature of Christianity as a religion based on writings regarded as peculiarly authoritative and on historical events and developments that makes arguments concerning the NT and other early Christian evidence important in justifying priestly understandings of the ordained. The early post-NT evidence becomes particularly important because such ideas and language are never unambiguously so used in the NT, a fact that has become increasingly recognized among even those for whom that priestliness is vital.[57]

In spite of this, attempts at justification are still made on the basis of the NT. One way of doing this is to argue from apostolic succession. This can be seen in the decree 'Presbyterorum Ordinis' adopted by the Second Vatican Council: 'Christ sent the apostles just as He Himself had been sent by the Father.[58] Through these same apostles He made their successors, the bishops, sharers in His consecration and mission. Their ministerial role has been handed down to priests in a limited degree.'[59]

Galot similarly traces the institution of the ministerial priesthood back to the institution of the twelve apostles.[60] He also argues that, whilst 'a priesthood conceived only as a cultic and ritual function does not correspond to Paul's conception of his own mission ..., Paul does not hesitate to use cultic terminology when describing his own apostolic mission.' He cites Romans 1:9, 15:15-16 and Philippians 2:17 as evidence.[61]

These last passages, then, are sometimes used to justify the application of priestly ideas to the ordained. Even as radical a Roman Catholic as Schillebeeckx finds that they indicate 'indirect tendencies'

---

[57] For example, Congar, *Lay People*, 136 and 139.
[58] Here reference is made, in a footnote, to Jn. 20:21.
[59] Abbott, 534.
[60] Galot, 71-91. O'Neill, 103, also argues that 'the priest role was implicit in the Church from the beginning and is clearly part of the identification of Christ's role and mission'.
[61] Galot, 95-6 and 23-8.

in the direction of talking 'about the priestly service of ministers.'[62]

Moberly is expressing the exegesis of an earlier time in his arguments to prove that presbyters and bishops were the ones who led eucharistic services in NT times,[63] but his centring of the origins of the ministerial priesthood in Christ's institution of the memorial of his self-sacrifice and his arguments to show that that memorial was understood sacrificially[64] enjoy more widespread support. Congar, for example, whilst acknowledging that 'the application of a sacrificial and sacerdotal vocabulary to external Christian worship is relatively late, and at the beginning was obviously shunned', finds continuity in 'the eucharist and its sacrificial import: from Irenaeus back to Justin, from Justin to Ignatius and the *Didache*, from thence to Clement and the apostolic writings, the celebration of the eucharist as a sacrificial worship can be followed.'[65]

Brown takes the view that 'the Eucharist was seen as an unbloody sacrifice ... in Christian writings about the end of the 1st century or the beginning of the 2nd', citing the *Didache* and *1 Clement*, but also argues that, 'by giving special significance to the elements of the (Passover?) meal that he ate with his disciples on the night before he died, Jesus supplied his followers with a community rite that would ultimately be seen as a sacrifice and whose celebrants would hence be understood as priests.'[66]

Brown's main argument to justify viewing the ordained as priests, however, is that the priesthood, the papacy and episcopacy are 'given institutions of grace within the Roman Catholic Church whose development has been guided by the Spirit.' Although aware that not 'every development within the Church is the work of the Spirit,' he states, 'I would not know what guidance of the Church by the Spirit could mean if it did not include the fundamental shaping of the special ministry which is so intimately concerned with Christian communal and sacramental life.'[67]

Tillard, the Anglican-Roman Catholic International Commision and the Faith and Order Advisory Group of the Church of England also

---

[62] Schillebeeckx, 144. Rom. 15:16 is also referred to in the context of explaining and justifying the priesthood of the ordained in *BEM*, 23.

[63] Moberly, 266-8.

[64] Ibid., 265-272.

[65] Congar, *Lay People*, 139. There is a lack of clarity in Congar's treatment as to how early he views the sacrificial understanding of the Eucharist as arising but this quotation implies that it is present in the apostolic, NT writings.

[66] Brown, *Priest and Bishop*, 19-20; see also 16-18.

[67] Ibid., 4. FOAG, 15-6, employs much the same kind of argument.

justify the application of priestly language to the ordained on the basis of the part they play in the eucharistic sacrifice and so in Christ's priesthood.[68]

As noted earlier, some justify the priesthood of the ordained on the basis of its derivation from Christ. This underlies the arguments already adduced that Christ instituted this priesthood in instituting the twelve apostles or in instituting the eucharist as a memorial of his self-sacrifice. Correspondingly, some justify it on the basis of its link with the priesthood of the Christian community. Whilst the basis for the latter priesthood is, of course, found in the NT writings, no such basis is usually sought for the link between the two. Nor is a basis sought in the early history of the church.

There are, however, different ways of presenting and arguing for the link between the priesthoods of the ordained and of the whole church. One is to point out the obvious, which is that since the ordained are baptized members of the church they necessarily share in the priesthood of the whole church. This makes their priesthood no different from that of the rest of the church, a view reflected in Wright's contention that 'we have no New Testament warrant for attributing to specific individuals a priestly function that goes beyond the range of functions appropriate to the priesthood of all the faithful.' And later: 'it is my contention that the New Testament's failure to designate ministers as priests, that is, to distinguish them qua priests in any way from the general Christian priesthood, must lead us to conclude that no-one in the body partakes in the priestly ministry of the risen Christ in a way that is different from the rest of the body's participation in it.'[69]

A second, and more popular, way of linking these two priesthoods is to argue that that of the ordained represents that of the whole Christian community in particular instances. So, for example, the Anglican-Roman Catholic International Commission argues that 'not only do [ministers] share through baptism in the priesthood of the people of God, but they are - particularly in presiding at the eucharist - representative of the whole Church in the fulfilment of its priestly vocation of self-offering to God as a living sacrifice (Rom. 12.1).'[70] The Hanson brothers are particularly fond of this kind of argument.[71]

A third way of connecting the priesthoods of the ordained and the whole church is to view the former as building up the latter. Indeed, the

---

[68] Tillard, 26-27; ARCIC, 41-2 and 35; and FOAG, 99.

[69] Wright, 'Ministry and Priesthood', *Anvil* 3 (1986), 206.

[70] ARCIC, 36.

[71] Hanson, R.P.C., *Groundwork*, 47. See too Hanson, R.P.C., *Christian Priesthood Examined*, 28 and 100-101 and Hanson, A.T. and R.P.C., 153.

Anglican-Roman Catholic International Commission uses this idea to support the view that the Christian ministry 'is not an extension of the common Christian priesthood but belongs to another realm of the gifts of the Spirit.' It continues immediately, 'It exists to help the Church to be "a royal priesthood", ...' This view is popular in ecumenical documents, being also found in *Baptism, Eucharist and Ministry* and the report of the Anglican-Reformed International Commission.[72]

Less popular in modern literature has been the attempt to trace a connection between the Levitical priesthood and that of the ordained. Tillard, having argued that the minister can be spoken of as priestly because of his words and gestures in the memorial of the Eucharist, points out that this belongs to the ritual realm, as did the Levitical sacrifices, and not to the existential, as do the priesthoods of Christ and of all Christians. Although the priesthood of the ordained is unique, there is a correct analogy to be drawn with the Levitical priesthood.[73]

A final kind of justification for a priestly understanding of the ordained is provided by R.P.C. Hanson, albeit only as a suggestion. He notes that 'a great many other religions besides Christianity, perhaps the majority of religions, have had priests', arguing that Christianity 'probably learnt from the example of pagan religions that most men find it difficult to understand or approach God without the aid of a man who in some sense stands for God, represents him, and feels called to devote himself to this representative ministry.' He concludes that this 'suggests that there is something natural and universal about priesthood.'[74] Harvey, however, views this sense of the need of a priesthood for these purposes as dying out today.[75]

Finally, as noted at the end of sections 2.2.2 and 2.3.1 above, some see great dangers in the continuing distinction between clergy and laity and others argue that priestly language and ideas hold dangers if applied to the ordained in any way differently from the way they are true of the church as a whole.

2.4 Summary and relevance of these issues to this study

Section 2.1 gave three general reasons for the importance of pursuing study of the roles of the ordained and the laity, particularly with regard to the understanding of their priesthoods and how these are to be

---

[72] ARCIC, 36; *BEM*, 23; ARIC, 50-51. The same view is expressed by Schillebeeckx in Grollenberg, 75.

[73] Tillard, 27, cf. Brown, *Priest and Bishop*, 5.

[74] Hanson, R.P.C., *Christian Priesthood Examined*, 100.

[75] Harvey, *Priest or President?*, 32-3.

expressed. Sections 2.2.1 and 2.3 showed the significance of examination of the evidence of the documents of the early church concerning these priesthoods. Section 2.2.2 demonstrated the need felt by some to question the distinction between the clergy and the laity, a distinction with which that between the priesthoods of the ordained and of the whole church has, recently at least, been closely linked. 2.3.1 illustrated the great variety of understandings of the centrality and importance of the priesthood of the ordained for the life of the church, from those who view it as absolutely essential to those who feel it is right to dispense with it completely, at least in some of its forms. 2.3.2 exhibited the wide disagreement over the nature and derivation of the priesthood of the ordained, especially between those who regard it as derived directly from Christ and those who hold it to be derived from the church, and between those who see an ontological difference and those who see no more than a functional difference between the priesthoods of the church and of the ordained. 2.3.3 to some extent linked the earlier sections to the different ways in which the application of priestly ideas to the ordained has been justified.

Although this study will examine evidence directly and indirectly relevant to the other issues mentioned, it is the questions posed by section 2.3.3 in particular which will be directly addressed. The central question underlying this study is: Is the application of priestly ideas and language to the ordained in a way different to the way in which they are applied to the church as a whole justified? The answer has obvious relevance to the other issues raised above, as have answers to subsidiary questions treated, which will be the nature of the two priesthoods under examination, their relationship to each other, and their relationship to Christ's.

Since some justifications seek a direct or implied basis in the NT we shall begin with an investigation of the NT evidence. It will seek to answer the questions: Is there evidence in the NT that church leaders were understood as priests in the earliest church, or that the eucharist was viewed as a sacrifice which implied the priesthood of those who presided at it? What evidence is there regarding attitudes to priesthood and cult, and what does this imply concerning the priesthood of church leaders?

Since other justifications relate to the development of a priestly understanding of church leaders in the post-NT period and the claim, whether explicit or implicit, that this occurred under the impetus of God the Holy Spirit, the study will continue with an examination of the evidence from the post-NT period up to AD 300. It will seek to address the questions: How soon, how, and why did the ordained come to be understood as priests in a way different from the Christian community in general, and are the reasons congruent with NT attitudes to priesthood and cult? In particular, is there evidence that the understanding of the ordained as priestly in a different way from the Christian community helped or hindered the sense of the priesthood of that community?[76] These questions are asked on the assumptions that the church, as understood and described by the writers of the NT, was inspired by the Holy Spirit and that the Holy Spirit would not subsequently lead the church in ways which contradicted or harmed the earlier ways in which he led it. It is not possible to present a defence of these assumptions here, but they are shared by many in the worldwide Christian community.

In order to answer these questions we shall examine the development of the understandings of the priesthoods of the ordained and of the whole church, and of the relationship between the clergy and the laity. In a conclusion we shall seek to relate what has been discovered to the issues raised in this chapter.

---

[76] Note here the comment by Hanson, R.P.C. in *Christian Priesthood Examined*, 98, that a sacerdotal, as opposed to a representative, view of the priesthood 'appears to obscure completely, if not actually to abolish, the doctrine of the priesthood of all believers. It drains believers' priesthood ... all away into the priesthood of the clergy.'

CHAPTER 3

Priesthood in the New Testament

In chapter 2 we noted that many of the arguments used to justify the application of priestly ideas to the ordained were based on the NT. In this chapter, we shall first consider these arguments and the passages used as a basis for them. Next, to help provide a foundation for assessing further whether priestly language and ideas are validly used for the ordained as far as the NT is concerned, we shall survey attitudes to priesthood and cult in the NT. Then, to enlarge that foundation, we shall investigate relevant NT teaching concerning the Christian, the church and the church's ministry. Finally, we shall seek to assess the significance of the evidence examined with regard to the overall view of priesthood in the NT and its relevance to understanding the ordained in priestly terms.

3.1 Are church leaders viewed as priests in the NT in a way different from other believers?

The investigation of justifications of a priestly understanding of the ordained in section 2.3.3 demonstrated that evidence derived from the NT is used in a variety of ways for this purpose. These will now be considered.

3.1.1 Evidence that Jesus instituted the Twelve to share and pass on his priestly mission

Galot is the most recent author studied to argue along these lines. He first points to Jesus' statement, 'Destroy this temple, and in three days I will raise it up'[1] (Jn. 2:19), as alluding both to Christ's resurrection and

---

[1] All quotations from the Bible are taken from *The Holy Bible containing the Old and New Testaments, Revised Standard Version* (London, 1952) or from K. Aland et al. (eds.), *The Greek New Testament*, (Stuttgart, 1983³), unless otherwise specified.

to 'the erection of a new temple, that is, of a new cult and of a new priesthood.'[2] Later, he argues that Jesus chose the Twelve in a new act of creation resulting in a new ontological priesthood for an essential role in establishing the church.[3] Whilst the Twelve's essential role may be conceded, Galot's exegetical arguments concerning Christ performing a new act of creation resulting in a new, ontological priesthood are not convincing. His first argument is that, in Greek, Mark writes, 'And he *made* twelve' (Mk. 3:14), the same verb as used in Genesis and Isaiah of God's work of creating the universe and as used in 1 Kings 13:33 and 2 Chronicles 13:9 of making priests (cf. Heb. 3:2 and Rev. 5:10). His second argument is that the apostles are given a new personality since three are given new names (Mk. 3:16-17) and they are all named apostles (Lk. 6:13). It is more likely that 'he made' should be translated and understood as 'he appointed', as would be perfectly natural in the other cases of the use of this verb with a personal object cited by Galot.[4] Moreover, the new names are more easily understood of their future functions than of any new personality.[5]

Galot further notes that the mission of the Twelve as described in Mark 3:14 is modelled on Jesus' mission and that the 'power to cast out devils' indicates 'a supernatural power' to carry out that mission. The privilege mentioned in Mark 4:11 and Matthew 13:11 is interpreted as indicating that the whole project of the kingdom is put into their hands, a contrast with everyone else being made in the words '"... for the rest there are only parables" (Lk. 8:10).'[6] It is not certain, however, that only the Twelve are being referred to in this last passage,[7] and there is no indication that the power mentioned in Mark 3:14 was to be restricted to the Twelve in the future.

Galot admits that, 'at the beginning, the Twelve represent God's new people' but argues from the eschatological saying in Matthew 19:28 that they are 'to rule over the new Israel. ... What we have here is a declaration relative not to the Second Coming but to the unfolding of the

---

[2] Galot, 35.
[3] Ibid., 72-4.
[4] So, for example, Taylor, V., *The Gospel According to St. Mark* (London, 1966), 230 and Cranfield, C.E.B., *The Cambridge Greek Testament Commentary: The Gospel according to St Mark* (Cambridge, 1972), 126-7.
[5] So ibid., 130-131.
[6] Galot, 74-5.
[7] Lk. 8:9 shows that Christ's disciples are being spoken to, and there can be no certainty that this meant only the Twelve since many women are also mentioned in Lk. 8:2-3 as having been travelling with Jesus at this time. Further, in Mk. 4:10 it is 'those who were about him with the twelve' to whom Jesus speaks.

New Israel, that is, to the life of the Church.'[8] It is more likely, however, that future rather than realized eschatology is meant here.[9] The idea of those who overcome ruling with Christ in the future is also found in Revelation 3:21 and 20:4, both of which imply future rather than realized eschatology.

Galot goes on to argue that, in the Lucan version of this passage (Lk. 22:28-30), 'the power to rule is associated with the power to eat and drink at the table of Christ, that is, to celebrate the Eucharist. Luke had just quoted Jesus' words: "Do this as a memorial of me" (Lk. 22:19), the words that establish the empowering of the apostles to preside at the eucharistic celebration.'[10] It is unlikely, however, that eating and drinking at Christ's table implies presiding at, rather than participating in, the eucharist, which is, in any case, a secondary allusion here, the primary being to the future messianic banquet.[11]

Finally, Galot interprets John 20:20-22 as showing that 'the power to remit sins is conferred by the risen Christ upon the disciples, ...'[12] More probable is Lindars' interpretation that 'the commissioning is of the disciples in the name of the whole Church for its mission to the world.'[13]

Not only is Galot's exegesis to be questioned, but none of the above passages clearly implies, much less explicitly states, the priesthood of the Twelve, except, perhaps, for presidency at the Eucharist, which will be examined below. Whether the Twelve enter into Christ's priestly mission in a way different from the rest of the church, and, if so, in what that difference consists, will also be examined further below. What is used by Galot to clarify the fact that the apostles and church leaders were seen as priests in the NT is evidence from Hebrews and from Paul.

3.1.2 Explicit evidence that apostles and church leaders were viewed as priests in the time of the NT

Many scholars view Paul's statement in Romans 15:15-16 as showing

---

[8] Galot, 76.

[9] See Büchsel in Kittel, G. and Friedrich, G. (eds.), *Theological Dictionary of the New Testament (TDNT* below: Grand Rapids, 1964-1976), vol.1, 688.

[10] Galot, 76.

[11] So Marshall, I.H., *The Gospel of Luke (New International Greek Testament Commentary)* (Exeter, 1978), 817.

[12] Galot, 77.

[13] Lindars, B., *The Gospel of John (NCB Commentary)* (London, 1972), 611; see too Brown, R.E., *The Gospel According to John* (London, 1966), vol.2, 1038-9.

that Paul understood his apostolate as a kind of priesthood.[14] In this verse Paul tells the Roman Christians that he has reminded them of certain things in his letter 'because of the grace given me by God to be a minister of Christ Jesus to the Gentiles in the priestly service of the gospel of God, so that the offering of the Gentiles may be acceptable, sanctified by the Holy Spirit.' As the commentators generally agree,[15] Paul is applying cultic and priestly language to his ministry here. What is debatable is whether Paul views his ministry as an apostle as priestly in a way different from Christians who are not apostles and, if he does, whether he views that priestly, apostolic ministry as to be transferred by him to those whom he ordains as leaders of the church. A reference to his special calling to preach the gospel to the Gentiles seems likely since he prefaces this passage with 'because of the grace given me by God ...' and in 1:5 states that through Christ 'we have received grace and apostleship to bring about the obedience of faith for the sake of his name among all the nations, ...' However, if Paul is alluding to his peculiar apostleship to the Gentiles (cf. Gal. 2:7-9),[16] this would probably not be transferable at all. Even if it were, it would fit itinerant evangelists far better than static church leaders.

On the other hand, the content of the sacrifice which Paul offers as a priest in preaching the gospel seems to be 'Gentile Christians who have been sanctified by the gift of the Holy Spirit.'[17] An alternative interpretation is therefore that he is describing as a priestly ministry the bringing of non-Christians to faith through the preaching of the gospel, and not just his own, peculiar calling to preach to the Gentiles. But the preaching of the gospel to unbelievers, whilst a major part of what the apostles were called to do, was also a part of what a more static church leader such as Timothy was told to do (2 Tim. 4:5) and was not seen as

---

[14] For example, Scott, W.M.F., 'Priesthood in the New Testament', *Scottish Journal of Theology* 10 (1957), 413-4; Colson, J., *La fonction diaconale aux origines de l'Église* (Bruges, 1960), 74-6 and *Ministre de Jésus-Christ ou le sacerdoce de l'évangile* (Paris, 1966), 182; Sesboüé in Delorme, J. (ed.), *Le ministère et les ministères selon le Nouveau Testament* (Paris, 1974), 407, n.65; Vidal in ibid., 476; Galot, 95-6; and Schillebeeckx, 144.
[15] The distinction made by Barth and supported by Cranfield, C.E.B., *A Critical and Exegetical Commentary on the Epistle to the Romans (ICC)* (Edinburgh, 1975-1979), vol.2, 755, that Paul likens himself to a Levite serving the priestly ministry of Christ is rightly condemned as 'too strained' by Dunn, J.D.G., *Romans 9-16 (Word Biblical Commentary)* (Dallas, 1988), 859.
[16] So Käsemann, E., *Commentary on Romans* (London, 1980), 392.
[17] Cranfield, *Romans*, vol.2, 757. Dunn, 860, rightly regards it as impossible to be sure whether Paul had the Gentile Christians' self-offering in mind, a view upheld by several scholars: Congar, *Lay People*, 126; Grelot, Sesboüé and Vidal in Delorme, 54, 407 and 476; and Vanhoye, A., *Old Testament Priests and the New Priest According to the New Testament* (Petersham, 1986), 269.

confined to apostles and church leaders. This is clear from the way in which those who left Jerusalem because of the persecution which arose there on Stephen's martyrdom are presented as having gone about 'preaching the word' (Acts 8:4).[18] Further evidence of this will be examined below in section 3.3.2. The Roman Catholic scholar, Daly, points out that the function of the general Christian priesthood in 1 Peter 2:9 is to 'declare the wonderful deeds of him who called you out of darkness into his marvellous light' which 'approximates rather closely Paul's description of the purpose of his ministry in Romans 15,16 ....' This makes preaching the gospel a specification of the 'spiritual sacrifices' of 1 Peter 2:5.[19] Such a view removes the basis for arguing that Paul viewed his 'priesthood'[20] as essentially different from that of all other Christians.

The same arguments against using Romans 15:15-16 to argue that Paul viewed apostles as priestly in a way different to other Christians apply to the other NT passages suggested as showing this. These will therefore be considered more briefly.

The next most frequently cited verse is Philippians 2:17, sometimes in conjunction with 2 Timothy 4:6. In both the verb *spendomai* ('pour a drink offering') is employed to refer to Paul's death, although 2 Timothy 4:6 has no equivalent to Philippians 2:17's 'upon the sacrifice and service of your faith.'[21] At least one scholar views 'service (*leitourgia*)' here as designating 'the function thanks to which Christ, acting through his apostle, offers men to God in sacrifice.'[22] However, although there are those who argue that Paul is the subject, giving "'If I should rather bleed to death in sacrifice to your faith,'"[23] it is more likely that the 'sacrifice' and 'service' refer to the Philippian believers' sacrifice and priestly service which consist of their faith or their gifts to Paul.[24]

Spendomai is clearly used to depict Paul's death as his being poured

---

[18] So Scott, 'Priesthood', *Scot J Th*, 414.

[19] Daly, R.J., *Christian Sacrifice: The Judaeo-Christian Background Before Origen* (Washington, 1978), 256.

[20] As can be discovered from Moulton W.F. Geden, A.S., and Moulton, H.K. (eds.), *A Concordance to the Greek Testament* (Edinburgh, 1963⁴), entries on *hiereus* and *archiereus*, there are no uses of these words in the Pauline corpus or in that often considered to be deutero-Pauline.

[21] A literal translation of the Greek.

[22] Grelot in Delorme, 53-4.

[23] So noted by Michel, *TDNT*, vol.7, 535, n.47.

[24] So Martin, R.P., *Philippians* (*NCB Commentary*) (London, 1976), 107. This view is noted in a footnote by Grelot in Delorme, 54, where he adds, 'one would then simply rejoin the perspective of Rm 12,1.'

out as a libation. Although Bauer, Arndt and Gingrich speak of Paul's shedding his blood as a sacrifice,[25] the verb is in the passive on both occasions and the identity of the offerer is not explicit. In any case, even if references to Paul's self-sacrifice were correctly discerned in Philippians 2:17 and 2 Timothy 4:6, there is no indication in either that it is viewed as peculiar to an apostle rather than as a particular instance of the self-giving to God Paul urges on all Christians in Romans. 12:1.

The same is true of Romans 1:9,[26] in which the verb *latreuein*, consistently used of religious, though not only of priestly, service in the Septuagint,[27] is employed by Paul with regard to his service of God; of 1 Corinthians 9:13-14,[28] in which Paul argues that those who proclaim the gospel should get their living by it as those who serve at the altar share in the offerings; and of 2 Corinthians 2:15-17,[29] in which Paul depicts himself and his fellow-preachers as 'the aroma of Christ to God.'

None of the NT passages adduced as evidence that the apostles were viewed as uniquely priestly in NT times in fact clearly asserts or supports that view.

3.1.3 Evidence that the special priesthood of apostles and church leaders was implied in the NT

Evidence that the sacrificial understanding of the eucharist shows that the special priesthood of apostles and church leaders is implied in the NT is important enough to warrant a separate section in this treatment. Here, other passages will be examined.

Vidal argues that the application of priestly vocabulary is justified by 'johannine expressions that correlate ... *consecration* or sanctification ... and the *sending* in mission (Jn 10,36 and 17,17-19).' He recognizes, however, 'the ambiguity that remains regarding those being addressed with these words and the general nature of the term consecration ...',[30] factors which rule such a correlation out.[31]

---

[25] Bauer, W., Arndt, W.F. and Gingrich, F.W., *A Greek-English Lexicon of the New Testament and Other Early Christian Literature* (Chicago, 1952⁴) on *spendo*; also Michel, *TDNT*, vol.7, 536.

[26] Viewed as a reference to Paul's apostolate as priestly by Colson, *Ministre de Jésus-Christ*, 182 and Grelot in Delorme, 53.

[27] So Strathmann, *TDNT*, vol.4, 61.

[28] Seen by Vanhoye, 267-8, as showing that 'Paul ... is likening the Christian apostolate to a priesthood.'

[29] Daly, *Christian Sacrifice*, 249-250, claims that in this passage 'Paul is thinking of his apostolic life in terms of a cultic offering'.

[30] Vidal in Delorme, 476-7.

[31] Cf. Brown, *John*, vol.2, 773-4.

Equally unconvincing are the attempts of Vanhoye, in a recent work, to argue that the existence of a priestly hierarchy is to be discerned in some of the later books of the NT. In his most successful, he recognizes that the author 'does not use a priestly title at this point' and that there is 'no explicit connection' between 1 Peter 5:1-4 and 2:1-10, but still argues that the parallels between them justify a connection between the concepts of presbyter and priest other than that involved in the general priesthood. His weightiest argument is that, in depicting the presbyters as shepherds of the flock in 5:2-3 and Christ as 'the chief shepherd' in 5:4, the author presents 'the charge of the presbyters as a realization of the very mission of Christ' which involves mediation such that 'Peter has initiated a priestly understanding of their role.'[32] However, there is no definite link between priestliness and presbyters in 1 Peter itself.

None of these passages imply that apostles and church leaders were viewed as priests in a way different from the way in which all believers were.

3.1.4 Evidence that the sacrificial understanding of the eucharist implied the special priesthood of those who presided at it

The amount of discussion surrounding this subject precludes an extensive treatment here. Only the nature of the sacrificial connotations surrounding the eucharist, and the lack of interest in who administers it can be dealt with.

Turning first to the Synoptic and Pauline accounts of the institution of the eucharist, three main arguments are used to show that they exhibit a sacrificial understanding of it. One is that clear parallels are drawn in them between the sacrifice performed by Moses to ratify the Sinaitic covenant and Christ's death memorialized in the eucharist as the sacrifice ratifying and establishing the New Covenant.[33] Another is that the Last Supper is depicted in these accounts as a Passover sacrifice,[34] and a third is that expiatory, atoning significance is ascribed to Jesus' death and so to the eucharist.[35]

These arguments clearly prove that Christ's death was interpreted as a sacrifice in NT times and that sacrificial ideas were attached to the eucharist. However, they do not demonstrate that the eucharist was

[32] Vanhoye, 264-7. See also his less successful arguments in 262-4 and 288.
[33] So Hein, K., *Eucharist and Excommunication* (Berne, 1973), 22; Daly, *Christian Sacrifice*, 221; Young, F.M., *The Use of Sacrificial Ideas in Greek Christian Writers from the New Testament to John Chrysostom* (Cambridge, Mass., 1979), 271-3; and Vanhoye, 53-4.
[34] So, for example, Daly, *Christian Sacrifice*, 220-221; but cf. Young, 306-9.
[35] So Young, 266-7 and Vanhoye, 54.

viewed simply as a sacrifice performed by a priest. Both the fact that Christ is depicted as identifying his body and blood with the bread and wine and the fact that he is presented as having said, "'Do this in remembrance of me'" in 1 Corinthians 11:24-25, suggest that the eucharist was a symbol of Christ's body and blood which reminded its participants of Christ's death, the benefits it provided, and their union with him and enjoyment of those benefits, making his death and its benefits present again for them. If this interpretation is correct, the eucharist is not seen as a sacrifice but as a reminder and 'making present' of Christ's sacrificial death.

Certainly it is unlikely that the authors were presenting any strict identification of the bread and wine with Christ's body and blood, since 'the words are ascribed to Jesus himself, present in the body ... and physically distinct from the loaf of which he spoke.'[36] Moreover, *anamnésis* probably means 'recollection' and thus 'making present'.[37] This understanding is supported by the way in which, in 1 Corinthians 11:26, the two instructions to 'do this in remembrance of me' are followed by the statement that 'as often as you eat this bread and drink the cup, you proclaim the Lord's death until he comes.'

The fact that the eucharist was a reminder of the union of its participants with Christ is brought out more clearly in 1 Corinthians 10:16-21, particularly in the descriptions of the cup and bread as a *koinônia* in Christ's blood and body, which involves participation[38] and fellowship.[39] Although some interpret these verses as evidence that Paul saw the Eucharist as a communion sacrifice,[40] and sacrificial connotations are present, the point of Paul's comparison of the partaking of the eucharist and the Jewish and pagan eating of certain sacrifices is not the sacrificial nature of the eating and drinking but the nature of the partaking involved. This is suggested by the fact that verses 18 and 20 are more likely dependent on verse 16 than vice versa, and by the way in which *koinônoi* is used in verses 18 and 20 and *metechein* in verses 17 and 21. Sacrifice is not mentioned until verse 18, and the main point of the comparison is brought out in verses 20 and 21. It involves

---

[36] Barrett, C.K., *The First Epistle to the Corinthians* (London, 1971²) 266.

[37] So Behm, *TDNT*, vol.1, 349. See too Marshall, *Luke*, 805, and Evans, C.F., *Saint Luke* (London, 1990), 790.

[38] So Bauer, Arndt and Gingrich, 440.

[39] This is the emphasis in Behm and Hauck, *TDNT*, vol.3, 738-9 and 805-6 and in Barrett, 233.

[40] For example, Daly, *Christian Sacrifice*, 231; Young, 240-242; Lietzmann, H., *Mass and Lord's Supper: A Study in the History of the Liturgy* with Richardson, R.D., *Introduction and Further Inquiry* (Leiden, 1979), 182-4.

participation, fellowship and partaking, not sacrifice.[41]

Several scholars argue that the eucharist is understood and presented in sacrificial terms in Hebrews, especially in chapters 10 and 13.[42] To take the most recent example, Vanhoye argues that 10:19-21 includes an allusion to the eucharist on the basis first that 'the author mentions the "flesh" and "blood of Christ" ... in two parts of parallel phrases', and second that 'the entire sentence corresponds as closely as possible to the reality of a eucharistic celebration.' Since Hebrews appears to be a sermon rather than a letter, this passage suggests that it was originally intended for a gathering (cf. 10:25) 'that included a eucharistic celebration.'[43] There is here, however, no clear allusion to the Eucharist, since the references to Christ's blood and flesh need refer to no more than Christ's historical death[44] and, without such a reference, the proof that Hebrews was intended for a eucharistic celebration falls.

The same is true of the references to 'the blood of the covenant' in Hebrews 10:29 and 13:20. Although Daly, echoing Betz, asks, 'how could these texts ... fail to suggest the Eucharistic cup to a Christian of the second generation?',[45] there is no clear reason why 'the blood of the covenant' must mean any more or other than the blood of Christ shed on the cross.[46]

Vanhoye regards 13:7-17 as especially significant, arguing that

> it is ... difficult to see as simply accidental the fact that the twofold mention of the "leaders" (13:7, 17) frames a passage which defines Christian worship and which irresistibly suggests the eucharistic celebration under its triple aspect of the sacrificial meal where only Christians have the right to eat (13:10), of "sacrifice of praise" which they raise up to God through Jesus Christ (13:15), and of unique opportunity for the expression of community love (13:16).[47]

Again, however, if the assumption that this was being delivered at a eucharistic celebration is removed, there is nothing which demands such

---

[41] On this see Behm, *TDNT*, vol.3, 184 and 740 and Barrett, 235.

[42] See Moberly, 269-271; Dabin, P., *Le sacerdoce royal dans les livres saints* (Paris, 1941), 368; Colson, *Ministre de Jésus-Christ*, 167-8 and 205; Hein, 147-8; Daly, *Christian Sacrifice*, 262-3 and 281-2; Young, 265; and Vanhoye, 228-235.

[43] Vanhoye, 228.

[44] So Montefiore, H., *A Commentary on the Epistle to the Hebrews* (London, 1964), 172-4; Bruce, F.F., *The Epistle to the Hebrews* (Grand Rapids, 1964), 244-9; and Guthrie, D., *Hebrews* (Leicester, 1983), 211-2.

[45] Daly, *Christian Sacrifice*, 262, n.90. Colson, *Ministre de Jésus-Christ*, 167, regards the reference to the same in Heb. 9:20 as suggesting the eucharist.

[46] So Bruce, 259 and Guthrie, 219, although Montefiore, 178-9, does see 'eucharistic overtones' here.

[47] Vanhoye, 231.

an interpretation. Even Daly concludes on 13:10 that 'the Eucharistic meaning cannot be excluded, but ... it alone is far too narrow an explanation of the text. The author of Heb seems to have in mind the total saving action of Christ.'[48] Indeed, the author goes on, in 13:11, to give a justification of what he is saying based on the regulations for the sin-offering in Leviticus 16:27, and follows it up by referring, in 13:12, to Christ as, like the sin-offering, suffering 'outside the gate in order to sanctify the people through his own blood.' Since, as elsewhere in Hebrews,[49] the sin-offering is Christ and never the eucharist, the reference to the altar in 13:10 is most likely an allusion to the cross on which Christ offered himself.[50] This is not to deny that the thanksgiving which probably accompanied the celebration of the eucharist in the early church could well have been viewed as a 'sacrifice of praise' such as is mentioned in Hebrews 13:15, but there is no need to narrow the latter down to that and, in any case, this would be the sacrifice of the whole church and not that of any group within it.[51] The same is true with regard to the perceptions of eucharistic references in the context of 1 Peter 2:5 and 9.[52]

Although, then, the eucharist had sacrificial connotations in the NT, it was not itself viewed as a sacrifice but as a memorial and making present of Christ's sacrifice. Moreover, there is little or no interest in who presided at it. Whilst the likelihood that the apostles initially, and the recognized leaders later, did so may be admitted, there is no evidence whatsoever that that role was viewed as priestly or as implying priestliness in NT times.

3.1.5 Other Arguments

Other arguments are based less directly on the NT evidence. One is that priestly language is rightly used of church leaders because they mediate Christ's mediation in an unique way. Some relate this to presidency at the eucharist,[53] an issue just discussed; some link it with preaching God's word and use Romans 15:16 in support,[54] an interpretation also

---

[48] Daly, *Christian Sacrifice*, 281-2.

[49] As is pointed out by Best, E., 'Spiritual Sacrifice: General Priesthood in the New Testament', *Interpretation* 14 (1960), 284.

[50] So Montefiore, 244; Bruce, 399-402, which see for suggested reasons why 'our author avoids mentioning the Eucharist when he has every opportunity to do so'; and Guthrie, 273.

[51] So Best E., 'Spiritual Sacrifices' in *Interp* 14 (1960), 284.

[52] See Colson, *Ministre de Jesus-Christ*, 171-6, on one side, and, on the other, Torrance, 17-22 and Best, E., 'Spiritual Sacrifices' in *Interp* 14 (1960), 279.

[53] For examples, see section 2.3.3 earlier.

[54] For example, Vidal in Delorme, 476-7.

discussed above; some connect it to enabling the church to be priestly or to carry out Christ's priestly mission, but the passages in the NT which have been adduced as supporting this do not in fact do so.[55] Vanhoye and Congar argue that there are two aspects of Christ's priesthood portrayed in the NT, corresponding to two types of priesthood in the church. Vanhoye calls them 'the aspect of existential offering and the aspect of mediation', the former being found in the general Christian priesthood and the latter in ministers as instruments of Christ's mediation.[56] The problem here is again the total lack of clear evidence in the NT to support the latter contention in particular. Yet to be considered is evidence which suggests that all Christians were viewed as mediating Christ in the NT.

The arguments that a priestly role validly attaches to the ordained in a way not shared with the rest of the Christian community because of the similarities of their roles and functions to those of the OT priests, because the NT is not anti-sacerdotal in its outlook, because this role developed under the guidance of the Holy Spirit, and because the ordained represent the church's priesthood, will be addressed after the rest of the evidence from the NT has been considered. Thus far the question asked at the outset of this section (are church leaders viewed as priests in the NT in a way different from other Christians?) has to be answered in the negative.

3.2 Attitudes towards priesthood, temple and cult in the NT

Only a survey of the attitudes apparent in the various writings of the NT can be attempted here, but this will have the merit of exposing the main lines of thought in these. Attitudes towards the temple-cultus in general are examined here because the Jewish priests' main functions in NT times were integrally connected with that cultus.[57]

3.2.1 The Synoptic Gospels

There is evidence in these gospels of both normal respect for and unusual attitudes to the temple-cultus. Respect is shown when God is depicted as using it to make his plans known to the priest Zechariah in Luke 1:8-23, when the prescriptions of the Mosaic Law are depicted as

---

[55] Torrance, 81, adduces Eph. 4:13 in which there is no priestly reference at all, and Vanhoye, 267 and 315-6, adduces Heb. 13:7 and 17, 1 Pet. 5:1-4 (cf. 2:1-10) and Rom. 15:16, all of which have been considered above.

[56] Vanhoye, 315-6; cf. Congar, *Lay People*, 159-161.

[57] So Best, E., 'Spiritual Sacrifices' in *Interp* 14 (1960), 274.

fulfilled for Jesus, and when two godly Jews are portrayed as welcoming his advent in Luke 2:22-39, the second not departing 'from the temple, worshipping with fasting and prayer night and day'. Further, Jesus is presented as treating the temple-cultus with normal respect when he tells the cleansed leper to show himself to the priest and offer what Moses had commanded (Mk. 1:44 and parallels), when he accepts the offering of a gift at the altar (Mt. 5:23-24), when he argues that the temple makes the gold on it sacred (Mt. 23:17), and when he accepts that God dwells in it (Mt. 23:21).[58]

On the other hand, unusual attitudes to the cultus are seen in the depictions of Jesus as claiming that 'something greater than the temple is here' and clearly meaning himself (Mt. 12:6 and 8), as emphatically stating that God desires mercy and not sacrifice (Mt. 9:13 and 12:7), as contrasting the behaviour of a priest and a Levite unfavourably with that of a Samaritan (Lk. 10:30-37), and as cleansing the temple of those who were misusing it (Mk. 11:15-19 and parallels).

It is possible that these teachings were meant and/or viewed in the early church as teaching no more than that God condemned misuse of temple and sacrifice, particularly the placing of right observance on a higher level than caring obedience, and that Christ was greater than the temple and its cultus, without implying anything with regard to the continuance of that cultus. This is, however, an irreduceable minimum of what they were understood to mean. [59]

In addition to this, there is much evidence that Christ's death was interpreted in terms of sacrifice. For one thing, there is the likening of his self-giving to a 'ransom for many ' in Mark 10:45.[60] For another, there is all the evidence of a sacrificial understanding of Christ's death in the synoptic accounts of the Last Supper noted earlier.

3.2.2 Acts

Here too a dual attitude can be discerned on the part of the early Christian community towards the Jerusalem temple and cult. On the one

---

[58] On these passages see Daly, *Christian Sacrifice*, 210-212 and Vanhoye, 3-5.

[59] See Daly, *Christian Sacrifice*, 213-5 and Vanhoye, 6-7 for fuller and at some points differing evaluations of the significance of these passages. Consideration of Jesus' reported statement regarding the destruction and replacement of the temple (Mk. 14:58 and parallel) will be given in considering the evidence from John's gospel.

[60] Vanhoye, 51, argues that this verse 'does not contain the slightest allusion to sacrifice', but Daly, *Christian Sacrifice*, 217-8, argues that it does because of the cultic, alongside the secular, use of *lutron* in the Septuagint, the likely allusion to Is. 53:10-12 and the suffering servant's self-offering as a sacrifice for sin, and the probable sacrificial connotations of 'to give his life'.

hand, according to Acts, many early Jewish Christians prayed in the temple and probably took part in the temple services like other Jews, in view of 2:46, 3:1, 21:26 and 22:17. In all likelihood these included the 'great many of the priests' who became 'obedient to the faith' (6:7). On the other hand, there is no suggestion that these priests received any special status in the church,[61] the later leader of it in Jerusalem being James who, as 'the Lord's brother' (Gal.1:19), could not have been a Levite.

The material concerning Stephen in Acts 6 and 7 is capable of being interpreted as containing varying degrees of hostility towards the temple-cultus.[62] The accusation in 6:13-14 could indicate only awareness of Jesus' prophecy of the temple's destruction,[63] but, in his speech, Stephen focuses on the time before Israel had the temple and implies strongly that God's presence 'is not restricted to any one land or any material building', at the beginning and end especially.[64] He further accuses the Israelites of idolatry from their earliest days (7:39-43),[65] and implies that, even in their worship in the temple, they are tending towards it, 'especially in the statement (v. 48): "the Most High does not dwell in houses made with hands ...." ["Made with hands"] was at that time a Jewish technical term used in the polemic against idolatry.'[66]

The brevity and nature of Stephen's treatment of the building of the temple in verses 48 and 49 implies definite disapproval of it.[67] His emphasis on the rejection of Jesus in 7:52 could suggest that he saw Jesus as superseding the temple, but does not definitely imply it.[68]

It is likely, then, that some Jewish Christians continued to view the temple as a valid place of worship, whilst others, in the Jerusalem area

---

[61] So Schweizer, E., *Church Order in the New Testament* (London, 1961), 47.

[62] For a view which maximises the anti-temple polemic, see Daly, *Christian Sacrifice*, 228-230; for a more 'minimalist' view, see Bruce, F.F., *Commentary on the Book of the Acts* (London, 1954), 153-161. Williams, C.S.C., *The Acts of the Apostles* (London, 1964²) 100-102, gives a helpful summary of different views.

[63] So Bruce, *Acts*, 135.

[64] So ibid., 141.

[65] So ibid., 153-6. Daly, *Christian Sacrifice*, 229, goes too far when he argues that, in 7:41-46, Stephen interprets Amos 5:25-27 'as claiming that the Israelites did indeed offer sacrifice in the desert, not to God, however, but to idols, thus implying that idolatry is at the very root of the Jewish sacrificial institution.'

[66] Daly, *Christian Sacrifice*, 229-230. He again goes too far, adding, 'Stephen was equating the temple with a pagan temple.' Rather, '"made with hands" has an undercurrent of meaning denoting idolatry' (Williams C.S.C., 110).

[67] So Bruce, *Acts*, 159.

[68] So ibid., 158 and Neil, W. *The Acts of the Apostles* (London, 1973), 114. All the justification for seeing an implied reference to Christ as the new temple given in Bruce is significantly taken from outside this passage.

at least, and probably elsewhere,[69] perceived it as a hindrance to the true worship of God, especially now that Christ had come. These may well have been aware of Jesus' prophecy of the temple's destruction, which will be examined below.

3.2.3 The Pauline epistles[70]

In spite of his respect for the temple as evinced, if this event is reported accurately, in Acts 21:20-26, it would be unwise to hold that Paul viewed the temple and its cult as having continuing validity on this basis. This is because he may well have been acting according to the principle he enunciates in 1 Corinthians 9:20, viz., he would act as a Jew in order to win Jews, and, in any case, 'the motives expressed in vs.24 were probably not his own, but James'.'[71]

It is clear from his correspondence that he viewed the church and the individual Christian as the temple in which God dwelt. The individual Christian's body is 'a temple of the Holy Spirit within you, which you have from God' (1 Cor. 6:19), and the Corinthian church is told 'you are God's temple and ... God's Spirit dwells in you' (1 Cor. 3:16-17) and 'we are the temple of the living God' (2 Cor. 6:16). This metaphor is further developed in Ephesians 2:19-22 in which Christians are told that they are 'built upon the foundation of the apostles and prophets, Christ Jesus himself being the cornerstone, in whom the whole structure is joined together and grows into a holy temple in the Lord; in whom you also are built into it for a dwelling place of God in the Spirit.'

Although no explicit statement shows how Paul viewed the Jerusalem temple, the fact that he and others[72] saw the church and those who made it up as God's dwelling-place proves that he did not regard the temple as God's exclusive dwelling-place. This and the development of the temple theme in Ephesians 2:20-21 implies also that he considered it to have

---

[69] Young, 81, argues that the anti-sacrificial position of Stephen's party had little ultimate influence because the importance of sacrifice decreased outside of Jerusalem and the Gentiles had no need to keep the Law or motivation to go to the temple. Bruce, *Acts*, 141-4, argues cogently that it was more widely held in Hellenistic Judaism.

[70] As Daly, *Christian Sacrifice*, 230, argues, it is valid to treat together the generally accepted Pauline letters and those considered by many as 'deutero-Pauline' since the latter do 'not add anything essentially new or introduce any radically new developments over and above what is already contained in the uncontested Pauline corpus.' They may well derive from a Pauline school, in any case.

[71] Williams C.S.C., 240, which see for the related discussion of whether Paul could have acted as he is portrayed in this passage.

[72] Daly, *Christian Sacrifice*, 232: the 'do you not know' of 1 Cor. 3:16 and 6:19 implies that Paul is recalling 'something which is already known and accepted by Paul's readers'.

been superseded in Christ, in whom the church exists.

The same is true of sacrifice. Though willing to offer it in the Jerusalem temple (Acts 21:26), for Paul it was primarily Christ's death and secondarily the self-giving of Christians to God which were the sacrifices which God wanted. In 1 Corinthians 5:7 he clearly writes that 'Christ, our paschal lamb, has been sacrificed.' As Daly argues, Paul expresses this 'in a context of practical exhortation which indicates that he is referring to something that is taken for granted as part of the Christian belief.'[73]

Further, in Romans 3:25 Christ is called a *hilastérion*. The debate over whether this is to be understood as propitiation, expiation or sin-offering is irrelevant here,[74] since a sacrificial allusion is accepted in any case. This is true of Ephesians 5:2 as well: 'Christ ... gave himself up for us, a fragrant offering and sacrifice to God.' There are other possible sacrificial allusions to Christ's death in the Pauline epistles,[75] but doubts attach to their sacrificial interpretation.[76]

Paul also describes the self-offering of Christians in sacrificial terms. This is seen most clearly and comprehensively in Romans 12:1 in which he appeals to the Roman Christians to 'present your bodies as a living sacrifice, holy and acceptable to God, which is your spiritual worship.' 'Your bodies' means '"yourselves" ... "the totality of which we are composed"',[77] while *latreia* ('worship') is the Septuagint equivalent of *abodah* which, used in connection with God, almost always denotes cultic service in the OT and

> implies that the true worship which God desires embraces the whole of the Christian's life from day to day. It implies that any cultic worship which is not accompanied by obedience in the ordinary affairs of life must be regarded as false worship. ... But it would be quite unjustifiable to argue that the logical implication of Paul's use of $\lambda\alpha\tau\rho\epsilon\iota/\alpha$ here is that no room is left for a Christian cultic worship ....[78]

Similarly, *logiké* ('spiritual') is likely to mean 'being consistent with a proper understanding of the truth of God revealed in Jesus Christ',

---

[73] Daly, *Christian Sacrifice*, 237.

[74] See Young, 161-7 for a discussion ending in favour of expiation; Cranfield, *Romans*, vol.1, 214-7 for one ending in favour of propitiation; and Daly, *Christian Sacrifice*, 239-240 for one in favour of sin-offering.

[75] See Daly, *Christian Sacrifice*,. 237-240

[76] See, for example, Cranfield, *Romans*, vol.1, 382, on Rom. 8:3.

[77] Ibid., vol.2, 598-9, quoting Calvin. So too Best, E., 'Spiritual Sacrifices' in *Interp* 14 (1960), 287

[78] Cranfield, *Romans*, vol.2, 601-2.

rather than 'spiritual' in the sense of 'inward' in view of Paul's use of 'bodies' earlier in the verse.[79]

Paul also wrote of the gifts sent by the Philippian Christians as 'a fragrant offering, a sacrifice acceptable and pleasing to God' (Phil. 4:18), three phrases 'each of which is a technical term which described the acceptability of a sacrifice before God, ...'[80] His use of sacrificial and priestly imagery to describe his own ministry and imminent death has been discussed earlier (see section 3.1.2 above).

In his teaching, then, Paul had no reason or desire to give the Jerusalem temple and its cultus any lasting significance. Although he never comments explicitly on its relevance, the presumption is that he regarded it as at its most peripherally relevant to his mainly Gentile converts and at its least completely irrelevant. He is not afraid, however, to use cultic vocabulary, but now to refer to Christ, and especially to his death, and to refer to the Christians, individually and collectively. It is likely, then, that he viewed the temple and its cultus as being superseded in Christ and in the church. It is also likely that, although never formulating his statements in the same way, he would have concurred with the viewpoint next to be examined in 1 Peter 2:1-10.[81]

3.2.4 1 Peter

The author of 1 Peter is another who makes no explicit statements about the Jerusalem temple cultus. Like Paul, however, he used sacrificial ideas to understand Christ's death. In 1:18-19 Christians are said to 'know that you were ransomed ... with the precious blood of Christ, like that of a lamb without blemish or spot.' The 'you know' suggests that what is being introduced is traditional and well-known and accepted teaching.[82]

Where the author goes beyond the evidence considered thus far is in his explicit description of Christians as a priesthood in 2:4 and 9 and his linking of that idea with the depictions of Christians as a spiritual house and as offering spiritual sacrifices, a high and deliberate concentration of cultic vocabulary and ideas. Although many scholars have argued that this passage is drawn from an early baptismal catachesis,[83] Vanhoye

---

[79] Ibid., 604-5.

[80] Daly, *Christian Sacrifice*, 242.

[81] Note Dabin, *Le sacerdoce royal dans les livres saints*, 200: 'The royal priesthood is only literally absent in the Pauline writings. His vocabulary does not know it, but what the word expresses is found in other words in Saint Paul as much as in Saint Peter.'

[82] See Michaels, J.R., *1 Peter* (Waco, 1988), 63.

[83] So, e.g., Dabin, *Le sacerdoce royal dans les livres saints*, 181; Ryan, L., 'Patristic Teaching

is right to point out that 'in this first part of the Epistle (1:1 - 2:10), Peter never mentions baptism explicitly .... What he is bringing out is the reality of the new birth',[84] as is clearly seen in 1:23 ('you have been born anew ...').

In 1 Peter 2:4-8 the author is taking up an idea fairly common in early Christian thinking (cf. Mk. 12:10 and parallels, Acts 4:11 and Rom. 9:33) that Christ is 'that living stone, rejected by men but in God's sight chosen and precious', quoting from Isaiah 28:16, Psalm 118:22 and Isaiah 8:14-15 in verses 6-8. Probably drawing also on the building-metaphor which was clearly known in Pauline and other circles (cf. Eph. 2:19-21, 1 Cor. 3:9-17, Mt. 16:18 and Mk. 14:58),[85] the author develops it and tells Christians: 'like living stones be yourselves built into a spiritual house, to be a holy priesthood, to offer spiritual sacrifices acceptable to God through Jesus Christ.' Although Elliott argues that 'house' here does not mean temple but house and household,[86] the use of cultic terms in the following context suggests that the temple-idea was in the author's mind.[87] The use of 'spiritual' to describe the house probably has connotations both of metaphorical rather than literal and of 'where the Spirit of God dwells'.[88]

Elliott and others have reacted very strongly against the use of the expressions 'holy priesthood' and 'royal priesthood' in 2:5 and 9 to support the view that each Christian is a ministering priest: 'it rather explicates the elect and holy character of the eschatological covenant community, its relation to Jesus, the elect and holy one of God, and its missionary responsibility in the world.'[89] A searching semantic analysis of 'a royal priesthood' and its use in Exodus 19:6 and in 1 Peter 2:5 and 9 leads Elliott to assert that they mean '"royal residence or dwelling place"' and '"body of priests"' and so 'it is semantically inadmissible to attempt to reduce either of these words to an individual-distributive classification and thereby to suggest that each individual believer is

---

on the Priesthood of the Faithful', *Irish Theological Quarterly*, 29 (1962), 26; Elliott, J.H., *The Elect and the Holy* (Leiden, 1966), 11 and 207; as well as several commentators.

[84] Vanhoye, 274, footnote 4, following Chevallier.

[85] So Michaels, 96-7.

[86] Elliott, *The Elect and the Holy*, 159.

[87] So Colson, *Ministre de Jésus-Christ*, 22-3 and Michaels, 100. Colson, Vanhoye, 258-9 and Best, E. '1 Peter 2:4-10 – A Reconsideration' in *Novum Testamentum* 11 (1969), 280, also adduce the use of *oikos* for the temple in the Septuagint.

[88] So Michaels, 100; see too Cranfield, C.E.B., *The First Epistle of Peter* (London, 1950), 47; Kelly, J.N.D., *The Epistles of Peter and of Jude* (London, 1963), 90; Best, E., '1 Peter 2:4-10', *Nov Test* 11 (1969), 292-3 and *1 Peter* (London, 1971), 102; Daly, *Christian Sacrifice*, 253.

[89] Elliott, J.H., 'Ministry and Church Order in the NT: A Traditio-Historical Analysis (1 Pt 5,1-5 & plls.)', *Catholic Biblical Quarterly* 32 (1970), 370.

being depicted as a "king" and a "priest.""[90]

The main emphasis here is definitely on the corporate character of the people of God, as shown by the collective nouns 'priesthood', 'race', 'kingdom',[91] 'nation', and 'people', as well as by 'house'. Moreover, the themes of election and holiness are present in verse 4 with reference to Christ ('chosen') and in verses 5 and 9 with reference to God's people ('holy' and 'chosen'). However, Elliott seems to be overreacting in his desire to correct an abuse of these verses. As Vanhoye rightly points out, 'the orientation of the whole Epistle does not favor restricting the perspective' to solely communal exercise of the Christian priesthood because 'it always implies a personal engagement of each Christian in "his whole conduct" (1:15) and not simply a contribution to common activities.'[92] This is supported by the use of the plural 'living stones' in verse 5. As Michaels writes, 'only momentarily does [the author] focus attention on Christian believers individually (i.e., as a plurality of "stones"), for his real interest is in their corporate identity',[93] but the fact is that he does briefly consider them as an aggregate of individuals in this context. Further, that it was possible to hold all Christians to be priests is shown by the plural 'priests' in Revelation 1:6 and 5:10.[94] Finally, there is the question as to what belief in only a communal priesthood would imply: would the church only be a priesthood when gathered together for worship or for giving or self-giving to God for others? In the light of all these arguments, then, it seems unlikely that the author would see any contradiction involved between viewing the whole church as a priesthood and considering individual Christians as priests.

Elliott also denies that the use of 'priesthood' in 1 Peter 2:5 and 9 has anything to do with the Levitical priesthood since it draws on Exodus 19:6 for the idea of the common priesthood and, right down through the history of Judaism and Christianity thus far, this was a separate tradition.[95] On the other hand, there is a 'close connection between the

---

[90] Elliott, *The Elect and the Holy*, 223: see 124ff. for arguments to show that the community's elect and holy nature are the main emphases in these verses and 68f. on the corporate nature of *hierateuma* ('priesthood').

[91] If this is to be taken as a noun: see Elliott, *The Elect and the Holy*, 72ff., Colson, *Ministre de Jésus-Christ*, 25 and Best, E.. '1 Peter 2:4-10' in *Nov Test* 11 (1969), 288ff. in favour of it being understood substantively and Schrenk, *TDNT*, vol.3, 250, Otranto, G., 'Il sacerdozio comune dei fedeli nei reflessi della 1 Petr. 2,9 (I e II secolo)', *Vetera Christianorum* 7 (1970), 228-9 and Michaels, 108-9, in favour of it being understood adjectivally.

[92] Vanhoye, 262.

[93] Michaels, 99.

[94] So Best, E., '1 Peter 2:4-10', *Nov Test* 11 (1969), 286-7.

[95] Elliott, *The Elect and the Holy*, 173 and 210.

Petrine complex of ideas in ii 4-10 and those of the primitive Christian tradition',[96] in which ideas connected with priesthood and sacrifice drawn from the Levitical tradition were already present, as we have shown in Paul. There is also the development of Exodus 19:6 in 1 Peter 2:5: Christians are a holy priesthood 'to offer spiritual sacrifices'. The offering of sacrifice was the business of the Levitical priests above all in the OT and, in Weiss' opinion at least,[97] the Septuagint is the basis of the NT use of 'offer' here and the Septuagint's use is 'almost exclusively' for offering sacrifice. It is unlikely that it could have been used without some of its connotations involving ideas connected with the Levitical priesthood.

Although Kelly goes too far in summarising Elliott's view as that *hierateuma* 'carries no specifically priestly implications',[98] Elliott does play down the priestly and sacrificial aspects of these verses.[99] Whilst the emphasis is on God's people's election and holiness above all in verse 9 and this theme is present in verse 5, the development of Exodus 19:6 in the way just noted above makes it certain that, though subordinate, the idea of priestly offering of sacrifice is certainly present.

There is nothing explicit in verse 5 to indicate what the 'spiritual sacrifices' are to consist of, although Michaels may be right to see 'a holy priesthood' and 1 Peter 1:15-16 as implying that holiness of life is one.[100] 'Spiritual' here will have the same connotations noted earlier in 'spiritual house'. Elliott is one who interprets verse 9 as indicating that proclamation of the gospel is an expression of the church's priesthood. More likely, however, is Michaels' view that what is involved is 'the praise of God by his people' in worship.[101]

1 Peter is significant, then, in that it explicitly calls God's people, the church, a priesthood and links this with being a temple and offering spiritual sacrifices, sacrifices which include holiness of life and worship. This implies, without explicitly stating, the supersession of the Jerusalem temple-cultus. It thus has much in common with Paul but does not go as far as Hebrews in rejection of that cultus.

---

[96] Best, E., '1 Peter 2:4-10', *Nov Test* 11 (1969), 284.

[97] Weiss, *TDNT*, vol.9, 60-61.

[98] Kelly, *Peter and Jude*, 98.

[99] See Elliott, *The Elect and the Holy*, 224-5 but cf. 217-8.

[100] Michaels, 101-2.

[101] Elliott, *The Elect and the Holy*, 192-9; Michaels, 110. Best, E., 'Spiritual Sacrifice' in *Interpretation* 14 (1960), 279 and elsewhere argues that proclamation is the purpose of the church as described in all four of the expressions used in verse 9 and not particularly of the church as priesthood. Elliott and Michaels argue that it is natural to interpret the metaphors of verse 5 in the light of the explicit statement at the end of verse 9.

3.2.5 Hebrews

Christ's high priesthood is central to Hebrews and dominates chapters 5-10 in particular. Although some have argued that Christ is viewed as high priest only from his death or exaltation, others have argued for the whole of his earthly life as well. Scholer comments: 'Most recent scholars do not propose an "either/or" situation ..., but instead see the strange paradox of his earthly high priest activity being mentioned simultaneously and even immediately adjacent to the heavenly high priest role.'[102]

Jesus' main priestly activity in his earthly life was to offer himself once-for-all as a sacrifice for sin (see, e.g., 7:27, 9:11-14 and 25-28). However,

> even ['in the days of his flesh'] Jesus performed priestly offering consisting of prayers of loud cries and tears. The term ['flesh'] in Heb. encompasses Jesus' entire earthly existence (5.7; 10.20), so that his whole earthly life attained to that high priestly objective which had forever evaded the former priests: access through the curtain into the heavenly holy of holies.

As heavenly high priest, Jesus no longer offers sacrifice or sprinkles blood, since that has been accomplished 'once for all'. Rather he intercedes on the basis of his self-offering (9:24-28, cf. 5:20 and 7:25).[103]

In the sections of the letter developing the theme of Christ's high priesthood, Christ is depicted mainly as fulfilling the OT legislation concerning the Day of Atonement. Whilst elements of similarity to the Levitical priesthood are pointed out, e.g., in 5:1-5, it is the differences and the superiority of Christ's high priesthood after the order of Melchizedek which receive most emphasis, especially in chapter 7. Here the discontinuity in the priesthood and the law is called a 'change' in verse 12 and a 'setting aside' in verse 18. Guthrie is right to point out that 'the writer does not here mean that the law itself is annulled, but that it can be discounted as a means of gaining perfection.'[104] But this was the main purpose of the priesthood via the offering of sacrifice, as far as the author of Hebrews is concerned (cf. 5:1, 7:11, 8:3 and 9:8-10), so that the Jewish priesthood is no longer necessary. This is implied above all in the statements that Christ has offered up the one sacrifice necessary on the cross 'once for all' (7:27, 9:11-12, 26b and 28).

---

[102] Scholer, J.M., *Proleptic Priests: Priesthood in the Epistle to the Hebrews* (Sheffield, 1991), 82.

[103] Ibid., 85-7

[104] Guthrie, 164.

The contrast of the old and the new continues to be drawn in chapters 8-10, first regarding the covenant, the old covenant being described as 'obsolete and growing old ... ready to vanish away' in 8:13; then concerning the cultus, the old being imposed 'until the time of reformation' (9:10); and finally with reference to the sacrifices, Christ being said to abolish the first to establish the second (10:9). Although the first two of these references could possibly be understood of the end of all things, the last cannot[105] and makes clear that the Levitical sacrificial system has been abolished as well as superseded in Christ.

On balance, Daly is right to consider the theme of the Christian community as the new temple 'totally absent' from Hebrews.[106] The priesthood of Christians, however, is implied, though never made explicit. This is clearest in 13:15-16, in which Christians are exhorted, 'let us continually offer up a sacrifice of praise', and to do good and share what they have, 'for such sacrifices are pleasing to God.' This is supported by the way in which *proserchesthai* ('draw near'), *eiserchesthai* ('enter') and *teleioun* ('be made perfect') are used of priestly access to God in the Levitical cultic system in the Septuagint and are applied to Christians' access to God in Hebrews.[107] So, for example, in 4:16 (cf. 10:22), Christians are exhorted, 'Let us ... draw near to the throne of grace'. This priestly activity, however, is never viewed as atoning in Hebrews but rather as a result of, and response to, the once-for-all atonement achieved by Christ.[108]

3.2.6 John and 1 John[109]

The statement, 'And the Word became flesh and dwelt [*eskénôsen*] among us' in John 1:14 suggests that 'the flesh of Jesus Christ is the new localization of God's presence on earth, and that Jesus is the replacement of the ancient Tabernacle' in the light of the use of *skéné* ('tent') in the Septuagint and intertestamental writings to refer to the temple's predecessor.[110] Confirmation comes in the Johannine account of the cleansing of the temple in 2:13-22, especially in verses 18-22.

---

[105] So Montefiore, 142 on 8:13, 150 on 9:10 and 168 on 10:9-10. Guthrie, 178 and 184-5, finds a reference to the time inaugurated by Christ in 8:13 and 9:10 as well as in 10:9.

[106] Daly, *Christian Sacrifice*, 262. See Montefiore, 73-4 on the interpretation of 3:1-6, the only passage in which this theme might be alluded to.

[107] For detailed argument, see Scholer, 91-207.

[108] See ibid., 205.

[109] These are treated together on the basis that similarities between them suggest a common general provenance: see especially Brown, R.E., *The Epistles of John* (London, 1982), 69-71.

[110] Brown, *John*, 33.

Whatever, if anything, Jesus actually said and meant,[111] the author of John clearly interpreted the statement he recorded as indicating that Christ's body was the temple replacing the Jerusalem temple. Further, John 4:21 suggests an abrogation of worship in Jerusalem in the words 'the hour is coming when neither on this mountain nor in Jerusalem will you worship the Father.' In contrast, verse 23 adds, 'the hour is coming, and now is, when the true worshippers will worship the Father in spirit and truth, ...' The precise meaning of the last four words is much discussed. They assert at least the priority of right internal dispositions in worship and, together with verse 21, suggest a new system of worship 'not tied to any particular holy place.'[112] A further reference to Christ as the temple may well be implied in 7:37-38, although whether this implies 'that those who believe in him ... also become the new temple'[113] is less certain because of exegetical problems.

Jesus' death is interpreted in sacrificial terms in both John and 1 John. This is clearest in 1 John 2:2 and 4:10 in which Jesus is called the expiation for our sins. Another sacrificial reference is almost certain in 1 John 1:7 which states that 'the blood of Jesus ... cleanses us from all sin' with all the ideas of 'the atoning function of blood'[114] in the OT background to this. In John's gospel Christ's death seems to be depicted as a Passover sacrifice[115] whilst the depictions of his voluntary laying down of his life on behalf of others probably also held sacrificial connotations.[116] Moreover, in John 15:12-14, 1 John 3:16 and 4:10-11, Jesus' followers are told to imitate him in this.

Jesus' priesthood may well also be implied in John and 1 John. Concerning the latter Brown argues that 'the manner in which Jesus is a *parakletos* in 2:1 must be interpreted through the reference to him as a *hilasmos*, "atonement", in 2:2' and that these verses were 'written in light of the Jewish ritual for the Day of Atonement,' thus supporting the view that Jesus is being depicted as 'a high priest in a heavenly temple.' He holds the same about the Gospel, especially John 10:36 and 17:19, where Jesus is portrayed as speaking of his consecration and sending by the Father.[117]

---

[111] See the discussions in Brown, *John*, 122-3; Morris, L., *The Gospel according to John* (London, 1971), 202-3; and Lindars, 142-3.

[112] Morris, 270.

[113] Daly, *Christian Sacrifice*, 291. See Brown, *John*, 319-321 for an explanation of the exegetical problems and the view that only Christ is referred to here.

[114] Daly, *Christian Sacrifice*, 292-3.

[115] See ibid., 294-5 and Brown, *John*, 883 and 895-6.

[116] So Daly, *Christian Sacrifice*, 292 and Lindars, 361.

[117] Brown, *The Epistles of John*, 217 and 220-221.

3.2.7 Revelation

From 4:1-22:5 'the basic scenery of the visions ... is the heavenly sanctuary seen after the model of the Jerusalem temple.'[118] This is shown by the references to the temple and its surroundings as the site of the visions in 7:15, 11:1, 14:15 and 17, 15:8, 16:1 and 16:17, as well as by numerous other references to items connected with the temple-cultus. This temple centres on God the Father and the Son, but includes those 'who have come out of the great tribulation' as worshippers (7:14-15, cf. 3:12).

That Christ's death is interpreted in sacrificial terms is proved, above all, by the fact that 'the lamb', 'with 28 occurrences, is the most frequently used Christological title' in Revelation.[119] Its strongly sacrificial connotations are expressed in the first description of it in 5:6 as 'standing, as though it had been slain' and the declaration in 5:9: 'thou wast slain and by thy blood didst ransom men for God'. Ideas of the Passover lamb, the Suffering Servant and the sin-offering are probably connoted by this title.[120]

It is likely that the depictions of the heavenly beings as holding 'bowls full of incense, which are the prayers of the saints' (5:8) and as mingling incense with 'the prayers of all the saints upon the golden altar' (8:3-4) involve Christians being seen as offering sacrifices of prayer. It is the heavenly beings who act in priestly fashion, but the saints must have offered up these prayers first and the prayers are likened to the incense-offering. Martyrdom and sacrifice may also be connected in the depiction of the martyrs' souls as 'under the altar' in 6:9.[121]

Although Vanhoye disputes it,[122] Christ is probably depicted as the high priest in 1:13 when described as 'clothed with a long robe' (*endedumenon podere*). *Podere* is used in other ways too in the Septuagint, but it is used there of the high priest's robe and the references to Christ's death as a sacrifice noted earlier enhance the likelihood that the author of Revelation viewed him as the priest of his own sacrifice.[123]

Exodus 19:6 is alluded to three times in Revelation. According to 1:6, Christ 'made us a kingdom, priests to his God and Father, ...' The

[118] Daly, *Christian Sacrifice*, 295.
[119] Ibid., 298.
[120] So ibid., 300.
[121] See ibid., 302-3 for an inconclusive discussion.
[122] See Vanhoye, 280-281. For the contrary view see Caird, G.B., *A Commentary on the Revelation of St. John the Divine* (London, 1966), 25.
[123] Vanhoye, 282, himself sees this as likely in 5:6.

aorist 'made' and its paralleling that in 'freed us from our sins by his blood', suggests that Christ established Christians as a kingdom and priests through his redeeming and sacrificial death. The use of the plural 'priests' here and in 5:10 shows that Christians can be seen as priests individually, though not individualistically, in view of the collective ''kingdom' with which it is in apposition.[124] What this priesthood involved is uncertain because of the lack of explanation.[125] The same problem arises in 5:10. Whilst 'kingdom' is developed in 'and they shall reign on earth', 'priests' is again not explained at all.

It is most likely that only martyrs are envisaged in 20:4-6[126] in which it is said that 'they shall be priests of God and of Christ, and they shall reign with him a thousand years.' They are probably presented as enjoying a fuller exercise of priesthood and rule during a millennium than had been possible earlier,[127] although the priesthood and rule are not explained.

In 7:9-17 the worship of the redeemed[128] in heaven is depicted in priestly terms. Although 'priests' is not used, *latreuein*, 'serve', frequently used of cultic worship in the Septuagint,[129] is (in verse 15) and the site is the temple. Worship in the New Jerusalem is depicted in priestly terms in 22:3.[130]

Not surprisingly, then, the priesthood of Christians is portrayed mainly, if not solely, in terms of heaven in Revelation. Nevertheless, the fact that its inauguration is connected with Christ's redeeming and sanctifying death implies that it is already a present reality which will have fuller expression later, as with so much in the NT's depiction of salvation. Its main expression is in worship, both praise and prayer being implied.[131]

---

[124] So Fiorenza, E.S., *Priester für Gott: Studien zum Herrschafts- und Priestermotiv in der Apokalypse*, (Münster, 1972), 227 and Vanhoye, 287 against Elliott, *The Elect and the Holy*, 113-4.

[125] See discussions in Caird, 17; Fiorenza, 232-4; and Vanhoye, 289.

[126] So Caird, 252-3; Beasley-Murray, G.R., *The Book of Revelation* (London, 1974), 294; and Vanhoye, 301-2. Fiorenza, 342, argues that all believers who decide for God's worship and against the Beast's are potential if not actual martyrs.

[127] Rather than an actual instead of a potential priesthood and rule as Fiorenza, 342, argues; cf. Caird, 252-3 and Vanhoye, 301-2.

[128] So Fiorenza, 392-5 and Beasley-Murray, 146-7. Caird, 100-103 and Vanhoye, 301-2, see only martyrs referred to because of 7:14.

[129] So Strathmann, *TDNT*, vol.4, 60-61.

[130] See especially Fiorenza, 379ff.

[131] Daly, *Christian Sacrifice*, 304-5, underestimates the significance of the priesthood of Christians in Revelation when he writes that its author 'was either not directly conscious of, or not particularly interested' in it.

3.2.8 Summary

Although there are passages, in the Synoptic Gospels and Acts in particular, in which reverence and respect for the Jerusalem temple and its cultus are exhibited, there are others in which criticisms are made, especially of mere performance without right attitudes and behaviour. Moreover, aspects of Christ's person, life and, above all, death are described in terms drawn from that cultus: he is the temple, the high priest and the sacrifice. Apart from the book of Hebrews, the supersession of the old cultus is only implied, but in that book it is made explicit and the old cultus is depicted as obsolete and dying away. Whilst the author of Hebrews thus goes further than other NT writings, it would be wrong to play down what he wrote,[132] since there is complete congruence between that and other parts of the NT, a good deal of it also being stated elsewhere in the NT. Further, Christians are described in cultic terms: as the temple, as sacrifices, and as priests who are to offer sacrifices, sacrifices which involve worship, material giving, holiness, and their whole selves.

3.3 NT teaching on the Christian, the church and ministry

An attempt is made here to summarize important relevant aspects of the NT's teaching on the Christian, the church and ministry both to demonstrate the congruence of what we have noted in section 3.2 with this and to form a broader foundation with which later developments can be compared.

3.3.1 The fundamental unity of all Christians

Much in the NT assumes or expresses what Christians have or are in common. Foundationally all are in Christ, benefit from what he has done, and are indwelt by the Spirit. As a result there is a unity and equality between Christians at the deepest levels that the NT envisages. This is expressed in various ways, including the description of all as 'disciples', 'believers' and 'saints' and the dissolving of the traditional distinctions of the day.[133] One of these is between priests and laity. Not only is the offering of sacrifice the prerogative and duty of all Christians, but the term used in the Septuagint for peculiarly priestly

---

[132] As does Brown, *Priest and Bishop*, 14.
[133] On this see especially Banks, R., *Paul's Idea of Community: The Early House Churches in their Historical Setting* (Exeter, 1980), 113-121; also Faivre, A., *Les laïcs aux origines de l'Église* (Paris, 1984), 15-6 and Küng, 19-23.

service, *leitourgia* and its cognates,[134] is used of activities open to, and expected of, all believers, such as the collection for the congregation in Jerusalem (Rom. 15:27 and 2 Cor. 9:12). Moreover, 'apart from its occurrence in Old Testament quotations and in direct references to the Jewish nation ..., *laos* refers only to Christians as a whole, as those upon whom the promises of God concerning the creation of a "people" of his own have fallen (2 Cor. 6:6). Nowhere does the term refer to only part of the community, or in opposition to *kléros*, clergy.'[135] It forms a boundary, not within the church, but between the whole people of God and those outside it. Further, *kléros* and its cognates are employed in the NT for privileges and a reality which belong to the whole people of God, as in the use of *kléronomos* ('inheritor') and *kléronomia* ('inheritance') in Acts 20:32, Romans 8:17, Galatians 3:29, and 4:7, and 1 Peter 1:4, and *kléros* in Acts 8:21, 26:18, Colossians 1:12, and, significantly for the point being made here, in 1 Peter 5:1-3 where the elders are told to behave 'not as domineering over those in your charge (*tôn klérôn*) but being examples to the flock.'[136]

The oneness within the church is also expressed in corporate metaphors, such as the body, the building and the bride, the first of which is developed to bring out the fundamental interdependence and importance, alongside the variety, of all believers in Christ (see especially 1 Cor. 12:4-26).

3.3.2 The ministry of all Christians

Another result and expression of this deep unity and equality is the possession by each Christian of at least one gift from God with which to serve and build up whole the community. This is seen in 'the fact that "to each one" occurs in connexion with the distribution of gifts in all the three passages (1 Cor.12:7, 11, cf. v.18; Rom.12.3f.; Eph.4:7)' in which this distribution is mentioned.[137] This in turn results in each Christian having a ministry or service to perform for the good of the community, as is recognized in much recent literature and confirmed by study of the use of the *diakonia* word-group in the NT. Not only is it the most used

---

[134] So Torrance, 15-16 and Strathmann, *TDNT*, vol.4, 220-221.

[135] Kraemer, 49; see also Cooke, 197; Delorme in Delorme, 312; Wingren, 'Der Begriff "Laie"' in Schröder and Müller, *Vom Amt des Laien*, 3-4; Hanson, A.T. and R.P.C., 127; and Strathmann, *TDNT*, vol.4, 54-7.

[136] See on this topic Foerster, *TDNT*, vol.3, 763-4 and 781-5; and Faivre, *Les laïcs*, 16-7.

[137] Fung, R.Y.K., 'Ministry, Community and Spiritual Gifts', *The Evangelical Quarterly* 56.1 (1984), 8-9.

for service,[138] but 'every activity or function which contributed to the upbuilding of the Christian community was brought under the category of diakonia. All Christians are *diakonoi*, ministers, called to a ministry.'[139] There is no exclusive caste which ministers.

This view has been challenged by John Collins in an extensive survey of the use of *diakonia* in both ancient, non-Christian Greek sources and early Christian writings, including the NT. He argues cogently that, in the former, the basic meaning is not that of service but that of go-between.[140] He further argues that this basic meaning is there in the NT also. He makes out a good case for this and provides a helpful corrective to the normal over-emphasis on service, an aspect of *diakonia*'s meaning that he accepts as present too. However, he goes beyond the evidence in maintaining that, 'the "gifts" that Paul acknowledged in 1 Cor. 12:4 may well have been "ministries" in 1 Cor. 12:5 only by virtue of having been recognized and endorsed by the community or its leaders; ....'[141] and in implying that 'ministry' should only be employed concerning the use of such recognized and endorsed gifts. As argued above, the fact that each part of the body has been given a gift resulting in 'varieties of service' shows that each Christian was seen as having a *diakonia*, even if its character as mediating God should be emphasized more than its character as serving God or others.

The fact that all Christians have an anointing, whether that refers only to the Spirit or to the word as well,[142] means, for the author of 1 John, that they 'have no need that any one should teach [them]' (2:27, cf. 2:20). This is compatible with the existence of teachers in the church as is clear from the context which is the discernment of false from true teaching. However, if there is any reference to the work of the Spirit at all here, then, as in the use of Jeremiah 31:33-34 in Hebrews 8:10-11, a degree of direct knowledge of God is implied, which has no need for mediation. Further, it is unlikely that this knowledge is only experienced when Christians are all together, suggesting that each has it.

Not only are all Christians able to evaluate teaching, they are all to mediate the results of Christ's salvific mediation to others in witness. This is seen in a number of ways in the NT. For one thing, the promises

---

[138] Moulton, Geden and Moulton list 95 occurrences, most of which relate to general Christian service, as against 15 of the *leitourgia* word-group and 26 of the *latreia*-group.
[139] Kraemer, 139; see too Beyer, *TDNT*, vol.2, 81-93.
[140] Collins, J.N., *Diakonia: Re-interpreting the Ancient Sources* (Oxford, 1990), 73-189.
[141] Ibid., 258-9.
[142] Bultmann, R., *The Johannine Epistles* (Philadelphia, 1973), 37-8; Marshall, I.H., *The Epistles of John* (Grand Rapids, 1978), 155; and Brown, *The Epistles of John*, 348, find a reference to the Spirit's work here, the first two alongside teaching of the word.

of the Spirit to enable in witness, though made to the Twelve or the Eleven in John 15:26-27 and Acts 1:8, were fulfilled for the whole Christian community (Acts 2:1-4). The promised Spirit of prophecy is presented as poured out on the same in Acts 2:16-18 and it is the whole community who pray for and receive boldness to speak God's word according to Acts 4:29-31. As noted earlier, the whole church 'went about preaching the word' in Acts 8:4 (cf. 8:1). Further, Paul rejoices in his imprisonment because 'most of the brethren have been made confident in the Lord ... and are much more bold to speak the word of God without fear' (Phil. 1:14).[143]

3.3.3 The understanding of authority and leadership

Authority and leadership clearly were exercised in the early church. At the beginning, the apostles are depicted as exercising authority over the church in Jerusalem and elsewhere both in Acts and in Paul's letters. Although there is no indication that the apostles were seen as passing their authority on to later leaders, such were appointed, whether called 'presbyters', as in Acts and the Pastoral Epistles, 'bishops and deacons', as in Philippians 1:1, 'those ... who are over you' (*proistamenoi*), as in 1 Thessalonians 5:12, or 'leaders' (*hégoumenoi*), as in Hebrews 13:7 and 17.

This authority was not based on force and power, however, but on a spirit of service and humility. As Paul says in 2 Corinthians 1:24, 'Not that we lord it over your faith; we work with you ...', and as the elders are exhorted to behave in 1 Peter 5:3, 'not as domineering over those in your charge, but being examples to the flock.' Indeed, Delorme notes that 'the received vocabulary for designating generally the constituted authorities of political or religious society is never applied to the ministers of the Church in the New Testament.' Küng sees the reason for this as the fact that it denoted domination, which is probable in view of the disclaimers of ruling as 'lord' noted above.[144]

Further, whilst subjection to and respect for leaders are encouraged (e.g., in 1 Thess. 5:12-13), their presence does not remove all authority from the congregation. This is seen from the appointment of a replacement for Judas when it is 'the brethren' who put forward two candidates in Acts 1:15-26, the appointment of the seven in Acts 6:1-6 where it is 'the whole multitude' who chose them, and the 'Jerusalem council' since the final decision 'seemed good to the apostles and the

---

[143] On this see Cooke, 49, 219 and 329-330.
[144] Delorme in Delorme, 317; Küng, 26. See too Banks, 134-7.

elders, with the whole church' (Acts 15.22).[145]

Finally, the gifts necessary for leadership are depicted by Paul as necessary but equal to other gifts. Although apostles, prophets and teachers head the list in 1 Corinthians 12:28, *ho proistamenos* (literally, 'the president' or 'the one presiding') is one gift alongside others in Romans 12:6-8.

3.3.4 The significance of this teaching

The leaders of the church, then, are never called priests or mediators in a way different from all Christians. Although they had authority and were to be heeded and obeyed, the gifts necessary for that authority were not viewed as making of them a separate caste but rather as manifestations of the Spirit who distributed gifts to every Christian. Authority, therefore, is all of grace and should be exercised in that light. Whilst leaders are to be respected, they are not elevated to a higher plane of holiness (all are called 'saints'), much less to a different ontological level of participation in Christ's priesthood. What all Christians have in common far outweighs the differences created between them by different gifts. Moreover, they are all to minister with the gifts God has provided, including mediating God's grace in Christ to those outside the church through their witness. The congruence of these ideas with that of the general priesthood is clear as is their incongruity with all ideas of an elevated priesthood within the church.

3.4 Conclusion

This survey of the relevant NT material has shown that a priesthood of church leaders separate or different from that of the Christian community is absent from the earliest church's writings. It has also shown that ideas are present in the NT which tell against the presence of a priestly group within the church. The main one is that Christ has offered the only effective sacrifice for sin so that the kinds of sacrifice which are now appropriate are those of people's lives and various aspects of those lives which are honouring to God. But these sacrifices are all such as can be, and are, offered by each Christian. Relevant too is the fact that all Christians can and should mediate Christ's presence and blessings through their exercise of the gift(s) they have been given and through their witness to those outside the church. The fundamental difference between church leaders and the rest of the church is that the

---

[145] See Hanson, R.P.C., *Christian Priesthood Examined*, 19-20 and 27.

former have been given the gift(s) necessary to exercise that leadership.

Further, the other arguments noted in section 2.3.3 to justify the application of priestly ideas to church leaders in a way different from the rest of the church receive no support in the NT and there are elements of NT teaching which tell against some of them. The argument that it is justified on the basis of the similarities of church leaders' roles and functions to those of the OT priests falls foul of the emphasis on the supersession of the Levitical priesthood in and through Christ found in Hebrews especially but implied in much of the NT. The argument that it is justified because the NT is not anti-sacerdotal, if sacerdotal refers to a specialized priesthood, runs aground on the same emphasis and the indications that mediation is not restricted to any part of the church. The argument that it is justified because church leaders represent or focus the church's priesthood is not contradicted by anything in the NT, although it is not supported by anything in it either. Indeed, the dangers noted by some[146] concerning what they view as a sacerdotal as opposed to a representative understanding of the ordained's priesthood will be present to some extent in any specialized use of priestly terminology.

It is with this background in mind that the writings of the post-NT church are now to be examined. This is, first, because of the NT's significance for all Christians as in some way(s) normative; second, with the argument in mind, also adduced in section 2.3.3, that the priestly understanding of church leaders developed under the guidance of the Spirit.[147] If this were so, then it would seem highly likely that the emphases noted above on the general priesthood and the dignity and ministry of all Christians should not be harmed by the development of the priestly understanding of church leaders, since the former were major expressions of the life of the Spirit in the earliest church and, unless the later development could be shown to have facilitated the work of the Spirit better, should be maintained as such.[148] It is the question of whether the development of the priestly understanding of church leaders did harm the appreciation of the general priesthood and the dignity and ministry of all Christians which will be addressed in the rest of this thesis. After tracing that development, the ongoing use of the

---

[146] See especially ibid., 96ff.

[147] So Brown, *Priest and Bishop*, 4 and Noll, R.R., *Christian Ministerial Priesthood: A Search for Its Beginnings In the Primary Documents Of the Apostolic Fathers* (San Francisco, 1993), 326.

[148] Schillebeeckx, 121-2 rightly argues that the Spirit-baptism of all believers was and should remain the matrix of all Christian ministry so that the shift from a charisma of the many to that of the few brings the danger of the Spirit being quenched and of the faithful becoming the objects of priestly or ministerial concern rather than the subjects and expressions of faith.

general priesthood will be examined as will the evolving understanding of the place of the non-ordained, especially vis-à-vis the ordained.

CHAPTER 4

The Developing Understanding of Church Leaders as Priests in the First Three Centuries

The evidence on this subject will now be examined in the Christian literature of the first three centuries. The treatment will be basically chronological with some allowance for geographical proximity. It will also seek to be exhaustive, except for Origen's writings which were too voluminous to be so treated.

4.1 The Apostolic Fathers[1]

The main relevant passages are *1 Clement* 40-41, *Didache* 13:3, and three passages in Ignatius' letters: *Smyrnaeans* 7:1, *Philadelphians* 9:1 and *Trallians* 7:2. In addition, a priestly understanding of those who presided at the eucharist has been inferred on the basis of *1 Clement* 44:4, *Didache* 14 and other passages which suggest a sacrificial understanding of that service and that church leaders presided at it.

4.1.1 1 Clement 40-41 and 44.4

Written from the Roman to the Corinthian church, *1 Clement* is probably the earliest Christian document outside the NT, dating from around the end of the first century AD,[2] although there are those who have argued for dates as early as 69 or 80.[3]

In the context of an exhortation to follow God's established order in

---

[1] Grant, R.M., *The Apostolic Fathers. A New Translation and Commentary*, vol. 1: *An Introduction* (Camden, N.J., 1964), vi: 'For our purposes, the Apostolic Fathers will consist of the writings from the early second century or late first century ascribed to Clement, Ignatius, Polycarp, Barnabas, and Hermas, together with the Didache, the fragments of Papias, and the Martyrdom of Polycarp.' The abbreviations used for these writings in this thesis are those of ibid., xi.

[2] Geerard, M., *Clavis Patrum Graecorum*, vol.1: *Patres Antenicaeni* (Turnhout, 1983), 5 gives 92-101 for Clement's episcopate, and Snyder, R.F., in Ferguson, E. (ed.), *Encyclopedia of Early Christianity* (London, 1990), 216, gives c.88-97. Noll, *Christian Ministerial Priesthood*, 57, states that *1 Clement* 'was written according to the general consensus of scholars in 95 or 96 A.D.'

[3] See Noll, *Christian Ministerial Priesthood*, 17-19.

the church, and especially to submit to leadership, Clement points to the OT example of God's commands that 'the offerings and services ... be performed diligently, and not ... carelessly or in disorder, but at designated times and seasons' (40:2). Not only has God commanded the times, but also the places and the people so that acceptable sacrifices may be made (40:3-4): 'For to the high priest the proper services have been given, and to the priests the proper office has been assigned, and upon the Levites the proper ministries have been imposed. The layman is bound by the layman's rules' (40:5). Clement adds: 'Let each of you, brothers, in his proper order give thanks to God, ... not overstepping the designated rule of his ministry, but acting with reverence' (41:1), following this up by a reminder that sacrifices are offered only at the altar in Jerusalem and after inspection 'by the high priest and the previously mentioned ministers.'[4]

Clement then points out that God sent Christ, Christ sent the apostles, the apostles appointed bishops and deacons (42), in a similar way to that in which Moses appointed Aaron and his tribe to the priesthood (43). In the light of the apostles' appointment of bishops and deacons (44:1-2), such ministers should not be removed (44:3), 'for it will be no small sin for us, if we depose from the bishop's office those who have offered the gifts blamelessly and in holiness.'(44:4)[5]

Commenting on past research concerning these passages, Noll wrote that 'about as many Catholic scholars ... find a reference to Christian ministerial priesthood ... as ... Protestant scholars ... do not.'[6] The strongest argument for finding such a reference is the parallel drawn between 'the "offerings" performed by the high priest or under his guidance (40:2, 4; 41:2) [and] the offering of gifts by those who hold the office of the episcopate (44:4).'[7]

Daly aptly notes that 'the gifts' of 44:4

remain something of a puzzle. ... There is no indication that the elements of bread and wine were so understood in Clement's time. He may well have understood by this phrase the general Christian spiritual sacrifice of praise, but this does not seem to explain satisfactorily the use of so concrete a phrase as ['the gifts'], nor the emphasis with which he suggests that offering them is the special function of the bishop qua bishop.[8]

[4] Lightfoot, J.B., Harmer, J.R. and Holmes, M.W. (eds.), *The Apostolic Fathers: Greek Texts and English Translations of their Writings* (Grand Rapids, 1992[2]), 73 and 75.
[5] Ibid., 79.
[6] Noll, R.R., 'The Search for a Christian Ministerial Priestood in 1 Clement', *Studia Patristica* 13 (1975), 250.
[7] Grant, *Introduction*, 163-4.
[8] Daly, *Christian Sacrifice*, 317.

He is right to note Clement's inclination to spiritualize the idea of sacrifice 'by placing in emphatic positions at the end of three different chapters (chaps. 18; 35; 52) some of the well-known spiritualizing Psalm texts from the LXX.'[9] Although it is impossible to be certain, this makes it most likely that 'the gifts' in 44:4 is used of the presidency of the presbyter or bishop at church services in which he was the spokesman of the people's prayers of praise and thanksgiving, including prayers offered over the bread and wine.[10]

Turning to the question of whether Clement was using OT terminology to describe a NT sacerdotal hierarchy, we must note the context. In 40-41 we have part of the most extended of four illustrations, 'all of which deal with the duty of observing order .... Thus it seems quite clear that first and foremost the Old Testament ["*tagma*"] *qua* ["*tagma*"] is placed in parallel with the New Testament ["*tagma*"]; ....'[11] R.P.C. Hanson therefore sees Clement's references to the OT cultic priesthood as 'made only to emphasize the necessity of order (i.e., orderliness) in the ministry',[12] and this is the most definite conclusion one can come to. Clement identifies the officers mentioned in 40:5 as those of the Jerusalem temple cultus (41:2)[13] so no literal reference to Christian ministers as priests is involved. Moreover, while Clement recognizes three orders of OT ministry, he is only aware of two in the church, the overseer or presbyter and the deacon. Equivalence is thereby ruled out.[14]

Noll's conclusion that 'we do indeed find in Clement a sort of neo-levitical mentality at work that ... would like to see the Christian

---

[9] Ibid., 314. Noll, *Christian Ministerial Priesthood*, 73-4, notes the same.

[10] So Eastwood, C., *The Royal Priesthood of the Faithful* (London, 1963), 58; Grant, R.M. in Grant, R.M. and Graham, H.H. (eds.), *The Apostolic Fathers. A New Translation and Commentary* vol. 2: *First and Second Clement* (Camden, N.J., 1965), 74; and Daly, *Christian Sacrifice*, 503. However, Noll, *Christian Ministerial Priesthood*, 77, concludes, 'the precise function of the *presbyter-episkopoi* in *1 Clement*, i.e. exactly what they said and did when they "offered the gifts", remains a mystery.'

[11] Noll, 'Search', *Studia Patristica* 13 (1975), 251.

[12] Hanson, R.P.C., *Studies in Christian Antiquity* (Edinburgh, 1985), 122. Faivre, *Les laics*, 31, and Noll, *Christian Ministerial Priesthood*, 66, agree.

[13] Noll, 'Search', *Studia Patristica* 13 (1975), 252.

[14] Hanson, R.P.C., *Christian Priesthood Examined*, 37; cf. Grant, *Introduction*, 163. Noll, *Christian Ministerial Priesthood*, 67, also points out that 'if Clement goes to the trouble of pointing out a parallel between one of the LXX non-cultic uses for the word *episkopoi* and the same title then being used for the leaders of the Christian community – a mere question of terminology hardly as important as the existence of a Christian priesthood – would he not *a fortiori* point out a direct parallel between the Old Testament priesthood or priestly functions and that in the New Covenant, had it been possible? This is something he certainly does not do, although he would have had an ideal opportunity to immediately after 40:5.'

ministry, whose terminology and actual boundaries of the areas of competence were still quite unfixed, develop in the direction of a spiritualized version of the Levitical order'[15] and that '*1 Clement* is beginning to suggest a subtle transfer of priesthood terminology to the broader work of the Christian overseers'[16]is suggestive but lacks conclusive proof and goes beyond the evidence.

The likeliest interpretation of these passages, then, is that Clement, by drawing on the order of the OT cult, is inculcating that order should reign in the church, an order that involved remaining in one's allotted position. The presbyter-bishop has the privileged position of offering the people's gifts of praise and thanksgiving, including those at the celebration of the eucharist, as their mouthpiece to God. It is unlikely that Clement viewed this person as a priest in a different way from the rest of the congregation.

4.1.2 Didache 13.3 and 14

In Kraft's view, 'the *Didache* contains a great deal of material which derives from very early (i.e., first-century and early second-century) forms of (Jewish-) Christianity; but it would be difficult to argue convincingly that the present form of the *Didache* is earlier than the mid-second century.'[17] The exact date of any part of it is fairly unimportant for our purposes. It is enough to note that here we have very early, post-NT testimony to church practices, probably from Syria.[18]

Lohse argues that the special priesthood of the ordained developed through comparison of bishops and deacons with OT priests, as in *1 Clement* 40ff. and in *Didache* 13:3, and through the picturing of ideas of sacrifice, at first figuratively, as in *Didache* 14:1.[19] Colson offers the tightest line of argument that they were: *Didache* 15:1 recommends the election of bishops and deacons to fulfil the service of the prophets and teachers, that is, for a ministry of teaching and of celebrating the

---

[15] Noll, 'Search', *Studia Patristica* 13 (1975), 253-4.

[16] Noll, *Christian Ministerial Priesthood*, 12.

[17] Kraft, R.A. (ed.), *The Apostolic Fathers. A New Translation and Commentary*, vol. 3: *The Didache and Barnabas* (Camden, N.J., 1965), 76.

[18] Very recently, Noll, *Christian Ministerial Priesthood*, 34, notes that recent, major critical studies have rejected 'the notion of a later artificial construction and consider the text as appearing during the late first century or beginning of the second, and all seem to prefer Syria or the Syrian-Palestinian border area as the place of origin.'

[19] Lohse in *Religion in Geschichte und Gegenwart*, (Tübingen, 1957-1965[3]), vol. 5, 578-9. Von Campenhausen, H., *Tradition and Life in the Church. Essays and Lectures in Church History* (London, 1968), 220, argues similarly.

eucharist, the latter in view of the instruction in 14:1.[20]

True prophets and, by implication from 13:1-2, true teachers, are identified as the Christians' high priests in 13:3: '... give these firstfruits to the prophets, for they are your high priests.'[21] The sole point of the comparison is that, as the high priests were provided with their food, so the prophets and teachers should be.[22] It is unwarranted, therefore, to state in general terms that 'the status of the resident prophets is equivalent to that of the high priests in the Old Testament'.[23] Nor is there any link between the 'priesthood' of the prophets and teachers and the offering of sacrifice except that of the firstfruits provided by the faithful. The exhortation in 15:1 to appoint bishops and deacons to fulfil the prophets' and teachers' ministry implies that the former are to be provided for like the latter, but that is all.

The relationships between the instructions in chapters 9 and 10 and those in chapter 14, and between the eucharist and a love-feast in them, have been much discussed.[24] That the eucharistic cup and bread are involved in 9:2-4 seems likely, since prayers over cup and bread are prescribed and the cup and bread, not just the prayer over them, are called the eucharist in 9:5 ('let no one eat or drink of your Eucharist except those who have been baptized ...').[25] However, the positioning of the instruction 'permit the prophets to give thanks however they wish' (10:7)[26] after the feast probably does not refer only to giving thanks over the elements, although it may include that.[27] In any case, possible sacrificial allusions in 9-10 remain no more than possible, as Daly allows.[28]

It is 14:1-3 which has been seen by many as showing that the eucharist was viewed as a sacrifice.[29] That a sacrifice is mentioned is clear in each verse of this chapter. In favour of the view that it is the

---

[20] Colson, *La fonction diaconale*, 92-3. So, too, in a more nuanced way, Grant, *Introduction*, 161-2.

[21] Lightfoot, Harmer and Holmes, 267.

[22] André de Hallieux offers this as likely in a quotation given in Noll, *Christian Ministerial Priesthood*, 33.

[23] Grant, *Introduction*, 161.

[24] See, for example, Kraft, 165-8 and 173-4; Lietzmann, 189-190; and Stevenson, 14.

[25] Lightfoot, Harmer and Holmes, 261.

[26] Ibid., 263.

[27] This holds even if 10:7 is considered a later addition made in the light of 11:3-12 as Kraft, 64, maintains.

[28] Daly, *Christian Sacrifice*, 311.

[29] So Palmer, P.F., 'The Lay Priesthood: Real or Metaphorical', *Theological Studies* 8 (1947), 596; Colson, *La fonction diaconale*, 92-3; von Campenhausen, *Tradition and Life*, 220; Daly, *Christian Sacrifice*, 312-3 and 502; Lietzmann, 193; Hanson, R.P.C., *Studies*, 85; and Stevenson, 15.

eucharistic celebration with the bread and cup that is being referred to
are the instructions 'break bread and give thanks' and the situation 'on
the Lord's own day gather together'.[30] However, 'break bread' could be
referring to 'a regular community meal', and the 'give thanks' could be
referring to the giving of thanks over such a meal or the giving of thanks
in general, so that the references to sacrifices could have no more than
'prayers and praise' in mind.[31] Of those who are certain that the
eucharist is involved, Palmer acknowledges that the emphasis is on the
inward dispositions, but points out that this is not in opposition to the
objective sacrifice of the eucharist, and Daly acknowledges that
Didache 14

> neither describes the content of this Eucharist (or Eucharistic prayer) nor
> explains its understanding of the term sacrifice. Falling back, therefore, on the
> larger context provided by this study, we can only conclude that the sacrifice
> of Did 14 apparently has primarily the spiritualized meaning of a prayer of
> praise and thanksgiving recited over the elements of bread and wine which
> evokes ... the Lord's saving presence.

Moreover, R.P.C. Hanson holds that 'the [sacrifice] here is the
Christian's offering of himself, his heart and his conscience' and
Stevenson argues that the eucharist was then seen as sacrificial 'because
it best expressed the Christian insight that worship presupposes a
sacrificial disposition on the part of the worshipper.'[32]

Noll considers that a reference in *Didache* 15.1 to bishops and
deacons ministering the ministry of prophets and deacons shows that
'the vocabulary of Levitical priestly service [is] applied here to that of
prophets, teachers, *epískopoi* and *diakonoi*, and the tie-in with the use of
thusía in ch. 14 is obvious.' He continues, however, 'but whether this is
simply meant to demonstrate a continuity between Christian ministers
and the Old Testament "types" or whether the four groups mentioned
here were actually considered to constitute a Christian priesthood is
impossible to say in the light of the meager data given here.'[33] The fact
that there are no other references to these groups being considered a

---

[30] Lightfoot, Harmer and Holmes, 267.

[31] Kraft, 174. Young, 249, also argues that it is the purity necessary for participation in the
church's eschatological fellowship-meal which is in view here.

[32] Palmer, P.F., 'The Lay Priesthood', *Th St* 8 (1947), 596; Daly, *Christian Sacrifice*, 502-3;
Hanson, R.P.C., *Studies*, 86; and Stevenson in Buchanan, C. (ed.), *Essays on Eucharistic
Sacrifice in the Early Church* (Bramcote, 1984), 28. Noll, *Christian Ministerial Priesthood*,
275, argues that breaking of bread, 'with the material elements involved', is part of the
sacrifice referred to in this passage. While possible, this is not necessarily so.

[33] Noll, *Christian Ministerial Priesthood*, 278.

Christian priesthood in this period militates against the likelihood that they are being so considered here. Even so, this passage demonstrates the way in which the drawing of parallels between OT and Christian usage played a part in the eventual identification of Christian leaders with OT priests.

Noll notes another usage of 'Levitical sacral-cultic terminology' regarding the eucharist in *Didache* 9.5, in which a warning is given against allowing other than the baptized to eat or drink of the eucharist because it is holy.[34] If he is right, it demonstrates the way in which sacral terminology became attached to the eucharist and/or an agape-meal, and prepared the way for later developments.

In conclusion, the use of priestly terminology in 13:3 indicates no more than that the analogy being made necessitated a reference to the prophets as high priests, and the reference to breaking bread and giving thanks as a sacrifice in 14:1-3 is as likely to refer to praise and thanksgiving as a sacrifice as to the eucharistic elements. In any case, it is an offering by the Christians in general that is referred to. The reference to church leaders 'ministering the ministry' in 15.1 is too vague to allow a definite reference to their priestly status, but, like the reference to the eucharist as holy in 9.5, it may show how sacral language was being used and prepared the way for later developments. There is, however, no clear warrant here for seeing the priesthood of the ordained as referred to.

4.1.3 Ignatius

Writing as bishop of Antioch in Syria some time in the reign of Trajan,[35] Ignatius' one possibly ambiguous use of *hiereis* ('priests') comes in *Philadelphians* 9:1 where we read, 'The priests, too, were good, but the High Priest ... is better'.[36] However, recent scholarship rightly views the priests referred to as the OT priests and the high priest as Christ, as the following context makes clear.[37]

On the other hand, Ignatius held the presidency of the bishop or his appointee at the eucharist to be necessary, as is seen in *Smyrnaeans* 8:1 in particular ('only that Eucharist which is under the authority of the bishop (or whomever he himself designates) is to be considered

---

[34] Ibid., 279.

[35] So Grant, 47-8.

[36] Lightfoot, Harmer and Holmes, 183.

[37] So Lawson, 135; Grant, R.M. (ed.), *The Apostolic Fathers. A New Translation and Commentary*, vol. 4: *Ignatius of Antioch* (Camden, N.J., 1966), 106-7; and Hanson, R.P.C., *Christian Priesthood Examined*, 36, where he refers to *Philippians* 9:1 but quotes *Philad* 9:1.

valid'[38]), and a number of scholars argue that he also conceived of the eucharist in sacrificial terms. This is done on the basis of the way in which he connects the eucharist with the sanctuary in several passages.[39] In *Philadelphians* 4:1, after a warning 'to participate in one Eucharist', there is a reference to the 'one flesh of our Lord Jesus Christ, and one cup which leads to unity through his blood; ... one altar, just as there is one bishop, together with the presbytery and the deacons ....'[40] In *Ephesians* 5:2, an eucharistic allusion is found in 'if anyone is not within the sanctuary, he lacks the bread of God.'[41] Further references to the sanctuary and the bishop, but not the eucharist, are found in *Trallians* 7:2 and *Magnesians* 7:1-2.[42]

Ignatius clearly does make connections between the eucharist, the bishop and the altar. It is difficult to know just what they are. He never uses 'sacrifice' of the eucharist nor 'priest' of the bishop. Lampe interprets altar here as 'altar-precincts, sanctuary ... met[aphorically], of place or sphere of worship',[43] suggesting a rather vague, but sacral, allusion to 'the Church (i.e. the gathered community)'.[44] Daly, moreover, argues that 'there is no need for us to interpret the image of the altar as Church; Ignatius himself does this for us in *Trall* 7,2', which says, 'The one who is within the sanctuary is clean, but the one who is outside the sanctuary is not clean. That is, whoever does anything without bishop and presbytery and deacons does not have a clean conscience.'[45] Noll, too, states, '*Thusiastérion* ... is an image which primarily signifies the whole Christian assembly together with its bishop.'[46] He further notes that 'the only place in the Letters where one could deduce theologically a "condition sacerdotale" is in the efficacious prayer "of the bishop and the whole assembly" (*Eph* 5:2), i.e. in "the public *prayer* of the Church, more especially that which accompanied the eucharist." Thus the *thusía* which is offered within the

---

[38] Lightfoot, Harmer and Holmes, 189.

[39] So Colson, *La fonction diaconale*, 86; Daly, *Christian Sacrifice*, 503; Young, 250; Williams R., *Eucharistic Sacrifice – The Roots of a Metaphor* (Bramcote, 1982), 18; and Stevenson, 17.

[40] Lightfoot, Harmer and Holmes, 179.

[41] Ibid., 141.

[42] Daly, *Christian Sacrifice*, 504. Daly argues that sacrificial overtones are also present in *Smyrn* 6:2, in which the eucharist is called 'the flesh of our Savior Jesus Christ, which suffered for our sins', but the only sacrificial reference concerns Jesus' death here. Daly further views *Rom* 2:2 as 'suggestive of the Eucharistic liturgy' and *Rom* 4:1f. as containing an eucharistic allusion, but these are yet more tenuous.

[43] Lampe, G.W.H. (ed.), *A Patristic Greek Lexicon* (Oxford, 1961), 660.

[44] Daly, *Christian Sacrifice*, 503.

[45] Ibid., 319 and Lightfoot, Harmer and Holmes, 163.

[46] Noll, *Christian Ministerial Priesthood*, 116.

thusiastérion … is the public prayer of thanksgiving.'[47]

In the church, Ignatius clearly wants the bishop and the eucharist to play central roles. It seems likely, then, that what we have here is another use of OT cultic language and ideas to apply to the church's worship, without the elements of the eucharist themselves being called a sacrifice or the presider being called a priest.

4.1.4 Summary

In this material from the earliest period of the church's history outside the NT, we find language and ideas drawn from OT cultic practice. They are used to illustrate particular points regarding the church: the need for order (*1 Clement* 40-41), the fact of the presbyter-bishop's presidency in worship (*1 Clement* 44.4), the need to provide for prophets and teachers (*Didache* 13:3), the need for purity in worship (*Didache* 14), for only the baptized to partake of the eucharist (*Didache* 9.5), and the sacral nature of the church's worship (Ignatius). It is also likely that they are used of church leaders' general functions in *Didache* 15.1. Sacrificial ideas are not yet being employed specifically and distinctively of the eucharistic elements, and there is evidence in *1 Clement* and *Barnabas* of polemic against literal sacrifices (*1 Clement* 52:1-3; *Barnabas* 2:4-8). However, the sacrificial understanding of Christians' repentant self-offering, found in *1 Clement* 18:17 and 52:4 and in *Barnabas* 2:9-10, Ignatius' martyrdom (*Romans* 4:2), and God's people's praise, found in *1 Clement* 35:12 (cf. 36:1) and 52:3, may well have been leading to sacrificial ideas becoming attached to the eucharistic celebration in general because of the prominence of thanksgiving and self-offering connected with that celebration. Church leaders are not called priests but sacral terminology and ideas are used of them in ways that adumbrate future developments.

4.2 The period of the second-century Apologists

Since the two largest and most significant bodies of extant material are those of Justin Martyr and Irenaeus, their views will be dealt with in turn, those of other second-century writers, where known, being referred to in a third section.

---

[47] Ibid., 120.

4.2.1 Justin Martyr

As far as is known, Justin was not ordained.[48] In his writings he never calls a church leader a priest, but he does have quite a developed understanding of sacrifice. On the one hand, he has a strong polemic against both pagan and Jewish sacrifices,[49] and on the other, he employs sacrificial language and ideas for some things which Christians do. Indeed, he asserts in *Dialogue with Trypho*[50] 29:1, that God 'accepts our [Gentile] sacrifices more willingly than he does yours [the Jews'].'[51] Important here are those passages in which he uses such ideas concerning the eucharist.

In *Dialogue* 117, having written at some length of Jesus' fulfilment of Zechariah's prophecies concerning Joshua the high priest (Zech. 2:10-3.2), and called Christians 'the true [high]priestly family of God', who offer 'pleasing sacrifices' (116:3), Justin writes, 'God has therefore announced in advance that all the sacrifices offered in his name, which Jesus Christ commanded to be offered, that is, in the Eucharist of the Bread and of the Chalice, which are offered by us Christians in every part of the world, are pleasing to him' (117:1).[52] The words 'that is, in the Eucharist of the Bread and of the Chalice', in apposition to 'all the sacrifices, etc.,' clearly identify the Christians' sacrifices with the eucharist.[53] Justin then accepts that 'prayers and thanksgivings, offered by worthy persons, are the only perfect and acceptable sacrifices to God' (117:2). He identifies these sacrifices, however, with the eucharist in the immediately following words, 'For Christians were instructed to offer only such prayers, even at their thanksgiving for their food, both liquid and solid, whereby the Passion which the Son of God endured for us is commemorated' (117:3). A further comparison of 'true and spiritual praises and thanksgivings' with sacrifices is made in 118:2.

Justin had already identified the sacrifices that God would accept according to Malachi 1:10-12 with 'the Eucharistic Bread and the Eucharistic Chalice' in *Dialogue* 41:3. He had also stated, in 41:1, that the flour-offering to be presented for those cleansed from leprosy was 'a

---

[48] Grant, R.M., *Greek Apologists of the Second Century* (London, 1988), 51: 'he became a Christian, though not a cleric, turning toward teaching as his Christian vocation.'

[49] On this see Daly, *Christian Sacrifice*, 325-8 and Young, 89-94.

[50] The abbreviations *Apol.* 1, *Apol.* 2, and *Dial.* will be used in references below for Justin's apologies and his *Dialogue with Trypho, a Jew.*

[51] Falls, T.B., *The Fathers of the Church: A New Translation: Writings of Justin Martyr* (Washington, 1948), 190. My additions in square brackets.

[52] Ibid., 328-9. My addition in light of the Greek text in Goodspeed, E.J. (ed.), *Die ältesten Apologeten* (Göttingen, 1914), 234-6.

[53] So, for example, Daly, *Christian Sacrifice*, 333.

prototype of the Eucharistic Bread'.[54] Justin again quotes Malachi 1:10-12 in *Dialogue* 28:4-5. There he has been explaining that true circumcision is a matter of knowing Christ and obeying God's righteous commands: such an one 'is circumcised with the only good and useful circumcision, and both he and his offerings are pleasing to God.'[55] He does not develop what those sacrifices consist of, however.

As Daly points out, Justin calls Christians' sacrifices those of 'prayer, praise and thanksgiving; but in every case where Justin becomes more specific than this, he is speaking of the Eucharist; i.e. Christian sacrifice is the Eucharist'. He goes on to assert that 'Christian sacrifice is for Justin primarily the Eucharistic prayer of praise and thanksgiving.' He does this mainly on the basis of *Apology* 1:66, in which, likening the change to that involved in the incarnation, Justin writes, 'So, ... the food which has been made the Eucharist by the prayer of his word, and which nourishes our flesh and blood by assimilation, is both the flesh and blood of that Jesus who was made flesh' (66:2).[56] The elements thus become the eucharist (cf. 66:1: 'We call this food the Eucharist, ...') through 'the prayer of praise and thanksgiving pronounced "over" or "before" or "on the occasion of the offering of the bread and the cup.'[57] This seems the best way of reconciling Justin's statements about the Christians' sacrifices being the eucharist of the bread and the cup and those about them being prayer and praise. Justin, then, or others who have influenced him at this point, has taken a new step in viewing the elements themselves, once prayed over, as eucharist and as sacrifice. Apart from Irenaeus, the other second century Apologists do not share this view of the eucharistic elements, but we have very little of their works to judge by.[58]

In spite of this understanding of both the prayer over the elements and then of the elements themselves as sacrifice, Justin does not relate it to the priesthood of the one presiding, but only, in *Dialogue* 116-117, to the priesthood of Christians in general. It is true that he twice, in *Apology* 1:65:3-5 and 67:5, depicts the *proestôs*, 'the one presiding, the president', as the one who receives bread and wine, gives thanks and praise over them and then hands them to the deacons for distribution to the people. The term 'deacons' here seems to be used as a title, since Justin explains that they are 'those whom we call deacons', thus making

---

[54] Falls, 209-210.
[55] So Falls, 190. However, Goodspeed, 122: '... is a friend of God and he rejoices over his gifts and offerings.' The difference does not affect the point made here.
[56] Falls, 105-6.
[57] Daly, *Christian Sacrifice*, 335-6 and 504-5.
[58] Their view of sacrifice will be further examined in section 5.

it likely that the *proestôs* was also a recognized leader, whether a
presbyter or a bishop. Further, the functions ascribed to the president are
sufficiently important not to be given to just any Christian.[59] Justin's
choice of *proestôs* rather than any other term is intriguing, but his
motivation remains obscure.[60]

Justin's understanding of the eucharistic prayer and of the
'eucharistized' elements as Christian sacrifices, then, was not translated
by him, as far as we can tell, into a peculiarly priestly view of the one
who presided.

4.2.2 Irenaeus

In his extant works, the five books of the *Against Heresies*, the
Demonstration of the Apostolic Preaching,[61] and various fragments,
Irenaeus, like Justin, never clearly uses *hiereus*, 'priest', to refer to
church leaders. Again, therefore, we must look at his understanding of
sacrifice, especially of the eucharist as sacrifice, and at his view of the
leader of eucharistic services.

Irenaeus also condemns pagan sacrifices, though with less revulsion
than Justin,[62] probably because he was not an apologist but emphasized
the continuity of OT and NT in his battle with Gnosticism. Further, in
contrast to Justin, Irenaeus views the difference between Jewish and
Christian sacrifice as 'one of species, not genus' so that 'what has been
rejected is not sacrifice in general, but only the Jewish species of it.'[63]
Indeed, he sees the OT sacrifices as revealed to Moses by God in order
to aid men to know and draw near to him, so prefiguring the NT ones
(*AH* 4:8:2, 17:1 and 19:1).

This continuity is also evinced in Irenaeus' frequent use of the OT
law of firstfruits to illustrate the Christian obligation to offer sacrifices

---

[59] So Faivre, *Les laics*, 48-9.

[60] See Harvey, A.E., 'Elders', *Journal of Theological Studies* 25 (1974), 318, Wartelle, A.
(ed.), *Saint Justin: Apologies* (Paris, 1987), 295 and Daly, *Christian Sacrifice*, 336, for the
view that 'the pagan addressees of the *Apology* would explain why Justin chose a general
secular term rather than the specific Christian liturgical one'. See Faivre, *Les laics*, 47-9, for
the view that 'the title seems to be completely secondary to him in comparison with the
service rendered to the community.' His argument that Justin took the trouble to explain the
meaning of 'deacons' and so could have done the same for a title which might have been less
known to outsiders carries some weight.

[61] Abbreviated to *AH* and *DAP* in references below. The chapter divisions of *AH* given in
Rousseau et al (eds.), *Irénée de Lyon: Contre les hérésies*, 5 vols. (Paris, various dates) are
adopted in this thesis rather than those used by Daly and others following Harvey's edition.

[62] So Daly, *Christian Sacrifice*, 340. The following treatment owes a good deal to Daly,
Christian Sacrifice, 340-344, 349-354 and 505-6.

[63] Daly, *Christian Sacrifice*, 342. See *AH* 4:18:2.

(e.g., in *AH* 4:17:5 and 18:1). That the eucharist is one of these is clear in *Against Heresies* 4:17:5. Having emphasized that God wants right dispositions and deeds rather than sacrifice, he refers to Christ instructing his disciples 'to offer God the firstfruits of his own creatures'.[64] He then describes Christ's actions and words respecting the bread and cup at the last supper, adding, 'and he taught what the new offering of the new covenant was. It is this offering that the church received from the apostles and that, in the whole world, she offers to the God who gives us food, as firstfruits of God's own gifts, under the new covenant. About this, among the twelve prophets, Malachi spoke in advance in these terms: ...[Mal. 1:10-11].'

Irenaeus clearly did not regard the eucharist alone as the church's sacrifice, since, after again quoting from Malachi 1:11, he adds, 'This incense, John says in the Apocalypse, is the prayers of the saints' (*AH* 4:17:6). This results in a degree of ambiguity, for us, in the following section until the eucharist is definitely referred to again at the end of 4:18:4.[65] The impression that by 'the church's offering', mentioned again in 18:1, Irenaeus has a variety of sacrifices in mind, is strengthened by the plurals in 'We must therefore offer to God the firstfruits of his own creatures, ...' (18:1) and by the reference to the Philippian Christians' gifts to Paul as a 'pure sacrifice' (18:4).

After a denial that the Jews and heretics make such a sacrifice, Irenaeus returns to the subject of the eucharist, stating concerning it, 'For we offer to him what is his, ...' (18:5). The idea of a change being produced in at least the significance of the bread and the cup when thanks have been given over them is present in both 18:4 and 5. The juxtaposition of different kinds of Christian sacrifices returns in 18:6 in which, after a reference to the fact that 'we need to offer something to God', Irenaeus adds, 'he accepts our good actions, ...' Then, after another reference to the fact that God 'wants us too to offer our present at the altar continually', he states that, 'There is then an altar in the heavens, - it is there that our prayers and offerings ascend - ....' Although the second is ambiguous, since 'prayers' and 'offerings' may not be in apposition, the first clearly implies that God accepts Christians' good works as offered to him.

Answering the question: 'in what way is the Eucharist a sacrifice?' Daly holds that 'Irenaeus seems to associate the essence of the

---

[64] This and other quotations from *AH* 4:17-18 are taken from Rousseau, A. et al. (eds.), *Irénée de Lyon: Contre les hérésies, Livre IV* (Paris, 1965), 590ff. The same editors are responsible for editions of the rest of *Against Heresies* so references below to these will be abbreviated to 'Rousseau et al.' with the volume appropriate to the relevant Book being cited assumed.

[65] On this and what follows, see Daly, *Christian Sacrifice*, 351-3.

Eucharistic sacrifice with prayer.' This is, first, because *Against Heresies* 4:17:5 'describes the Eucharistic offering as the new oblation which the Church offers', and, second, because *Against Heresies* 4:17:6 'refers to Rev 8,4 to show that the "incense" of the Malachi prophecy is "the prayers of the saints."' He further points to the understanding of the church's offering in 4:18:1-4 and to 'the Early Church's spiritualization of the ideas of sacrifice' before concluding that 'it was not in the Eucharist as a cultic action that Irenaeus seemed to see its sacrificial element ... [but rather] in its [prayers and thanksgivings]'.[66]

These arguments make it highly likely that it was the thanksgiving offered over the elements which Irenaeus above all viewed as sacrificial. However, the way he uses the OT law of firstfruits and refers to the elements of the eucharist as deriving from God's gifts in creation suggests that he saw the elements as well as the prayers as a sacrifice of thanksgiving. The implication of this is present in *Against Heresies* 4:17:5 where, in addition to the reference to Christ's instruction to the disciples 'to offer God the firstfruits of his own creatures', he writes that Jesus at the last supper 'took bread that comes from creation ... and the cup similarly that comes from creation to which we belong.'[67] This is a new direction as compared with Justin,[68] resulting from the anti-Gnostic desire to trace continuity between Old and New Testaments noted earlier.

A further new direction, possibly resulting from the same cause, is that Irenaeus on one occasion views the Christian sacrifice as propitiatory. This is in *Against Heresies* 4:17:2, where Irenaeus writes of the true sacrifice 'by the offering of which they would render God favourable to themselves [*quod offerentes propitiabuntur Deum*].' Irenaeus 'may well have meant nothing more than the common Christian conviction that God heeds the prayers and good works of those who live according to His will' but it is significant that 'the language of propitiation ... has been taken up into the mainstream of Christian tradition.'[69]

Although Irenaeus thus regards the eucharist as sacrificial, he does

---

[66] Ibid., 505-6.

[67] Young, 261-4, argues along these lines. Garrett, J.L., 'The Pre-Cyprianic Doctrine of the Priesthood of All Christians' in Church, F.F. and George, T. (eds.), *Continuity And Discontinuity in Church History* (Leiden, 1979), 52, basically holds the same as Daly, but it seems to me more likely that Irenaeus views the elements themselves, probably as and when consecrated as sacrifices.

[68] So Hanson, R.P.C., *Studies*, 92.

[69] Daly, *Christian Sacrifice*, 356-9.

not view it as the sacrifice of Christ[70] and he considers it the whole church's sacrifice.[71] The only passage in his extant writings in which he says anything about who led eucharistic services is in a letter to Victor of Rome, preserved by Eusebius of Caesarea, in which he notes that, '... in church Anicetus made way for Polycarp to celebrate the Eucharist ....'[72] As Faivre writes of the evidence of Irenaeus' works, 'is there a specific sacrificial function exercised by particular people? Nothing allows us to say so.'[73]

4.2.3 Other second-century authors

The works and remnants of works by other second-century authors do not add a great deal to what has already been discovered, but do serve to fill out the overall picture and to confirm a number of the ideas concerning sacrifice already noted. None of them refer to a church leader as a priest or as an offerer of sacrifice. Some polemicize against pagan and Jewish sacrifices and/or maintain views of Christian sacrifice similar to those noted above.

A Jewish-Christian document probably from the second century, the *Odes of Solomon* contains a passage in which the author describes himself as a priest offering the sacrifice of God's thought and adds that 'the sacrifice of the Lord is righteousness and purity of heart and lips. Present your reins before Him blamelessly; ....'[74] Although Justin does not describe justice, mercy and virtue sacrificially, he does contrast them with sacrifice as what God prefers. It is likely that what Young calls the Jewish 'prophetic moralising' tradition[75] is to be discerned behind both, the *Odes* here presenting an early example of these virtues being called sacrifices.

During an exposition of God's self-sufficiency, in the Greek text of his *Apology* 1, Aristides says that God does not need sacrifice and libation, an idea found again in the Syriac text of chapter 13.[76] In his

---

[70] So Hanson, R.P.C., *Studies*, 92. Note too Garrett, 'Pre-Cyprianic Doctrine' in Church and George, *Continuity and Discontinuity*, 52, n.57.

[71] So Eastwood, 69; Daly, *Christian Sacrifice*, 350; Hanson, R.P.C., *Christian Priesthood Examined*, 48; and Faivre, *Les laïcs*, 53.

[72] *Historia Ecclesiastica* (*HE*) 5:24: Williamson, G.A. and Louth, A. (eds.), *Eusebius: The History of the Church* (London, 1989²), 173.

[73] Faivre, *Les laïcs*, 53.

[74] *Odes* 20:3-4 from Harris, J.R. (ed.), *The Odes and Psalms of Solomon* (Cambridge, 1909), 117. Hanson, R.P.C., *Studies*, 85, says it is from the Judaeo-Christian period in the second century and probably from Antioch.

[75] See Young, 103-7.

[76] Goodspeed, 4 and 17.

Supplication 13, Athenagoras, significantly replying to the accusation that Christians do not sacrifice, likewise denies that God needs sacrifices, since he lacks nothing, adding that the greatest sacrifice in God's eyes would be to know and worship him and 'rational worship as an unbloody sacrifice',[77] probably alluding to Romans 12:1. The author of *The Epistle to Diognetus* scorns the way that pagans worship their gods 'with the blood and fat of victims' (2:8) and the Jews for thinking that God needs such sacrifices (3:3-5).[78] The Valentinian Gnostic author of *The Letter of Ptolemaus to Flora* says that 'the Saviour instructed us to make offerings, but not those which are made by means of irrational beasts or with incense, but ... through spiritual praise and glorification and thanksgiving, and through liberality and kindness to our neighbours.'[79]

Similarly the author of *The Sentences of Sextus* 46b and 47 states, 'A pure and sinless heart is the finest altar dedicated to God. The only suitable offering to God is to do good deeds for men because of God.'[80] A Christian section in *The Sibylline Oracles*, dated by some to around AD 200,[81] says that 'God needs no sacrifice or libation but rather works of mercy: ... give to the hungry bread and to the thirsty drink ... and present this living sacrifice to me, the living God, ...'[82] Here is a direct reference to Romans 12:1, like that noted in Athenagoras above.

In *The Martyrdom of Apollonius* Apollonius explains, 'With all Christians I offer a pure and unbloody sacrifice ..., a sacrifice of prayer ...', whilst he desires the proconsul to 'offer prayers to him alone, as a pure and blameless sacrifice to God' (8 and 44).[83] In addition, the idea of the martyr's death as a sacrifice is frequent in the *Acts* of the martyrs.[84]

In the apocryphal *Acts of Peter*, dated to the late second century by Schneemelcher, Peter is said to have raised someone from the dead who then offered himself as a 'speaking sacrifice' to God.[85] And 'a contrite heart is the acceptable sacrifice' is found in the late second- or early third-century *Teaching of Silvanus*.[86]

---

[77] Schoedel, W.R. (ed.), *Athenagoras 'Legatio' and 'De Resurrectione'* (Oxford, 1992), 29.
[78] Lightfoot, Harmer and Holmes, 537 and 539.
[79] Foerster, W. (ed.), *Gnosis: A Selection of Gnostic Texts*, (Oxford, 1972), vol.1, 158-9.
[80] Edwards, R.A. and Wild, R.A. (eds.), *The Sentences of Sextus* (Chico, 1981), 21.
[81] So Hanson, R.P.C., *Studies*, 87.
[82] Schneemelcher, W. and Wilson, R. McL. (eds.), *New Testament Apocrypha* (Cambridge, 1991), vol.2, 678.
[83] Musurillo, H. (ed.), *The Acts of the Christian Martyrs* (Oxford, 1972), 93 and 103.
[84] On this see especially Daly, *Christian Sacrifice*, 378-385.
[85] *Acts of Peter* 2:8:29: Scheemelcher and Wilson, vol.2, 311.
[86] Robinson, J.M. (ed.), *The Nag Hammadi Library in English* (Leiden, 1977), 347 for the

There are also instances of the eucharist being referred to as a sacrifice. In the *Acts of Peter* 2:1:2, the eucharist, consisting of bread and water, is clearly called a sacrifice,[87] although without any indication of what the sacrificial aspect consisted in. Further, in the anonymous *On the Passover*, recently dated to the second half of the second century,[88] a close association or identification of the Passover with the eucharist is made in chapter 26: 'It is at night that the flesh is eaten for the light of the world has fallen asleep on the great body of Christ: "Take, eat, it's my body."'[89] Daly cites other passages which suggest the same identification.[90] If this document does come from the second half of the second century, then it provides us with the first evidence of the eucharist,[91] rather than only Christ's death, being identified as the Christian Passover and so, given the way in which it is linked with the Passover-story in Exodus 12, as a sacrifice. Doubt regarding the dating, however, leaves some uncertainty here.

4.2.4 Summary

We have seen, then, that in the mid to late second century AD neither church leaders nor the leaders of Christian worship are ever called 'priests', nor are they explicitly said to perform sacrificial acts. It is true that what little information there is makes it likely that the normal leaders of the church presided at worship which included the eucharist. It is also true that the eucharist is at times referred to in sacrificial language. However, the general view of sacrifice amongst second-century Christians, as far as that can be ascertained from the evidence available, was that God did not want or need literal, bloody sacrifices, but that he did want, mainly to demonstrate gratitude and willingness to obey and serve him, a penitent heart, heartfelt prayer and praise, and kindness towards others, these at times being spoken of in sacrificial terms. It therefore seems likely that when the eucharist is spoken of in

---

date and 355 for the text.

[87] Scheemelcher and Wilson, vol.2, 288: 'And they brought bread and water to Paul for the sacrifice so that after the prayer he should distribute to everyone.'

[88] So Daly, *Christian Sacrifice*, 373, n.1, in which see the relevant literature. Nautin, P. (ed.), *Homélies Pascales: I Une homélie inspirée du traité sur la pâque d'Hippolyte*, (Paris, 1950), 46-8, however, argues that it shows evidence of having been written after Arianism in the early fifth century. Daly's abbreviation of *IP* has been used for this below.

[89] Ibid., 153.

[90] Daly, *Christian Sacrifice*, 375, cites also chapters 4, 32, 40, 41 and 49 as containing passages which identify the Passover and eucharist.

[91] Daly, *Christian Sacrifice*, 375, n.8, acknowledges that *IP* never uses 'eucharist', but the quotation of Mt. 26:26 strongly suggests that the eucharist is in the author's mind.

such terms, it is the gratitude and self-giving expressed in the prayers of thanks and worship over the bread and cup which are mainly in mind. With Justin and Irenaeus, however, arrives the additional idea of the elements themselves as sacrifices of what God has given in creation, although probably those elements as consecrated, in Justin's case, rather than the elements in themselves. Further, if the anonymous *On the Passover* is from the second century, then it provides further evidence that a sacrificial understanding of the eucharist was prevalent.

<h3 style="text-align:center">4.3 Tertullian</h3>

Although Clement of Alexandria flourished a little earlier than Tertullian or Hippolytus, the close links between the former and Origen make it useful for purposes of comparison to treat these two consecutively. Since Tertullian flourished a few years earlier than Hippolytus, he will be treated first in this period.

   While the *Passion of Perpetua* also comes from North Africa in this period, it contains nothing relevant to this discussion, so only Tertullian's works are referred to.

<h4 style="text-align:center">4.3.1 Situation</h4>

The issue of whether Tertullian remained a layman all his life or was ordained has never received a generally accepted answer since Koch first questioned Jerome's assertion that he was a presbyter. No attempt to give a definitive answer can be made here, but Tertullian's question, 'For are not we lay people also priests?' in *On the Exhortation to Chastity* 7:3,[92] suggests that he was a layman when he wrote this work which is generally considered to come from his Montanist period.[93] The evidence of *On Monogamy* 12:2 is less certain, since he could be writing only rhetorically in the words 'whenever we are minded to exalt ourselves with swelling pride at the expense of the clergy, ...'[94] Together with the fact that Tertullian never aligns himself with the clergy, and the possibility that Jerome concluded that Tertullian must

---

[92] Le Saint, W.P., *Tertullan: Treatises on Marriage and Remarriage* (London, 1951), 53. This seems to me to be the likeliest inference from this passage in spite of arguments to the contrary, for which see, for example, Otranto, G., 'Nonne et laici sacerdotes sumus? (Exh. cast. 7,3)', *Vetera Christianorum* 8 (1971), 38-9. *On the Exhortation to Chastity* will be abbreviated to *Chastity* below.

[93] So Dekkers, E., *Clavis Patrum Latinorum* (Bruges, 1961²), 4; Barnes, T.D., *Tertullian, A Historical and Literary Study* (Oxford, 1985²), 55; and Moreschini, C. in Moreschini, C. and Fredouille, J.-C. (eds.), *Tertullien: Exhortation à la chasteté* (Paris, 1985), 8.

[94] Le Saint, 99.

have been a presbyter because he could not conceive of someone like him otherwise, it seems more likely than not that Tertullian remained a layman all his life.[95] If so, this may be a reason why he took the views we are going to examine, with regard to the priestliness of the laity in particular.

The other issue whose effect on Tertullian's views has been much discussed, is that of his conversion to Montanism. Although there is some disagreement with regard to which of his writings exhibit Montanist beliefs or influences, it is necessary to look at evidence from documents from as many periods of his work as possible in order to discern any changes or developments which may have been caused by his exposure to Montanism.

4.3.2 Church leaders as priests

Most scholars agree that Tertullian was the first writer to use the word 'priest' of church leaders.[96] The earliest such reference is in *On Baptism* 17:1. Explaining who can give baptism, he writes, 'The supreme right of giving it belongs to the high priest, which is the bishop [*si qui est, episcopus*]: after him, to the presbyters and deacons, yet not without commission from the bishop .... Except for that, even laymen have the right: ....'[97]

This is taken as a straightforward reference to the bishop as high priest by such as Bardy and Kilmartin but Bévenot has queried it.[98] He makes it the more significant by maintaining that it is the only occasion in his early period in which Tertullian names the bishop 'summus sacerdos'. He translates, or interprets, the beginning of 17:1 as: '"The supreme right to confer baptism belongs to the 'chief-priest', if he may be so called, i.e. the bishop", or better, if less elegantly, "to the chief-

---

[95] This conclusion seems to have been becoming more generally accepted in recent publications, although it is too early to say that it has reached general acceptance. In favour, using the kinds of arguments I have used, and others, see Barnes, 11 and 323; Evans, R.F., *One and Holy. The Church in Latin Patristic Thought* (London, 1972), 4; Faivre, *Les laics*, 64; Neymeyr, U., *Die christlichen Lehrer im zweiten Jahrhundert* (Leiden, 1989), 108-112.

[96] So von Campenhausen, *Tradition and Life*, 220 and Hanson, R.P.C., *Christian Priesthood Examined*, 38. Kilmartin in Ferguson, E. (ed.), *Encyclopedia of Early Christianity*, 754, cites Polycrates of Ephesus (c.195) as calling the apostle John a teacher and priest (*hiereus*) who wears the 'sacerdotal tiara' according to Eusebius, *HE* 5:24:3. This is not a reference to contemporary church leaders, although it may reflect current practice concerning them.

[97] Evans, E. (ed.), *Tertullian's Homily on Baptism* (London, 1964), 35.

[98] Bardy, G, 'Le sacerdoce chrétien d'après Tertullien', *La Vie spirituelle* 58 (1939), 112; Kilmartin in Ferguson, E. (ed.), *Encyclopedia of Early Christianity*, 754; cf. Bévenot, M., 'Tertullian's thoughts about the christian priesthood' in de Smedt, A.M., et al. (eds.), *Corona Gratiarum* (Bruges, 1975), 128-131, which see for the following arguments.

priest - if there is such a thing - I mean, the bishop".' His reasons are 'that nowhere else does Tertullian call the bishop "summus sacerdos" and only once or twice (as a Montanist) "sacerdos"....' Somewhat tentatively, he suggests that Tertullian wrote thus here on the model of *1 Clement* 40:5, and concludes that, 'if he had *1 Clem.* in mind, we could understand "summus sacerdos" as a literary transcript of [the Greek "high priest"], and it would thus in this context not imply that a bishop was then generally so regarded or so called.'

'*Si qui est*' is difficult to interpret with any certainty, but alternatives are possible. Neither Evans nor Refoulé and Drouzy translate as does Bévenot, the former, as we have already noted, giving 'which is the bishop', and the latter, 'that is, the bishop, if he is there.'[99] Bévenot's translation, then, does not force itself on the interpreter. Since his main reason for this interpretation is the lack of evidence of Tertullian calling the bishop 'priest' elsewhere, while admitting that he does so later and as a Montanist, further conclusions concerning Bévenot's view must await our further study of other passages in which Tertullian so uses 'priest'.

A second, pre-Montanist passage to be considered is found in *A Prescription of the Heretics*[100] 41:8. Criticising the ordination practices of heretical Christian groups, Tertullian writes, 'And so today they have one bishop, tomorrow another; today a deacon who tomorrow will be a lector; today a presbyter who tomorrow will be a layman. For they charge even laymen with priestly functions.'[101] The 'priestly functions' are likely to refer to those functions appropriate to the bishop, the deacon and the presbyter in view of the immediately preceding references to them. It is likely, then, that we have here a second reference to the bishop as priestly and a first which includes the deacon and the presbyter in that description. Bévenot alludes to this passage only to comment, 'this public attack on the goings on of heretics would have been impossible if the same practices were current in the Church which he was himself defending'.[102] He does not clarify whether he includes the calling of the clergy 'priests' among these practices.

---

[99] Evans, E., *Baptism*, 35 and Refoulé, R.F. and Drouzy, M. (eds.), *Tertullien: Traité du baptême* (Paris, 1952), 90. A possibility suggested by consultation of Glare, P.G.W. (ed.), *Oxford Latin Dictionary* (Oxford, 1982), articles on 'qui', B. 15 b and on 'quis' 6, would give the translation, 'the high priest, whoever it is, the bishop', meaning whoever the individual may be at the time who is the bishop.

[100] Abbreviated to *Prescription* below.

[101] Refoulé, R.F. and de Labriolle, P. (eds.), *Tertullien: Traité de la Prescription contre les hérétiques* (Paris, 1957), 148.

[102] Bévenot, 'Tertullian's thoughts' in de Smedt, A.M., et al. (eds.), *Corona Gratiarum*, 130.

However, there is no indication that Tertullian is so condemning this practice, indeed, he uses 'priestly' 'without explanation, as if the title was a familiar one to his readers.'[103]

A final, possible, pre-Montanist reference to Christian leadership as priestly is in *To His Wife* 1:7:4-5. Criticising second marriages, Tertullian points to Paul's declarations, presumably in 1 Timothy 3:2, 5:9 and Titus 1:6, 'For men who have been married twice are not allowed to preside in the Church nor is it possible that a widow be chosen unless she was the wife of but one man. ... The altar of God must be an altar of manifest purity and all the glory which surrounds the Church is the glory of sanctity. The pagans have a priesthood of widows and celibates ....'[104] The connection between 'the pagans have a priesthood of widows and celibates' and Paul's unwillingness for the twice-married to preside in the church is rather distant and so, whilst a priestly allusion to church leadership may be implied, it would be unwise to insist that it is.[105]

During his Montanist period, Tertullian writes in *The Chaplet* 3:2 describing baptism, 'When we are going to enter the water, but a little before, in the presence of the congregation and under the hand of the president [*antistitis*], we solemnly profess that we disown the devil, and his pomp, and his angels.'[106] The most frequent meaning of *antistes* in Latin literature is 'a (high-) priest or priestess'[107] and it can mean this in Tertullian's writings (cf. *To the Nations* 1:12:1: '"the priesthood of a cross"'[108]). Although his use of it as the equivalent of *praeses* (cf. *Apology* 1:1: 'Magistrates of the Roman Empire'[109]) leaves a margin of doubt whether it means 'priest' or 'president' here, the association of the bishop as 'high priest' with baptism in *On Baptism* 17:1 tells in favour of 'priest'.

Further, in *On the Veiling of Virgins* 9:2 Tertullian lists what is forbidden to women in the church, ending with 'a priestly office'.[110] This clearly implies a restricted priestly office held by selected males.

---

[103] Hanson, R.P.C., *Christian Priesthood Examined*, 38. Bardy, 'Le sacerdoce', *La Vie spirituelle* 58 (1939), 111, also takes this as a reference to priestly functions of the ordained.
[104] Le Saint, 20.
[105] Garrett, 'Pre-Cyprianic Doctrine' in Church and George, *Continuity and Discontinuity*, 59, so takes it.
[106] Roberts, A.R., Donaldson, J and Coxe, A.C. (eds.), *The Ante-Nicene Fathers* (Grand Rapids, 1973[2]), vol. 3, 172-3.
[107] Glare, 'antistes', 1 b.
[108] Roberts, Donaldson and Coxe, vol. 3, 222.
[109] Arbesmann, R., Daly, E.J. and Quain, E.A. (eds.), *Tertullian: Apologetical Works and Minucius Felix: Octavius* (Washington, 1950), 7.
[110] Schulz-Flügel, E. and Mattei, P. (eds.), *Tertullien: Le Voile des Vierges* (Paris, 1997), 161.

Tertullian precedes this by stating, 'A woman is not permitted to speak in church, nor to teach either, to baptize, to offer the sacrifice, nor to exercise any masculine function, ...' suggesting that the clergy as a whole have priestly office, since baptism is ascribed elsewhere to presbyters and deacons (cf. *On Baptism* 17:1 above).

In *Chastity* 7:2, Tertullian returns to the subject of the prohibition of second marriages, noted earlier in *To His Wife* 1:7:4-5. He recalls a passage in Leviticus prohibiting priests from more than one marriage, a passage which no-one else can find,[111] and reminds his readers that Paul 'requires that none but monogamists are to be chosen for the order of the priesthood. ... So true is this that, as I recall, there have been men deposed from office for digamy. Well, then, you will say, it follows that all whom the Apostle does not mention in this law are free. It would be folly to imagine that lay people may do what priests may not.'[112] After a reference to the general priesthoood, Tertullian adds, 'where there is no ... hierarchy, you yourself offer sacrifice, you baptize, and you are your own priest' (7:3), a passage which suggests that offering sacrifice and baptizing are vital constituents of being priestly. This impression is reinforced when, in 7:4, he argues that, 'if in time of necessity you have the right to exercise a priestly power, you must also needs be living according to priestly discipline even when it is not necessary for you to exercise priestly powers. As a digamist will you baptize? As a digamist will you offer sacrifice?'

Bévenot says that here Tertullian 'forces the [Pauline] text to enable him to apply it to all the faithful whom he had encouraged to think of themselves as "sacerdotes"'.[113] While this is the ultimate end Tertullian attains, on the way he makes a clear distinction between 'priests' and 'laymen', one, moreover, which he places on the lips of his opponents (cf. 'you will say, ...') as well as his own. He also mentions that some twice-married were thrown out of their place, which is more likely to refer to clergymen than to laity. This, then, is another reference to the clergy, not only the bishop, as 'the order of priesthood' and as 'priests'.[114]

In *Chastity* 11:2, still dealing with second marriages, Tertullian refers

---

[111] So Garrett in Church and George, *Continuity and Discontinuity*, 59. For possible explanations of why Tertullian writes this, see Le Saint, 139, n.47 and Otranto, 'Nonne', *Vetera Christianorum* 8 (1971), 35-6.

[112] Le Saint, 53.

[113] Bévenot, 'Tertullian's thoughts' in de Smedt, A.M., et al., *Corona Gratiarum*, 136.

[114] So Garrett in Church and George, *Continuity and Discontinuity*, 59 and Faivre, *Les laics*, 64. Vilela, A., *La condition collégiale des prêtres au IIIe siècle* (Paris, 1971), 242, wrongly restricts the reference to presbyters.

to the practice of offering sacrifices on behalf of the dead wife and asks, 'Do you wish, then, to stand before the Lord with as many wives as you remember in your prayers? Will you offer the Sacrifice for two wives and have recommendation made of both through the ministry of a priest whose monogamy is a necessary condition of his ordination, ...?'[115] Even Bévenot acknowledges that this is 'a possible exception' to Tertullian's normal custom of not referring to the celebrant of the eucharist as a 'priest', but adds, 'his use of the term in this very Montanist passage is no proof that the bishop was currently so called in the Carthaginian church.'[116] Hanson notes this passage as referring to a presbyter.[117]

In *On Monogamy* 12:2, Tertullian argues in the opposite direction from *Chastity* 7:2.[118] Countering the suggestion that Paul insisted on monogamy only for the clergy, Tertullian castigates the laity:

Indeed, whenever we are minded to exalt ourselves with swelling pride at the expense of the clergy, then "we are all one", then we are all priests, for "He hath made us priests to God and His Father"! But when we are called upon to be the peers of priests in discipline, we lay aside our fillets – and pair off! The question under consideration concerned the qualities required in men who were to receive orders in the Church.[119]

Clearly, the two priesthoods were not universally seen as exactly the same. Further, the clergy, not only the bishops, are assumed to be priests by Tertullian here.

A considerable degree of sarcasm is evident in his reference, in *On Modesty* 1:6, to a 'bishop of bishops' as 'most high priest'[120] so that little store should be set by it. Discussing who can forgive sin in *On Modesty* 21:17, however, he argues that it is 'the Church of the Spirit, through a spiritual man, and not the Church constituted by many bishops. Indeed, it is a right and decision of the Lord and not of the servant, of God himself and not of the priest.'[121] The parallel requires the equation of the bishop with the priest. Bévenot agrees, but points out

[115] Le Saint, 59-60.
[116] Bévenot, 'Tertullian's thoughts' in de Smedt, A.M., et al. (eds.), *Corona Gratiarum*, 132-3.
[117] Hanson, R.P.C., *Christian Priesthood Examined*, 38. He mistakes the numbering, calling it 11:20.
[118] So Garrett, 'Pre-Cyprianic Doctrine' in Church and George, *Continuity and Discontinuity*, 59-60.
[119] Le Saint, 99.
[120] Micaelli,C. and Munier, C. (eds.) *Tertullien: La Pudicité* (Paris, 1993), vol. 1, 147.
[121] Ibid., 275.

that this 'was not meant to be complimentary'. This is true but does not remove the priestly reference to the bishop. Tertullian's other, non-pejorative priestly allusions to the bishop and clergy demonstrate that it did not regularly have such negative significance for him. Bévenot's futher arguments for an evolution of his usage in this direction over the years are not convincing either.[122]

Drawing on this evidence, certain conclusions can be drawn. One is that, on two occasions (in *On Baptism* 17:1 and *On Modesty* 21:17), the bishop is referred to as a priest. Another is that, in *On Monogamy* 12:2, the clergy are referred to as priests. This is probably so in the references to 'priestly office' in *On the Veiling of Virgins* 9:2, 'priestly order' in *Chastity* 7:2, and 'priestly functions' in *Prescription* 41:8. The mentions of bishop, deacons and presbyters together over against the laity in *On Baptism* 17:1 and *Prescription* 41:8, the description of them as 'leaders' over against the 'layman', and their identification with the 'clergy' in *On Flight in Persecution* 11:1-2,[123] show that all three made up the clergy[124] and were regarded as priestly.

Gy argues that Tertullian never calls the presbyter 'priest' so that 'the *presbyter* participates in the bishop's priesthood.'[125] Since Tertullian never distinguishes the priesthood of the (rest of the) clergy from that of the bishop, nor explains the relationship between their priesthoods, Gy's second point must remain a possibility. Tertullian does, however, refer to the clergy, which certainly included the presbyters, as 'priests' in *On Monogamy* 12:28. The question if, or how far, presbyters and deacons were seen as priestly apart from the bishop's priesthood remains open.

Tertullian's lack of reflection on the meaning of this priesthood[126] makes it somewhat uncertain what it consists in for him. Nonetheless, there are some suggestive indications. The most significant statement is 'you yourself offer sacrifice, you baptize, and you are your own priest' in *Chastity* 7:3, and the ensuing reference in 7:4. This strongly suggests that baptizing and offering sacrifice are the most important parts of what constitutes priesthood, especially that of the ordained, for Tertullian. This is confirmed by the references to the bishop as 'high priest' having

---

[122] Bévenot, 'Tertullian's thoughts' in de Smedt, A.M., et al. (eds.), *Corona Gratiarum*, 135-7.

[123] Arbesmann et al., 297.

[124] So Faivre, *Les laics*, 64.

[125] Gy, P.-M., 'Remarques sur le vocabulaire antique du sacerdoce chrétien' in *Études sur les sacrements de l'ordre* (Paris, 1957), 142.

[126] Hanson, R.P.C., *Christian Priesthood Examined*, 38-9: 'it is to be observed that Tertullian does not draw any theological inferences from this use of the term priest for bishops and presbyters. The term seems to come naturally to his lips, but he does not seem to want to use it in order to build any particular doctrine of the episcopal or presbyteral ministry.'

the supreme right to baptize in *On Baptism* 17:1, the offering of a commemorative eucharist through a priest in *Chastity* 11:2 and the juxtaposition of offering and baptizing with the 'priestly office' in *On the Veiling of Virgins* 9:1. There is only one reference to the bishop as 'priest' in the context of church discipline (*On Modesty* 21:17), but, in view of later developments, this too may have been a significant aspect of the bishop's priestliness.

Finally, the fact that Tertullian makes such priestly references to the bishop and the clergy so infrequently (seven times where such a reference is very likely and three where it is less likely but quite possible) and without any apparent need to justify that usage suggests that it was well established in the North African church in Tertullian's day.[127] Although his attitude to bishops may have changed through his becoming a Montanist, his calling the clergy priests does not seem to have done so.

4.3.3 View of sacrifice

Tertullian frequently interprets Christian sacrifice in terms of 'spiritual sacrifices'. As Catholic and as Montanist he stresses the prophetic cult criticism that God prefers mercy to sacrifice,[128] teaching that even in the case of the sacrifices of the old covenant it was the attitude behind the offering that God was really interested in.[129] In line with this, he depicts a contrite and humble heart, various aspects of self-denial, and martyrdom, as appropriate sacrifices,[130] also quoting Romans 12:1 of the living sacrifice of our bodies.[131] He further refers to the sacrifices of praise and prayer.[132]

It is against this background that what Tertullian writes of the eucharist as a sacrifice must be evaluated. In his Catholic period, he says of Mithra, in *Prescription* 40:4, that 'he too celebrates the offering of bread' after a reference to 'things of the divine sacraments' which

---

[127] Against Bévenot's view noted earlier. Although Tertullian's priestly references to the bishop and clergy are infrequent, they are not as infrequent as Bévenot suggests.

[128] E.g., in *On Repentance* 8:3, *Against Marcion* 2:13:5, 2:17:2, and 4:10:4.

[129] *Against Marcion* 2:22:2-4.

[130] See *Against the Jews* 5:5, *On Patience* 13:2, *On Women's Apparel* 2:9:7, *On the Resurrection of the Dead* 8:4, *On Fasting* 3:4, 9:8, 16:1, 16:8, *Scorpiace* 7:7, 15:2, and *On Flight in Persecution* 12:7.

[131] *On the Resurrection of the Dead* 47:16.

[132] Of praise: *Against the Jews* 5:5, *Against Marcion* 3:22:6, 4:35:11; of prayer: *Apology* 30:5, *On Prayer* 18:5, 18:27, 28:1-4, *Against Marcion* 4:1:8, *To Scapula* 2:8, and *On Fasting* 10:13.

probably refers to the eucharistic bread.[133] In *On Prayer* 19:1-4 receiving the Lord's body in the eucharist is identified with participating in a sacrifice.[134] These examples make it likely that the eucharist is meant when the offering of a sacrifice is mentioned between the visiting of the sick and the giving of a sermon as occasions when women would appear in public in *On Women's Apparel* 2:11:2, when 'sacrifices' are amongst the matters attended to by a Christian couple in *To His Wife* 2:8:8 and when an 'offering' is celebrated at weddings according to *To His Wife* 2:8:6.[135]

Three likely references to the eucharist as a sacrifice from Tertullian's Montanist period relate to the practice of offering eucharists on behalf of the dead. First, in *The Chaplet* 3:3, just after mentioning 'the sacrament of the eucharist', he writes of 'offerings for the dead as birthday honours'.[136] Second, in *Chastity* 11:1, he refers to the making of 'annual sacrifices' on behalf of the dead partner, following this with the statement quoted earlier about offering through a priest. Two references to prayer (11:2: 'Do you wish, then, to stand before the Lord with as many wives as you remember in your prayers?' and 'as your sacrifice ascends') in the immediate context suggest that 'even as [Tertullian] calls the rite a sacrifice he explains that it is a sacrifice only of prayers'.[137] Third, in *On Monogamy* 10:4, Tertullian says that the woman bereaved of her husband 'offers the sacrifice each year on the anniversary of his falling asleep.'[138]

Tertullian, then, clearly denominated the eucharist as a sacrifice, but only as one action amongst a number of actions and attitudes which he regarded as sacrificial. Moreover, there is some indication (in *Chastity* 11:1-2) that it was the prayers offered with or over the elements which formed what was sacrificial about the eucharist for him. Kelly writes, 'what the sacrifice consists in, he does not specify. No doubt he views it primarily as an offering of prayer and worship, but worship in the context of the Saviour's passion and of the elements which "represent" His sacrificed body and blood.'[139]

Another way of understanding the sacrificial aspect of the eucharist is

---

[133] Refoulé and de Labriolle, 144. So understood by Hanson, R.P.C., *Studies*, 94, n.40 and by Stevenson, 19.

[134] Arbesmann et al., 174-5.

[135] Ibid., 145; Le Saint, 34-5. All three are taken as references to the eucharist by Hanson, R.P.C., *Studies*, 94, n.40, as is the last by Stevenson, 19.

[136] Roberts, Donaldson and Coxe, vol. 3, 173. This too is taken as a reference to the eucharist by Hanson, R.P.C., *Studies*, 94, n. 40.

[137] Ibid., 94.

[138] Le Saint, 92. This also appears in Hanson's list in Hanson, R.P.C., *Studies*, 94, n. 40.

[139] Kelly, J.N.D., *Early Christian Doctrines* (London, 1977⁵), 214.

suggested by Le Saint: '*oblatio* can mean ... the gifts which the faithful offer when Mass is celebrated.' This may be reflected in the references to the offerings made on the anniversaries of Christians' deaths,[140] but it is not clear. Certainly, as R.P.C. Hanson points out, Tertullian never speaks of 'offering Christ in the eucharist.'[141] However, the offering of sacrifice is one of the main connotations of priestliness for Tertullian, as we noted earlier, and it is likely that it was the eucharist which he saw as the sacrifice that the clergy were to be particularly responsible for.

4.4 Hippolytus

4.4.1 Life and writings

The problems involved here are legion and this is not the place to deal with them in detail. All that will be attempted is to mention some major issues and their most recent solutions.

Frickel and Botte conclude that Hippolytus was a schismatic bishop of Rome who was reconciled to the generally recognized church before his martyrdom, flourishing c.222-235.[142] Although some have questioned it, most scholars accept the attribution of the work, *Refutation of All Heresies*, to him.[143] The attributions to him of *Contra Noetum*, commentaries on Daniel and the Song of Songs, and *The Antichrist* have also been generally accepted,[144] but there has been much more controversy over the work generally known as the *Apostolic Tradition*.

For one thing, the original text of this work is uncertain because of the number of somewhat different parallel texts extant now generally considered to depend on the original.[145] In this thesis, Botte's latest

---

[140] Le Saint, 146, n. 92.

[141] Hanson, R.P.C., *Studies*, 95.

[142] Frickel, J., *Das Dunkel um Hippolyt von Rom* (Graz, 1988), 45-63 and 119; Botte, B. (ed.), *La Tradition apostolique de Saint Hippolyte: Essai de reconstitution* (Münster, 1989[5]), XIV-XV. Brent, A., *Hippolytus and the Roman Church in the Third Century: Communities in Tension before the Emergence of a Monarch-Bishop* (Leiden, 1995), denies that the concept of schism has any meaning in the early third-century situation in Rome, largely because of the lack of a monarchical bishop and the existence of several house-churches, but, generally speaking, accepts the same date and place.

[143] See Frickel, 99-122 for an account of the controversy. Frickel, 204 and 299; Geerard, vol.1, nos. 1870-1925; Marcovich, M. (ed.), *Refutatio Omnium Haeresium* (Berlin, 1986), 10-16; and Botte, XV, accept this attribution. Brent, 289-290 and elsewhere, does not.

[144] On *Contra Noetum*, see Butterworth, R. (ed.), *Contra Noetum* (London, 1977), 7-33.

[145] On this see Botte, XI-XII and XVII-XXVIII. Brent, 195, even questions whether there ever was a single text called 'The Apostolic Tradition'.

reconstruction is used.[146] For another, the ascription to Hippolytus is less than completely secure.[147] However, Botte still accepts it[148] and his position is adopted here. Further, some have argued it derives from an Alexandrian background. Botte concludes, however, that 'there is ... no valid reason' for doing so.[149]

A final issue is how far the *Apostolic Tradition* represents a liturgical usage at Rome which had existed for some time. Botte presents a finely balanced view:

> The stage of improvisation has not yet passed, and Hippolytus gives his prayers as models and not as fixed formulas. Besides, it is not likely that, writing in Rome, he presents as the true tradition things that had nothing to do with Roman customs. No doubt he has specified certain points on his own authority. But, on the whole, we are right to think that the *Tradition* represents well Roman discipline at the beginning of the third century.[150]

4.4.2 The priesthood of the ordained

It is generally accepted[151] that Hippolytus is writing self-consciously as a bishop in the preface to *Refutation of All Heresies* 6. He here describes the Holy Spirit as given to the apostles and transmitted to those who have rightly believed, continuing, 'whose successors we chance to be and partakers of the same grace of high priesthood and of teaching, ...'[152]

The bishop is again called 'priest' in the *Apostolic Tradition* 3,[153] in

---

[146] The translations of the *Apostolic Tradition* have been made from Botte's French translation with the help of Cuming, G.J. (ed.), *Hippolytus: A Text for Students*, (Bramcote, 1976).

[147] E.g., Geerard, vol.1, 226-228, places it among the 'Iuris Ps.-Apostolici opera singula' and not amongst Hippolytus' works, and Brent, 458, sees it as a composite work.

[148] Botte, XIII.

[149] Botte, XVI-XVII. See too Chadwick, H. in Dix, G. and Chadwick, H, *The Apostolic Tradition of St. Hippolytus* (London, 1968²), g-i. Cuming, 5, is more cautious. Quasten, J., *Patrology* (Utrecht, 1953), vol. 2, 163, takes the opposing view.

[150] Botte, XVI. See too Faivre, A., *Naissance d'une hiérarchie* (Paris, 1977), 50, who views it as reflecting rites c.180-200, while Vilela, 343, sees it as written c.215 but reflecting earlier practice. Brent, 458, claims that it is creating a new social reality rather than reflecting an old one, but Botte's arguments are more convincing.

[151] E.g., by von Campenhausen, H., *Ecclesiastical Authority and Spiritual Power in the Church of the First Three Centuries* (London, 1969), 175-6 and Hanson, R.P.C., *Christian Priesthood Examined*, 39 and *Studies*, 95, n. 48.

[152] Legge, F. (ed.), *Philosophumena or the Refutation of All Heresies* (London, 1922), vol. 1, 34.

[153] Botte, 6-10. Brent, 302, sees this and the reference in *Refutation* just mentioned as 'the earliest usage of such sacral and hierarchical terminology in Christian literature ....'

which the ordination-prayer of a bishop is given. Its opening includes the description of God as instituting the 'leaders and priests' of Israel, continuing the cultic allusions with the words, 'and you did not leave your sanctuary without a ministry.' That this sanctuary is now continued in the church is implied in the following reference to God having poured out the power of his Spirit on his beloved son Jesus, which he has given to his holy apostles, 'who established the church in every place as your sanctuary, ...' The intercession for the one being consecrated then begins, 'You, Father, who know people's hearts, grant to this your servant, whom you have chosen for the episcopate, to feed your holy flock and to exercise the high priesthood before you blamelessly, serving night and day; to propitiate you unceasingly and to offer to you your holy church's gifts; and, by the spirit of high priesthood, to have the power to forgive sins ....' The powers asked for are clearly believed to come as a result of this prayer, since section 4 begins, 'When he has been made bishop, let all offer him the kiss of peace, greeting him because he has been made worthy.' The laying-on of hands, referred to at the end of section 2, must also have been viewed as having a part to play in the conferring of these powers. Further, the Greek and Latin constructions involved suggest strongly that the power to forgive sins derives from the bishop's 'high priestly spirit',[154] which is given in this ordination. Moreover, the placing of the exercising of the high priesthood alongside the feeding of the flock as the main attributes of the oversight being given, implies that the one involves the other. Finally, there is a natural link between the bishop's high priesthood and the power 'to propitiate you unceasingly and to offer to you your holy church's gifts'. However, we cannot simply assume that this refers to the eucharist, since the prayer continues with a plea that the bishop be enabled 'to please you in gentleness and a pure heart, offering to you a sweet-smelling savour', showing that Hippolytus viewed the offering of a pure heart as a sacrifice also.[155]

Consideration of the reference to priesthood in the *Apostolic Tradition* 4 will be left until section 5.4 of this thesis, since it could well refer to all those present as priests. There is no reference to priesthood in the *Apostolic Tradition* 7, where the ordination of presbyters is prescribed, but there is one in section 8, in which the deacon's ordination or institution is dealt with:

---

[154] Hanson, R.P.C., *Studies*, 96: 'it may be that this highpriesthood refers particularly to the bishop's power of forgiving sins'.

[155] Hanson, R.P.C., *Christian Priesthood Examined*, 49 and *Studies*, 96, sees this as an indication of the 'pure offering' tradition, and Young, 100, views it as a spiritual sacrifice.

> In the ordination of a deacon, the bishop alone should lay on hands, because he is not being ordained to the priesthood, but to the bishop's service, to do what the bishop tells him. For he does not share in the counsel of the clergy, but administers and informs the bishop of what is necessary. He does not receive the common spirit in which the presbyters[156] share, but that which is entrusted to him under the power of the bishop. [157]

Priesthood here is connected, not with offering the eucharistic sacrifice,[158] but with participating in the counsel among the clergy. There is nothing immediately priestly or sacrificial about this, but this priesthood is in virtue of participating in the clergy, whose main function is helping and governing the people, according to the *Apostolic Tradition* 7,[159] so it relates to these activities. Clearly, it implies that the presbyters as well as the bishop, but not the deacons, belonged to the clergy and the priesthood envisaged.[160]

The fact that the author finds it necessary to explain why only the bishop should lay hands on the deacon and how the deacon differs from the presbyter suggests that this work was written at a time when there was discussion, and probably some dissension, over the relationships between bishops, presbyters, deacons and others. This is also suggested by the way in which the deacon is said not to 'share in the counsel of the clergy' in the *Apostolic Tradition* 8, but it is implied that he does belong to the clergy in the *Apostolic Tradition* 10, in which instruction is given not to ordain or lay hands on a widow 'because she does not offer the offering nor has she a liturgical duty (*liturgia*). Ordination is done with the clergy on account of their liturgical duties.'[161] It is noteworthy that 'the members of the clergy (*kleros*) receive the laying on of hands ... because they have a role to play in the liturgical service (*leitourgia*). The functions that have no cultic role to play do not have to receive a laying on of hands.'[162] As Faivre goes on to point out, this is a much more restricted view of service or ministry, both in terms of those who can exercise it and in terms of its content, than in NT times.

---

[156] Botte has 'prêtres' here, but it is '*presbyteri*' in the Latin versions.

[157] Botte, 22-24. The two main texts are not exactly the same in detail, but are the same on the point being treated here.

[158] So Powell, D., 'Ordo Presbyterii', *Journal of Theological Studies, New Series* 26 (1975), 308.

[159] Botte, 20-21.

[160] So Kilmartin in Ferguson, E. (ed.), *Encyclopedia of Early Christianity*, 754; Hanson, R.P.C., *Studies*, 96.

[161] Botte, 30-31.

[162] Faivre, *Emergence*, 76.

Further references to the bishop's priesthood are found in the *Apostolic Tradition* 8 where God is asked to give 'the Spirit of grace and caring to your servant [the deacon] whom you have chosen to serve your Church and to present in your sanctuary what is offered to you by him who is established as your high priest, ...',[163] and in section 34, in which deacons are told to inform the bishop of those who are ill so that he may visit them, 'for a sick man is comforted when the high priest remembers him.'[164]

Hippolytus, then, was very happy to use high priestly terminology of the bishop, and saw no need to justify it, suggesting, as with Tertullian, that it was a generally accepted usage. He also regarded presbyters as part of the priesthood. This is apparent in two passages and the fact that the bishop is called the 'high priest (*summus sacerdos*)' and the 'chief of priests (*princeps sacerdotum*)' may also suggest that others held a special priesthood under him. Like Tertullian, but more definitely and prominently, he links the bishop's high priesthood and the ability to forgive sin. He also connects it with teaching, caring for the flock, and offering gifts. He further relates priesthood to caring for and ruling the people when the presbyters are included and to offering sacrifice and having a 'liturgical duty ' when the whole clergy is referred to.

4.4.3 View of the eucharist as a sacrifice

We noted above Hippolytus' allusion to the bishop as offering a pleasing perfume to God by his gentleness and pure heart in the ordination-prayer for the bishop in the *Apostolic Tradition* 3. In addition, there are three passages in his *Commentary on the Song of Solomon* in which references to incense are interpreted as the offering of themselves by Christians in self-denial and righteous living.

The first interprets Song 4:6b 'if some people crucify ... their bodies with strength and desire, then they become "hills of incense" and joyous.'[165] This is immediately followed by a related interpretation of Song 4:7 which is that 'those who mortify their bodies thereupon smell like incense through their righteousness.'

The second such passage comes soon after these. The same phrase, found in both Song 4:10c and 4:11c, is interpreted twice. The first is: 'if anyone with right heart and the right faith knows God, then he smells

---

[163] Botte, 26-7. Cf. the way the deacons bring the people's gifts to the bishop in sections 4 and 22.

[164] Botte, 80-81.

[165] Bonwetsch, G.N. in Bonwetsch, G.N. and Achelis, H. (eds.), *Hippolytus Werke, exegetische und homiletische Schriften* (Leipzig, 1897), 371-3.

better to him than all incense'; and the second: 'we are clothed by Christ who put us on in baptism; and only those from whose clothes comes such a fragrance of incense are righteous and worthy to be sister and bride of Christ and God: "sister" to succeed him, and "bride" to be indissolubly united in his love.'

The final such passage interprets '"the flower with nard, saffron, bamboo and cinnamon with all the trees of Lebanon, myrrhs and aloes with all the best kinds of incense"' (Song 4:13-14) as 'good deeds', especially loving one's enemies which is true righteousness.

Although the objection could be raised that the incense mentioned in Song does not appear in sacrificial contexts and so need not have sacrificial connotations, it probably did have such connotations for Christians because of its association with the Israelite sacrificial system and with prayer in Revelation 5:8 and 8:3-4. Also telling in favour of sacrificial connotations here is the way in which self-denial and right living were sometimes described in sacrificial ways by other second- and third-century Christian authors including Tertullian.

Hippolytus' main emphasis, however, is on material offerings brought by believers as sacrifices. These include the bread and wine used for the eucharist.

The procedure for the celebration of the eucharist is outlined first in the *Apostolic Tradition* 4[166] after that for the ordination of the bishop. This begins, 'Let the deacons present the offering to him and let him, laying his hands on it with all the presbytery, say, giving thanks: ....' This offering consists of the bread and the cup, as is made clear later in the prayer in the words, 'we offer to you the bread and the cup, giving you thanks ....' The link with offering is taken up again in the immediately following words '... because you have considered us worthy to stand before you and minister to you (or, to practise the priesthood: *tibi sacerdotium exhibere*).[167] And we ask you to send your Holy Spirit on the offering of the holy church.'[168] There ensues a plea for the filling of the Holy Spirit for all those partaking.

It will be argued in section 5.4 of this thesis that this involves a reference to the priesthood of all partaking. It is possible that 'the offering of the holy church' at the end of the passage quoted is the participants themselves, but it is more likely that it alludes to the bread

---

[166] The quotations from this section which follow are found in Botte, 10-17.

[167] See discussion in section 5.4.1 below.

[168] Daly, *Christian Sacrifice*, 367, n. 69, points out that the reference to the eucharist as 'the offering of the holy church' 'recalls Irenaeus' "new offering of the new testament" and "offering of the church"'.

and cup, in view of the earlier use of 'offering' for them.[169] The link, then, is primarily between the general priesthood and the bread and cup as an offering. However, it is the bishop and the presbyters who lay hands on these and the deacon who brings them (cf. the *Apostolic Tradition* 8 above), suggesting that the reference to the clergy having a 'liturgical duty' and offering sacrifice in the *Apostolic Tradition* 10 at least includes these actions, and that they perform them on the general priesthood's behalf. On the other hand, this offering delimits the clergy in the *Apostolic Tradition* 10 and suggests that only they could perform it.

That other materials can be offered is clear in the *Apostolic Tradition* 5 and 6, which begin, 'If anyone offers oil, let him (the bishop) give thanks in the same way as for the offering of bread and wine, ...' and 'Likewise, if anyone offers cheese and olives, let him say, ...'[170] Further references to offerings brought by the people to God via the bishop which do not refer only or at all to the bread and wine occur in the *Apostolic Tradition* 23, which shows that the faithful may bring something at any time, probably for a fellowship- or agape-meal,[171] in section 31, in which literal firstfruits are presented, and in section 32, where fruits and flowers are offered.

In section 21, however, where, after a baptism has taken place, 'the offering shall be presented by the deacons to the bishop', there follows, 'and he will give thanks over the bread that it may be the symbol of Christ's body and over the cup of wine that it may be the likeness of the blood that was poured out for all those who believe in him; ....'[172] The elements are called an offering before they are prayed over, suggesting that they are viewed as offerings in the same way as other material gifts, although they receive greater and different significance after the prayer. This is confirmed by the references which immediately follow to prayers over mixed milk and honey, and water, which is said to be presented 'as an offering' as a symbol of cleansing. These are partaken of by the worshippers as well as the cup. However, it is the bread and wine which are above all referred to as 'the holy offering' in the conclusion to 21 which says, 'We have handed on to you briefly these things about holy baptism and the holy offering, ...'[173]

Section 20 says, 'Those to be baptized shall not bring with them any other thing except what each brings for the eucharist (*propter*

---

[169] Against Stevenson, 21.

[170] Botte, 18-9.

[171] So ibid., 61, n. (6).

[172] Ibid., 54-5. See 55, note (2), for Botte's reconstruction of this text.

[173] Ibid., 58-9.

eucharistiam). For it is appropriate that he who has been made worthy should offer an offering at the same time (*eadem hora*).'[174] '*Eadem hora*' seems to be referring to the morning of the baptism, so this is probably an offering of materials which do not involve the bread and wine being received as Christ's body and blood, since those present are not yet baptized and the eucharist proper takes place after that. It is said to be 'propter eucharistiam', meaning 'for thanksgiving'.

In the *Apostolic Tradition* 25, there is a general reference to the offering which may include the eucharist, and a description of how 'the bishop has offered the cup' which has already been called 'the cup of the offering'.[175] This may be a reference to the eucharist but the lack of reference to the bread or to Christ means that it may rather be a *eulogia*, meaning bread received from the bishop's hand, 'and not a eucharist, the symbol of the Lord's body', as described in section 26.[176] Finally, the association of an 'offering' with Easter in section 33[177] makes a eucharistic reference very likely there.

The over-all picture given by these references to offering is of many different materials, especially foodstuffs, being offered to God and blessed by the bishop. This may well combine ideas of gift-sacrifice, particularly in the literal offering of the firstfruits, an idea already noted in Irenaeus,[178] and of communion-sacrifice, in the eucharist and agape-meal.[179] There is a difference, however, between the offering of gifts by any of the faithful, the deacons' bringing them to the bishop, and the blessing of them and the prayer over the bread and cup which will then be seen as Christ's body and blood normally done by the bishop, although they are all closely related.[180] The presbyters lay hands on the bread and cup with the bishop while he prays (section 4), hold offerings for those who partake (21), break the bread and distribute it to the people (22), and may have performed the whole eucharist under the bishop's orders.[181] The deacons bring the people's offerings to the bishop for him to pray over them (4 and 21), hold the offerings if there

---

[174] Ibid., 44-5.
[175] Ibid., 66-7.
[176] Ibid.
[177] Ibid., 78-9.
[178] So Daly, *Christian Sacrifice*, 363-4.
[179] Young, 100, sees the eucharist as among the offerings in kind which are communion-sacrifices.
[180] The 'three distinct meanings which "offer" can have for Hippolytus', according to Daly, *Christian Sacrifice*, 367, n. 70.
[181] Hein, 302-3, n. 44: although the *Apostolic Tradition* 'describes the bishop alone as president of the eucharistic service', section 22 says, 'On other days they shall receive communion as the bishop directs' (Botte, 60-61).

are insufficient presbyters (21), and break the bread (22). All three, then, have a part to play in the liturgy which, according to section 8, differentiates them from the non-clergy. This evidence also suggests that it is the laying hands on the bread and cup while the bishop prays over them that means the presbyters and bishop are the *sacerdotium* ('priesthood') while the deacon is not.[182]

The reference to the bishop propitiating God in the *Apostolic Tradition* 3 demonstrates that Irenaeus' one reference to propitiatory sacrifice had at least one successor. Its accompaniment by 'offering the church's gifts' which, as we have seen, can have much wider connotations than just the bread and cup, and its being an isolated reference which may refer to prayer, reduce the probability of it referring to the eucharist proper or alone. The offering of eucharistic worship was an important part of the bishop's task for Hippolytus, but his view of sacrificial offering was much wider than this and 'offering the church's gifts', a defining aspect of what makes a bishop a bishop according to the *Apostolic Tradition* 3, probably reflects this rather than narrowing the bishop's function down to the consecration of the bread and wine. Leadership of the congregation's sacrificial worship in general, an important part of which was the eucharist proper, was a vital constituent of what made the clergy priestly for him. Thanksgiving is strongly emphasized in the eucharistic prayers in the *Apostolic Tradition* 4, and, although the idea of firstfruits is only mentioned in section 31, it fits with the offerings made and suggests that the ideas of thank-offering and thanksgiving are the predominant sacrificial aspects of the eucharist for Hippolytus.

4.5 Clement of Alexandria[183]

4.5.1 Life and works

Clement flourished around or just before the time of Tertullian's earlier literary activity.[184] It has been disputed whether he was ordained a presbyter and whether he held any official teaching position in the

---

[182] Implied in Garrett, 'Pre-Cyprianic Doctrine' in Church and George, *Continuity and Discontinuity*, 61.

[183] In this section, 'Clement' will mean Clement of Alexandria unless otherwise indicated.

[184] Bigg, C., *The Christian Platonists of Alexandria* (Oxford, 1913), 72-3, Mondésert, C. and Plassart, A. (eds.), *Le Protreptique* (Paris, 1949²), 11-12, Osborn, E.F., *The Philosophy of Clement of Alexandria* (Cambridge, 1957), 3-4, and Quasten, vol.2, 5, all give c.150-c.215. Osborn dates his writings to 175-202.

church.

Bigg cites *Paidagogos* 1:6:37 as evidence that he was ordained,[185] but the text is somewhat spoilt and probably read, 'on the model of the good shepherd, the leaders of the churches are the shepherds and we are the sheep',[186] rather than '... we are the good shepherds, etc.',[187] leaving the question unresolved. Osborn views the reference to Clement as 'the blessed presbyter' in a letter by Alexander of Jerusalem, preserved by Eusebius, as 'the chief piece of evidence for Clement's having been ordained a presbyter.'[188] On the other hand, Koch argues that it was normal to name the church to which a cleric belonged so that the fact that Alexander does not do this shows that he was using 'presbyteros' in a different sense, which was to indicate that Clement was an outstanding teacher. Quatember counters that 'the title "Presbyter", in an official document by a bishop cannot be otherwise understood',[189] meaning other than as an ordained presbyter. The weight of the external evidence, then, must be deemed to lie on the side of Clement's ordination as a presbyter.[190]

Eusebius of Caesarea believed that Clement had succeeded Pantaenus as head of catechetical instruction in the church of Alexandria with Origen as one of his pupils.[191] Recent scholarship, however, has tended towards the view that he was not head of an official catechetical school of the church, but rather an independent teacher and philosopher who gathered any who were interested to hear him, on the model of other such teachers and philosophers of the time.[192] Most recently Wilken has followed Méhat in arguing that the two views should not be so sharply contrasted. Rather what began as 'private' instruction for those interested was eventually transformed into ecclesiastical instruction associated with the catechumenate. Nonetheless, 'the teaching of

---

[185] Bigg, 73, n. 2.

[186] Marrou, H.-I. and Harl, M. (eds.), *Le Pédagogue*, vol.1 (Paris, 1960), 178.

[187] As translated in Wood, S.P. (ed.), *Clement of Alexandria: Christ the Educator* (Washington, 1954), 36.

[188] Osborn, 3-4; see *HE* 6:11:6.

[189] Quatember, F., *Die christliche Lebenshaltung des Klemens von Alexandrien nach seinem Pädagogus* (Vienna, 1946), 14-7, countering points made by H. Koch in an article in the *Zeitschrift für neutestamentliche Wissenschaft* (1921), 43-8 which I have been unable to obtain.

[190] So Vilela, 28. Neymeyr, 92-3, leaves the question undecided.

[191] *HE* 6:6:1.

[192] So Bardy, G., *La Théologie de l'Église de saint Irénée au concile de Nicée* (Paris, 1947), 111; Mondésert in Mondésert and Plassart, 7-10; von Campenhausen, *Ecclesiastical Authority*, 197; Cooke, 237 and 242; against Quasten, vol.2, 5 and Osborn, 3. See also the history of views given in Wilken, R.L., 'Alexandria: A School for Training in Virtue' in Henry, P. (ed.), *Schools of Thought in the Christian Tradition* (Philadelphia, 1984), 16-7.

Pantaenus and Clement, and later Origen, is to be understood in the light of the model of the contemporary philosophical schools.'[193] Neymeyr also has pointed out that the two extremes are not the only two possibilities and has taken the view that Clement must have had a circle of pupils which included unbaptized, catechumens and Christians and that his teaching was not purely private.[194] Probably what began unofficially became officially recognized by the church. As will be seen, Clement's understanding of the truly gnostic teacher was an important part of his view of the Christian life and, as von Campenhausen has pointed out,[195] reflected his understanding of his own situation.

The question of the relationship between Clement's three major works has been much discussed among scholars, but has very little relevance for this thesis and no agreed solution has been reached.[196] What is relevant is that Clement's extant writings are not his complete output,[197] and nowhere deal with the subjects we are discussing at all systematically. We must therefore beware of drawing wide-ranging conclusions from his silence on certain subjects, and we have to infer some of his teaching from what he does say clearly. His apologetic and educational aims also have to be kept in mind as they influence what he deals with and how he deals with it, especially as he saw teaching as needing to be related to the stage which anyone had reached, some being withheld from unbelievers and some from immature Christians.[198] Nonetheless, as Marrou argues, Clement's portrait of Alexandria, its church and its thought-world, for all its shortcomings, has definite historical value.[199]

4.5.2 The gnostic Christian as priest

As Von Campenhausen writes, 'the pattern of the "priestly" man is for [Clement] not the bishop or priest [sc. presbyter] of the official hierarchy but the gnostic and the gnostic teacher.' He rightly adds, 'this does not, of course, exclude the possibility that someone holding an official position in the church may also be included among the

---

[193] Ibid., 17-8.

[194] Neymeyr, 92-5.

[195] Von Campenhausen, *Ecclesiastical Authority*, 198.

[196] So Daly, *Christian Sacrifice*, 443.

[197] See Mondésert in Mondésert and Plassart, 15-16 and Völker, W., *Der wahre Gnostiker nach Clemens Alexandrinus* (Berlin, 1952), 2-3.

[198] On this see Mondésert in Mondésert C. and Caster, M. (eds.), *Les Stromates, Stromate I* (Paris, 1951), 20-21.

[199] In Marrou and Harl, 88.

gnostics.'[200] Clement nowhere calls the clergy 'priests'[201] but does at times draw comparisons between the gnostic Christian and the church's hierarchy which need examination to see whether they imply the hierarchy's priesthood. First, passages will be examined which show that Clement viewed the Christian gnostic as priestly, to lay the foundation for studying those comparisons.

One such passage is found in *Stromateis* 4:25:158:1 where Clement writes, 'Now only those living purely are priests of God.'[202] This clause is in the context of a discussion of *gnôsis* and the contemplation of God. In 159:2, having continued to expound the theme of priesthood in 158:2-159:1 and so in the same context, he interprets the seven days of purification for a priest on the death of a close relative as 'the Gnostic ought to rise out of the sphere of creation and of sin.' Clearly, the gnostic Christian is being referred to as priest throughout this passage.[203]

Second, in *Stromateis* 5:6:39:3-4, Clement interprets the high priest's putting off of 'the sanctified tunic' and his putting on of 'the other tunic, that of the holy of holies, as it were' in terms of both Christ's incarnation and the Christian gnostic. So in 39:4 he writes,

> It seems to me that he indicates thus that the Levite is also the gnostic inasmuch as he can be above the other priests. These have been washed by water, clothed in faith alone and receive the dwelling appropriate to them, but he who can discern intelligible things from sensible things, who hastens, passing other priests, in his ascension towards the entrance to the spiritual world, is washed from things here below no longer by water, as before when he was purified on his admission to the Levitical tribe, but already by the word of knowledge.[204]

The beginning of this passage clearly identifies the Levite and gnostic as the one ruling other priests.[205] The questions then arise: who are the other priests and to whom are they being compared in the earlier dispensation? Since the high priest's use of his tunics is the subject

---

[200] Von Campenhausen, *Ecclesiastical Authority*, 201. Others who point to the priesthood of the Christian gnostic in Clement's writings include Bigg, 134; Völker, W*ahre Gnostiker*, 510-511; Osborn, 107; Eastwood, 72-3; Hanson, R.P.C., *Christian Priesthood Examined*, 51; and Garrett, 'Pre-Cyprianic Doctrine' in Church and George, *Continuity and Discontinuity*, 53.

[201] So Hanson, R.P.C., *Christian Priesthood Examined*, 51.

[202] Roberts, Donaldson and Coxe, vol. 2, 877-8.

[203] So understood by Völker, *Wahre Gnostiker*, 510; von Campenhausen, *Ecclesiastical Authority*, 201, n. 152; and Hanson, R.P.C., *Christian Priesthood Examined*, 51.

[204] The passages quoted here and below from *Strom* 5.6.39-41 are based on Le Boulluec and Voulet, 88-91.

[205] So understood by von Campenhausen, *Ecclesiastical Authority*, 201, n. 152; Hanson, R.P.C., *Christian Priesthood Examined*, 51; and Le Boulluec in Le Boulluec and Voulet, 159.

being interpreted, the gnostic is being likened to him. The other priests must be the other priestly Levites. As these other priests are said here to have been washed with water and to have put on faith, they are the ordinary, non-gnostic Christians of Clement's day.[206] This passage will therefore be mentioned again in section 5.

This contrast is still present in *Stromateis* 5:6:40:1, which continues from 39:4: 'Pure in his whole heart, having perfectly directed his conduct to the summit, having grown far beyond the measure of the simple priest, in short, sanctified in word and life, clothed in more brightness of glory, receiving the inexpressible inheritance of the spiritual and perfect man, ...' The gnostic Christian is regarded as having surpassed the ordinary priest in the clause, 'having grown far beyond the measure of the simple priest'.[207]

There is another passage, in *Excerpta ex Theodoto* 27, in which Clement interprets the high priest's entrance into the holy of holies in a similarly dual way to that just treated. There too the gnostic Christian becomes high priestly.[208]

Another passage in *Stromateis* in which Clement alludes to the priestliness of the gnostic Christian is found in 7:3:14:5. He has been describing the gnostic from the beginning of 7:3, and has asserted that his virtues are 'an offering approved by God' (14:1). In 14:5 he writes, 'That is why, knowingly, we do not sacrifice to God, who has no needs, and who has given everything to everyone. Rather we give glory to him who has been sacrificed (*hiereuthenta*) for us by sacrificing (*hiereuontes*) ourselves through the absence of need for the sake of the one who has no need, and through the absence of passion for the sake of the one who has no passion.[209] Lampe too gives 'sacrifice' as the meaning of the two uses of *hiereuô* here, but a reference to acting as a *hiereus*, a priest, is implicit.[210] Finally,[211] in *Stromateis* 7:7:36:2, in a discussion of the gnostic Christian's converse with, and praise of God, Clement writes, 'Now this is the royal man, the worthy priest of God,

---

[206] So Völker, *Wahre Gnostiker*, 151, n. 2.

[207] This interpretation is further reinforced in 40:3-41:1. On 40:3, see Le Boulluec in Le Boulluec and Voulet, 165-6.

[208] Cf. Sagnard, F. (ed.), *Extraits de Théodote* (Paris, 1970), 11.

[209] Le Boulluec, A. (ed.), *Clément d'Alexandrie: Les Stromates: Stromate VII* (Paris, 1997), 70-73.

[210] Lampe, 670; cf. Le Boulluec, 72-3, fn. 4, and Garrett, 'Pre-Cyprianic Doctrine' in Church and George, *Continuity and Discontinuity*, 53, who refers to the early part of the passage referred to here as evidence of the gnostic priesthood.

[211] There are less certain allusions to the priestliness of the gnostic Christian in *Strom* 2.4.19.4 and 5.6.34.3.

For Clement, then, the priest, after Christ himself, is the gnostic Christian who is closely assimilated to Christ. The qualities connoted by priestliness for Clement are holiness, knowledge, devotion and ascent to God, and assimilation to the Logos. The relationship between the gnostic and other Christians will be examined in section 5. The relationship between the gnostic Christian and the ordained will be examined next.

4.5.3 The gnostic Christian and the ordained

In *Stromateis* 6:13, having stated that the gnostic Christian is 'equal to the angels' and may be enrolled 'in the chosen body of the apostles', Clement continues,

> Such an one is in reality a presbyter of the Church, and a true minister (deacon) of the will of God, if he do and teach what is the Lord's; not as being ordained by men, nor regarded as righteous because a presbyter, but enrolled in the presbyterate because righteous. And although here upon earth he be not honored with the chief seat, he will sit down on the twenty-four thrones, juding the people, as John says in the Apocalypse. (106:2).

After a digression about the unity of the covenant of salvation, and a reference to the gnostics as 'the chosen of the chosen', being honoured in heaven, Clement adds,

> according to my opinion, the grades here in the Church of bishops, presbyters, deacons, are imitations of the angelic glory, and of that economy which ... awaits those who, following the footsteps of the apostles, have lived in perfection of righteousness, according to the Gospel. For these taken up in the clouds, the apostle writes, will first minister [sc. as deacons], then be classed in the presbyterate, by promotion in glory (for glory differs from glory) till they grow into a perfect man. (107:2-3)[213]

Clement's main point here is the gnostic Christian's real value in God's eyes. In 106:2 he argues that gnostic Christians are true presbyters, deacons and bishops, not as appointed by men but because of what they are, and this will be seen in heaven.[214] In 107:2-3, it is clear

---

[212] Le Boulluec, 132-3. Völker, *Wahre Gnostiker*, 510; von Campenhausen, *Ecclesiastical Authority*, 201, n. 152; Hanson, R.P.C., *Christian Priesthood Examined*, 51; and Garrett, 'Pre-Cyprianic Doctrine' in Church and George, *Continuity and Discontinuity*, 53, find a reference to the gnostic Christian here.

[213] Roberts, Donaldson and Coxe, vol. 2, 1020-1021.

[214] Vilela, 32, argues that this passage is about the gnostic who has been ordained a presbyter,

that ultimate reality, for him, lies in heaven among the angels and deceased gnostics where there are degrees of glory to be attained. These degrees are imitated by those involved in the church's earthly hierarchy. Faivre appositely comments, 'Clement sacralized the hierarchy of the church at the same time as relativizing it, because he regarded it as an imitation of the steps toward heavenly glory, human deacons and presbyters being, in his view, no more than imitations, but, it should be noted, in spite of everything very faithful imitations. It would seem therefore that he regarded the perfect man as a heavenly episkopos.'[215]

A somewhat similar passage is found in *Stromateis* 7:1:3:3-4. In 3:1, Clement has been explaining in what the gnostic's service of God consists, pointing to the ways in which different kinds of service to men have different aims. In 3:3-4 he makes the following comparison: 'Similarly, in the case of the church, the presbyters preserve the image of improvement and the deacons that of submission. This double kind of help is exercised as much by the angels in their submission to God for the administration of earthly matters as by the gnostic himself; ....'[216] The similar language used of the service involved indicates a degree of equivalence, although that of the presbyter and deacons deals with men, whilst that of the angels and the gnostic is rendered to God. However, this difference is not to be over-stressed and no disapproval is implied.

In both these cases, then, a three-way comparison is involved with the main point in each case being the value of the gnostic Christian and his service. As just stated, no disapproval of the church's hierarchy is implied[217] and it is viewed as an imitation of that in heaven, having real, if indeterminate, value. Clement takes the church's hierarchy and its value for granted; clearly he felt a great need to defend and uphold that of the gnostic Christian. This evidence does not enable us to state for certain that Clement knew of or viewed the clergy as priestly, but the degree of equivalence implied in these comparisons with the gnostic suggests that he did.

4.5.4 View of sacrifice

Clement holds a view of sacrifice very like that of others of the apologists at whom we have already looked. For one thing he stresses that God does not need sacrifice. On the other hand, it is clear that on

---

but see the criticisms of Gryson, R., 'Review of Vilela, A., *La condition collégiale des prêtres au IIIe siècle*', *Revue d'histoire ecclésiastique* (1974), 110-111.

[215] Faivre, *Emergence*, 59. See also von Campenhausen, *Ecclesiastical Authority*, 210, n. 217.

[216] Le Boulluec, 44-5.

[217] So von Campenhausen, *Ecclesiastical Authority*, 211.

this subject, as on others, Clement was more influenced by Hellenistic Judaism and Greek philosophy than any Christian writer before him.[218]

On the other hand, Clement also at times, like the other apologists, simply quotes the OT cult criticism, with little of his own comment, e.g., in *Paidagogos* 3:12:90:1-4. Moreover, he frequently combines philosophical analysis, quotation of OT cult-criticism and quotation of pagan cult-criticism.[219]

Alongside this strenuous rejection of literal sacrifice goes a strong positive teaching on the kinds of sacrifices which are appropriate. Daly points out that Clement likes to interpret some realities in the OT as the symbols of moral realities, a method which often results in seeing sacrifice in terms of the gnostic Christian's life and worship. Indeed, he asserts that 'for Clement, ... the idea of the worship of the gnostic is practically coterminous with that of the sacrifice and prayer of the gnostic.'[220] As an example he again adduces *Stromateis* 5:11:67:1ff., which begins, 'Now sacrifice approved by God consists in unchanging separation from the body and its passions.'[221]

There is a merging of the gnostic Christian's sacrifice with that of the whole church in Clement's major explanation of Christian sacrifice in *Stromateis* 7:6-7. He says prayer is 'the best and holiest sacrifice', the terrestrial altar is 'the earthly gathering of gifts dedicated by our prayers', the church's sacrifice is 'the word breathed out by holy souls', the truly holy altar is 'the righteous soul' and its incense 'worthy prayer', the sacrifices of the OT Law are 'allegories of the godliness that is ours', the sacrifices God loves consist of prayer and different nations and natures gathered for prayer, 'with a pure mind, a just and right way of life, thanks to worthy deeds and righteous prayer' (7:6:31:7-8, 32:4-5 and 7, 34:2).[222]

More passages could be cited,[223] but enough have been adduced to show how strongly spiritualized was Clement's view of sacrifice. As Daly notes concerning the church's sacrifice in *Stromateis* 7:6:32:4,

---

[218] So Daly, *Christian Sacrifice*, 449 and ff.

[219] So ibid., which see for references.

[220] Ibid., 444-8 and 466. Daly argues that Clement's exegesis 'is quite different from the (relatively) sober, traditional typology found in Justin, Irenaeus and Hippolytus', using 'the more flamboyant allegorizing exegesis which was developed by Philo, "baptized" by Barnabas, and finally brought to perfection by Origen.'

[221] Le Boulluec, 136-7.

[222] Le Boulluec, 116-127. Völker, *Wahre Gnostiker*, 549, says of this passage, 'it is not only apologetic interest that allows him to grasp this thought, but he uses it in defence because it is an expression of his innermost conviction and really reaches the heart of the matter.'

[223] *Prot* 4:59:2; *Paid* 3:12:90:3; *Strom* 2:18:78:4 and 96:3; 4:16:104:2 (martyrs as a sacrifice); 4:18:113:3; 5:11:67:1.

whilst in Irenaeus' and Hippolytus' writings the church's sacrifice is seen mainly as the eucharist, 'the most that can be said for Clement's text is merely that it is open to Eucharistic connotations.'[224]

4.5.5 View of the eucharist as sacrifice

In *Stromateis* 1:19:96:1, Clement condemns heretical groups who use only bread and water for the eucharist 'in their offering contrary to the rules of the Church.'[225] In *Stromateis* 6:14:113:3, Clement writes of the need to keep the soul pure 'and giving thanks always for all things to God, by righteous hearing and divine reading, by true investigation, by holy oblation, by blessed prayer; lauding hymning, blessing, praising, ...'[226] The setting of 'by holy oblation' alongside giving thanks, hearing, reading and investigating suggests that it means the eucharist.[227]

The question of Clement's view of the eucharist has been a Roman Catholic-Protestant battle-ground in the past.[228] The fact that he does not, in either of these references, explain in what way it is a sacrifice, means that we only speculate from what he does say. His highly spiritualized view of sacrifice makes an understanding of the sacrificial nature of the eucharist along the lines of thanksgiving most likely.[229] The lack of a developed understanding of the relationship between Christ's self-sacrifice on the cross and the eucharist elsewhere at this time makes it unlikely that Clement possessed one either.[230]

The fact that he never links church leadership with presidency at the eucharist[231] suggests that this presidency was of little or no importance to him. He certainly makes no links between it and any putative priesthood of the president.

4.5.6 Conclusion

Clement shows much less interest in the ordained and their position in

---

[224] Daly, *Christian Sacrifice*, 471.

[225] Ferguson, J. (ed.), *Clement of Alexandria: Stromateis Books One to Three* (Washington, 1991), 96, except that I have changed his 'offertory' to 'offering' as a translation of *prosfora* that retains the sacrificial connotations more clearly.

[226] Roberts, Donaldson and Coxe, vol. 2, 1024.

[227] Hanson, R.P.C., *Studies*, 100, n. 74.

[228] See Völker, *Wahre Gnostiker*, 598-600, and Kelly, *Early Christian Doctrines*, 213.

[229] Daly, *Christian Sacrifice*, 471, points out that the possibility of material sacrifice (as in the firstfruits perhaps) cannot be ruled out, but there is nothing to indicate it clearly.

[230] So Hanson, R.P.C., *Studies*, 100.

[231] A point made by ibid., 51.

the church than his contemporaries, Tertullian and Hippolytus. This is explained by their situations, the character of their writings and the nature of their interests as compared with his.[232] R.P.C. Hanson argues that the lack of sign of the practice of calling the clergy priests in Clement's writings confirms that 'the practice only arose at the beginning of the 3rd century.'[233] We have noted, however, that he may well have been aware of it, although he never finds it necessary to state it. Even so, the lack of mention of it in literature up to Clement, combined with his virtual silence on it, Origen's awareness of it, and Clement's emphasis on the gnostic Christian's priesthood, which shows that he was quite happy with priestly ideas, suggests quite strongly that it was only developing at this time.

4.6 Origen[234]

4.6.1 Life and work

Origen's writings betray his community of interest with Clement, although, strangely, he never names him or uses 'gnostic' of the spiritual Christian.[235] After his father's martyrdom in c.202, he maintained himself and his family by teaching, which from c.203-c.231 included being head of Alexandria's catechetical school with bishop Demetrius' approval. His relationship with Bishop Demetrius was stormy, and may well have had an effect on his view of bishops.[236] Their disputes resulted in Origen being ordained by Theoctetus of Caesarea, leaving Alexandria for good and continuing his work in Caearea until his death some time after 251.

---

[232] See section 6.5 below for what he does say.

[233] Hanson, R.P.C., *Christian Priesthood Examined*, 51.

[234] The volume of his works, the paucity of modern translations, and lack of time have meant that Origen's are the only Church Father's works used in this thesis not to have been read in their entirety. Nonetheless, as the references to them will show, many have been studied and enough to give a fair view of his teaching.
The following abbreviations are used in references below for Origen's non-exegetical works: *CC*: *Contra Celsum*; *DH*: *Dialogus cum Heraclide*; *EM*: *Exhortatio ad martyrium*; *PA*: *Peri archon* or *De principiis*; *PE*: *Peri euches* or *De oratione*. His exegetical works are abbreviated to *C.* (*Commentarii*), *H.* (*Homiliae*), *C. Ser.* (*Commentariorum series*), *Sel.* (*Selecta*) or *Frag.* (*Fragmenta*) with the abbreviation of the biblical book commented on.

[235] Crouzel, H., *Origène et la 'connaissance mystique'* (Paris, 1961), 397, notes that *gnôstikos* is so used only once by Origen and that in a not particularly authentic fragment. In *Origène* (Paris, 1985), 25, he questions whether Origen ever heard Clement, as Eusebius (*HE* 6:3:1) suggests, but accepts that he had read Clement's writings.

[236] See further in section 6.6.3 below on this relationship.

Problems have been raised for students of Origen by three main facts: first, a number of his writings are available only in Latin editions by Rufinus and Jerome; second, some have survived only in fragments; and third, most of his extant works are exegetical and homiletical rather than doctrinal and systematic. Regarding the first, although it is clearly better to be able to use what remains in Greek, de Lubac has been followed by others in arguing that, 'to have the likelihood of reaching the authentic Origen, one must multiply the quotations. Then parallel passages control, determine, and comment on one another, especially when, for example, a phrase of Rufinus' Latin, another of Jerome's, and another in the original come into consideration. Now this is not rare, and from these comparisons comes an impression of unity.'[237] This method will be followed as far as possible.

Regarding the second, it is helpful for this study that Origen's extant work includes so many homilies and commentaries in which he deals with the subject of sacrifice and priesthood in some detail. These are sufficient to give a fair impression of its importance for him and his overall view of it. Regarding the third, Origen's method of commenting on a text, in both his commentaries and homilies, gave him frequent and ample scope for developing his ideas quite fully on any subject in which he was interested, and this clearly included that of sacrifice and priesthood. It is fair to conclude, then, that we can arrive at a fairly complete, though not exhaustive, comprehension of his views on this subject.

Origen's interpretation of Scripture and its scriptural and Hellenistic roots have been extensively studied elsewhere.[238] Here it is only necessary to note that he can arrive at more than one meaning of any passage because of his view of revelation which is that the shadows were revealed to Israel in the OT and the Law, the images to the church in the NT and the gospel, and the realities eschatologically. The Christian can, to some extent, ascend in knowledge and understanding of these in this life by moral and intellectual effort and graces and gifts imparted by Christ through the Spirit.[239]

---

[237] Quoted with approval by Schäfer, T., *Das Priester-Bild im Leben und Werk des Origenes* (Frankfurt am Main, 1978), 23 and Crouzel, *Origène*, 78.

[238] See especially, Crouzel, *Origène*, 95ff. and many parts of Crouzel, *Origène et la 'connaissance mystique'*.

[239] For full accounts of this spiritual ascent, see Völker, W., *Das Vollkommenheitsideal des Origenes* (Tübingen, 1930) and Crouzel, *Origène et la 'connaissance mystique'*. For a brief account, see Crouzel, *Origène*, 155ff.

4.6.2 General view of priests: priesthood of the perfect

In the light of what we have just noted, it is not surprising to find that Origen is very insistent that the old priesthood and temple cultus have passed away to be replaced by the new which is centred on Christ.[240] Nonetheless, the Jewish priests and sacrifices 'contain countless symbols which are explained by those who are learned'[241] and 'the apostle says somewhere that the discussion about the sacrifices ought to be understood about certain heavenly mysteries, "Which serve for an example and shadow of heavenly things."'[242]

Turning to Origen's exegesis of the Levitical priesthood, we face the problem that he interprets it of the clergy, Christ and his angels, the faithful, and the perfect.[243] This means that we have to examine passages closely in their contexts to try to ascertain what Origen is saying. It also means that it is at times unclear to whom he is referring and that his interpretation can change 'in mid-stream', as it were.Treatments of priesthood in Origen, and many of Origen in general, acknowledge that he viewed perfect Christians as priests.[244] Such a generally accepted view needs no validation here, especially as it will become apparent in various texts that we shall study concerning his view of the priesthood of the ordained and of the faithful, as will what being a perfect Christian involved for him. A prior point worth making, however, is that he does not consider them totally, but only relatively, perfect, especially in this life.[245]

The similarities between his conception of the perfect and Clement's idea of the gnostic Christian suggest that Origen was familiar with

---

[240] See especially *C. Jn.* 10:24(16), 28:12(11), *H. Lev.* 10:1 and *H. Josh.* 2:1.

[241] *CC* 4:31: Chadwick, H. (ed.), *Origen: Contra Celsum* (Cambridge, 1965), 208.

[242] *C. Jn.* 6:266: Heine, R.E. (ed.), *Origen: Commentary on the Gospel according to John Books 1-10* (Washington, 1989), 240.

[243] So Crouzel, *Origène*, 288. See the very similar outlines of Origen's view of the historical development of the priesthood in Vilela, 51 and Schäfer, 153.

[244] So Völker, *Vollkommenheitsideal*, 181ff.; Rahner, K. 'La doctrine d'Origène sur la pénitence', *Recherches de Science Religieuse* 37 (1950), 52 and 259; Daniélou, J., *Origen* (London, 1955), 44-50; Crouzel, *Origène et la 'connaissance mystique'*, 86, 157-161 and 409; von Campenhausen, *Ecclesiastical Authority*, 255-6; Lécuyer, J., 'Sacerdoce des fidèles et sacerdoce ministériel chez Origène', *Vetera Christianorum* 7 (1970), 258; Vilela, 57, 79 and 128-136; Lies, L., *Wort und Eucharistie bei Origenes* (1978), 200; Vogt, H.J., *Das Kirchenverständnis des Origenes* (Cologne, 1974), 90-91; Nautin, P, *Origène et son œuvre* (Paris, 1977), 426-7; Schäfer, 60-63, etc.; Garrett, 'Pre-Cyprianic Doctrine' in Church and George, *Continuity and Discontinuity*, 56; Trigg, J.W., 'The Charismatic Intellectual: Origen's Understanding of Religious Leadership', *Church History* 50 (1981), 7-19; Trigg, J.W., *Origen: The Bible and Philosophy in the Third-century Church* (Atlanta, 1983), 140ff.; Crouzel, *Origène*, 289 and 301.

[245] Crouzel, *Origène et la 'connaissance mystique'*, 483.

Clement's views and that they reflect a general view of some in the Alexandrian church. Origen himself provides abundant evidence that he regarded very few in the church as among the perfect. It seems therefore more likely to represent the view of those who regarded themselves as a spiritual élite, and of those who honoured such as a spiritual élite. Crouzel, however, rightly notes that 'the contrasting of Christians of simple faith with the perfect does not involve any élitism but the recognition that Christians are not at the same point in their relationships with God, especially because of their moral behaviour. The spiritual or perfect do not form a closed élite; every Christian is called to it.'[246]

4.6.3 The priesthood of the ordained

Largely as a result of Origen's complex hermeneutics, scholars have arrived at different views of how he regarded the relationship between the priesthood of the ordained and the priesthood of the perfect. At one extreme, Trigg holds that the priesthood of the perfect is essential for Origen to the extent that he never approvingly identifies the ordained as priests.[247] The others studied hold that, although the internal priesthood of the perfect was very important for Origen, so was the external priesthood of the ordained. They find varying degrees of identification of the two, Rahner being at the other extreme in regarding them as both ideally and, largely, in practice the same, whereas the rest acknowledge that, whilst this may have been the ideal for Origen, reality was different, so that the two hierarchies existed side by side and overlapped to some extent.[248]

Since we have it in Greek, a very important witness to whether Origen called church officials 'priests' non-disparagingly is a passage in *Homilies on Jeremiah* 12:3: 'Hence, if anyone among these *priests* sins – I am pointing to us presbyters – or among those Levites who stood

---

[246] Ibid., 494.

[247] Trigg, *Origen*, 143, states, 'unquestionably Origen did not identify priests with the existing officials of the church', although in 'The Charismatic Intellectual', *Church History* 50 (1981), 12, n. 37, he admits that 'Origen seems to refer to this practice, though disparagingly' and gives two references. Völker, *Vollkommenheitsideal*, 181-2, acknowledges that in *H. Lev.* 5 Origen views the cleric as the priest and the spiritual as the high priest, but otherwise emphasizes that Origen views the perfect as priest.

[248] Rahner, 'La doctrine d'Origène', *Recher Sci Rel* 37 (1950), 51-2 and 276-7. Others studied: Daniélou, 44-7; Crouzel, *Origène et la 'connaissance mystique'*, 86, 157-162, 174-8, 409, 485, 492; von Campenhausen, *Ecclesiastical Authority*, 254-6; Lécuyer, 'Sacerdoce des fidèles', *Vetera Christianorum* 7 (1970), 258-262; Vilela, 57, 79-83; Vogt, 70-79; Schäfer, 54, 60, 63, 141-2.

around the people – yet I mean these deacons – he will have this punishment.'[249] Whilst this is a warning against such people sinning, it affords no evidence of disapproval of the likening of the presbyters and deacons to the OT priests and Levites.[250] Indeed, part of the continuation of the passage just quoted is 'but there are also priestly blessings'. This may imply, as Vogt argues, 'that the clergy are contrasted with the community not only for practial, organisational reasons, but that God's will stands behind this differentiation.'[251] This is equally true of calling the clergy 'priests'.

Other passages of Origen preserved in Greek which have been cited as showing that he called church officials 'priests' are *Commentary on Matthew* 15:26, 16:25 and 17:3. The first is unlikely, since the priestly reference in the Latin is attributable to the editor, the Greek containing none.[252] Schäfer cites *Commentary on Matthew* 16:25 and 17:3 as passages in which bishops are called 'high priests'.[253] In the former, Origen likens the 'culpable ... high priests and scribes' to 'certain culpable high priests who do not adorn the name of bishop with their way of life ....' He describes them in a thoroughly negative way, but does liken the chief priests of Jesus' day to bishops of his own. In 17:3 he writes, 'and even now in the temple, the church, is Christ and he teaches in it and some, resembling those chief priests and elders of the people, learn of him ....' In view of the clearer reference in 16:25, this too probably involves a likening of the bishops to the high priests and presbyters to the elders.

We thus have three Greek passages, in two of which Origen is happy to liken bishops to the chief priests of Jesus' day, in the other identifying OT priests and Levites with presbyters and deacons. These are important in that they make it the more likely that when the Latin editors of his works use *sacerdos* of church leaders, Origen himself had used *hiereus*, and it is not an addition of their own, reflecting practice in their own, later day. As we shall see, the context often ensures that such is the case anyway. All these Greek texts, however, involve disparaging references to the clergy, betraying an important aspect of Origen's

---

[249] Smith, J.C. (ed.), *Origen: Homilies on Jeremiah. Homily on 1 Kings 28* (Washington, 1998), 115.

[250] As Trigg, 'The Charismatic Intellectual', *Ch H* 50 (1981), 12, n. 37, implies.

[251] Vogt, 4. Vilela, 84; and Schäfer, 85 and 217, see references to the presbyters as priests here, whereas Hanson, R.P.C., *Studies*, 100, mistakenly cites this passage to support the view that 'throughout his work Origen refers to bishops as priests or high priests'.

[252] Daniélou, 43, cites this but cf. the texts in Klostermann, E. and Benz, E. (eds.), *Origenes Werke*, vol. 10 (Leipzig, 1935), 426.

[253] Schäfer, 67-68. For the texts discussed below see Klostermann and Benz, 558-9 and 585.

general attitude to them. Further, in that the chief priests' main task was to rule the people in Jesus' day, this is the primary connotation of the bishops' priesthood here.

Not surprisingly, there are many references to priesthood in Origen's homilies, especially in those on Leviticus, Numbers and Joshua. These will be presented here to demonstrate, first, how they depict the relationships amongst the clergy and between the clergy and the rest of the church, and, second, to show the major connotations of priesthood for Origen, including the priesthood of the ordained.

As we have already noted from *Commentary on Matthew* 16:25 and 17:3, Origen sometimes likens the bishop to the high priest, a custom also found in *Homilies on Leviticus* 6:6, where he encourages each priest to assess his degrees of merit and 'know that he has obtained the highest priesthood not only in name but in merit.'[254] On the other hand, the presbyters are included with the bishop in the 'priestly order' as over against the deacons, when he differentiates between that and the Levitical order, or the priests and the Levites, as in *Homilies on Numbers* 2:1, *Homilies on Joshua* 4:1 and *Homilies on Judges* 3:2. Then again a contrast between bishops and presbyter-priests is implied in *Homilies on Exodus* 11:6, where Origen asks, 'But who today of those who preside over the people ... sees fit to accept counsel from even a lower priest, much less from a layman or a Gentile?'[255] He may well be thinking of bishops and presbyters in *Homilies on Leviticus* 7:1 where he mentions priests and high priests.[256]

Origen also contrasts the ordained as priests with the rest of the church. He does this explicitly in *Homilies on Numbers* 22:4, where he asks, concerning the choice of church leaders, 'who then will dare, whether among the people itself ... or among even the priests themselves, who will dare to judge himself capable of pronouncing on this, ...?'[257] He also does it explicitly in *Homilies on Numbers* 2:1, when he contrasts the 'eminent order of the priesthood' with 'an order of inferior ministry' and 'the common multitude'.[258] He implies it in writing of the 'priestly order', as noted above, and of the 'priestly assembly' in *Homilies on Joshua* 9:5,[259] in his reference to the need for

---

[254] Barkley, G.W. (ed.), *Origen: Homilies on Leviticus 1-16* (Washington, 1990), 126.
[255] Heine, R.E. (ed.), *Origen: Homilies on Genesis and Exodus* (Washington, 1982), 364. Vilela, 91 and Schäfer, 56, see bishops and presbyters referred to here.
[256] Barkley, 129.
[257] Méhat, A. (ed.), *Origène: Homélies sur les Nombres* (Paris, 1951), 431. Cited in Vilela, 85, as a reference to the priesthood of the presbyters or bishop.
[258] Doutreleau, L. (ed.), *Origène: Homélies sur les Nombres I* (Paris, 1996), 59.
[259] Jaubert, A. (ed.), *Origène: Homélies sur Josué* (Paris, 1960), 255.

the people to be present at the ordination of a priest in *Homilies on Leviticus* 6:3, and in his allusions to the upkeep of the priestly clergy by the laity in *Homilies on Leviticus* 3:6, *Homilies on Numbers* 11:1-2 and *Homilies on Joshua* 17:2-3. He also implies it and the way in which the priestly hierarchy were now being regarded in his reference to those who 'come to church and bow their heads to the priests' in *Homilies on Joshua* 10:3.[260]

In spite of this differentiation, Origen repeatedly refers to the priestly ordained disparagingly, pointing out their failings and need to live up to their priestly calling in holiness, study and knowledge of the word, and growth toward perfection. In a number of these passages, the call to perfection means that it is unclear whether he is referring to the ordained or to the perfect as priests.

A general reference to the pride of the priestly bishops and presbyters and to the deacons not living as befits their position is found in *Homilies on Numbers* 2:1:

> Do you think that those charged with the priesthood, when they boast of belonging to the priestly order, behave as appropriate to their order and fulfil their function according to the dignity of this order? Similarly for the deacons, do you believe they behave as appropriate to the order of their ministry? How does it happen that we often hear people blaspheming and saying, "Look what a bishop or presbyter or deacon!" Are these things not said when a priest or minister of God is seen contravening his order in some way and behaving inappropriately for the priestly or Levitical order?[261]

Another reference to pride among the priestly ordained as well as the people is found in *Homilies on Judges* 3:2, where Origen states, 'But sometimes this malady of pride not only reaches the poor of the people but pursues even the priestly and Levitical order.'[262] Further, in *Homilies on Joshua* 4:2, he rhetorically asks concerning the priests who led the Israelites to the promised land, 'Who today among the priests is such as to deserve to be enrolled in that order?'[263] And in *Homilies on Numbers* 10:3, he asks, 'who can hold the rank and honour of the priesthood without on the other hand fulfilling the activities and ministry of the priesthood, …?'[264]

---

[260] Ibid., 276; cf. Vilela, 86.

[261] Doutreleau, 58-61. See Vogt, 61 and Schäfer, 56.

[262] Messié, P., Neyrand, L. and Borret, M. (eds.), *Origène: Homélies sur les Juges* (Paris, 1993), 100-101. Cited in Vilela, 86 as referring to the presbyters and deacons.

[263] Jaubert, 150. Schäfer, 89, sees a reference to church leaders here.

[264] Doutreleau, 284-5. Vilela, 85, cites the passage immediately preceding this as referring to presbyters.

That Origen sees priestly living, involving holiness, detachment from this world, and dedication to God, as of paramount importance for the ordained and for other Christians is clear in *Homilies on Joshua* 9:5: 'All those, indeed, who live out their religion in a priestly and holy way, not only those who are seen sitting in priestly assemblies, but rather those who behave in a priestly way, whose share is the Lord and who have no portion in the world, they are truly priests and Levites of the Lord, ...'[265]

A similar emphasis on the need for holiness to accompany priesthood is apparent in *Homilies on 1 Kings* 1:7. Here he is reflecting on the fact that there are two priests in Scripture called Phineas: 'today too each Phineas is found among the priests of the Lord, as is Eleazar, who is called the first bishop in the scriptures .... There are priests from whose mouths no scandal, no falsehood, no deceit nor any wrong is produced, and those are rightly likened to the Phineas who was the son of Aaron. But there are also some priests like that Phineas who was the son of Eli, ...'[266]

In *Homilies on Leviticus* 7:1, Origen is commenting on the prohibition on Aaron and his sons drinking alcohol in Lev 10:8-11. He then argues that Paul confirms these laws by those of the NT, in which, 'setting up the rules of life for the priests or the chief priests to this, he tells them they ought not to be enslaved "to much wine", but to be "sober."'[267]

This priestly holiness extends to the thought-life and affects the judgment:

> For it happens often that he who produces a shallow and common judgment and understands earthly things sits in the eminent order of the priesthood or occupies a teacher's chair while another, who is spiritual and so free from earthly behaviour that he can judge everything and not himself be judged by anyone, holds an order of inferior ministry or even is left in the common multitude.[268]

---

[265] Jaubert, 255. Völker, *Vollkommenheitsideal*, 182, Trigg, 'The Charismatic Intellectual', *Ch H* 50 (1981), 12, and Schäfer, 60, point out that this passage implies the priesthood either of all Christians or of the perfect, while Vilela, 86 and Schäfer, 60, rightly find a reference to the ordained in the 'priestly assembly.'

[266] Quoted in Vilela, 86, as referring to presbyters. The description of Eleazar as 'first bishop' means that bishops are in Origen's mind, although presbyters could also be included.

[267] Barkley, 130. He is probably referring to Titus 1:7-8 and/or 2:2-3. The latter refers to older men and women, but Origen may have confused it with the former which refers to the bishop. A reference to church leaders is therefore likely. So Vogt, 42, and Schäfer, 217, as against Völker, *Vollkommenheitsideal*, 187, who finds the perfect meant.

[268] *H. Num.* 2:1 (Doutreleau, 56-9).

It should also be accompanied by a priestly scholarship and understanding of Scripture. This is apparent in *Homilies on Leviticus* 6:3 where Origen writes, 'For in ordaining a priest, the presence of the people is also required that all may know and be certain that from all the people one is chosen for the priesthood who is more excellent, who is more wise, who is more holy, who is more eminent in every virtue, lest afterwards, when he stands before the people, any hesitation or any doubt should remain.'

Völker sees a reference to the perfect teacher in this section because of the later statement, 'He is high priest who has knowledge of the Law and understands the reasons for each mystery and, in brief, who knew the Law both according to the spirit and according to the letter.'[269] Others, however, find a reference to the external priesthood.[270] The likeliest explanation is that Origen begins by referring to the external priesthood of the ordained, but develops his exposition increasingly in terms of the internal priesthood of the perfect, to which the external ought to conform. The references to ordination, the people's presence, and Paul's requirements for a bishop in 1 Timothy 3:7 make an initial reference to the official hierarchy certain.

Similar points are illustrated in *Homilies on Leviticus* 6:6. Commenting on the difference between the high priest's and the priests' clothing, Origen examines 'what is the difference between minor priests and major priests':

> These therefore receive the grace of the priesthood and they perform the office but not as that one .... From this I think it is one thing for the priests to perform their office, another thing to be instructed and prepared in all things. For anyone can perform the religious ministry, but few there are who are adorned with morals, instructed in doctrine, educated in wisdom, very well adapted to communicate the truth of things and who expound the wisdom of the faith, not omitting the ornament of understandings and the splendor of assertions .... One then is the name of a priest, but there is not one dignity either by the worth of his life or by the virtues of his soul.[271]

Schäfer is caught in two minds on this passage. In one place he argues that Origen means the difference between the priestly laity and the ordained and in another the difference between the bishop and the presbyters.[272] Probably, Origen is here combining the internal and

---

[269] Barkley. 120-121. Völker, *Vollkommenheitsideal*, 170.
[270] Rahner, 'La doctrine d'Origène', *Recher Sci Rel* 37 (1950), 52, Daniélou, 50, Vogt, 11, and Schäfer, 94.
[271] Barkley, 126.
[272] Schäfer, 52, cf. 57.

external priesthoods, judging the external ('it is one thing for the priests to perform their office') by the internal ('another ... to be instructed and prepared in all things'). Indeed, he goes on to encourage each priest to assess his degrees of merit and seems to have the bishop in mind since he describes him as having 'the highest priesthood not only in name but in merit' if he has the required qualities but 'otherwise he would know that he is placed in an inferior degree although he receives the name of the first.'

As well as the connotations of leadership and rule of the people involved in Origen's likening of bishops to the high priests of Jesus' day which we noted in *Commentary on Matthew* 16:25 and 17:3, there are three references to the priests leading and ruling the people or the church. They are found in *Homilies on Exodus* 11:6 ('those who preside over the people'), *Homilies on Leviticus* 5:4 ('the priests of the Lord who preside in the churches') and in *Homilies on Joshua* 7:6 ('the priests who preside over the people').[273] The context in each case makes it likely that the bishops are meant.

Leadership and ministry are also implied in those texts where Origen speaks of the priesthood's upkeep by the laity. For example, in *Homilies on Leviticus* 3:6, he writes of 'the prayers and offerings which are presented in the churches of God for the use of the saints and the ministry of the priesthood or for the need of the poor by devoted and religious minds.'[274] In *Homilies on Numbers* 11:2 he condemns the Christian who worships God and enters his church, 'who knows that the priests and the ministers stand at the altar and serve zealously either the word of God or the ministry of the Church, ... and does not offer the firstfruits to the priests.'[275]

Another passage in which the support of the priests by the laity is dealt with is *Homilies on Joshua* 17:2-3. This is not as straightforward since Origen begins the section by speaking of those in the church who 'surpass all others in goodness of character and in merits for whom the Lord himself is said to be the inheritance.' He then contrasts those who 'believe simply' with those who 'work hard at wisdom and knowledge, etc.', concluding, 'such perhaps are indicated here under the name of Levites and priests, whose inheritance is the Lord himself, ...' 17:3 continues this interpretation, referring to the 'inheritance of the perfect and outstanding' as being the Lord and wisdom. Such live on earth to

---

[273] Heine, 364, Barkley, 98, and Jaubert, 208.

[274] Barkley, 64.

[275] Méhat, 207. Vogt, 46 and Schäfer, 52-3, find a reference to the presbyters and bishop as priests and the deacons as ministers here.

help others share in this inheritance: 'Therefore thus also now, the Levite and priest, who has no land, is commanded to live with the Israelite, who has land, in order that the priest and the Levite may receive from the Israelite earthly things, that he does not have, and, in return, the Israelite may receive from the priest and Levite heavenly and divine things that he does not have.' The passage continues with the fact that priests are to be dedicated to God's word, 'but again, so that they may have time for it, they must use the ministries of the lay people.'[276] The reference to the laity suggests that Origen now has the external hierarchy of the church in mind, although all that led up to it implies the hierarchy of perfection. Probably, he began with a reference solely to the perfect, but transferred his reference to the external hierarchy which ideally conformed with the internal.[277]

In these last two passages we have noted that Origen referred to priests as serving, and giving themselves to, the word of God so that they can explain it to others. Moreover, it is obvious that other connotations of priesthood at which we have looked make the priest pre-eminently suited to teach. However, it is precisely those qualities which characterize the perfect, so that the question arises whether Origen envisaged teachers who did not belong to the clergy. This will be examined further in section 6.6.3, where it will be shown that teaching was becoming increasingly the exclusive function of the clergy. Thus, allusions in Origen's writings to priests teaching mainly involve his urging of the ordained as priests to conform to that internal priestliness which most suited them to be teachers, although he probably wished that non-clergy who were so suited could teach publicly too.

In *Homilies on Leviticus* 6:6, Origen states, 'These are the two works of the high priest: that he either learn from God by reading the divine Scriptures and by meditating often on them, or teach the people'[278] at the end of a long section in which the link between teaching and priesthood is expounded. Again, in *Homilies on Leviticus* 5:8, he states, 'The flesh, which is allotted to the priests from the sacrifices, is 'the word of God' that they teach in the Church.'[279] He goes on to refer to them delivering a sermon to the people, confirming that he has a real church situation in mind.[280]

Further, in *Homilies on Numbers* 4:3, Origen begins by explaining

---

[276] Jaubert, 374ff.

[277] Vilela, 86; Vogt, 47, and Schäfer, 88-91, all see a reference to the external hierarchy here, only Schäfer seeing an initial reference to the perfect.

[278] Barkley, 128. Vilela, 85 and Vogt, 61 see the clergy as teachers meant here.

[279] Barkley, 105.

[280] Vilela, 84; Lies, 161 and Schäfer, 85, see this as a reference to the ordained.

that a true priest is one to whom the secrets of wisdom have been given. He warns his hearers that they should not reveal these secrets easily to the people, since 'they are mysteries hidden in secret and are open to priests alone ....' A little further on he adds, 'we must show ourselves such that we are proved worthy of the order of priesthood....'[281] Similarly, in *Homilies on Leviticus* 5:3 he writes, 'There also are other teachings of the Church to which the Levites can likewise attain, but they are lower than these which were granted to the priests to approach.'[282] However, he alludes to the teaching function of the priests again in *Homilies on Joshua* 4:2 where he explains that 'it is the priestly and Levitical order that stands by the ark of the covenant of the Lord in which the law of God is carried, doubtless so that they may enlighten the people concerning God's commandments.'[283]

The priestly link with understanding mysteries is apparent in *Homilies on Joshua* 4:1 where Origen likens Israel's journey from Egypt to the crossing of the Jordan to the progress from spiritual darkness to baptism, concluding, 'If, indeed, you reach the mystical spring of baptism, and, with the priestly and Levitical order standing by, you are initiated into those revered and wonderful mysteries that those know who have the right to know, then, having crossed the Jordan thanks to the ministries of the priests, you will enter the land of promise, ...'[284] The reference to an actual baptism makes an allusion to the ordained highly likely.[285]

There is another set of passages in which priestliness is closely connected with ability to deal with people's sins. These have given rise to the same question whether Origen envisaged non-clergy as able to perform this ministry as we noted regarding teaching. This also will be examined in section 6.6.3 with the same result. In these passages too, then, Origen probably has the ordained in mind in practice, whilst unwilling to rule out the possibility of the non-clerical perfect doing the same in theory. For example, in *Homilies on Leviticus* 5:3, Origen states that the 'ministers and priests of the Church receive "the sins of the people" according to the example of the one who gave the priesthood to the Church. Imitating their teacher, let them grant the people forgiveness of sins. Therefore, these priests of the Church ought to be ... perfected

---

[281] Doutreleau, 108-113. Cited in Vilela, 85 as a reference to the ordained. Schäfer, 56 agrees against Völker, *Vollkommenheitsideal*, 179 and Crouzel, *Origène et la 'connaissance mystique'*, 157, 409 and 492.

[282] Barkley, 96.

[283] Jaubert, 154-5. Vilela, 85 and Schäfer, 220 find references to the ordained here.

[284] Jaubert, 148-9.

[285] Vilela, 85 and Schäfer, 86 and 157, view this as a reference to church leaders.

and learned in the priestly duties ....' Thus far he clearly has the external church hierarchy in mind, summoning them to perfection. He goes on, however, to liken the holy place in which sin is consumed to 'a sound faith and holy conduct' and the consequent purificatory sacrifice to killing 'the sacrifice of God's word' and offering 'sacrifices of "holy doctrine."' Finally, he speaks of some doctrines which only the high priest has access to, some to which only priests have access, some only Levites and some the laity.[286] This suggests that Origen has 'almost without noticing changed from one meaning of the Levitical priesthood to another',[287] although a consistent reference to the external hierarchy is possible.

Homilies on Numbers 10:1 is similar. Origen begins this section with the words 'those who are better take upon themselves the faults and sins of those who are inferior.' He continues, 'If an Israelite, that is a layman, sins, he cannot efface his own sin himself, but looks for a Levite, he needs a priest, indeed, he seeks more and even higher than that: he needs the High Priest so that he may obtain the remission of his sins. But if a priest or the High Priest sins, he can purify himself of it, if, however, he does not sin against God.'[288] Vogt argues against a reference to the ordained here, but it is probably to be explained as we noted above.[289]

Finally, in *Homilies on Leviticus* 2:4 Origen mentions a 'remission of sins through penitence, ... when the sinner washes "his couch in tears" ..., when he is not ashamed to make known his sin to the priest of the Lord and to seek a cure ....'[290]

Vilela has made an inventory of twenty-six texts in Origen's works referring to the priesthood of presbyters. He has compiled this by perusal of Origen's works with the help of the index to the Berlin corpus.[291] All of these have been dealt with above, except for three whose reference to the priesthood of the ordained is very uncertain.[292] Five have been included which he does not mention in that list.[293]

---

[286] Barkley, 95-6.

[287] Vogt, 72. Völker, *Vollkommenheitsideal*, 143 and 188, sees a reference to the perfect here, while Rahner, 'La doctrine d'Origène', *Recher Sci Rel* 37 (1950), 275 and Vilela, 84 see the reference as to the ordained.

[288] Doutreleau, 270-271.

[289] Vogt, 74. Faivre, *Emergence*, 60, finds a reference to the ordained.

[290] Barkley, 47.

[291] Vilela, 84-6, see 86, n. 3.

[292] The passage quoted from *H. Josh.* 25:4 is referring to the resurrection; that from *H. Num.* 28:2 gives nothing in the context from which to judge who is being referred to; and that in *H. Gen.* 16:5 could as well refer to the general priesthood as to the ordained.

[293] They are from *C. Mt.* 16:25, *H. Num.* 11:1-2, *H. Lev.* 2:4, 6:3 and 7:1.

Although this is exhaustive, it does give sufficient data on which to base conclusions, including those noted earlier regarding the differentiations amongst the clergy and between the clergy and the people.

One conclusion is that Origen undoubtedly describes the ordained as priests at times. Although he repeatedly criticizes them for not living appropriately, he never attacks the practice of viewing them as priestly, nor does he seek to justify it, suggesting that it was an accepted part of his environment. It is not possible to assess whether there was any kind of evolution in Origen's thought on this subject as all the extant references come from fairly late in his life-time.

Further, it was vital for priests to be holy, which means detached from this world, its interests and desires, and devoted to God. The main priestly task, for Origen, was undoubtedly that of studying the word and teaching the people. Priests were also to be involved in church discipline and to rule the people. There remains the issue of Origen's view of sacrifice, especially concerning the eucharist, and its connection with priesthood.

4.6.4 The clergy, priesthood, sacrifice and the eucharist

Origen's emphasis regarding Christian sacrifice does not lie on the eucharist. Vogt can conclude 'that he never directly describes the eucharist as sacrifice'.[294] Whilst this may be going too far, there is uncertainty over his possible references to the eucharist as sacrifice, some of which have also been seen as showing that Origen mentions the presidency of the clergy at the eucharist.

For example, Lécuyer cites *Dialogus cum Heraclide* 4:22 and 5:7 as texts which specialists agree relate to the eucharistic gathering.[295] However, although it contains references to bishops, presbyters and the faithful as well as to an offering made to God through Christ in the context of a meeting, there is nothing to show that the offering is the eucharist rather than prayers and praise. In fact the need to be right in one's prayers is mentioned soon after the offering and could suggest that they are meant.

The same is true of a passage in *Homilies on Leviticus* 7:1 in which Origen links the need for the OT priests to be sober 'when they are present at the altar to pray to the Lord and to offer sacrifices in his presence' with Paul's instruction, originally concerning bishops but

---

[294] Vogt, 42.

[295] Lécuyer, 'Sacerdoce des fidèles', *Vetera Christianorum* 7 (1970), 260. For *DH* 4:22 and 5:7 see Scherer, (ed.), *Origène: Dialogue avec Héraclide* (Paris, 1960), 62-4.

interpreted by Origen as 'for the priests or the chief priests'.[296] Again, although the 'offer sacrifices' could refer to the eucharist, it could refer to prayer, as, a few lines earlier, Origen has quoted from Leviticus 9:7 regarding the priests 'who "approach the altar of God to pray for the people" [and] ought also to intervene for the transgressions of others'.

The likeliest reference to the practice of the offering of the eucharist as a sacrifice by priests is found in *Homilies on Leviticus* 1:3. Origen is explaining that Jesus offered himself as a victim for both those on earth and those in heaven where, 'if there are those who minister as priests there, he offered the vital strength of his body as some kind of spiritual sacrifice.'[297] He probably gained his idea of there being such from earth.

Indeed, Origen's favoured understanding of sacrifice is mainly in terms of holy living, self-denial and prayer. Daly notes that Christian sacrifice for him involves martyrdom, the whole of the Christian life, proper dispositions, ascetic and prayerful living. He concludes: 'foremost in [Origen's] consciousness was apparently not a liturgical rite of the Church, but rather that interior liturgy of the Christian heart and spirit by which a man offered himself and all his prayers, works and thoughts through Jesus Christ to God the Father.'[298]

To give just a few examples:[299] in *Contra Celsum* 8:17, he writes, 'our altars are the mind of each righteous man, from which true and intelligible incense with a sweet savour is sent up, prayers from a pure conscience'; in *Homilies on Leviticus* 9:9 he gives a list of sacrifices: renunciation of all possessions to follow Christ, martyrdom motivated by love for others, mortification of the body; in *Homilies on Exodus* 9:4, he describes vices as well as good deeds as sacrifices.[300]

Further, whilst at times Origen places the teaching of God's word on a par with the eucharist,[301] once he clearly depicts the former as the more important. This is in *Commentary on John* 32:310, where he writes, 'Let the simple understand the bread and the cup according to the more common interpretation concerning the Eucharist, but let those who have learned to hear in a deeper way understand them in accordance with the promise that is more excellent and concerns the

---

[296] Barkley, 130. Vilela, 139, views this as a reference to the eucharist.

[297] Barkley, 34. See on this Schäfer, 177.

[298] Daly, R.J., 'Sacrifice in Origen' in Cross, F.L. (ed.), *Studia Patristica*, vol. 11 (Berlin, 1972), 126-9.

[299] Ibid.,126: 'by rough count, Origen speaks of sacrifice or related subjects in about 550 different places ....'

[300] Chadwick, 464; Barkley, 196-7; Heine, *Origen: Homilies on Genesis and Exodus*, 341.

[301] *H. Num.* 16:9 and *H. Ex.* 13:3.

nourishing word of truth.'[302] Moreover, as Daniélou points out, Origen's preferred interpretation of Christ's words at the last supper is:

> This bread which God the Word declares is his body is the word that feeds men's souls, ... And this drink which God the Word declares to be his blood is the word which is pre-eminently the heart's drink, the word that more than any other makes the drinkers of it drunk in their hearts .... What God the Word called his body was not the visible bread he was holding in his hands but the word in sign or sacrament of which this bread was to be broken. ... Can the body and blood of God the Word be anything but the word that gives nourishment, the word that makes men exult?[303]

Finally, although there is evidence that Origen was aware of and accepted the real presence of Christ once the bread and wine had been consecrated,[304] he sometimes so emphasized the need for the right attitude of heart and mind that there was little room for an objective presence of Christ in the elements.[305]

Origen, then, was aware that the eucharist was thought of in sacrificial terms, and that priestly clergy presided at it, but these concepts receive so little attention in his writings that, for one thing, he did not derive his conception of priesthood from them, but accepted them as part of his environment, and, for another, the offering of the eucharistic sacrifice was not a major aspect of his understanding of priesthood.

4.6.5 Conclusion

In view of his lack of explicit justification for the use of *hiereus* for the bishop and presbyters, Origen probably found and accepted it as an established custom, which cautions us against viewing Clement's silence as indicating ignorance of this practice.

On the other hand, Origen's reasons for choosing the priest as his major OT model for the perfect may have had little to do with the reasons why the presbyters and bishops were being thought of in priestly terms by the church in general in his time. Certainly the major connotations of priesthood for him differ to a considerable extent from those of Tertullian and Hippolytus. While holiness was a general

---

[302] Heine, R.E. (ed.), *Origen: Commentary on the Gospel according to John Books 13-32* (Washington, 1993), 400.
[303] *Ser. C. Mt.* 85 as quoted in Daniélou, 67.
[304] In *H. Num.* 16:9 and *H. Ex.* 13:3, cf. *CC* 8:33 on the importance of the consecratory prayer.
[305] See especially *C. Mt.* 11:14 and note Daniélou, 63.

connotation of priesthood for them, Tertullian and Hippolytus do not link the latter so insistently and emphatically to dedication to understanding and teaching God's word and so to dealing with sin also as do Origen and Clement. There is little indication that the latter did this because of the teaching-role of the priest in either OT or NT times. One reason, as Trigg argues, was probably that, in the OT especially, 'priests were a tribe apart, entirely consecrated to God's service.' Another is that 'priests, and the high priest in particular, also have privileged access to God.'[306] Since Origen's conception of the truly spiritual man involved spiritual knowledge and holiness above all, these were two central connections which inclined him in favour of choosing the priest for his OT model of the truly spiritual man.

Trigg argues that a further 'more significant reason why Origen picked' the priest and the apostle as symbols of authority was that 'they gave him a way to oppose the pretensions of official authority, which was rapidly appropriating these very symbols to legitimate episcopal authority. "Priest," in Origen's time, was just beginning to become the customary term to describe presbyters and bishops, and bishops were increasingly depicting themselves as successors to the apostles.'[307] It is clear from the texts studied already in section 4.6.3 that Origen criticizes the lack of holiness and spiritual perception of many presbyters and bishops who were generally viewed as priests, but it is not clear that he was attacking these officials and their claims by using the priest and apostle as his biblical models. Rather, these officials did not conform to the ideal to which these models for him pointed, and that was the reason why he criticized them.

Teaching, then, was for Origen the most important priestly activity because it fitted his conception of the ideal Christian whom he viewed as priestly for the reasons outlined above. The fact that presbyters and bishops were generally viewed as priestly did not lead him to deny their priesthood but to criticize them for not living up to the true priesthood to which they, and all Christians, had been called.

As with other doctrines, Origen's theology of priesthood was so broad in including contradictory tendencies, that he could father opposing views. It is not difficult to see how his great emphasis on the priesthood of the truly spiritual, together with his general division of the Christian community into the simple and the perfect, tended to increase the sense of division of that community into the mediators of God's

---

[306] Trigg, 'The Charismatic Intellectual', *Ch H* 50 (1981), 9-10. He rightly points to *C. Jn.* 1:2 for evidence of the first.
[307] Ibid., 12.

grace and those to whom that grace was mediated. His acceptance of the 'status quo' with regard to the official hierarchy, together with his call for them to be perfect and so to exercise these mediatorial functions, formed part of the whole movement towards viewing that hierarchy as the dispensers of God's grace to the laity. On the other hand, the same emphasis led to his inspiration of that basically lay movement of spirituality and asceticism, often linked to mediation of grace, which resulted in monasticism.

4.7 Cyprian and the Western church in the mid-third century

There is little relevant evidence in the writings of the two other Western writers of this period of whose works some is extant. The only passage from Minucius Felix[308] is in his *Octavius* 9:4 in which an opponent of Christianity states that Christans 'worship the genitals of their pontiff and priest, adoring, it appears, the sex of their "father".'[309] Although this could reflect the Christian practice of calling the bishop 'priest', it could also be a general non-Christian reference to the Christian clergy in terms which non-Christians understood, implying nothing regarding this Christian practice.[310] Cyprian's contemporary in Rome, Novatian, has two references to Cyprian himself as priest.[311] In the first, Roman presbyters and confessors ask for Cyprian's prayers, the priestly allusion to Cyprian occasioned by the reference to themselves as 'destined to be sacrificial victims', but implying his prayers will be especially effective.[312] In the second, the lapsed are to show honour to God's priest 'to draw upon themselves the mercy of God', mediatorial connotations being apparent.

4.7.1 Cyprian's life and significance

Important for the present study is the fact that as the bishop of Carthage

---

[308] DeSimone, R.J. (ed.), *Novation: The Trinity, The Spectacles, Jewish Foods, In Praise of Purity, Letters* (Washington, 1973), 13, says he wrote in Rome. Clarke, G.W. (ed.), *The Octavius of Marcus Minucius Felix* (New York, 1974), 7-11, argues for his African background and dates him between Tertullan and Cyprian. Quispel, G., 'African Christianity before Minucius Felix and Tertullian' in den Boeff, J., and Kessels, A.H.M. (eds.), *Actus: Studies in Honour of H.L.W. Nelson* (Utrecht, 1982), 309-321, however, argues for Minucius' priority to Tertullian. McHugh in Ferguson (ed.), *Encyclopedia of Early Christianity*, 600, is uncertain.

[309] Clarke, *Octavius*, 64.

[310] See ibid., 218-9, n. 119 for an inconclusive discussion on this point.

[311] *Epp.* 31:5:2 and 36:3:3 of the Cyprianic corpus. For texts quoted below see Clarke, G.W. (ed.), *The Letters of St. Cyprian of Carthage* (New York, 1984-1989), vol. 2, 36 and 48.

[312] So Clarke, *Letters*, vol. 2, 137, n. 21.

Cyprian faced a number of important practical problems, including persecution and threats to his authority from within the church, for much of the time up to his martyrdom in 258.

Some have reproached Cyprian with being 'a practical man of the Church rather than a real theologian.'[313] However, as Wiles so rightly points out,

> a religious leader can no more help talking theology, whether consciously intending to do so or not, than Molière's M. Jourdain could help talking prose. An unconscious theology, indeed, can be every bit as important and as influential as a fully self-conscious one; in fact, its influence is very liable to be the greater, because succeeding generations are less likely to be aware of it and so less likely to submit it to critical scrutiny and review. In no case is this largely-unconscious influence more significant than in the case of Cyprian.

Wiles adds that the influence of Cyprian's teaching was enhanced for subsequent generations because 'not only does he stand out as the only substantial western writer of the third century to avoid the sin of schism, but his words had the added prestige of being the words of an outstanding bishop and, still more importantly, martyr.'[314] Indeed, Laurance argues that recently 'studies have been published that bring clarifications on Cyprian's originality in at least one theological area: ecclesiology.'[315] Wiles makes the same point and quotes Lightfoot approvingly to the effect that Cyprian has made the '"transition from the universal sacerdotalism of the New Testament to the particular sacerdotalism of a later age"' while '"Tertullian and Origen are still hovering on the border."' He judges this a 'comparatively small' development, but one which 'can be seen as a vital step over the threshold into a new domain.'[316]

4.7.2 The priesthood of bishops

There is no doubt that when Cyprian speaks or writes of *sacerdotes*, something he does very frequently indeed in his epistles in particular, he is referring to the bishops in the vast majority of cases, if not in every one. Often the context leaves no doubt that this is so. For example,

---

[313] Laurance, J.D., 'Le président de l'eucharistie selon Cyprien de Carthage: un nouvel examen', *La Maison-Dieu* 154 (1983), 151.

[314] Wiles, M.F., 'The Theological Legacy of St. Cyprian' in *Journal of Ecclesiastical History* 14 (1963), 139.

[315] Laurance, 'Le président', *La Maison-Dieu* 154 (1983), 151-2.

[316] Wiles, 'Theological Legacy', *J Eccle H* 14 (1963), 142 and 144.

when, in *Epistle* 3:3:2,[317] Cyprian writes, 'Therefore, it is proper that the deacon of whom you write should do penance for his outrageous conduct, thereby acknowledging the reverence due his priest and making amends with full humility to the bishop, his appointed leader',[318] it is clear that it is the bishop who is meant by 'priest' since the whole context is dealing with a deacon's rebellion against a bishop (cf. 3:3:1).

Many other instances can be given from both early and late works, suggesting that this was Cyprian's settled practice. One of his earliest treatises is *De habitu virginum*, usually dated to 249.[319] In chapter 1, he writes, 'Now if God chastises whom he loves, and chastises that he may correct, brethren also, and priests particularly, do not hate but love those whom they chastise that they may correct, ...'[320] The distinction implied between the brethren and the priests here means the general priesthood is not intended, and the role of the bishop in church discipline, to be examined later, makes it likely that the bishops are being referred to as priests. The same is true of a reference to the 'priest of the Lord' in *De lapsis* 14,[321] written in 251,[322] and in a very similar context of disciplining the wayward. Several other passages refer to the bishop as priest in *De lapsis* in the context of different aspects of church discipline.[323] Those in chapters 22, 25, and 26 also mention the bishop's part as 'priest' in the offering of the eucharist.

Although references to the bishop as 'priest' are not found in the last treatises, *De bono patientiae, De zelo et livore,* and *Ad Fortunatum,*[324] this is more likely because their content did not lend itself to such references than owing to any changes in Cyprian's practice. This is confirmed by such references in the epistles, both early and late.

According to Clarke's chronology of the earlier epistles, the earliest

---

[317] The abbreviations of Cyprian's works used below are *Dem: Ad Demetrianum; Dom.: De dominica oratione; Don: Ad Donatum; Ep.(p)*: Epistula(e); *Fort: Ad Fortunatum; Hab. Virg.: De habitu virginum; Lap.: De lapsis; Mort.: De mortalitate; Op.: De opere et eleemosynis; Pat: De bono patientiae; Test: Testimonia or Ad Quirinum; Un.: De ecclesiae unitate; Zel: De zelo et livore.* Also used are *Vita: Vita Caecilii Cypriani* and *Sent: Sententiae episcoporum de haereticis baptizandis.*

[318] Clarke, *Letters*, vol. 1, 56, with my translation of *sacerdos* as 'priest' where Clarke translates 'bishop'. I have followed the same practice in other quotations from Clarke below.

[319] So Sage, M., *Cyprian* (Philadelphia, 1975), 381.

[320] Keenan, A.E. in Deferrari, R.J. (ed.), *Saint Cyprian: Treatises* (Washington, 1958).

[321] Bévenot, M. (ed.), *Cyprian: De Lapsis and De Ecclesiae Catholicae Unitate* (Oxford, 1971), 20-22 translates 'bishop of the Lord' but *sacerdos* is used in the Latin.

[322] So Bévenot in Weber, R. et al. (eds.), *Sancti Cypriani Episcopi Opera* (Turnhout, 1972 and 1976), vol. 1, 218 and Sage, 380.

[323] *Lap.* 16, 18, 22, 25, 26, 28, 29 and 36.

[324] For these dates see Sage, 380-383; and Weber and Moreschini in Weber et al., vol. 1, LIII and vol. 2, 116.

in which the bishop is called 'priest' is *Epistle* 15, dated to May 250.[325] In *Epistle* 15:1:2, he is warning martyrs and confessors in Carthage that 'those actions which you are taking yourselves and which manifest both due circumspection towards God and respect towards the priest of God, those actions are being undermined by certain presbyters who believe without a thought for fear of God or respect for their bishop.'[326] The context and the parallel between 'respect towards the priest' and 'or respect for their bishop' both ensure that the bishop is meant by 'priest' here.

It may be significant that the reference to the bishop as priest here, and the next in *Epistle* 17:2:1,[327] both involve Cyprian defending the honour of the bishop as priest from threats within the church. Although his earliest reference to the bishop as priest, noted above as in *De habitu virginum* 1, deals with discipline, there are no others in the treatises before these in *Epistles* 15 and 17. Since the two other references to the bishop as priest in the earliest epistles are likewise found in the context of threats to Cyprian's authority,[328] the possibility arises that Cyprian relied the more heavily on this designation because of its connotations, for him and his flock, of divine choice backed up by divine authority. This possibility is enhanced by the way in which he uses biblical passages which explicitly or implicitly warn of dire consequences for those who disobey priests chosen by God. These do not occur until after the Decian persecution is over, if Clarke's dating of *Epistle* 3 is to be adopted,[329] but the fact that he also uses such biblical stories and texts in *Epistles* 59:4-5 and 66:3 shows that there was a close link in his mind between the bishop's priesthood and his sacred authority, which link probably increased his predilection for this designation in situations which threatened his authority.

Turning to Cyprian's later epistles, his last designation of the bishop in priestly language comes in *Epistle* 76, dated to several months after August 257, and so less than a year before his death.[330] In *Epistle* 76:3:1, addressing Christian confessors in the mines, he writes, 'Moreover, dearly beloved brethren, there is no reason why you should regard it as any loss to your faith or piety that in your present circumstances priests of God are allowed no opportunity for offering and celebrating the

---

[325] Clarke, *Letters*, vol. 1, 270. See also his list on 12.
[326] Ibid., 90.
[327] Ibid., 292, dates this also to May 250.
[328] *Epp.* 19:1 and 20:2:3, dated by Clarke, *Epistles*, vol. 1, 300 and 304-5, to June and July 250.
[329] Ibid., vol.1, 164.
[330] Ibid., vol.4, 277.

divine sacrifices.'[331] Whether Cyprian envisaged presbyters as 'offering and celebrating the divine sacrifices' will be discussed below. Suffice it to note here that the bishops, nine of whom are mentioned among the addressees at the head of the letter, would have been included. That this is not an isolated instance of Cyprian denominating the bishop as 'priest' in his later letters is shown by other examples in *Epistles* 74 and 73, both of which are dated to mid-256 by Clarke.[332]

This practice was general in North Africa at this time, as is confirmed by Pontius' usage in the *Vita Caecilii Cypriani*, and by four different bishops according to the *Sententiae episcoporum de haereticis baptizandis*. It is also followed by Firmilian of Caesarea on one occasion, and by Novatian twice, showing it was an even wider custom.[333]

4.7.3 The priesthood of presbyters?

There is disagreement amongst scholars over whether Cyprian ever explicitly refers to presbyters as priests. Benson, von Campenhausen and Bévenot hold that by 'priests' he always means bishops, never presbyters, whilst Goetz, Bardy and Vilela hold that, although normally using 'priests' to refer to bishops, he does on occasion use it of presbyters. D'Alès, Walker and Kilmartin take more of a mediating position, seeing priesthood as fully possessed only by the bishop, in Cyprian's view, although presbyters can be associated with the bishop in his priestly honour.[334]

The passage most frequently cited[335] to show that Cyprian occasionally called presbyters 'priests' is in *Epistle* 40:1:2. Writing concerning the enrolment of the presbyter Numidicus in the Carthaginian presbyterate, Cyprian says he has been spared martyrdom so that 'the Lord could thus join him to our clergy and bring lustre to

---

[331] Ibid., 97.

[332] Ibid., 234-5 and 219-220. See 74:8:1, 8:3 and 10:3, and 73:2:3, 8:1, 23:20 and 26:2.

[333] See *Vita* 5, 10, 11, 13, 15, 18 and 19, *Sent.* 8, 18, 26 and 52, *Epp.* 75:16:2, 31:5:2 and 36:3:3.

[334] Benson, E.W., *Cyprian, His Life, His Times, His Work* (London, 1897), 33, n. 3; von Campenhausen, *Ecclesiastical Authority*, 282, n. 70; Bévenot, M., '"Sacerdos" as understood by Cyprian', *Journal of Theological Studies* 30 (1979), 414 and 423; Goetz, K.G., *Das Christentum Cyprians: Eine historisch-kritische Untersuchung* (Giessen, 1896), 99; Bardy, 'Le sacerdoce', *La Vie spirituelle* 58 (1939), 117-8; Vilela, 273; d'Alès, A., *La Théologie de Saint Cyprien* (Paris, 1922), 138; Walker, G.S.M., *The Churchmanship of St. Cyprian* (London, 1968), 38; and Kilmartin in Ferguson, E., *Encyclopedia of Early Christianity*, 754.

[335] By Goetz, 100; d'Alès, 314; Bardy, 'Le sacerdoce', *La Vie spirituelle* 58 (1939), 117-8, n. 106; and Vilela, 282-3.

our ranks, which have been left forlorn by the lapse of some of our
presbyters, by means of priests who have been graced with glory.'[336]
Clarke argues that Cyprian is being honorific and proleptic, anticipating
that Numidicus will be promoted to bishop. Indeed, the passage
continues, 'For God permitting, he will undoubtedly be promoted to a
more exalted ecclesiastical station when we have returned to you
through the protection of the Lord.' However, as Clarke recognizes,
'Cyprian can hardly mean that Numidicus will be elected to the see of
Carthage (he has the general view of one occupant per see). Does he
rather assume that the clergy and plebs of Numidicus' home diocese ...
must choose so honoured a presbyter for their (vacant) cathedra when
peace is restored?'[337]

As well as this there is the fact that the most obvious reference of
'[priests] who have been graced with glory' is to Numidicus and others
like him who are worthy to be added to the presbyters. It is the
abundance of presbyters which has been depleted and is now being
adorned with these priests. This, then, is probably an occasion when
Cyprian refers to presbyters as 'priests'.

The other passage often cited[338] is in *Epistle* 61:3:1 where Cyprian
describes presbyters as 'united with that bishop in the dignity of the
priesthood'.[339] Bévenot argues that, 'this can be taken as meaning *either*
that they were sacerdotes just as much as their bishop, *or* that they were
honourably associated with their bishop in *his* sacerdotal functions. In
the latter case, Cyprian would not be calling them "sacerdotes".'[340]

Probably the choice is not as stark as this. Cyprian's overwhelming
emphasis on the bishop's priesthood and its significance makes it
unlikely that he viewed any presbyteral priesthood as exactly the same,
but his likely application of 'priests' to presbyters in *Epistle* 40 means
he could well be referring to them as such here too.

Vilela points to three other passages in which he feels that Cyprian
calls presbyters 'priests'.[341] Justifying the choosing of priest-bishops in
the presence of the people in *Epistle* 67:4:3, Cyprian and his fellow
bishops add, 'And we notice that the apostles observed this rule not in
the appointment of priests and bishops only, but even in the case of

---

[336] Here and below see Clarke, *Epistles*, vol. 2, 58.
[337] Ibid., 198-9. Vilela, 282-3, acknowledges the possibility of the last suggestion.
[338] Bardy, 'Le sacerdoce', *La Vie spirituelle* 58 (1939), 118, n. 106; d'Alès, 138-9; Vilela, 284.
[339] Clarke, *Epistles* vol. 3, 93.
[340] Bévenot, '"Sacerdos"' in *J Th St* 30 (1979), 414.
[341] Vilela, 283-5.

deacons as well ....'[342] The reason for seeing the 'priests' here as including presbyters is that the authors mention the ordination of bishops and deacons but not that of presbyters, while Cyprian's normal practice is to mention the presbyters and bishops (as in *Epistles* 1:1:1, 48:2) or the presbyters and deacons (as in the addresses to many of his letters, e.g., *Epistles* 1 and 5) or all three together (as in *Epistles* 32:1:2, 71:1:1 and 80:1:2). Clarke argues against this because there is no other example of Cyprian calling presbyters 'priests'. This argument would not hold if *Epistle* 40:1:2 were interpreted as above. Further, 'in what immediately follows only two classes of unworthy appointment are considered: those who illegitimately make the way *ad altaris ministerium* (= deacon?) *vel ad sacerdotalem locum* (= bishop?).'[343] This argument also would not hold if *sacerdotalis* could apply to both bishop and presbyter. On balance, then, it is likely that this passage too indicates that Cyprian thought of presbyters, but not deacons, as priests.

Vilela also cites *Epistle* 72:2:2 in which Cyprian states that 'it is essential that priests and ministers, waiting as they do upon the sacrifices of the altar, should be men who are sound and without blemish.'[344] Clarke translates 'priests and ministers' as 'bishops and clergy', but Cyprian may be identifying the bishops and the presbyters with the 'priests' and the deacons with the 'ministers'.

Vilela's third passage is in *Epistle* 1:1:1 in which Cyprian is dealing with the issue of a presbyter being nominated as a guardian in someone's will. This is wrong because 'everyone honoured with the sacred priesthood and appointed to clerical office ought to dedicate himself exclusively to altar and sacrifices ....'[345] Since the context concerns a presbyter, he is included, but is he included in both descriptions, like the bishop, or only the latter? The fact that the presbyter could offer the eucharistic sacrifice (see below) suggests that he is referred to in both.

Cyprian continues in *Epistle* 1:1:2 by pointing to the non-provision of land for the Levites to encourage their dedication to temple and altar, stating, 'This is the arrangement and rule which applies to our clergy even today: those who are advanced in the Church of God by clerical appointment are not to be distracted in any way from their sacred duties; ....' As Clarke writes, 'Cyprian's argument here requires that Levite apply to all ranks of the clergy.'[346] We shall examine the constituents of

---

[342] Clarke, *Epistles*, vol. 4, 23.
[343] Ibid., 148.
[344] Ibid., 53.
[345] Ibid., vol. 1, 51.
[346] Ibid., 156.

the clergy for Cyprian later, but it certainly included the deacon, possibly reflecting the priest-Levite distinction noted in Origen.

There is general agreement that Cyprian did envisage presbyters as offering the sacrifice of the eucharist. This is clear in *Epistle* 5:2:1, which implies that they did so 'as a matter of course and not as a special privilege ... under emergency conditions.'[347] A number of other references also make this certain.[348] It is also clear that, when necessary, presbyters, and even deacons, could readmit the lapsed to communion, a function which, as we shall see further below, Cyprian often ascribes to the 'priest'. This is apparent in *Epistle* 18:1:2, in which he states that any lapsed who have certificates from martyrs and are ill, 'need not wait for our presence, but they may make confession of their sin before any presbyter in person, or if a presbyter cannot be found and their end is coming fast, even before a deacon. In this way, after hands have been laid upon them in forgiveness, they may come to the Lord with ... peace ....'[349]

We can conclude, then, that Cyprian did at times call presbyters 'priests' and he did view them as involved in some, at least, of the bishop's priestly ministries. Bévenot's arguments to rule out the view that Cyprian referred to presbyters as 'priests'[350] at most show that, on one occasion, Cyprian did not include presbyters and deacons among one group of bishops which he called 'priests'. It thus confirms what we have already noted that he normally means bishops when he writes 'priests', but it does not show that he never used it of presbyters.

4.7.4 The connotations of bishops' priesthood: sacral authority

We have already noted that Cyprian designated the bishop as 'priest' throughout his literary career and that it was one of his favourite designations for the bishop. This suggests that it was not just a practice adopted from his ecclesiastical environment so that it meant little more than a synonym for 'bishop', but 'priest' had important connotations for him. These are indicated by the ways in which he used it.

We have already noted one of these: he uses it in passages highly significant for him relating to the honour to be given to the priest. He often supports this by using biblical passages which relate God's punishment of transgressors against priestly honour and Jesus giving

---

[347] Ibid., 187.
[348] E.g., *Epp.* 16:4:2 and 34:1.
[349] Clarke, *Epistles*, vol. 1, 524; note Clarke's comments on 298. This directive is repeated in *Ep.* 19:2:1.
[350] Bévenot, '"Sacerdos"' in *J Th St* 30 (1979), 421-3.

honour to the priest. These have been noted in *Epistles* 3, 59 and 66. They can also be found in *Epistle* 69 and in *De ecclesiae unitate* 18, whilst it is above all as priests that he refers to bishops in the context of opposition to their rule in *De ecclesiae unitate* 17. Even if Cyprian adopted the use of 'priest' for the bishop from traditional custom, as is likely in view of Tertullian's practice, his reflection on it in the light of the Scriptures and opposition to bishops, not least himself, resulted in a predilection for its connotations of appointment by God and sacral rule of God's people. This predilection is stronger than in any extant writings before him except the *Didascalia Apostolorum* which is unlikely to have influenced him.[351]

4.7.5 The connotations of bishops' priesthood: discipline

Another context, already noted above, in which Cyprian frequently uses 'priest' of the bishop is that of church discipline. Since it was in this area that his authority was threatened by the confessors' practice of issuing certificates of forgiveness to the lapsed during and after the Decian persecution, it is not surprising that the twin motifs of discipline and authority are at times found together.

Regarding the bishop's and clergy's connection with the penitential system, Capelle argues that, 'while in his early letters [Cyprian] speaks of intervention "by bishop and clergy", later there is mention only of "priests". Is this an indication of a simplified procedure? It also seems that the claim of priestly authority became progressively more pronounced: it had been put into check!'[352]

It is true that in *Epistles* 15:1:2, 16:1:3 and 17:2:1, mention is made of the imposition of hands 'by the bishop and clergy' and 'of the bishop and clergy',[353] but 'priest' is also used of the bishop in *Epistles* 15:1:2 and 17:2:1, as noted above, and that in contexts in which the challenging of the Cyprian's authority with regard to discipline is involved. Whilst Capelle may be right that Cyprian came to simplify the procedure, the accentuation of the bishop's priestly authority had already taken place in the earliest letters relating to it.

---

[351] This is not to deny the role which his experience of Roman authority in Africa Proconsularis may have played in his authoritarian emphasis, although Clarke, *Epistles*, vol. 1, 19 probably exaggerates this. We shall note in the next section that the author of the *Didascalia* may well have predated him in this emphasis.

[352] Capelle, B., 'L'absolution sacerdotale chez S. Cyprien', *Recherche de Théologie Ancienne et Médiévale* 7 (1935), 228, n. 9. Eastwood, 87 and Vilela, 302 agree that Cyprian changed his procedure.

[353] Clarke, *Epistles*, vol. 1, 90, 94 and 97.

Certainly, it is as 'priest' that the bishop is often described in the context of reconciliation of the penitent, suggesting it had such connotations for Cyprian, connotations also evident in Tertullian's *On Modesty* 21:17. So in *Epistle* 19:1, he writes, 'Now he does penance who being mindful of this precept of God is meek and patient and obedient to the priests of God and he thereby earns the Lord's favour by his acts of submission and his just works.'[354] 'Obedient' and 'acts of submission' probably refer to compliance with the penitential discipline which the priests have imposed. Although, as we have noted, presbyters and even deacons may administer discipline when necessary, the fact that the plural 'priests' is primarily to be understood of the bishops is supported by more explicit references to the bishops as priests in the context of discipline, e.g., in *Epistle* 43:3:2. Here Cyprian is pouring scorn on the policies of those who oppose him. He writes of the lapsed, 'he is to be deprived even of repentance, no satisfaction is to be rendered to God through the bishops and priests; ....'[355] It is probable that 'bishops and priests' refers only to the bishops, especially as both are in the plural.[356] It is also likely that the allusion to satisfaction involves the priestly bishop's assigning of penance, through the performing of which satisfaction can be made.[357] Significantly, this passage is followed by one in which the priest's authority is defended against these threats.

Similarly, in *De lapsis* 29, Cyprian exhorts the lapsed to confess his sins 'while his confession can still be heard, while satisfaction and forgiveness granted through the priests are pleasing to God.' He immediately continues, 'Let us turn back to the Lord with our whole heart and, expressing our repentance in deep sorrow, implore God for His mercy',[358] again suggesting that the 'satisfaction' is likely to involve the bishop's assigning of penance,[359] whilst the 'forgiveness' probably involves his declaration of this based on the evidence of penitence. Certainly, the granting of peace or reconciliation to the church is closely connected with the remission of sins in *Epistle* 27:3:3 ('peace is to be granted and sins remitted'[360]).

The references in *Epistles* 15, 16, and 17 to the laying-on of hands by the bishop and clergy have already been noted. They indicate that the

[354] Ibid., 99.
[355] Ibid., vol. 2, 63.
[356] Ibid., 218, n. 13 assumes this.
[357] So Bardy, 'Le sacerdoce', *La Vie spirituelle* 58 (1939), 99.
[358] Bévenot, *De Lapsis*, 45.
[359] So Bardy, 'Le sacerdoce', *La Vie spirituelle* 58 (1939), 99.
[360] Clarke, *Epistles*, vol. 1, 114.

order is the doing of penance, confession of sin, the imposition of hands, and the taking of the eucharist (so 15:1:2, 16:2:3, 17:2:1). We have noted that the priestly bishop is involved in all these stages. Other references to the bishop as 'priest' being involved in this process are found in *De lapsis* 16, 18 and 36, *Epistles* 55:29 and 59:5:1. The last is significant in two ways. One is that it is in the context of one of the catenas of biblical texts relating the bishop's priesthood to his choice by God and his consequent sacral authority (see 4:1-3). The other is that it is clearly the bishop who is called 'priest and judge who acts in Christ's stead', since, in 5:2, Cyprian goes on to write of the choice of the priest 'after ... fellow bishops have expressed their concurrence, ...'.[361]

4.7.6 Connotations of bishops' priesthood: eucharistic sacrifice.

The third context in which Cyprian often uses 'priest' for the bishop is that of offering the eucharist as a sacrifice. Before looking at pertinent passages, it is worth noting that he has many ideas of Christian sacrifice which are similar to earlier ones. In one of his earliest works, *Ad Quirinum*, or *Testimonia*, he cites OT prophetic criticism of the sacrificial cult and refers to sacrifices of praise and justice (1:16), and quotes, "'a sacrifice to God is a contrite spirit'" (3:6).[362] He quotes the last again in *De mortalitate* 11 and *Epistle* 6:2:1, and has several references to martyrdoms as sacrifice,[363] an idea which, as we have noted, goes back at least to Ignatius and Paul. He calls peace, concord and unity among Christians and giving to the poor sacrifices in *De dominica oratione* 23 and 33.

There is no doubt that Cyprian viewed the eucharist as a sacrifice. Although he could refer to priests' prayers as sacrifices, as in *Epistle* 66:9:1, where he writes that to the Lord and his Christ 'I never cease to offer up sacrifices with pure and unstained lips',[364] his frequent mentions of prayers and sacrifices together probably refer to the prayers at the eucharistic sacrifices.[365] Moreover, in *Epistle* 76:3:1-2, Cyprian contrasts the fact that, in the mines, 'priests of God are allowed no opportunity for offering and celebrating the divine sacrifices' with the fact that all the confessors celebrate and offer 'a truly precious and glorious sacrifice'. He goes on to pile up the sacrificial references,

---

[361] Ibid., vol. 3, 72-3.
[362] Weber in Weber et al., vol. 1, 16-7, 94 and 124.
[363] *Ep.* 6.2.1, *Fort.* 11, and *Dom.* 24.
[364] Ibid., 122.
[365] E.g., *Epp.* 65.2.1 and 4.1. Cf. Clarke, *Epistles*, vol. 3, 319, n. 8 and elsewhere.

ending by quoting Romans 12:1-2.[366] The 'divine sacrifices', then, are the eucharists which the imprisoned bishops are not able to offer, suggesting that they are needed for this kind of sacrifice, but not for those which all the confessors are offering in their suffering.

A related kind of sacrifice is 'the presentation of material gifts by the faithful for the matter of the Mass or for the maintenance of the clergy or poor as part of the liturgical action',[367] a practice already noted in Hippolytus' *Apostolic Tradition*. In *De opere et eleemosynis* 15, Cyprian rebukes the rich because 'you celebrate the Lord's Feast, who do not at all consider the offering, who come to the Lord's Feast without a sacrifice, who take a part of the sacrifice which the poor man offered.'[368] The context makes it certain that money or goods are involved. The same practice is probably reflected in *De dominica oratione* 23, where Cyprian warns that 'neither does God receive the sacrifice of the dissident, and He orders him to turn back from the altar and first be reconciled with his brother, ...'[369] Clarke suggests that a passage in *Epistle* 34:1 may also refer to it. Here, Cyprian is commending his presbyters and deacons for no longer being in communion with a presbyter and his deacon who 'have been admitting the lapsed into communion [and] ... have been offering their oblations.'[370]

These uses of 'sacrifice' without reference to the priestly offering of the sacrifice of the eucharist by the bishop show that the former are far from lacking and that Cyprian has links in this area with earlier Christian thought and practice. Most frequently, however, he means the eucharist when referring to sacrifice, and then the bishop or offerer is usually called 'priest'.

Some clear examples of these two points are found in *Epistle* 63, 'the place where Cyprian expounds his views about the eucharist most fully', and 'our first extant extended study on the nature of the Eucharist.'[371] In *Epistle* 63:1:1, Cyprian indicates that he is writing about some who, 'when they consecrate the Lord's cup and administer it to their people, do not follow the precepts and practices of Jesus Christ our Lord and God, the Author and Teacher of this sacrifice.'[372] 'Sacrifice' here must refer to the eucharist, since he is talking about the consecration of the

---

[366] Ibid., 97.

[367] Ryan, 'Patristic Teaching', *Irish Theological Quarterly* 29 (1962), 48; d'Alès, 261-2.

[368] Deferrari, 240-241.

[369] Ibid., 148.

[370] Clarke, *Epistles*, vol. 2, 42. See too 157.

[371] Hanson, R.P.C., *Christian Priesthood Examined*, 56; Clarke, *Epistles*, vol. 3, 288.

[372] For this and the following quotations from *Ep.* 63, see ibid., 98-107.

Lord's cup. In 4:1, he calls Jesus' and Melchizedek's sacrifice 'bread
and wine, that is to say His own body and blood.' And in 9:3, he
concludes that 'the Lord's sacrifice is not duly consecrated and
celebrated unless the offering and sacrifice we make corresponds with
his passion.' This correspondence relates to both the sacrifice and the
priest as he says in 14:4:

> For if Christ Jesus, our Lord and our God, is Himself the great High Priest of
> God the Father and if He offered Himself as a sacrifice to the Father and
> directed that this should be done in remembrance of Him, then without a
> doubt that priest truly serves in Christ's place who imitates what Christ did
> and he offers up a true and complete sacrifice to God the Father in the Church
> when he proceeds to offer it just as he sees Christ Himself to have offered
> it.[373]

For the first time in extant Christian literature the priest at the
eucharist is said to act 'in Christ's place' in offering the sacrifice, and
the sacrifice is called 'true and complete'. Finally, in 17:1 Cyprian states
that 'the passion of the Lord is the sacrifice we offer ....' He still never
speaks explicitly of offering Christ as a sacrifice in the eucharist, but
this last quotation and references in 2:1 to offering the cup and in 4:1 to
offering Christ's blood indicate that he is much closer to it than anyone
before him. Hanson is probably true to Cyprian's thought when he
writes,

> the offering hitherto had been the offering made by men, the offering of
> praise, or of themselves, or of the bread and wine for God to bless. Now a
> new step has been taken: the bishop as priest offers the consecrated elements
> which have become Christ's body and blood, ... Irenaeus' hesitation about
> the thought that man could offer anything to God in any circumstances has
> become a confident declaration that the priest offers Christ and Christ's
> sacrifice to God.[374]

Elsewhere Hanson notes as an example of Cyprian's influence here that
the 'pseudo-Cyprianic third-century ... tract *De Aleatoribus* three times
refers to the eucharist as *sacrificium Christi.*'[375]

Young too sees Cyprian as the first to explicitly make the change
from viewing the eucharist as portraying the drama of Christ's suffering

---

[373] Other references to bishops and/or presbyters as 'priests' offering the eucharist as a
'sacrifice', or 'offering' include: *Epp.* 37.1.2, 57.3.2, 61.4.2, 62.5, 65.2.1, 67.1.1-2, 68.2.1,
69.1.4, , 69.5.2, 69.8.3, 72.2.2, 73.2.3, 76.3.1, *Lap.* 26, *Un.* 13 17 and 18, *Dom.* 4.
[374] Hanson, R.P.C., *Christian Priesthood Examined*, 58. Note to similar effect Wiles,
'Theological Legacy', *J Eccl H* 14 (1963), 147-8 and Walker, G.S.M., 38-9.
[375] Hanson, R.P.C., *Studies*, 105-6.

to reenacting it, one of the consequences being that, just as Christ's death was seen as a sacrifice for sin, so the eucharist came to be viewed also.[376] As Laurance in particular argues, Cyprian views the priestly celebrant at the eucharist as a living 'type' of Christ. He points to the statement, 'being priests ... we imitate Christ's teaching and example' in *Epistle* 55:19:2 and to 'that priest truly serves in Christ's place who imitates what Christ did and he offers up a true and complete sacrifice to God the Father in the Church when he proceeds to offer it just as he sees Christ Himself to have offered it' in 63:14:4.[377]

The viewing of the eucharist as a sacrifice for sin may also be related to the Jewish influences on the church in Carthage[378] and to Cyprian's strong dependence on OT ideas.[379] Although Cyprian does not explicitly ascribe propitiatory value to the eucharist, he does seem 'to imply some objective efficacy for the *sacrificium* which is ... denied to the deceased'[380] in *Epistle* 1:2:1 ('nor should the sacrifice be celebrated for his repose'[381]). Further, in *De opere et eleemosynis* 18, Cyprian likens Job's sacrifices for his children's sins to 'righteous works', especially almsgiving, by which Christian parents can commend their children to God.[382] The normal eucharistic sacrifices on the dead's behalf may also have had propitiatory connotations, although not in those to be celebrated in commemoration of the martyrs.[383]

Finally, Cyprian, like Hippolytus, defines the ordained priesthood partly in terms of the sacrifice. This is clearly illustrated in *Epistle* 1:1:1, in which he states that 'everyone honoured with the sacred priesthood and appointed to clerical office ought to dedicate himself exclusively to

---

[376] Young, 279.

[377] Laurance, 'Le président', *La Maison-Dieu* 154 (1983), 155-7 and 163-5; see also Bévenot, '"Sacerdos"' in *J Th St* 30 (1979), 428-9. For the passages of Cyprian cited see Clark, *Epistles*, vol. 3, 45 and 106.

[378] On this generally see especially Quispel, 'African Christianity', in den Boeff and Kessels, *Actus*; also Wiles, 'Theological Legacy', *J Eccl H* 14 (1963), 144 and Frend, W.H.C., 'Jews and Christians in Third Century Carthage' in Neill, S.C. and Weber, H.-R. (eds.), *Paganisme, Judaisme, Christianisme* (Paris, 1978), 191-3.

[379] On this generally see Wiles, 'Theological Legacy', *J Eccl H* 14 (1963), 145 and 148; Walker, G.S.M., 37; Zell, R.L., 'The Priesthood of Christ in Tertullian and St Cyprian' in Cross, F.L. (ed.), *Studia Patristica* 11 (Berlin, 1972), 282-6; Hein, 436; Hinchliff, P., *Cyprian of Carthage and the Unity of the Christian Church* (London, 1974), 103; Frend, 'Jews and Christians' in Neill and Weber, *Paganisme, Judaisme, Christianisme*, 191; and Hanson, R.P.C., *Studies*, 129.

[380] Clarke, *Epistles*, vol. 1, 159-160, n. 25. Note also Evans, R.F., *One and Holy*, 40-41, on the way in which Cyprian developed the theory of satisfaction, including 'almsgiving [as] one of the "remedies for propitiating God".'

[381] Clarke, *Epistles*, vol. 1, 52.

[382] Deferrari, 244.

[383] So Clarke, *Epistles*, vol. 1, 252, n. 15.

altar and sacrifices and devote himself entirely to prayer and supplication.'[384] It is unlikely that the sacrifices and altar referred to here mean the prayers also mentioned in view of the frequency of Cyprian's uses of 'sacrifice' to mean the eucharist and the rarity of his uses of it to mean prayers.

4.7.7 Summary and conclusion

Although Cyprian did not invent the application of 'priest' to the bishop, nor did he invent its connotations of sacral authority, offering eucharistic sacrifice and dealing with sin, he has clearly emphasized that priesthood and these connotations, particularly the first and third, more than anyone before him in the West. Particularly important for the development of his stress on this priesthood were his meditation on the Scriptures relating to the divine choice and support of priests, the threats to his episcopal authority, not least in the area of church discipline, his application of OT priestly law directly to bishops and presbyters,[385] and his meditation on the link between Christ's priesthood and self-sacrifice and the priestly celebrant of the eucharistic sacrifice. Moreover, he thus had a great influence on later understanding of the ministry in the West. Ironically, in view of modern depreciation of his originality, he marks something of a watershed in the church's appreciation of priesthood.

4.8 The *Didascalia Apostolorum*[386]

This is the only third-century document not so far dealt with in which the priesthood of the ordained is clearly mentioned.

4.8.1 Significance

Its significance arises first from its date and provenance. There is general agreement that it was produced in Syria in the third century AD, but not over when in that century. However, although some used to view it as from the first, and some from the second half of the century,[387] more recently the consensus has tilted towards the earlier part of the

---

[384] Ibid., 51.

[385] Cf. ibid., 167, n. 15: 'Cyprian ... finds in the Jewish *sacerdotes* of the old dispensation types of the bishops of the Christian church, and is prepared to read off practical disciplinary rules accordingly.' See too Wiles, 'Theological Legacy', *J Eccl H* 14 (1963), 144-6.

[386] This will be abbreviated to *Didasc* in footnotes below.

[387] See Connolly, R.H. (ed.), *Didascalia Apostolorum: The Syriac Version translated and accompanied by the Verona Latin Fragments* (Oxford, 1929), lxxxix-xci.

century.[388]

Von Campenhausen, Vilela and Faivre hold that the author might well have been a bishop concerned to defend the rights of bishops against those of the rest of the Christian community.[389] Whilst there is no conclusive proof of this, the internal evidence certainly fits such a situation. We must bear in mind, then, that the author's claims for the bishop or clergy may go beyond the reality of his day, but will relate to it.[390]

4.8.2 The (high) priesthood of the bishop

The most cogent proof for the contention that the author is a bishop concerned to promote and defend the authority of bishops is his presentation of such an exalted view of the position, office and functions of a bishop that two scholars can say that he almost deifies him.[391] Some point to his likely knowledge of, and indebtedness to, Ignatius' writings in this regard.[392] The bishop is not only pastor of God's flock, 'he is minister of the word and mediator; but to you a teacher, and your father after God, who begot you through the water. This is your chief and your leader, and he is your mighty king. He rules in the place of the Almighty: but let him be honoured by you as God, for the bishop sits for you in the place of God Almighty.'[393] These words follow immediately after the identification of the bishops as 'your high priests; but the priests and Levites now are the presbyters and deacons, and the orphans and widows: but the Levite and high priest is the bishop.' This in turn follows a reference to the general priesthood as a result of which Christians are told to 'set by part-offerings and tithes and firstfruits to Christ, the true High Priest, and to his ministers, even tithes of salvation ....' Between this and the passages already quoted, we find the further exhortation to, 'instead of the sacrifices which then were, offer now prayers and petitions and thanksgivings. Then were firstfruits and tithes and part-offerings and gifts; but today the oblations which are offered

---

[388] Tidner, E. (ed.), *Didascaliae Apostolorum, Canonum Ecclesiasticorum, Traditionis Apostolicae, Versiones Latinae* (Berlin, 1963), IX; Vilela, 197; Faivre, *Naissance*, 119; Stevenson, 30.

[389] von Campenhausen, *Ecclesiastical Authority*, 240; Vilela, 197; Faivre, *Emergence*, 85.

[390] Cf. Stevenson, 30: '[it] shows us more of the internal life of the Christian Church than anything else of the time.'

[391] Vilela, 199 and Gryson, R., 'Les élections ecclésiastiques au IIIe siècle', *Revue d'histoire ecclésiastique* 68 (1973), 389.

[392] Bârlea, O., *Die Weihe der Bischöfe, Presbyter und Diakone in vornicänischer Zeit* (Munich, 1969), 121 and Vilela, 200.

[393] For this and the following quotations from chapter 9 of the Syriac, see Connolly, 86-9.

through the bishops to the Lord God.' That the bringing of these gifts to be distributed by the high priestly bishop is the main point being made is illustrated by the way in which this section continues. Echoing *Didache* 13:3, the author has connected these offerings with the OT legislation concerning firstfruits and tithes. This causes him to link these sacrifices and the priesthood of the whole Christian community with Christ's high priesthood, the high priesthood of the bishop and the priesthood and 'Levitehood' of the presbyters, deacons, widows and orphans.

The initial connection of the bishop's priestliness here was with his distribution of the people's gifts. It is made into a support for his leadership by the author, as can be seen by the words, 'And as it was not lawful ... for one who was not a Levite to draw near to the altar or to offer aught without the high priest, so you also shall do nothing without the bishop.'[394] This suggests, as with Cyprian, that the practice of denominating the bishop 'priest', probably already current in the Christian community, has been taken up by this author and developed in authoritarian directions out of a sense of being threatened. The parallel with Cyprian is even stronger in chapter 23 in which the author warns that 'if any of you covet the primacy and dare to make a schism, he shall inherit the place of Korah and Dathan and Abiram, ... For even the adherents of Korah were Levites, ...; but they coveted the primacy, and desired the high priesthood ....'[395] This is not to suggest that there was any dependence of Cyprian on the *Didascalia* but to point out how a similar emphasis on priestly sacral authority probably resulted from threats to episcopal authority in each case.

There is also the possible implication in the above that there were problems in the Christian community over the whole issue of giving and the use and distribution of those gifts. This is reinforced in chapter 8[396] in which bishops are warned against misuse of these gifts for themselves alone, but their right is defended to be nourished by them once they have provided for the needy. This right is likened to the way in which the Levites 'were nourished from those things which were given as offerings to God by all the people - gifts, and part-offerings, and firstfruits, and tithes, and sacrifices, and offerings, and holocausts .... You also then to-day, O bishops, are priests to your people, and the

---

[394] 9: ibid., 89.

[395] Ibid., 194.

[396] Ibid., 78-80 for this and the passage quoted below. See too 98-100: 'Sell all thou hast, and give to the poor. So do, therefore, and keep the command through (him who is) bishop and priest and thy mediator with the Lord God. ... The Lord God ... delivered this stewardship into his hands and held him worthy of the priesthood of so great an office.'

Levites who minister to the tabernacle of God, the holy Catholic Church, who stand continually before the Lord God.'

The first quotation above from chapter 9 included a reference to the bishop as priest being 'minister of the word and mediator'. This last quotation from chapter 8 is immediately followed by 'you then are to your people priests and prophets, and princes and leaders and kings, and mediators between God and His faithful, and receivers of the word, and preachers and proclaimers thereof, and knowers of the Scriptures and of the utterances of God, and witnesses of His will, who bear the sins of all, and are to give any answer for all.' Similarly to Origen and Clement, the priest is seen as the mediator of the knowledge of God in study, preaching and teaching.

One of the most important tasks of the priestly bishop is caring for the wayward. In this last quotation he is said to 'bear the sins of all'. In chapter 7 also he is told to 'have a care of all, that none may stumble and perish by reason of thee. ... As therefore thou carriest the burden of all, be watchful; for it is written: "The Lord said unto Moses: Thou and Aaron shall take upon you the sins of the priesthood."'[397] The author follows this with a list of duties the bishop should carry out in the discipline of the congregation.

He also links the bishop's priestliness and his holiness. In chapter 4, when dealing with the qualifications necessary to be a bishop, he writes, with an allusion to Leviticus 21:17, 'and let him be proved whether he be without blemish in the things of the world, and likewise in his body; for it is written: See that there be no blemish in him that standeth up to be priest.'[398] With another reference to OT priests, a similar point is made further on in the same section: 'for when the pastor shall be remote from all evil, he will be able to constrain his disciples also and encourage them by his good manners to be imitators of his good works; as the Lord has said in the Twelve Prophets: "The people shall be even as the priest."'[399]

Hanson notes that 'in this work we find, as we did in Hippolytus, a developed doctrine of Christian priesthood but little development in its thought about eucharistic offering.'[400] Distinguishing between the indissoluble Law and the temporary and dissoluble 'Second Legislation', the author states that in the former there is 'no burden, nor distinction of meats, nor incensings, nor offerings of sacrifices and burnt

---

[397] Ibid., 56.
[398] Ibid., 32.
[399] Ibid., 36.
[400] Hanson, R.P.C., *Studies*, 97-8.

offerings.' Further on, he states, 'for God had no need of sacrifices'.[401] Elsewhere he tells his hearers that God has freed them from 'sacrifices and oblations, and ... sin offerings ..., and holocausts, and burnt offerings ...; tithes and firstfruits, and part-offerings, and gifts and oblations'.[402] Noted earlier was the passage in which he says, 'instead of the sacrifices which then were, offer now prayers and petitions and thanksgivings, etc.' In this passage, ideas of thank-offerings and gift-offerings have been joined with sin-offerings, as happened in Cyprian also, but the eucharist is not one of these. Even so, they are offered through the bishop as high priest. In line with this is the way in which a needy man and widows and orphans are called 'the altar of God' and 'the altar of Christ' as the recipients of people's gifts in chapter 18.[403]

In chapter 9 'the Eucharist of the oblation' is referred to in the context of the bishop's priestly stewardship of the people's gifts. The context indicates that this refers to the people's gifts: 'when thou hast received the Eucharist of the oblation, that which comes into thy hands cast (in), that thou mayest share it with strangers: for this is collected (and brought) to the bishop for the entertainment of all strangers.'[404] The likeliest explanation is that 'eucharist' refers to the thanksgiving represented in the gifts, which may include the bread and wine for the eucharist in a practice like that noted in the *Apostolic Tradition*.[405]

'Thanksgiving' could be all that is meant by 'eucharist' in a passage in chapter 11 translated, 'now the gift of God is our prayer and our Eucharist.' It is in the context of a warning that, 'If then thou keep any malice against thy brother, or he against thee, thy prayer is not heard and thy Eucharist is not accepted; and thou shalt be found void (both) of prayer and Eucharist by reason of the anger which thou keepest.'[406] The ensuing context deals only with prayer, ending 'and forgive thy neighbour, that thou mayest be heard when thou prayest, and mayest offer an acceptable oblation to the Lord.' However, if Hanson is right to see a reminiscence of *Didache* 14:1-2 here,[407] in which the eucharist as bread and cup clearly is in mind, then it probably means the same in the passage quoted above.

This likelihood is increased by the unambiguous reference to the

---

[401] 26: Connolly, 218-220.

[402] 9: ibid., 98.

[403] Ibid., 154-6. Hanson, R.P.C., *Studies*, 98, sees the former as 'a poor man praying for his benefactor' being 'esteemed as the altar of God', but there is no reason to suppose this.

[404] Connolly, 100.

[405] Note also the reference given below to 'the oblations of the Eucharist' in chapter 12.

[406] Connolly, 115-7, for the passage quoted and the context.

[407] Hanson, R.P.C., *Studies*, 98-9.

eucharist as 'the likeness of the royal body of Christ' in chapter 26 which says that Christians can 'come together even in the cemeteries, and read the holy Scriptures, and without demur perform your ministry and your supplication to God; and offer an acceptable Eucharist, the likeness of the royal body of Christ, ... pure bread that is made with fire and sanctified with invocations ....'[408] As Hanson points out, 'this is not a doctrine of the offering of the body of Christ, but the text does speak of the offering of the antitype of the body of Christ.'[409]

Other illustrations of the fact that the author thought of the eucharist as a sacrifice are found in chapter 12. In one passage he writes, 'but of the deacons let one stand always by the oblations of the Eucharist; ... and afterwards, when you [the bishop] offer, let them minister together in the Church', and in another, 'when you offer the oblation, let him [a visiting bishop] speak. But if he is wise and gives the honour to thee, and is unwilling to offer, at least let him speak over the cup.'[410] Although there is no doubt, then, that the author of *Didascalia* viewed the bishop as the one who normally presided at the eucharist, or that he used sacrificial language concerning it, he nowhere relates the bishop's priesthood specifically to this function.

Whenever the priestliness of the bishop is mentioned, the author draws something out of that priestliness, illustrating that, whether or not it has become a commonplace synonym for 'bishop' in his environment, it has not for him. His normal word for the bishop is *episkopos*. The main connotations of the bishop's priesthood are holiness, sacral authority and centrality to the church's life, reception, distribution and partaking of the people's offerings, mediation of God's word, and bearing and dealing with the people's sins. The frequent quotations from the OT when the bishop's priesthood is mentioned show that the OT priesthood is seen as the priestly pattern for bishops to follow, though with the modifications noted.

4.8.3 The priesthood of presbyters and deacons?

We have already noted the one passage in which the presbyters and deacons are likened to the priests and Levites of the OT. It came in chapter 9 after the bishops had been called 'your high priests.' It

[408] Connolly, 252.
[409] Hanson, R.P.C., *Studies*, 99. He has just noted that 'we may here accept the *Apostolic Constitutions* as a reliable guide when it gives us [antitypos] as the original Greek of this word.' Connolly, liii, notes that 'the application to the Eucharist of [antitypos], or [antitypon] as a substantive, is first met with ... in the *Apostolic Tradition* of Hippolytus'.
[410] Ibid., 120 and 122.

continues, 'the priests and Levites now are the presbyters and deacons, and the orphans and widows.'[411] Clearly, the priesthood of the rest is overshadowed by that of the bishop, called as he is 'high priest' and 'Levite' and the passage going on to focus as it does on his mediatorial rule and offering of the people's gifts. The only place left for others is as his helpers and delegates.[412] Moreover, the 'priesthood' of the presbyters and deacons consists only in the fact that they benefit from the people's offerings as do the widows and orphans.

Further, the information in the *Didascalia* concerning the functions of presbyters and deacons does not indicate that they were viewed as priestly. It is possible that they were so regarded because they shared in judging disputes with the bishop,[413] or that the presbyters were because they were the bishop's 'counsellors and assessors', the 'moderators and councillors of the Church', to be honoured as the Apostles, being seated in a place of honour in the meetings,[414] or the deacons were because they helped the bishop in the reception and distribution of the people's gifts, could be likened to Aaron as Moses', i.e., the bishop's, mouthpiece, shepherd the people with the bishop, and visit the sick on his behalf,[415] but this is never stated either implicitly or explicitly by the author himself.[416] It is likely, then, that he was unaware of it, although he could have been uninterested in it or setting the bishop's priesthood in the highest relief.

4.8.4 Conclusion

The *Didascalia* is, then, an important witness to the development in Syria of the priestly understanding of the bishop at a time probably between the *Apostolic Tradition* and Cyprian and contemporary with Origen. It also provides ample further evidence of the influence of OT priestly categories on this development.

It further bears witness to the variety of major connotations which priestliness could have in the third century AD As with Origen, the need for the community to support the bishop and the need for holiness are important points of contact with the priesthood of the OT. Unlike Cyprian, and more like Origen and others, it is the people's gifts and praises which are the offerings to be made through the bishop, the

---

[411] Ibid., 86 and 87.
[412] So Faivre, *Naissance*, 119.
[413] See 11: Connolly, 111.
[414] See 9 and 12: ibid., 96-7, 90-91, and 119, cf. 120-121.
[415] See 9, 11, 15 and 16: ibid., 88-92, 109, 140, 148 and 150.
[416] Faivre, *Naissance*, 119: 'the presbyters ... do not appear to fulfil any "priestly" function'.

sacrifice of the eucharist receiving nothing like the prominence which it does in Cyprian. Another similarity to Origen and difference from Cyprian is in the emphasis on the priestly bishop as mediating God's word. Where it is like Cyprian, however, is in its emphasis on the sacral authority of priesthood, probably because of similar circumstances of threat to the bishop's authority.

4.9 Summary and conclusion

4.9.1 Summary of origins, connotations and factors

We have noted that the use of priestly terminology and ideas for the ordained in distinction from the rest of the church first appears in the writings of Tertullian soon after AD 200. Before this, Christian writers had used a number of cultic and priestly ideas, drawn mostly if not solely from the OT, to illustrate particular points about the contemporary church. These included the need for order, as illustrated in the OT hierarchy (*1 Clement* 40-41), the presbyter-bishop's presidency of the church's worship, called his offering of its gifts (*1 Clement* 44:4), and the need to provide for its prophets and teachers, and possibly its bishops and deacons, as illustrated by the Israelites' provision for their high priests (*Didache* 13:3, cf. 15:1). They also included the use of sacrificial language to describe the church's prayers and praise, gifts for the upkeep of its dependents, penitent self-offering, martyrdom and worship, and probably the eucharist as an occasion of the church's offering of praise and prayer.

The eucharist is itself first clearly called a sacrifice by Justin, though solely in contexts suggesting offerings of praise and thanksgiving for blessings received. Irenaeus adds to this the idea of the bread and wine being like the OT offering of the firstfruits, also likened to the provisions for the prophets and teachers in the *Didache*, probably with connotations of thanksgiving and the sanctifying of creation. In just one passage Irenaeus also views sacrifice, though not specifically that of the eucharist, as propitiatory (*AH* 4:17:2).

Up to this point, then, Christian authors were not frightened to use cultic, sacrificial, and, as we shall note in the next chapter, priestly imagery, but never of a church leader in a way different from other Christians. The example of Justin is particularly significant, in that he could well have used *hiereus* of church leaders in his *Apology*, since this would have been readily understood by his non-Christian readers. His not doing so suggests that it was not general practice then. It seems very likely that the lack of tradition of doing so going back to NT times was the major reason. Several of these authors are aware of Christ's priesthood and it may be that the definitive nature of this contributed to their inhibitions against using priestly language in ways not sanctioned by the NT.

Tertullian unambiguously refers to the bishop both as 'priest' and as 'high priest'. He also clearly refers to the clergy, which probably included bishops, presbyters and deacons, in priestly terms without ever calling them 'priests'. The fact that he does not feel the need to offer any kind of justification of doing this suggests that this was by then an established practice in North Africa. His virtual definition of this priesthood in terms of baptizing and offering sacrifice, but also in connection with the forgiving of sin, provides fuel for the argument that these were the main connotations of church leaders' priestliness in North Africa when the practice arose. The sacrifice for which the church leaders were responsible in a special way at least included, and possibly consisted mainly in, the eucharist. Tertullian viewed this as one Christian sacrifice among many and probably saw its sacrificial aspects as involving thanksgiving and, less clearly, the gifts the faithful offer when the eucharist is celebrated.

Most of these developments are also found in the slightly later writings of Hippolytus, especially in the *Apostolic Tradition* which probably reflects the usage of the Roman church in the late second and early third centuries. He refers to the bishop in high priestly terms three times and clearly implies that the presbyter, though not the deacon, in contrast to Tertullian, was ordained to the priesthood. Whilst there are suggestions that priestliness was connected with authority to rule, it is especially with the authority to forgive sins that the bishop's priesthood was linked on one occasion, although it is also linked with serving, propitiating God and offering the church's gifts. The bishop and clergy are clearly linked with offering sacrifice, as the language of propitiation also indicates.

Apart from one reference to living in gentleness and with a pure heart as offering a sweet-smelling savour, sacrifice means material gifts in the *Apostolic Tradition*. These gifts are brought by the congregation and taken to the bishop by the deacons. They include oil, cheese, olives, honey, milk and water, as well as bread and wine. The bishop was to give thanks over all of them, he and the presbyters laying hands on the bread and wine while he did so and thus changing their significance. Likened once to the OT offering of firstfruits, the sacrificial aspects of the eucharist seem to have consisted of grateful offering of the church's gifts and thanksgiving. As with Irenaeus, however, there is the one reference to propitiation.

For Clement, writing near the end of the second century in Alexandria, the priest is above all the gnostic Christian, whose priestly characteristics include pure living, access to divine truth, knowledge, devotion and ascent to God and assimilation to the Logos. The degree of equivalence involved in his comparisons of the gnostic Christian and the church hierarchy, together with the fact that Origen clearly accepted the practice, suggest that he was aware that priestly ideas were being used of the clergy. His priestly emphasis clearly lay strongly elsewhere, however, and it is likely that he was living in Alexandria when use of priestly ideas for the clergy was only just beginning. Like others of the Apologists, he saw the eucharist as one Christian sacrifice among many. It is impossible to know in what its sacrificial aspect consisted for him.

With most of his relevant comments deriving from c.230-250, Origen continues Clement's strong emphasis on the priestliness of the Christian who is completely dedicated to God and his word. Unlike Clement, he shows explicit awareness of the application of priestly categories to the ordained. Proof is lacking that he disapproved of this practice, although he was very critical of the ordained. He likens the bishop to the high priest and the priest, identifies the OT priests and Levites with the presbyters and deacons respectively, and fairly often refers to church leaders as priests in such a way that it is difficult to know whether he has bishops alone, presbyters alone, or both, in mind.

His choice of the priest as his main OT paradigm of the godly man, like Clement's, related above all to the OT picture of the priest and the high priest as completely dedicated to God and his service and having access to God and so to the highest knowledge of God. This fitted the Christian 'priest' for teaching, the priestly task *par excellence* for Origen, but not a task which he related to the picture of the priest in Scripture except through his allegorical exegesis. It probably owed more to his picture of the ideal Christian, therefore, which itself derived from a mixture of biblical and neo-Platonist emphases, and to his allegorical hermeneutics, than to biblical priesthood. The qualities of the ideal Christian also fitted him for the exercise of church discipline and this and allegorical exegesis were probably the main reasons why Origen emphasized this as a 'priestly' task. Although he calls the eucharist a sacrifice on occasion, his understanding of sacrifice focused very much on other matters, especially holy living, self-denial and prayer. It is therefore unlikely that he connected his idea of priestliness specifically to the offering of the eucharist. He sometimes links it with leadership, however.

It is, in fact, impossible to know how far his and Clement's peculiar emphases were shared by other Christians in Alexandria and Caesarea, although those who regarded themselves as belonging to the priestly élite and those who honoured them as such clearly shared it. There are such significant overlaps between his conception of priesthood and those of Tertullian, Hippolytus and Cyprian, however, that he was not far from mainstream thinking on this subject.

Returning to North Africa, the fullest development of the special priesthood up to AD 300 is that of Cyprian. Writing in the years 248-258, he uses 'priest' of the bishop especially far more often than any Christian writer before him. His corpus provides wider evidence of this practice also, in letters from Novatian in Rome and Firmilian of Caesarea, and in the *Sententiae* of North African bishops, four of whose statements witness to it.

Although Cyprian uses 'priest' of the bishop in the vast majority of cases, there are a few passages in which it is likely that he uses it of the presbyter as well. Whilst Cyprian must have found this custom in his ecclesiastical environment, he developed it to connote sacral, God-given and God-protected authority in a far greater way than anyone before in the West, doubtless because of the threats to his own episcopal authority. He also uses it often concerning the bishop's role in church discipline and the offering of the eucharist. Retaining some earlier non-eucharistic understandings, but adding propitiatory overtones, he most frequently refers to the eucharist as the Christian sacrifice. Moreover, he links the eucharist to the priestliness of the bishop in a new way in that he regards him as acting in Christ's place and offering Christ's passion in it. Further, somewhat like Tertullian, he defines the priesthood of bishops and presbyters in terms of dedication to offering sacrifices and prayer. Cyprian has thus moved far towards the view of the ordained Christian priest as the mediator of God's grace in ruling, judging, forgiving sin and offering sacrifice for sin.

Finally, the *Didascalia* is a witness to the fact that the priestly understanding of the bishop was present in Syria also in the early to mid-third century, although the priesthood of presbyters is not made clear. It further witnesses to the strong influence of OT categories of thought on this development in ways at times similar to Origen and at times to Cyprian. All three share the idea that the bishop as priest should be holy, supported by the faithful and care for and discipline the wayward. It shares with Cyprian the view that the bishop as priest has sacral authority, while it shares with Origen the view that he mediates the knowledge of God in study and teaching. It departs widely from Origen in seeing him as doing this as bishop and not as a 'perfect' Christian, thus coming closer to Cyprian again. Its view of sacrifice centres on prayer and praise. It does see the eucharist as a sacrifice but does not relate the bishop's priestliness to this. It explicitly teaches the priestly bishop's mediatorial role.

From this overview of the development of the priesthood of the ordained in Christian writings up to 300, we can conclude that the practice of thinking of the ordained as priests grew up in the late second century, becoming widespread at its end. Clearly it was the bishop who was the main church leader designated as 'priest' in a special way, almost certainly because of his leading role in the activities we have already noted as closely linked to priesthood. Whether or not presbyters and deacons were initially known individually as priests remains somewhat uncertain, although the evidence suggests that the presbyters were in North Africa as early as Tertullian, in Rome with Hippolytus and in Alexandria by the time of Origen. The lack of evidence of this for Syria in the *Didascalia* may demonstrate that this was not a uniform apprehension or it may be the result of the author's attempts to throw the bishop's priesthood into the highest relief or another reason for not mentioning it. The presbyters certainly formed a priestly group around the bishop from close to, if not at, the inception of the practice, no doubt for basically the same main reasons as the bishop. There was some uncertainty and, probably, some dispute over who should be included in what was meant by the clergy and the priesthood, the deacons apparently being included in both by Tertullian, included in the clergy and excluded from the priesthood in the *Apostolic Tradition*, and viewed as the Levites by Origen. Cyprian seems to have included only the presbyters in the priesthood, whilst it is unclear what the situation reflected in the *Didascalia* was.

4.9.2 Reasons for this development; theological reflection

The influence of the OT is apparent throughout and was one of the most important factors. Although it is never used explicitly to justify the bishops' and presbyters' special priesthood, an aspect of OT Law concerning priests is used by Tertullian, and his references to priestly order, discipline, office and tasks reflect OT patterns of thought. The prayer for the bishop in Hippolytus' *Apostolic Tradition* 3 is redolent with OT priestly and sacrificial allusions, while Clement's and Origen's explanations of priesthood derive most often from their interpretation of OT laws and stories concerning priests and especially the high priest.

Cyprian transfers some OT priestly laws directly to the priestly bishop and presbyters as well as supporting the bishop's sacral authority partly by OT stories, and the *Didascalia* links the bishop's priesthood to OT laws concerning the people's offerings, and backs his sacral authority with OT stories. In many ways, then, the development of the special priesthood was a reversion to OT categories of thought.

Second, the leading of worship, and the offering of the eucharist in particular, both conceived of in sacrificial terms, were also of primary importance. Worship and the eucharist were understood partially in sacrificial terms from NT times, and we have traced this, and the offering of the people's gifts having sacrifial overtones, through the second century, though without any connection with the president's priesthood. Tertullian almost defines priesthood in terms of baptizing and offering, probably referring to offering the eucharistic sacrifice above all. Hippolytus refers to the bishop serving night and day, propitiating God and offering the church's gifts, to ordination being for offering an oblation and having an apparently cultic ministry, and to the high priestly bishop offering in the holy of holies. The eucharist is certainly included among the sacrifices alluded to, but was probably not the only one in view of all the other gifts mentioned as offered by him. This emphasis is missing in Clement owing to his general lack of interest in the church's public worship. It is also toned well down in Origen because of his other interests regarding priesthood. It is probably present in his references to the priestly clergy presiding over the church, baptizing, and serving in the sanctuary. These relate more to knowing and teaching God and his word than to leading in worship, but teaching God's word was the most important part of leading worship to Origen. Offering the eucharistic sacrifice was a vital part of being a priest for Cyprian, and offering the people's gifts, including the eucharist, was so for the author of the *Didascalia*. It was probably this aspect of the bishops' and, to a lesser extent, presbyters' functions which first led to people making a connection between them and priesthood.

Cyprian links priestly presidency at the eucharistic sacrifice with Christ's high priesthood. This is in *Epistle* 63, where he views the priestly president as imitating Christ's priestly self-offering to the Father, acting in his place, and offering a true and full sacrifice. This emphasis is not found elsewhere, except in Origen's and Clement's interpretations of the OT high priesthood in terms of Christ's and that of the perfect. It may also lie behind the references to the bishop as high priest in Tertullian and Hippolytus, but this cannot be certain. It does not, then, appear to be a strong general factor in the early development of the special priesthood, perhaps because of the emphasis on the finality of Christ's priesthood and self-sacrifice in Hebrews. It may be that the practice of calling bishops priests in a special way had to be established on other bases before this could be overlooked.

Another significant factor was the exercise of church discipline. This is a minor emphasis in Tertullian but comes to the fore in the ordination-prayer in the *Apostolic Tradition* 3 where the bishop's authority to forgive sin is in virtue of his high priestly spirit. Origen's view of the truly spiritual and priestly man makes that man most apt to deal with people's sins, while the author of the *Didascalia* presents this as the bishop, and Cyprian depicts the priestly bishop as in charge of all aspects of church discipline. This connection is most likely to be explained by the intimate link between the OT priest and dealing with sin, although this is clearly apparent only in Origen and the *Didascalia*.

Threats to the bishop's authority in the third century led to the development of a strong emphasis on the priest's sacral authority. An emphasis on the priest as leader is not clear in Tertullian, but may be present in Hippolytus' references to priesthood relating to the 'counsel of the clergy' (*Apostolic Tradition* 8). Again, Clement's and Origen's views of the spiritual, priestly man suit him best to be leader of God's people, although he may not be so in practice. It is, however, in Cyprian and the *Didascalia* that this connotation is most stressed. Cyprian and Origen relate this priestly leadership both to the OT and to the respect shown to priests in the NT. This was probably the main reason for this emphasis. Contemporary respect for priestly leaders may also have been a factor,[417] but it is impossible to discern if this was so. The way in which this is not an important factor for Tertullian or Hippolytus suggests that it was less part of the original impetus for the special priesthood than presidency in worship and in discipline.

Underlying all these factors was the perception, again explicitly based on the OT, that the priest was especially holy, being completely dedicated to God and his service and so needing to be supported by God's people. On the other hand, this is not such a dominant, early motif as to suggest that it was a major reason for priestly ideas being attached to the bishops and presbyters in a special way.

It was very important in Alexandria, however, where priestliness was understood in a way which only partially overlapped with that of the ordained but, in so far as it started out from the OT, related to complete dedication and access to God. The emphasis there on priesthood relating

---

[417] So Hanson, R.P.C., *Christian Priesthood Examined*, 43-4, regarding the general development of the special priesthood.

above all to purity, self-denial, and study and teaching of God's word is also found in the *Didascalia*, where the only priest is the bishop. It is, however, unlikely that this was an important general factor in the rise of the special priesthood, since teaching and special knowledge of God and his word are not mentioned in connection with that priesthood in Tertullian, although teaching is once in Hippolytus.

Most important, then, were a great interest in the OT and its categories of thought, probably stimulated in reaction to Marcion and Gnosticism in general; and the presidency of the bishop and, to some extent, presbyters in public worship generally and at the eucharist in particular, for both of which sacrificial ideas were of some importance. Attaching also to the bishops especially were priestly ideas linked to their administration of the church's discipline. As time went on, ideas of sacral authority were added, the need to support them financially was justified, and links with Christ's high priesthood were developed, on the basis of the clergy's priestliness. In the background throughout were ideas of priestly holiness viewed as particularly appropriate to church leaders.

The idea of sacrifice was thus vital in this development. Beginning and continuing throughout the second century with a strong rejection of literal sacrifice, both Jewish and pagan, it was understood and applied to Christian sacrifice, again largely in terms of the OT and of the early Christians' reinterpretation of it, in the areas of worship (including the eucharist), self-denial and martyrdom, and returning gifts to God. Thanksgiving thus predominated and the idea of sacrifice for sin was seen as pertaining to Christ's sacrifice alone. Even these ideas of sacrifice were adequate for the bishop's presidency in worship to contribute to him being viewed as priestly, however. Vague and isolated references to propitiation attaching to other than Christ's self-sacrifice in the second century become more frequent in some, but not all, writers in the third, resulting in Cyprian's view of the bishop as priest offering the sacrifice of the eucharist in the place of Christ and identifying that sacrifice with Christ's passion and so almost with Christ himself.

Considerable changes have taken place with regard to priesthood and sacrifice between the situation reflected in the NT and that portrayed in Cyprian, in particular. From a time when the only sacrifices, apart from the one offered once and for all by Christ, were ones which could be offered by all Christians and when, apart from Christ, the only priests were Christians in general, we have arrived at a time when the main, though not the only, Christian sacrifice is the eucharist which is well on its way to being identified with Christ and to being seen as an offering for sin, and when the Christian priest is the bishop, together with the presbyters.

We shall now trace the fortunes and understanding of the general priesthood in this period, and then developments in the relationship between the priestly clergy and the laity, in order to facilitate our evaluation of the rise of the special priesthood in an overall conclusion.

CHAPTER 5

Developments in the Understanding of the General Priesthood in the First Three Centuries[1]

The aim in tracing these developments will be to note if, and if so, how strongly, this priesthood continued to be believed in and how it was understood. In particular, we shall be looking for evidence whether there is any correlation between the increasing emphasis on the priesthood of the ordained and a decreasing interest in that of Christians in general.

5.1 The Apostolic Fathers

The priesthood of the whole church is never explicitly mentioned in the writings of the Apostolic Fathers, but ideas connected to it in the NT are present. Most significant are those of 'spiritual sacrifices' offered by the 'holy priesthood' (1 Pet. 2:5) and the temple individually or corporately indwelt by God (1 Pet. 2:5, 1 Cor. 6:19, etc.).

5.1.1 Cultic imagery in 1 and 2 Clement

Mentioned concerning what the sacrificial aspect of the eucharist consisted in at that time in section 4.1, these passages will be dealt with in more detail now.

Turning firstly to *1 Clement*, we noted earlier part of Daly's statement that, 'following the lead of the NT, and in harmony with most other early Christian writers, Clement also is inclined to spiritualize the idea of sacrifice. He does so not in his own words but by placing in emphatic positions at the end of three different chapters (chaps. 18; 35; 52) some of the well-known spiritualizing Psalm texts from the LXX.'[2] In chapter

---

[1] Garrett, 'Pre-Cyprianic Doctrine' in Church and George, *Continuity and Discontinuity*, 45, wrote in 1979, 'the doctrine of the priesthood of all Christians as taught during the patristic era has been the subject of detailed research by neither patristic scholars nor historians of this particular doctrine.' This is still true for the period covered in this book as far as I have been able to discover.

[2] Daly, *Christian Sacrifice*, 314.

18, after quoting almost the whole of Psalm 51 (50 in the Septuagint), he ends with the statements, "'For if you had desired sacrifice, I would have given it; but in whole burnt offerings you will take no pleasure. The sacrifice for God is a broken spirit; a broken and humbled heart God will not despise.'" He concludes chapter 35 by quoting Psalm 50 (49):16-23, ending, "'The sacrifice of praise will glorify me, and that is the way by which I will show him the salvation of God.'"And he ends chapter 52 by quoting Psalm 50 (49):14, "'For the sacrifice of God is a broken spirit'" and Psalm 51 (50):17 again.[3]

Clement also uses the concept of firstfruits, in *1 Clement* 29:3 of God choosing Israel, in 24:1 of Jesus as the firstfruits of those raised and in 42:4 of Christians who are the first converts in one place,[4] in the last echoing Paul's idea in 1 Corinthians 16:15 and Romans 16:5, an idea which suggests the Christian's sacrificial dedication to God.

In *1 Clement* 36:1 Jesus is called 'the High Priest of our offerings',[5] 'our offerings' relating primarily to the 'sacrifice of praise' mentioned in 35:12. The same idea is present in 61:3, together with that of the Christians themselves being the offering made to the Father through Christ since he is the high priest 'of our souls'.[6] This reappears in 64:1, where God is asked to give Christians a series of virtues 'that they may be pleasing to his name through our high priest and guardian, Jesus Christ, ...',[7] 'pleasing' being used of sacrifices in Romans 12:1 and Philippians 4:18. Several scholars have seen these passages as evidence of the continuation of ideas connected with the general priesthood in the church, Otranto in particular noting their cultic settings.[8]

Garrett further sees what we noted in section 4.1.1 concerning *1 Clement* 40:5 as relevant in that 'Clement likens the proper conduct of Christian worship to the divine prescriptions for the sacrifices in ancient Israel's worship ... [and] extends this analogy to apply to a single place of worship, ...'[9] The way in which the example of the OT priestly organisation is followed by, 'Let each of you, brothers, in his proper

---

[3] Lightfoot, Harmer and Holmes, 51, 69 and 87.

[4] So Daly, *Christian Sacrifice*, 315.

[5] Lightfoot, Harmer and Holmes, 69.

[6] Ibid., 99

[7] Ibid., 101.

[8] Dabin, *Le sacerdoce royal des fidèles*, 509, and Lécuyer, J., 'Essai sur le sacerdoce des fidèles chez les pères', *La Maison-Dieu* 27 (1951), 22, n. 48 cite 36:1; Garrett, 'Pre-Cyprianic Doctrine' in Church and George, *Continuity and Discontinuity*, 46-7, cites 61:3, 64 and 52:1-4; and Otranto, 'Il sacerdozio', *Vetera Christianorum* 7 (1970), 234-5, cites all three. Garrett calls these passages 'pertinent to this priesthood'.

[9] Garrett, 'Pre-Cyprianic Doctrine' in Church and George, *Continuity and Discontinuity*, 46-7, citing 40:5 and 41:2.

order give thanks to God',[10] implies the involvement of all Christians in sacrificial worship.

Clement, then, has a firm grasp of the belief that all Christians can offer sacrifices of a penitent heart, praise, and themselves. Similar ideas are also present in *2 Clement*, which is not by Clement, but comes from the second century.[11] As Young points out, 'the offering of spiritual sacrifices is regarded simply as a repayment made by Christians in gratitude for their salvation through Christ.'[12] This is clear in 1:3: 'What repayment, then, shall we give to him, or what fruit worthy of what he has given to us?', 1:5: 'What praise, then, shall we give him, or what repayment in return for what we received?', 9:7: 'While we still have time to be healed, let us place ourselves in the hands of God the Physician, and pay him what is due', and 15:2: 'For this is the return which we are able to repay to God who created us: ...'.[13] The idea of sacrifice is conveyed in these via the verb 'give' and its compounds and the noun 'repayment'. Further, in 3:1-5, the author contrasts Christians not sacrificing to dead gods with their wholehearted obedience, whilst, in 9:7-8, the recompense God wants is 'sincere, heartfelt repentance'.[14] Their own selves, obedience and repentance are offerings to God.

The analogy of the temple is not used for the Christian or the church by Clement but it does appear in *2 Clement*. In quite a Pauline manner, the author states that, 'We must, therefore, guard the flesh as a temple of God.'[15]

5.1.2 Cultic imagery in the Didache

The only figures explicitly likened to the OT high priests in the *Didache* (13:3) are prophets and, probably, teachers, as noted in section 4.1.2. The significance of this lies in the fact that, whilst these were officially recognized as bringing God's word, this was probably on the basis of some gift previously demonstrated, not on the basis of appointment, whereas the 'bishops and deacons' who were coming to replace them (cf. 15:1-2) were appointed by the congregation. The prophets and teachers would thus have been what we now know as 'lay' figures,

---

[10] 41:1 in Lightfoot, Harmer and Holmes, 73 and 75.

[11] Geerard, vol. 1, 6, dates it to 120-140; Donfried, K.P., *The Setting of Second Clement in Early Christianity* (Leiden, 1974), 1, to c.98-100; and Snyder in Ferguson, E., *Encyclopedia of Early Christianity*, 217, agrees that it reflects the second century.

[12] Young, 130.

[13] Lightfoot, Harmer and Holmes, 101, 115, 123.

[14] Ibid., 109 and 115. Young, 130, links these statements and the exhortation in 9:10 to the issue of spiritual sacrifice.

[15] 9:3: Lightfoot, Harmer and Holmes, 114.

although the distinction between clergy and laity had not apparently been made at this time and it is uncertain how ordination was regarded and exercised.

We also noted earlier that the analogy made in 13:3 related only to the provision of the prophets' needs by the rest of the congregation and involved the identification of the firstfruit-offering with the gifts of the faithful. Young plausibly suggests that this is evidence that Christians continued the Jewish practice of offering firstfruits.[16] Certainly it is Christians in general who are to bring these offerings.

Again noted in section 4.1.2 was the use of sacrificial language in *Didache* 14:1-3. It was argued that the instruction 'give thanks', after 'on the Lord's own day gather together and break bread', could refer to giving thanks over bread which was part of a community-meal, or to giving thanks in general, as well as, or better than, it could refer to the eucharist. Then, the sacrifice referred to would be one of thanksgiving. Even if it were, or included a reference to the eucharist as a sacrifice, it is clearly that of the whole church, and the emphasis lies on giving thanks and on the inner dispositions of the participants, as is shown by the instructions which follow.[17] These emphases lessen still further the likelihood that the eucharist as an objective sacrifice is referred to here.[18]

Otranto and Daly note the possible sacrificial overtones involved in the use of *sunerchomai* ('gather together') in 14:1 and 2.[19] They point also to the use of *proserchomai* ('approach') in 4:14, where we find, 'In church you shall confess your transgressions, and you shall not approach your prayer with an evil conscience.'[20] The similarities of these instructions to 14:1-3 where there is a clear reference to sacrifice tell in favour of such a reference here.

We have found, then, two of the three main cultic images in the *Didache*, that of the temple not being employed. They are mainly used of sacrifices which all Christians can offer to God, viz., worship, thanksgiving and gifts in kind. The one reference to priests involves the priesthood of prophets and probably of teachers, but does not clearly relate to any sacrificial functions except that of being supported by the

---

[16] Young, 98-9. Daly, *Christian Sacrifice*, 313, views this 'as a Christian continuation of the OT law', pointing to the 'according to the commandment' in 13:5 and 7.

[17] Lightfoot, Harmer and Holmes, 267.

[18] Against Palmer, 'Lay Priesthood', *Th St* 8 (1947), 596 and Ryan, 'Patristic Teaching', *Irish Theological Quarterly* 29 (1962), 45. For other relevant views, see section 4.1.2 above.

[19] Otranto, 'Il sacerdozio', *Vetera Christianorum* 7 (1970), 229 and Daly, *Christian Sacrifice*, 312-3.

[20] Lightfoot, Harmer and Holmes, 257.

people.

5.1.3 Cultic imagery in Ignatius' writings

In section 4.1.3, Ignatius' connecting of the eucharist, the bishop and the altar was discussed. Although Young argues that this shows that he thought the eucharist 'a sacrifice of some sort', it was argued, with Lampe, that 'altar' means the church as gathered for worship which is being likened to a sanctuary.[21] Indeed, Noll's argument was noted that the only priestly condition known in Ignatius' writings is a collective one, 'i.e. inclusive of the whole assembly.'[22] If correct, this approaches viewing the church as the temple, as is confirmed by the close connection of the two images in *Magnesians* 7:2, in which Ignatius urges, 'Let all of you run together as to one temple of God, as to one altar, to one Jesus Christ, ...'.[23] This was an image which Ignatius liked, his fullest exposition of it coming in *Ephesians* 9:1-2. Complimenting the Ephesian believers on refusing to listen to false doctrine, he likens them to 'the stones of a temple, prepared beforehand for the building of God the Father, hoisted up to the heights by the crane of Jesus Christ, which is the cross, using as a rope the Holy Spirit; your faith is what lifts you up, and love is the way that leads up to God. So you are all fellow pilgrims, carrying your God and your shrine, your Christ and your holy things, ...'[24] Daly notes that

> this text takes up the principle [sic] elements of the Pauline idea of the Christian community as in the process of being built up into the temple of God .... But it resembles most closely 1 Pt 2,4-10 where this Pauline idea received its fullest NT expression ... The idea of Christians as individual stones or construction elements in the building of the temple is taken up and developed much farther than it was in the NT ... the Cross is specifically introduced ..., and the whole of it is also made more consciously trinitarian.[25]

The final four epithets quoted all point to God's indwelling of the individual Christian, whilst the reference to Christians as 'stones of a temple, prepared beforehand for the building of God the Father', brings

---

[21] Young, 250; Lampe, 660.

[22] Noll, *Christian Ministerial Priesthood*, 123.

[23] Lightfoot, Harmer and Holmes, 155.

[24] Lightfoot, Harmer and Holmes, 143.

[25] Daly, *Christian Sacrifice*, 318-9. Otranto, 'Il sacerdozio', *Vetera Christianorum* 7 (1970), 237-8 and Dabin, *Le sacerdoce royal des fidèles*, 509, emphasize this text's affinities with 1 Pet. 2:9, but quote from Migne's text of *Eph.* 9:2, which includes a clear quotation from 1 Pet. 2:9 that does not belong to the original according to Lightfoot, Harmer and Holmes.

out the collective aspect without losing the individual.

However, to quote Daly again,

> the community that Ignatius is thinking of is also far more 'ecclesiastical' (in the sense of an institutionalized Church) than was the case with Paul. *Philadelphians* 7,2, for example, is quite similar to 1 Cor 3,16; 6,19 when it exhorts: "Keep your bodies as the temples of God - ...." But, being sandwiched between the exhortation to "Do nothing without the bishop," and to "love unity; avoid divisions," the phrase receives an ecclesiastical dimension not present in Paul.[26]

Ignatius' main use of sacrificial language concerns his own martyrdom, 'in contrast to Paul who concentrates his attention on the sacrificial aspect of the whole of Christian life (Rom. 12,1f) ....'[27] He depicts it in liturgical terms in *Romans* 2:2: 'Grant me nothing more than to be poured out as an offering to God while there is still an altar ready, ...', and in *Romans* 4:2: 'Pray to the Lord on my behalf, that through these instruments I might prove to be a sacrifice to God.'[28] Young persuasively argues for a Jewish background to this concept but goes on to recognize that 'these ideas have been transformed by the desire to imitate Christ .... In this, Ignatius is clearly influenced by St. Paul'.[29] Ignatius' exhortation of his readers to be fellow-initiates of the martyred Paul and imitators of Christ[30] amply illustrates that he viewed all Christians as able to offer this sacrifice.

Ignatius, then, takes up OT cultic concepts to describe the church as a whole and Christians as individuals, in particular to emphasize their unity in worship, their indwelling by God and so their need to be holy, and their ability to offer themselves to God in martyrdom. Again, all these concepts relate either to the church as a whole, or to individual Christians, and never to church leaders alone.

5.1.4 Cultic imagery in The Shepherd of Hermas

Written in Rome in the early to mid-second century,[31] this document contains little cultic imagery.

---

[26] Daly, *Christian Sacrifice*, 319.

[27] Daly, *Christian Sacrifice*, 320. Cf. Hanson, R.P.C., *Studies*, 87, who sees the former as an extension of the idea of self-offering from Rom. 12:1, as it may well be.

[28] Lightfoot, Harmer and Holmes, 169, 171.

[29] Young, 108-9.

[30] So Young, 109, citing *Eph.* 12:2 and *Philad.* 7:2.

[31] See Grant, *Introduction*, 85; Snyder, R.F. (ed.), *The Shepherd of Hermas* (Camden, 1968), 19 and 22-4; and Aune in Ferguson, E., *Encyclopedia of Early Christianity*, 421.

In *Similitudes* 5:3:8, or 56:8, it is stated that, 'If, then, you complete
the fast in this way, as I have commanded you, your sacrifice will be
acceptable in God's sight, ...'[32] The fast involves both literal fasting
with the giving of the cost of what would have been eaten to the poor,
and the moral fasting of abstention from evil (5:3:5-7). Young notes the
Jewish influence on this and that 'the spiritualising of the fast has not
led to abolishing actual observance, but exists alongside it and
transforms the act into charity.'[33]

Further, in *Similitudes* 9:28:5, or 105:5, those suffering for Christ are
told that they 'ought to glorify God, because God has considered you
worthy that you should bear this name and that all your sins be
healed.'[34] Young argues that 'in this case the pre-Christian Jewish
tradition seems to have been the dominant factor in the attribution of
atoning significance to the martyr's death.'[35] Whilst this is not a
reference to martyrdom as a sacrifice, it may throw light on the passages
in Ignatius which include such references.

Noll notes too the references to 'altar' in *Mandates* 10:3 and
Similitudes 8:2:5. The first refers to God's altar in heaven, to which
prayer ascends, while the reference in the second is most unclear but 'it
is highly improbable that this could have any bearing on a cultus in the
Christian community.'[36]

The only other possible cultic allusions in *The Shepherd* are found in
Visions 3:2-7, or 11:2-7.[37] Here the church is depicted as a tower under
construction by angels, the stones used are the individuals who make up
the church (3:5), whilst those rejected and thrown away are those
outside the church (3:6-7).[38] This is clearly a development of the kinds
of ideas we have noted earlier in the NT, including 1 Peter 2:4-10, and
in Ignatius (*Eph.* 9:1-2). Daly argues that 'since Hermas calls the
building a tower or building rather than a temple, the image may not
have been intended to carry a sacrificial connotation at all',[39] but this

---

[32] Lightfoot, Harmer and Holmes, 433.

[33] Young, 104 and 101. Noll, *Christian Ministerial Priesthood*, 237: 'The most we can say is
that *thusía* here appears to be part of a remembrance of phrases from Scripture and that true
fasting would seem to be approved as one possible substitute on a personal level for the
Jewish Temple cult.'

[34] Lightfoot, Harmer and Holmes, 513.

[35] Young, 108.

[36] Noll, *Christian Ministerial Priesthood*, 239.

[37] Garrett, 'Pre-Cyprianic Doctrine' in Church and George, *Continuity and Discontinuity*, 47,
sees *Sim.* 2:3 as containing a possible reference to the royal priesthood. He does not explain
why and the reason is not readily apparent.

[38] See Lightfoot, Harmer and Holmes, 351, 353.

[39] Daly, *Christian Sacrifice*, 322.

does not seem likely.

The paucity and insignificance of cultic allusions in *The Shepherd* can thus be seen.

5.1.5 Other cultic allusions

In his *Philippians* 4:3, Polycarp reminds the widows that they are 'God's altar'.[40] This idea 'appears here for the first time in extant Christian literature, although the context clearly indicates that it was hardly a novel idea for Polycarp or for his readers.'[41] It may have developed from that of the church as an altar which we noted in Ignatius' writings, just as the image of the church as temple had been extended to the individual.[42] Another factor may have been that the widows live from the church's offerings and so are the figurative altar on which these are made;[43] still another the connection of the widows with prayer.[44]

More likening of martydom to sacrifice is found in *The Martyrdom of Polycarp*. In 14:1, the hero is described as having been bound 'like a splendid ram chosen from a great flock for a sacrifice, a burnt offering prepared and acceptable to God' and in 14:2 as having prayed that he might share in the cup of Christ with the martyrs and 'be received among them in your presence today, as a rich and acceptable sacrifice, ...'[45] This is presented as a thank-offering, a gift-sacrifice, rather than as expiatory, as in Ignatius.[46]

The only other cultic references in the Apostolic Fathers are found in *The Epistle of Barnabas*, usually dated between AD 70 and 135 and originating from Alexandria.[47] Although this contains radical cult-criticism, it is the OT sacrificial cult which is rejected, not sacrifice as such. This is apparent as early as 1:7 in which the author states, 'we ought to make a richer and loftier offering out of reverence for him.'[48]

Indeed, the first main subject dealt with in the epistle is sacrifice in 2:4-10. Here OT prophetic cult criticism is interpreted as teaching that God 'needs neither sacrifices nor whole burnt offerings nor general

---

[40] Lightfoot, Harmer and Holmes, 211.

[41] Daly, *Christian Sacrifice*, 323.

[42] So ibid.

[43] So Camelot, P.T. (ed.), *Ignace d'Antioche, Polycarpe de Smyrne. Lettre, Martyre de Polycarpe* (Paris, 1958³), 208.

[44] So Noll, *Christian Ministerial Priesthood*, 150, quoting from Schoedel, W.L

[45] Lightfoot, Harmer and Holmes, 237, 239.

[46] So Young, 130.

[47] See Ferguson in Ferguson, E., *Encyclopedia of Early Christianity*, 138, and Kraft, 39-56.

[48] Lightfoot, Harmer and Holmes, 275, 277.

offerings'. 2:6 states that, 'Therefore he has abolished these things, in order that the new law of our Lord Jesus Christ, which is free from the yoke of compulsion, might have its offering, one not made by man.' More prophetic cult criticism is followed in 2:9-10 by an exhortation to understand the Father's loving intention on 'how we may approach him', which is knowing that, '"A sacrifice to God is a broken heart; an aroma pleasing to the Lord is a heart that glorifies its Maker."' [49]

Daly points out that 'not made by man' 'is a hapax legomenon in Greek literature. It seems quite likely that this unique coinage is intended to be an allusion to the word [*cheiropoiétos*: made by (human) hand] and its derogatory associations with idolatry .... In any case, it certainly expresses Barnabas' conviction that OT cultic sacrifice was the result of human invention and not of divine ordinance.' [50] What was of divine ordinance was the spiritual sacrifice of penitence and holy thinking and living. [51]

The temple theme is found in *Barnabas* 4:11; 6:14-15 and 16:1-10. In 4:11 Christians are exhorted, 'Let us become spiritual; let us become a perfect temple for God.' [52] This involves the collective use of the metaphor and is found in an exhortation to right living. It adumbrates the emphases we have found and shall find in Clement and Origen. The individual use is found in 6:15: 'For the dwelling-place of our heart, my brothers, is a holy temple dedicated to the Lord.' [53]

It is, however, in 16:1-10 that the author deals with this topic at greatest length. He begins by condemning those who 'set their hope on the building, as though it were God's house, and not on their God who created them. For they, almost like the heathen, consecrated him by means of the temple.' After quotations to support this (16:2-5), he argues that a temple still exists (16:6-7) and explains what it is (16:7-10). Before we believed, our heart was 'truly a temple built by human hands, because it was full of idolatry and was the home of demons'; when we believed, however, 'we became new, created again from the beginning. Consequently God truly dwells in our dwelling-place – that is, in us.' This happens as we confess Christ through the door of the

---

[49] Ibid., 277, 279.

[50] Daly, *Christian Sacrifice*, 427.

[51] This passage is cited as an example of the 'sacrifice of a holy life' by Ryan, 'Patristic Teaching', *Irish Theological Quarterly* 29 (1962), 45; of the '"pure offering" doctrine' by Hanson, R.P.C., *Studies*, 86; and, less convincingly, as involving a reflection of the general priesthood of 1 Pet. 2:9 by Otranto, 'Il sacerdozio', *Vetera Christianorum* 7 (1970), 233-4, although it is unclear what is meant by 'reflection' here

[52] Lightfoot, Harmer and Holmes, 283.

[53] Ibid., 291.

temple, our mouths. He concludes, 'This is the spiritual temple that is being built for the Lord.'[54]

Although Philo and the author of *Barnabas* have much in common, 'Philo had explicitly rejected the idea that the human body could be made in the image and likeness of God. ... Barnabas, on the other hand, is totally Christian and incarnational in outlook.'[55] He follows Paul's and 1 Peter's ideas, whilst going well beyond them.[56]

Whilst being so critical of the OT sacrificial cultus that he denies it derives from God, the author of *Barnabas* has a strong concept of the kind of cultus God does want. It is one which involves sacrifices of repentance and holy thinking and living, the individual Christian as a temple vibrantly indwelt by God, and the whole church as an 'incorruptible temple.'

5.1.6 Conclusion

Although, then, we have found no explicit allusions to the general priesthood in the writings of the Apostolic Fathers, and this throws doubt on whether belief in it continued after the NT period, we have found a good deal of evidence of ideas associated with it in 1 Peter 2:5. This, combined with what we shall see of its survival in the writings of Justin and others, points strongly in the direction of seeing its absence in the Apostolic Fathers as fortuitous.

However, clearly more important, because of the greater emphases on them in the writings which came to make up the NT and, as far as sacrifice is concerned, in the OT too, were ideas of spiritual sacrifices to be offered by all Christians and of all Christians individually or collectively as a temple indwelt by God. Another important factor was reaction against Judaism. The reinterpretation of cultic ideas begun by the earliest Christians evidently continued after the NT period, albeit mainly along the lines laid down in the NT writings. This was a general development, being seen in writings from Rome, Syria and Alexandria.

5.2 The period of the second-century Apologists

As in section 4.2, relevant material will be examined from Justin Martyr and Irenaeus and then from other second century sources.

---

[54] Ibid., 317, 319.
[55] Daly, *Christian Sacrifice*, 436.
[56] So ibid., 439; see also Otranto, 'Il sacerdozio', *Vetera Christianorum* 7 (1970), 234.

5.2.1 Cultic and priestly imagery in Justin Martyr

Justin's use of sacrificial ideas was explored in section 4.2.1 above and needs only to be summarized here. He has a strong polemic against both pagan and Jewish sacrifice and identifies Christians' sacrifices with the bread and cup of the eucharist (*Dial.* 41:3), and with their prayers and thanksgivings (*Dial.* 117:2). Whilst, therefore, Justin identifies the Christian sacrifice with the eucharist, it seems to be the prayers and thanks offered over the elements which he primarily sees as sacrifices, although he also speaks of the elements, at least when prayed over, sacrificially.

It is in the latter of the two passages referred to above that Justin also alludes to the priesthood of all the faithful, the first to do so in any extant documents after the NT. This occurs during Justin's exposition of the story concerning Joshua the high priest in Zechariah 3. After a reference to Jesus Christ as high priest (*Dial.* 116:1), Justin identifies Christians with that Joshua:

> For, just as that Jesus, who is called a priest by the prophet, was seen wearing filthy clothes (because he was said to have married a harlot), and is called a brand snatched out of the fire (because he was forgiven his sins when the devil that opposed him was rebuked), so we, who through the name of Jesus have as one man believed in God the Creator of all, have taken off our dirty clothes, that is, our sins, through the name of his first-begotten Son. Having been set on fire by the word of this calling, we are now of the true [high-] priestly family of God, as he himself testifies when he says that in every place among the Gentiles pure and pleasing sacrifices are offered up to him. But God receives sacrifices from no one, except through his priests (116:3).[57]

Clearly, a number of factors lead to Justin's description of Christians in general as 'the true high-priestly family of God.' First and foremost is the desire to show the Jews that the OT scriptures should be interpreted christologically, a point which becomes even clearer in 117:2 and 4, where he criticizes a Jewish interpretation of Malachi 1:10-12. Second is the implied union between Christ and his people.[58] Justin seems about to interpret the story concerning Joshua of Christ as high priest, but in fact interprets it of Christians who have believed in him. Third is Justin's awareness of Christian worship as centred on the bread and the cup as the only sacrifice acceptable to God,[59] as he makes clear in 117:1

---

[57] Falls, 327-8. My addition in square brackets based on the Greek text in Goodspeed, 234.

[58] Otranto, 'Il sacerdozio', *Vetera Christianorum* 7 (1970), 239-240: 'The priesthood of the faithful finds its reason for being in that of the Messiah ....' See the rest of this passage for an outline of some of Justin's teaching on Christ's high priesthood.

[59] Ryan, 'Patristic Teaching', *Irish Theological Quarterly* 29 (1962), 28, especially

and 3, with the admission of prayers and thanksgivings as such sacrifices in 117:2.

A possible fourth factor is Justin's awareness of 1 Peter 2:5 and/or 9. Palmer is caught in two minds on this, whilst Ryan finds it 'surprising, that when tradition first predicates a priesthood of all Christians, it should base this teaching not on the words of St. Peter or St. John but on the eucharistic prophecy of Malachy.' Otranto, on the other hand, is sure of a reference to 1 Peter 2 here.[60] There are two factors which argue for this. One is the reference to *genos*, meaning 'family' or 'race'.[61] The '[high]-priestly' is obviously conditioned by the exposition of Joshua as high priest, but *genos* alongside it suggests 1 Peter 2:9, 'a chosen race [*genos*], a royal priesthood'. Another, as Otranto argues,[62] is the way in which 117:1 continues from the passage quoted above with, 'Therefore all the sacrifices [offered] through this name',[63] as 1 Peter 2:5 states that Christians are a 'holy priesthood, to offer spiritual sacrifices acceptable to God through Jesus Christ.' It is likely, then, that Justin had 1 Peter 2:4-10 at least in the back of his mind when he wrote this passage. It also shows that ideas of Christian sacrifice could be connected with the general priesthood.

Three Roman Catholic scholars feel that Justin, in using 'true' or 'genuine' with 'the [high]-priestly ... race', was indicating that he viewed the high-priesthood of Christians as real rather than metaphorical.[64] It is more likely from the context that the contrast was between the OT Jewish and the Christian priesthoods. Daly's statement that it 'is not at all clear from this passage nor from its immediate context' what Justin means precisely by the reference to Christians being the true high-priestly race of God[65] is somewhat puzzling. The immediate context in 117:1 demonstrates unambiguously that Justin meant the offering of Christian sacrifices and in particular the eucharist in the sense outlined above. It is true, though, that it was only a step in

---

emphasizes this: 'Justin concludes that Christians are a high-priestly race from the fact that they have an active part in the Church's public worship.'

[60] Palmer, 'Lay Priesthood', *Th St* 8 (1947), 580: 'St. Justin does not appear to have the classical text of St. Peter in mind - an allusion may be seen in his reference to the "high-priestly race of God"'; Ryan, 'Patristic Teaching', *Irish Theological Quarterly* 29 (1962), 28; and Otranto, 'Il sacerdozio', *Vetera Christianorum* 7 (1970), 240.

[61] So Palmer, 'Lay Priesthood', *Th St* 8 (1947), 580.

[62] Otranto, 'Il sacerdozio', *Vetera Christianorum* 7 (1970), 240-241.

[63] This is a literal translation of the Greek text given by Goodspeed, 234. Falls, 328, has, 'all the sacrifices offered in his name'.

[64] Ryan, 'Patristic Teaching', *Irish Theological Quarterly* 29 (1962), 28; Quacquarelli, A., 'L'epiteto sacerdote ai cristiani in Giustino Martire', *Vetera Christianorum* 7.1 (1970), 18; and Otranto, 'Il sacerdozio', *Vetera Christianorum* 7 (1970), 240.

[65] Daly, *Christian Sacrifice*, 335.

his overall argument, and a minor one at that. It does, however, show that he was aware of the general priesthood and that he saw no need to justify it, referring to it as if it were well known to his fellow-Christians.

It is particularly significant for this study that the eucharist is viewed at this time as an offering by all Christians as priests and, in spite of the leading role of a president, never by a particular Christian as priest. Precisely that which is considered by some today to constitute the priestliness of the ordained was considered by Justin to involve the priestliness of the whole Christian community.

The one passage in Justin's writings which could involve a reference to the Christian community as a temple is found in *Dialogue* 86:6 where he likens the stick Elisha threw into the Jordan to recover the iron part of an axe which the sons of the prophets had taken to cut down trees to build a house to study the law in to Christ, who cleansed us from sin by the cross and baptism and 'made us a house of prayer and worship.'[66] Justin probably has Jesus' words about the temple in Matthew 21:13 in mind here.[67]

Justin, then, is significant for the purposes of this study, first because he is the first outside the NT explicitly to mention the general priesthood, and second, because he connects it with the offering of Christian sacrifices, and the eucharist in particular.

5.2.2 Cultic and priestly imagery in Irenaeus

As with Justin, Irenaeus' view of sacrifice was studied in section 4.2.2 above and needs only summarising here. He shares much of Justin's polemic against pagan and Jewish sacrifices but with less revulsion. One indication of this is his willingness to see the OT sacrifices as prefiguring NT ones. For example, he uses the OT firstfruits law with regard to the eucharist. Other Christian sacrifices are prayer and good works. Both the thanks and prayers over the elements and the elements themselves, even before they have been prayed over, are seen as sacrificial aspects of the eucharist. There is also one indication that Irenaeus saw Christian sacrifice as propitiatory. Throughout, however, the eucharist is seen as the sacrifice of the whole church: in *Against Heresies* 4:17:5, Irenaeus writes of the bread and cup that God 'taught what the new offering of the new covenant was. It is this offering that the church received from the apostles and that, in the whole world, she

---

[66] Falls, 286.

[67] Against Daly, *Christian Sacrifice*, 337, who says, 'the idea of the community as temple of God is totally absent' from Justin's writings.

offers to ... God'; in 4:18:1 it is called the 'church's offering'; and
4:18:4 begins, 'Therefore, because the church offers with simplicity,
....'[68]

In Garrett's view, there are passages in *Against Heresies*

> in which Irenaeus could easily have become more explicit about the royal
> priesthood of Christians. For example, mention of the Old Testament
> "sacerdotal and liturgical service" could have led to a comparable mention of
> the sacerdotal functions under the New Covenant, but instead Irenaeus refers
> to the giving of the Holy Spirit. Likewise, the prayers of the church ... are not
> described as a priestly sacrifice but as the opposite of "angelic invocations"
> and "incantations".[69]

However, there are factors which lessen the significance of Irenaeus'
omission of the general priesthood, especially in the first of these
passages. In this,[70] Irenaeus is pointing to the differences between how
the Word of God revealed himself to the patriarchs, under the Mosaic
law, in his incarnation, and finally through the sending of the Spirit, as a
parallel with his revelation of himself differently through the four
gospels. Allusion to the relationship between the 'priestly and liturgical
order' under the Law and the priesthood under Christ would only have
been relevant if accompanied by references to different priestly
arrangements in the times of the patriarchs, Christ, and the church.
Omission is therefore not surprising.

In the second passage Garrett referred to, there is no clear reason why
Irenaeus should have described prayers in sacrificial terms, either. In it[71]
he contrasts the purity and openness of Christians' prayers for miracles
with others' incantations and magic practices. There is no mention of
pagan or heretical priests or sacrificial practices which would have led
us to expect a reference to prayer as a Christian, priestly sacrifice.
Moreover, Irenaeus does view prayer, good works and the eucharist as
Christian sacrifices, as noted above, and he does mention the general
priesthood, as Garrett recognizes.[72]

The first passage to be considered as including a reference to the
general priesthood is in *Against Heresies* 4:8:3. While answering
Marcion's attempts to exclude Abraham from salvation by Christ

---

[68] Rousseau et al., 592f., 597f. and 606f.

[69] Garrett, 'Pre-Cyprianic Doctrine' in Church and George, *Continuity and Discontinuity*, 51,
referring to *AH* 3.11.8 and 2.32.5.

[70] *AH* 3.11.8: Rousseau et al., 168.

[71] *AH* 2.32.5: Rousseau et al., 342.

[72] Garrett, 'Pre-Cyprianic Doctrine' in Church and George, *Continuity and Discontinuity*, 51-
2.

(4:8:1), Irenaeus defends Jesus' healing of a woman on the sabbath and calling her "'a daughter of Abraham'" (4:8:2, quoting Lk. 13:15-16). In 4:8:3 he points to the distinction between the Law's permission of the hungry eating and its prohibition of reaping and gathering on the sabbath. He argues that this was why Jesus referred, in Luke 6:3-4, to David's eating and giving to his men to eat the bread before the Lord in the temple which only the priests were allowed to eat. He continues, either with a clear reference to the general priesthood as given in the Latin translation: 'for all the just have priestly rank', or with the narrower statement as given by John of Damascus and the Armenian translation: 'for every just king has priestly rank'. Rousseau et al. prefer the latter.[73] Although no explanation of this particular choice is given, the most likely is the general argument given by Rousseau: 'If one has two different readings, one of which is supported by a single witness and the other by two, it is right to presume that the latter reading reflects the lost original; however, this presumption should not be elevated to certainty and the reading in question should not be adopted unless it does complete justice to the demands of the context.'[74]

Although 'for all the just have priestly rank' is appropriate to a context in which both David and his men ate the holy bread, it is not more appropriate than 'for every just king has priestly rank', because it is preceded by a reference to David alone as priest. The reading given by John of Damascus and the Armenian translation is therefore to be preferred.

However, the passage continues, in both Latin and Greek, 'All the Lord's disciples were priests too, not having fields or houses here for an inheritance but always attending to the altar and God.' This statement is then illustrated by quotations from Deuteronomy 33:9, 10:9 and 18:1 regarding the priests' dependence on God and the offerings to him, whereupon the disciples are said to have 'the Levitical inheritance'.[75] The primary reference here is to the twelve disciples, but there may well be a secondary reference to Christians in general. Factors which suggest this are: the wider context, in 4:8:1 and the beginning of 4:8:2, deals with the church as the true descendants of Abraham; all Christians have to be like the disciples in the respects noted; Christians are elsewhere called 'disciples' by Irenaeus;[76] and the reference to this passage in *Against Heresies* 5:34:3.

---

[73] Rousseau et al., 472. See 68-9 for a description of the Greek evidence.

[74] Ibid., 164. See the justification of this on 165.

[75] Ibid., 474.

[76] E.g., in *AH* 4:33:1 (Rousseau et al., 802).

In this last, Irenaeus explains how various OT prophecies will be fulfilled in an earthly kingdom after the resurrection, ending with a description of the people's, including the priests', joy. He continues, 'We showed in the earlier book that the Levites and priests are all the Lord's disciples, who both profane the Sabbath in the temple and are blameless. Such promises mean clearly, then, the feasting that this creation will provide in the kingdom of the just and that God has promised to serve there.'[77] Here the primary reference of 'the Levites and priests are all the Lord's disciples' is to Christians in general. For one thing, 'all' seems unnecessary apart from the desire to indicate all Christians; for another, the context refers to the churches at the beginning of *Against Heresies* 5:34:3, and the 'kingdom of the righteous' in the sentence after the reference to the disciples. This makes a similar general reference in *Against Heresies* 4:8:3 more likely.[78]

These passages do not receive adequate treatment in the secondary literature on the general priesthood, but Daly does point out that Irenaeus has 'taken over and developed further the Dominical argument which implicitly ... made the Levitical priesthood a partial model for the Christian priesthood.'[79] The quotations from Deuteronomy make this a valid observation and a new departure as far as the general priesthood in extant literature is concerned. We noted the themes of the dependence of the ordained priesthood on the Lord alone and serving the altar and the Lord earlier. Here they are related to the general priesthood, showing that they were already known connotations of priesthood when the special priesthood arose.

From one point of view, these references are quite insignificant, since both occur as only one step in arguments about other matters, indicating that the general priesthood is not a subject which Irenaeus sees any need to develop. On the other hand, it is mentioned without any attempt to justify it, which, together with what we have noted concerning Irenaeus' understanding of sacrifices as offered by all Christians, suggests that it

---

[77] Rousseau et al., 432.

[78] Palmer, 'Lay Priesthood', *Th St* 8 (1947), and Lécuyer, J., 'Essai sur le sacerdoce des fidèles chez les pères', *La Maison-Dieu* 27 (1951), mention neither. Otranto, 'Il sacerdozio', *Vetera Christianorum* 7 (1970), 241, and Eastwood, 67, refer to only *AH* 4:8:3, accepting the Latin translation without any discussion of its textual reliability, and expounding it as meaning the general priesthood as does 1 Pet. 2:9. Dabin, *Le sacerdoce royal des fidèles*, 512, Daly, *Christian Sacrifice*, 347, and Garrett, 'Pre-Cyprianic Doctrine' in Church and George, *Continuity and Discontinuity*, 51, also mention only *AH* 4:8:3, but give both texts of it and see a reference to the general priesthood without any discussion. Faivre, *Emergence*, 36-7, alone mentions both *AH* 4.8.3 and 5.34.3, seeing them as teaching the general priesthood but without discussion.

[79] Daly, *Christian Sacrifice*, 347.

was a commonplace in the church of those days. This would not be surprising if any of the NT references to it were common knowledge.

Irenaeus does not make any allusion in either of these passages to those NT references because the latter are not germane to his argument. The main link is with the disciples and their priestly freedom and conformity with the Levitical regulations noted. These do not relate to offering sacrifice, the function of the general priesthood described by Justin, but to their complete dependence on God and service of the altar and God in 4:8:3, and to their blamelessness and enjoyment of God's eschatological blessings in 5:34:3. The last are not presented as especially priestly blessings.

Irenaeus does not mention the general priesthood elsewhere in his extant writings, but Daly finds it in a passage in *Demonstration of the Apostolic Preaching* 96. In this Irenaeus argues that Christians do not need the Mosaic Law as a tutor, since they have no desire to disobey it. He illustrates this from several laws, including, "'and there will be no command to remain idle one day of rest to him who is always a Sabbath keeper, who is in the temple of God which is the human body, rendering service to God and at all times working righteousness. He says, 'for I will have mercy and not sacrifice, and knowledge of God more than burnt offerings.'"[80] The idea of the Christian serving God in the temple of the human body certainly implies his priesthood, but it was probably not consciously in Irenaeus' mind. However, this passage again shows Irenaeus' connection of serving God with cultic concepts in appropriate contexts. This service is open to all.

Similar ideas are present in *Against Heresies* 5:6:2 in an argument for the resurrection of the body. This whole section consists mainly of quotations from the NT on the theme of the body.[81] In it Irenaeus has taken up the Pauline idea of the individual, not the community, and the body in particular, as the temple of God. Both are explicable by 'the need to emphasize against the Gnostics the physical reality of the incarnation, and of Christ's and our bodily resurrection.'[82]

Already noted in a footnote above was a quotation of 1 Corinthians 3:17 at the end of *Against Heresies* 4:8:3. Daly views this as the only place where Irenaeus was thinking of the Christian community as temple, since the allusion to Numbers 15:32-36 which precedes it, 'recounting as it does the violation of established ritual regulations,

---

[80] Daly, *Christian Sacrifice*, 348, citing the *Patrologia orientalis* 12.5, 728. This corresponds closely to the French translation of the Armenian in Froidevaux, L.M. (ed.), *Démonstration de la Prédication Apostolique* (Paris, 1959), 164-5.

[81] Rousseau et al., 80-82.

[82] Daly, *Christian Sacrifice*, 346.

supports more the idea of the temple as community or institution than the idea of the temple as individual.'[83] Williams, however, views this as 'an entirely inconclusive case' and argues that Irenaeus 'does not seem to pick up the idea of the church itself as temple.'[84] This is so, 1 Corinthians 3:17 being quoted mainly because of its mentions of temple and defilement which are key-words in the context, rather than with any intention of describing the church.

The church is referred to as God's building and tower in *Against Heresies* 4:25:1 and 4:36:2, but neither of these passages contains anything else that is cultic so that it is unlikely they involve references to the church as the temple.

In conclusion, Irenaeus has a more favourable attitude towards OT sacrifice than Justin, which may well be largely the result of his need and desire to show as much continuity as possible between the OT and the revelation in Christ in his attempts to combat Marcion's teaching. Like Justin, he views the eucharist as the main Christian offering, while regarding good works and prayer as such offerings too. He takes up ideas from Paul's teaching which involve cultic imagery, in particular that of the individual Christian as the temple of God, developing this in opposition to Gnostic ideas. He does not, however, take up Paul's collective application of the temple-image, nor does he clearly use that of the individual Christian's whole life as a sacrifice.[85] This was probably due to their irrelevance to his main preoccupations. Like Justin, he alludes to the general priesthood, but only twice and without making a significant issue of it on either occasion. Unlike him, he does not link it with offering Christian sacrifice since the context does not require it. In the first case, this is mainly that of a very minor support to his larger argument concerning the correctness of Jesus' use of the sabbath as compared with OT law and practice. He does, however, develop somewhat the connotations of complete dependence on God. When he refers back to this later, it is largely because of an OT quotation which mentioned priests near the end, although the inclusion of all Christians as priests and servants and so as enjoying the benefits promised in the OT passage made the allusion apposite. Whilst relatively unimportant in the picture of Irenaeus' overall teaching, these references demonstrate a general awareness of the Christian use of these cultic images in the ways indicated.

---

[83] Ibid., 348.
[84] Williams, R., 13, n. 1.
[85] So Daly, *Christian Sacrifice*, 359.

5.2.3 Cultic and priestly imagery in other second-century Christian literature

The attitude of other second-century Christian writers towards pagan and Jewish sacrifice and their use of sacrificial ideas to describe holiness, knowing and worshipping God, praise and generosity, prayer and martyrdom as well as the eucharist were noted in section 4.2.3 above, as was the fact that they never use priestly ideas of leaders of worship. There are also some passages which allude to the general priesthood and some which use the idea of the individual as the temple.

The clearest reference to the general priesthood is found in Melito's *On the Passover* 68, and consists of the words 'and made us a new priesthood and an eternal people personal to him.'[86] It comes in a series of statements of what Christ has done for his people and was suggested by the last of these which says that Christ 'is he that delivered us ... from tyranny to eternal royalty', because of the way 'kingdom' and 'priesthood' are linked in 1 Peter 2:9. Perler says that 'Melito seems to be the first to mention the expression "new priesthood"',[87] but the concept is not developed or explained.

A second allusion to the general priesthood, quoted in section 4.2.3 above, comes in Ode 20 of the *Odes of Solomon*: 'I am a priest of the Lord, and to Him I do priestly service: and to Him I offer the sacrifice of His thought.'[88] This links the priesthood of the individual Christian with sacrifice and service, albeit the sacrifice of God's thought which seems akin to God's word, and, further on, of righteousness, purity and the inward being, rather than of the eucharist and thanksgiving like Justin.

The only passage in the apocryphal NT writings to possibly allude to the general priesthood is in the Gnostic *Gospel of Philip*[89] in a discussion of knowing the truth and so becoming perfect. In sections 124-125a, the 'mysteries of the truth' are said to be hidden behind a curtain and 'if any belong to the tribe of the priesthood, they will be able to enter within the veil with the high priest.'[90] Wilson rightly views the spiritual as meant by 'any [who] belong to the tribe of priesthood.'[91]

---

[86] Perler, O. (ed.), *Méliton des Sardes: Sur la Pâque et fragments* (Paris, 1966), 98, gives this in brackets because it appears in only one of the two Greek manuscripts. Hall, S.G. (ed.), *Melito of Sardis: 'On Pascha' and fragments* (Oxford, 1979), 36, includes it unbracketed because it also appears in the Coptic and Georgian versions.

[87] Perler, 174.

[88] Harris, J.R. (ed.), *The Odes and Psalms of Solomon* (Cambridge, 1909), 116.

[89] So Garrett, 'Pre-Cyprianic Doctrine' in Church and George, *Continuity and Discontinuity*, 47-48.

[90] Schneemelcher and Wilson, vol.1, 205.

[91] Wilson, R.McL. (ed.), *The Gospel of Philip, translated from the Coptic text, with an Introduction and Commentary* (London, 1962), 192.

This, and the making of priesthood and entering the holiest of all into a symbol of knowing the truth, is similar to what we shall note later in Clement of Alexandria and Origen, which suggests the possibility of Gnostic influence on their view of priestliness or of common influences on both. It does not relate to anything else noted so far except to the exhortation 'Let us become spiritual; let us become a perfect temple for God' in *Barnabas* 4:11.

There are also some references in the late second-century or early third-century, non-Gnostic[92] *Teaching of Silvanus* which suggest an awareness of the general priesthood. In one, Wisdom summons all to receive understanding, which is described as 'a high priestly garment which is woven from every (kind of) wisdom'; a second, noted earlier, states that 'a contrite heart is the acceptable sacrifice'; a third urges Christians to 'cease being a tomb, and become (again) a temple, so that uprightness and divinity may remain in you'; and a fourth exhorts readers to allow Christ to enter the temple within to cast out the merchants, continuing, 'let him dwell in the temple which is within you, and may you become for him a priest and a Levite, entering in purity. Blessed are you, O soul, if you find this one in your temple. Blessed are you still more if you perform his service. But he who will defile the temple of God, that one God will destroy. For you lay yourself open, O man, if you cast this one out of your temple.'[93] This contains no allusions to the NT passages mentioning the general priesthood, but rather to 1 Corinthians 3:16-17 used of the individual Christian. Nonetheless, each aspect of cultic imagery noted in the NT is represented here and, along with the other evidence noted above, it is evidence of the widespread diffusion of these ideas in the second- to third-century church. Holiness, service and wisdom are the main connotations of priesthood and temple here.

Further uses of the temple-image in second-century literature are found in the *Acts of Paul* where there is the statement, inspired by 1 Corinthians 6:18-19, 'blessed are they who have kept the flesh pure, for they shall become a temple of God',[94] and Tatian who, discussing man being made in God's image, likens his body to a temple thus: 'If such a structure is like a shrine, "God" is willing to "dwell" in it through the "spirit", his representative.'[95] In both cases, we find the individual

---

[92] So Peel, Zandee and Wisse in Robinson, J.M. (ed.), *The Nag Hammadi Library in English* (Leiden, 1977), 347.

[93] Sections 89, 104, 106 and 109: Peel and Zandee in Robinson, 1977, 349 and 355-7.

[94] Schneemelcher and Wilson, vol. 2, 239.

[95] *Oratio ad Graecos* 15.2: Whittaker, M. (ed.), *Tatian 'Oratio ad Graecos' and Fragments*, (Oxford, 1982), 31.

application of this image and not the collective, as in Irenaeus.

5.2.4 Summary and conclusion

This survey of the available evidence in second-century Christian literature outside the writings of the Apostolic Fathers provides ample evidence of the widespread use of cultic imagery for the general Christian life. Undoubtedly sacrificial imagery is found most frequently, but we have found uses of priestly imagery in Justin, Irenaeus, Melito, the *Odes of Solomon*, the *Gospel of Philip*, and the *Teaching of Silvanus*, and uses of temple imagery in Irenaeus, the *Teaching of Silvanus*, the *Acts of Paul* and Tatian. These make it unlikely that the lack of priestly imagery in the Apostolic Fathers is significant.

The NT passages which allude to the general priesthood are referred to in Melito and possibly in Irenaeus. This suggests that they did not have much direct influence on these authors generally, although a common awareness of them is implied by the development of the cultic imagery we have noted. Another major factor was the desire to make the OT relevant to Christians, OT allusions being present in all the passages studied except Melito, whose reference to 1 Peter has OT echoes. Purity or blamelessness is mentioned in three of them (Irenaeus, *Against Heresies* 5:34:3, the *Odes of Solomon* and *the Teaching of Silvanus*), and spirituality implying it in another (the *Gospel of Philip*) suggesting that this was an important connotation of priesthood. Clearly, the offering of Christian sacrifice, with which it is connected by Justin and the *Odes of Solomon*, and priestly service in general, as in Irenaeus' *Against Heresies* 4:8:3, and *Odes of Solomon* 20, (cf. Irenaeus, *Demonstration of the Apostolic Preaching* 96) are other important connotations, whilst complete dependence upon God was one for Irenaeus, but not at this time for anyone else that we know of.

Paul plays a vitally important part for Irenaeus as a source for his use of temple imagery for the Christian's body, as his numerous quotations from 1 Corinthians in *Against Heresies* 5:6:2 show, its main connotation being God's indwelling of the body by the Spirit. This was probably true of the other references noted also. Only Paul's application of the temple imagery to the individual is clearly evidenced, suggesting that the Greek emphasis on the individual was becoming more influential than the early Christian equal emphasis on the community.

All this evidence shows that second-century Christianity was not afraid to use cultic imagery and used it of the whole church's activity and of the individual Christian. It thus continued NT applications of this imagery. This makes the silence of both the NT and the second-century evidence regarding the unique priesthood of church leaders more eloquent. Whilst it is possible that this priesthood was present from NT times and through the second century, the fact that it is not clearly mentioned in the extant literature and that cultic ideas were used in other ways must persuade the unbiased historian that this is rather less likely than more.

5.3 Tertullian

When Tertullian was dealt with in section 4.3 earlier, we noted that he calls the clergy 'priests' and has a fairly rich understanding of sacrifice. This includes the eucharist, praise, an afflicted and humble heart, self-denial, martyrdom, Christians' bodies and prayer. Although the offering of the eucharist is normally performed by the clergy, the rest of these can be offered by all Christians. We are now going to examine Tertullian's significant contribution to the understanding of the general priesthood and his use of temple imagery for the church and the individual Christian.

5.3.1 The general priesthood

Some older Catholic scholars have argued that Tertullian's adoption of Montanism played a significant role in the evolution of his understanding of priesthood, although more recent ones have not done so.[96] We have already found that this was not so regarding the special priesthood, but was it so with regard to the common priesthood? As chronological a treatment as possible will be followed, with special attention to Montanist influence. Since some of the texts deal with both priesthoods, there will be some necessary overlap with the discussion in section 4.3.2.

Although there is a possible reference to Christians in general as priests in *To the Nations* 1:12:1, it is not mentioned in the secondary literature studied, perhaps because *sacerdos* is not definitely used, there is doubt over whether *antistes* means 'priest', and the reference is set in the mouths of pagans and is meant metaphorically.[97] These factors render its value to our discussion negligible.

---

[96] See Bardy, 'Le sacerdoce', *La Vie spirituelle* 58 (1939), 119-123; Palmer, 'Lay Priesthood', *Th St* 8 (1947), 574; Dabin, *Le sacerdoce royal des fidèles*, 71; and Ryan, 'Patristic Teaching', *Irish Theological Quarterly* 29 (1962), 32-3; but cf. Otranto, 'Nonne et laici', *Vetera Christianorum* 8 (1971), 45-7 and Faivre, *Emergence*, 45-6.
[97] For the text see Borleffs in Dekkers, E. et al (eds.), *Tertulliani Opera* (Turnhout, 1954), 30.

Several scholars[98] find a reference to the common priesthood implied in the pre-Montanist *On Baptism* 7:1-2 where Tertullian likens the baptismal anointing to

> that ancient practice by which, ever since Aaron was anointed by Moses, there was a custom of anointing them for priesthood with oil out of a horn. That is why <the high priest> is called a christ, from "chrism" which is … "anointing": and from this also our Lord obtained his title, though it had become a spiritual anointing, in that he was anointed with the Spirit by God the Father: and so <it says> in the Acts, "For of a truth they are gathered together in this city against thy holy Son whom thou hast anointed." So also in our case, the unction flows upon the flesh, but turns to spiritual profit, just as in the baptism itself there is an act that touches the flesh, that we are immersed in water, but a spiritual effect, that we are set free from sins.[99]

All Christians are clearly meant here, since all were expected to undergo baptism. Although its nature is not clarified, a connection is implied between Christ's anointing with the Spirit at his baptism, that of Christians, and the priestly anointing with oil.

The clearest pre-Montanist mention of the general priesthood arises in *On Prayer* 28.[100] Having just referred to public prayer as 'a rich victim' in 27, Tertullian begins 28:1, 'Now, this is the spiritual victim which has set aside the earlier sacrifice', whereupon he quotes Isaiah 1:11 as indicating that God does not want sacrifices. In contrast, he states that, 'The Gospel teaches what God demands', quoting from John 4:23-24 to the effect that he wants true, spiritual worshippers. He continues,

> We are the true worshippers and true priests who, offering our prayer in the spirit, offer sacrifice in the spirit – that is, prayer – as a victim that is appropriate and acceptable to God: this is what He has demanded and what He has foreordained for Himself. This prayer, consecrated to Him with our whole heart, nurtured by faith, prepared with truth – a prayer that is without blemish because of our innocence, clean because of our chastity – a prayer that has received the victor's crown because of our love for one another – this prayer we should bring to the altar of God with a display of good works amid the singing of psalms and hymns and it will obtain for us all that we ask.

---

[98] Palmer, 'Lay Priesthood', *Th St* 8 (1947), 582; Dabin, *Le sacerdoce royal des fidèles*, 70; and Otranto, 'Nonne et laici', *Vetera Christianorum* 8 (1971), 28-30.

[99] Evans, E., *Baptism*, 17.

[100] Acknowledged by Bardy, 'Le sacerdoce', *La Vie spirituelle* 58 (1939), 120; Dabin, *Le sacerdoce royal des fidèles*, 70; Ryan, 'Patristic Teaching', *Irish Theological Quarterly* 29 (1962), 33; Otranto, 'Nonne et laici', *Vetera Christianorum* 8 (1971), 33-5; Bévenot, 'Tertullian's thoughts' in de Smedt et al., *Corona Gratiarum*, 127-8; and Garrett, 'Pre-Cyprianic Doctrine' in Church and George, *Continuity and Discontinuity*, 60.

$(28:3-4)^{101}$

The main connotation of this priesthood is indisputably that of offering the sacrifice of prayer, but not just any sacrifice of prayer, rather one which issues from total self-dedication to God which is expressed in action as well as abstention: in Bévenot's words, 'this prayer we must bring to God's altar prepared like any sacrificial victim - only spiritually.'[102]

This passage proves that 'in his Catholic days Tertullian taught that there is a priesthood of the laity.'[103] However, as Bardy points out, 'the *munera sacerdotalia* [priestly functions] are not in view here.'[104] Bévenot argues that all Christians are priests here only metaphorically.[105] But as long as Christian sacrifice was understood in the transferred sense already present in the NT, then it and the priesthood associated with it were both understood metaphorically, in that 'sacrifice' and 'priesthood' no longer had the same meaning as in the OT and much of current paganism. On the other hand, many early Christians believed that in offering 'spiritual sacrifices' they were behaving as priests as much as the OT priests. To this extent their priesthood and sacrifices were understood as literally as those of the OT. Bévenot contrasts the general priesthood offering prayer with the offering of the eucharist, but both prayer and eucharist are offered to God, according to Tertullian. The priesthoods of the ordained and of the church in general are presented equally 'really' and non-metaphorically by Tertullian.[106]

Otranto feels that 'the "acceptable sacrifice" is still in line with 1 Peter 2.5.'[107] Tertullian may have had 1 Peter 2 in his general awareness in writing this, but further than that the evidence does not take us. Otranto further likens this passage to Justin's in *Dialogue* 116:3. They have in common the connection of the general priesthood with the offering of sacrifice consisting above all in praise and prayer, but Justin connects this with the eucharist as Tertullian does not. This difference is probably due only to the context, however.

A further reference to general Christian priesthood from Tertullian's

---

[101] Arbesmann et al., 185-6.
[102] Bévenot, 'Tertullian's thoughts' in de Smedt et al., *Corona Gratiarum*, 127-8.
[103] Ryan, 'Patristic Teaching', *Irish Theological Quarterly* 29 (1962), 32-3.
[104] Bardy, 'Le sacerdoce', *La Vie spirituelle* 58 (1939), 120.
[105] Bévenot, 'Tertullian's thoughts' in de Smedt et al., *Corona Gratiarum*, 128.
[106] On this subject see Otranto, 'Il sacerdozio', *Vetera Christianorum* 7 (1970), 245, commenting on first- and second-century evidence in general.
[107] Ibid., 33.

Catholic period is found in *The Shows* 16:4. Sarcastically describing what happens at shows, he says that the result is that it 'progresses to outbursts of fury and passion and discord and to everything forbidden to the priests of peace.'[108] He clearly means Christians in general here.[109] Dabin calls it a metaphorical usage; Bévenot points out that, 'the Vestal virgins are priestesses of Satan – "gehennae sacerdotes" (*ad Uxor.* I 6.3 and 5). In contrast, christian virgins should be "sacerdotes pudicitiae" (*Cult. fem.* II 12.1), just as all christians should be "sacerdotes pacis" (*Spect*, 16.4).'[110]

It does seem that *sacerdotes* is being used in a metaphorical sense in the latter two references. Although the Vestals were literal priestesses, Christian virgins are only *sacerdotes pudicitiae* ('priests of modesty') and Christians *sacerdotes pacis* ('priests of peace') as consecrated servants of each. To this extent these uses are different from the literal use noted in *On Prayer* 28:3.

Since *On Baptism* 7:1-2 and *On Prayer* 28:3-4 render it certain that the general priesthood was part of Tertullian's thought-world before he became a Montanist, the difficulties of dating the parts of *Against Marcion*, particularly with regard to Tertullian's conversion to Montanism, are less important. Barnes' latest view would make a passage in 3:7:7 pre-Montanist, Dekkers sees the whole work as pre-Montanist and Hanson argues that Tertullian 'is not writing in a specifically Montanist interest'.[111] In this passage Tertullian is explaining the meaning of the two goats of the Day of Atonement. The second, 'made an offering for sins, and given as food to the priests of the temple, marked the tokens of his second manifestation, at which, when all sins have been done away, the priests of the spiritual temple, which is the Church, were to enjoy as it were a feast of our Lord's grace, while the rest remain without a taste of salvation.'[112] The last clause ensures that all Christians are being referred to as the 'priests of the spiritual temple, which is the Church', since it contrasts them with all others who will 'fast from salvation', while they enjoy the 'sacrificial feast' of God's grace.[113] This passage again illustrates how Tertullian

---

[108] Arbesmann et al., 85.

[109] So Dabin, *Le sacerdoce royal des fidèles*, 70, Otranto, 'Nonne et laici', *Vetera Christianorum* 8 (1971), 41 and Bévenot, 'Tertullian's thoughts' in de Smedt et al., *Corona Gratiarum*, 128.

[110] Dabin, *Le sacerdoce royal des fidèles*, 70; Bévenot, 'Tertullian's thoughts' in de Smedt et al., *Corona Gratiarum*, 128.

[111] Barnes, 327-8; Dekkers, 3; and Hanson, R.P.C., *Christian Priesthood Examined*, 29.

[112] Evans, E. (ed.), *Tertullian: Adversus Marcionem* (Oxford, 1972), 191.

[113] Hanson, R.P.C., *Christian Priesthood Examined*, 29, is the only one in the secondary literature studied who mentions this as a reference to the general priesthood.

was content to use a Levitical model for the priesthood of the faithful, as in *On Baptism* 7:1-2. As there, the main connotation concerns the enjoyment of salvation, viewed here as eschatological sacrificial feast rather than as present anointing.

Two further likely references to the general priesthood in this work are in books 4 and 5. Barnes, building on Quispel's studies, views these as written later than books 1-3, after Tertullian had become a Montanist.[114] In 4:23:10-11, Tertullian views Jesus' injunction, '"Leave the dead to bury their own dead; but as for you, go and proclaim the kingdom of God"' (Lk. 9:60) as confirming the prohibitions in Leviticus 21:1 and Numbers 6:6-7 on priests and Nazirites attending their parents' funerals. He then comments, 'and I suppose it was for the <nazirite> vow and for the priesthood that he intended this man whom he had begun to prepare for preaching the kingdom of God.'[115]

Hanson alone sees a reference to the general priesthood here,[116] but this seems correct. *On Baptism* 7 has already shown that Tertullian finds a dedication and consecration, likened to that of the OT priests, belonging to all who are baptized and he uses the same passages to argue for the general priesthood later in *On Monogamy* 7:8, as we shall note below. Although he does not develop what he understands by this priesthood, it again shows that he was happy to use a Levitical model for it and that one of its major connotations was consecration to God, as in his pre-Montanist period.

The final reference to the priesthood of all Christians in *Against Marcion* is in 5:9:9 and is not mentioned in the secondary literature studied. Christ is here called 'the pontifex of the uncircumcised priesthood' which Tertullian sees as appropriate for the priest in the order of Melchizedek who was himself uncircumcised.[117] That Tertullian here intends the general priesthood is rendered certain by his contrasting of Jews in general and Christians in general in the context. He links Christ's priesthood to that of Christians in general here as he connects their anointings in *On Baptism* 7.

Tertullian once more uses 'priest' in a metaphorical sense in *On the Resurrection of the Dead* 9:2. Emphasising God's love for man's flesh, Tertullian, in a highly rhetorical passage, writes, 'Away, away with the idea that God should abandon to eternal ruin the work of His hands, the object of His mind's care, the receptacle of His breath, the queen of His

---

[114] Barnes, 326-8.

[115] Evans, E., *Adversus Marcionem*, 389.

[116] Hanson, R.P.C., *Christian Priesthood Examined*, 29.

[117] Evans, E., *Adversus Marcionem*, 567.

effort, the heir of his bounty, the priest of his worship, ...'[118] Only
Dabin cites this as a reference to the general priesthood[119] and it is not
really an allusion to that but to man's flesh as a 'dedicated servant' of
God's religion.

A passage examined in section 4.3.2 because of its relevance to the
priesthood of the clergy is found in *Chastity* 7. As we noted then,
Tertullian is arguing against the propriety of second marriages. After a
summary of the evidence on this subject, Moreschini concludes that
'Montanism has not modified Tertullian's ideas: the *Ad uxorem*
contains, at least in germ, the greater part of the arguments developed in
the following treatises. ... Tertullian's evolution concerning the problem
of marriage, if it existed at all, was, above all, an evolution of tone;
....'[120] This means that we should not see the whole context of this
passage as due mainly to the influence of Montanism. The passage itself
remains to be considered.

Beginning by basing his case on what he believed to be Levitical
legislation, Tertullian then notes that Paul prescribed only one marriage
for those 'to be chosen for the order of the priesthood.' He makes it
clear that he means the clergy by adding, 'So true is this that, as I recall,
there have been men deposed from office for digamy.' Facing the
objection that this does not apply to others, he replies,

> It would be folly to imagine that lay people may do what prests may not. For
> are not we lay people also priests? It is written: "He hath made us also a
> kingdom, and priests to God and His father." It is ecclesiastical authority
> which distinguishes clergy and laity, this and the dignity which sets a man
> apart by reason of membership in the hierarchy. Hence, where there is no
> such hierarchy, you yourself offer sacrifice, you baptize, and you are your
> own priest. Obviously, where there are three gathered together, even though
> they are lay persons, there is a church. ... Therefore, if in time of necessity
> you have the right to exercise a priestly power, you must also needs be living
> accordingly (sic.) to priestly discipline even when it is not necessary for you
> to exercise priestly powers. As a digamist will you baptize? As a digamist
> will you offer sacrifice? How much more serious a crime is it for a lay
> digamist to perform sacerdotal functions, when a priest who becomes a
> digamist is removed from his priestly office! (7:2-5)[121]

Bardy uses this text as his main proof for the assertions that 'Montanism
inspired Tertullian with a new conception of priesthood', 'in his

---

[118] Souter, A., *Tertullian: Concerning the Resurrection of the Flesh* (London, 1922), 22-3.
[119] Dabin, *Le sacerdoce royal des fidèles*, 69-70.
[120] Moreschini in Moreschini and Fredouille, 16-7.
[121] Le Saint, 53-4.

Montanist writings, Tertullian ... attributes the exercise of functions reserved to the bishops and priests to all the faithful', and 'the Church of which he thinks when he affirms that wherever there are three believers there also is the Church is the spiritual Church of Montanus and the new prophecy.'[122] Palmer, Dabin, Le Saint, Ryan and Bévenot take the same view.[123] The last criticizes Otranto for suggesting that 'Tertullian maintained, throughout, a clear distinction between the functions of the clergy and those of the laity, and that no more than "the intransigent tone" characterized his Montanism'.[124] Hanson too views Tertullian as maintaining a distinction between clergy and laity throughout, although he feels that Montanism led him to over-emphasize the priesthood of the laity, whilst Faivre too sees more continuity than contrast between the two periods.[125]

How far, then, does the text under consideration support either of these views? First, there is no indication here that Tertullian wants to remove the distinction between the 'priestly order' and the 'lay people'. Not only does he make no criticism of the selecting of some for the priestly order, but he makes it clear that the laity can only baptize, offer and be a priest 'where there is no such hierarchy' and 'in time of necessity'. Bardy argues that Tertullian only added this 'to legitimate by the case of necessity an usurpation so contrary to all the customs',[126] but this is to make modern assumptions about the customs at the time. Rather, Tertullian viewed the clergy as those who normally baptized, offered and were priests, but recognized that, when or where there was no council of presbyters,[127] then it was right for the laity to do these things in virtue of their priesthood.

Further, Tertullian had already allowed the laity's right to administer baptism, without even mentioning necessity, in his Catholic period in *On Baptism* 17:2 ('even laymen have the right'[128]). The addition of offering in *Chastity* 7:3-4 need be due to no more than the fact that in *On Baptism* 17 he was dealing only with baptism, whereas here he is dealing with the most important aspects of the priest's work. Otranto's conclusion that Tertullian 'did not intend to substitute the universal for

---

[122] Bardy, 'Le sacerdoce', *La Vie spirituelle* 58 (1939), 119-122.

[123] Palmer, 'Lay Priesthood', *Th St* 8 (1947), 574; Dabin, *Le sacerdoce royal des fidèles*, 71; Le Saint, 140, n. 53; Ryan, 'Patristic Teaching', *Irish Theological Quarterly* 29 (1962), 33; and Bévenot, 'Tertullian's thoughts' in de Smedt et al., *Corona Gratiarum*, 134-5.

[124] Ibid., n. 3, citing Otranto, 'Nonne et laici', *Vetera Christianorum* 8 (1971), 40 and 47.

[125] Hanson, R.P.C., *Christian Priesthood Examined*, 29-30 and Faivre, *Emergence*, 43-7.

[126] Bardy, 'Le sacerdoce', *La Vie spirituelle* 58 (1939), 122.

[127] So Vilela, 230 and Moreschini in Moreschini and Fredouille, 163-4, following Vilela.

[128] Evans, E., *Baptism*, 35.

the ministerial priesthood'[129] seems warranted.

Ryan argues that, as a Catholic, Tertullian taught that 'the sacred functions which belong to priests may not be carried out by the laity' and that disregard for this among the heretics had been 'severely censured' by him in *Prescription* 41.[130] Faivre asks concerning this passage, 'Was Tertullian the Catholic here contradicting a Tertullian who let his Montanist sympathies become visible in his *Exhortation to Chastity*?' But he answers his own question: 'It is only an apparent contradiction. He is complaining above all of the arbitrary way in which the heretics behave.'[131] This is particularly evident in 41:6: 'Their ordinations are performed haphazardly, lightly, changeably', and 41:8: 'And so today they have one bishop, tomorrow another; today a deacon who tomorrow will be a lector; today a presbyter who tomorrow will be a layman. For they charge even laymen with priestly functions.'[132] In view of his allowing the laity to baptize in *On Baptism* 17 and his later identification of priesthood in *Chastity* 7:3-4 with baptizing and offering, Tertullian may well have meant that the heretics were bestowing such priestly functions on the laity on a regular rather than an exceptional basis. This would involve no contradiction at all.

There is some uncertainty over the correct Latin text of '... the dignity which sets a man apart by reason of membership in the hierarchy', but the details need not concern us here. It is the church's authority which makes the difference between the clergy and the laity. The rest of the sentence probably indicates that the honour conveyed by this difference is sanctified through the clergy's meeting.[133] This suggests that all are equally priestly but that some are constituted as a special priestly order by the Christian community.[134] The view that Tertullian wanted to underline the ecclesiastical rather than the divine origin of this distinction, as this passage has been generally

---

[129] Otranto, 'Nonne et laici', *Vetera Christianorum* 8 (1971), 39. Bardy, 'Le sacerdoce', *La Vie spirituelle* 58 (1939), 121-2, argues that Tertullian allows the laity to administer baptism because 'it's a question of an indispensable sacrament', but this is not the argument Tertullian uses in *Bapt.* 17.2 which is that, as Christ's disciples were given the right to baptize without being bishops, presbyters or deacons, so baptism can be administered by all. Evans, E., *Baptism*, 35, places these words in inverted commas and explains (98) that he views them as 'a supposed interlocutor's objection', producing 'a somewhat unwilling concession' from Tertullian, but this is not an interpretation necessitated by the text itself.

[130] Ryan, 'Patristic Teaching', *Irish Theological Quarterly* 29 (1962), 33.

[131] Faivre, *Emergence*, 47.

[132] Refoulé and de Labriolle, 147-8.

[133] This is suggested by Fredouille's translation in Moreschini and Fredouille, 163.

[134] Faivre, *Emergence*, 47, goes further, arguing that Tertullian was reminding the clergy that this distinction only existed by the assent of the whole church and not just of the hierarchy. This is possible but uncertain.

understood,[135] seems correct in view of the contrast between the implied
"'[Christ] made us also a kingdom, and priests to God and His father'"
and the 'It is ecclesiastical authority which distinguishes clergy and
laity, ...'.

Moreover, it is not clear how such an interpretation contradicts
anything in Tertullian's earlier, Catholic writings. Ryan argues that, in
that period, the 'priesthood of the laity is essentially distinct from, and
inferior to, the divinely instituted hierarchical priesthood, which has
definite authority and definite powers.'[136] Whilst, for the purposes of his
argument concerning second marriages, he plays down the inferiority
and distinction involved, there is no indication in *Chastity* 7 that
Tertullian denies them or the authority and powers of the clergy.

Finally, the significance of the sentence, 'Obviously, where there are
three gathered together, even though they are lay persons, there is a
church' (*Chastity* 7:3) must be considered. Bévenot argues that, as a
Catholic, Tertullian, in *On Baptism* 6, had interpreted 'where three' of
the Trinity, but, as a Montanist, of the faithful as constituting the church
and being as priestly as the clergy.[137] However, for one thing, Tertullian
uses both interpretations again in his Montanist period in *On Modesty*
21:16, and, for another, even as a Catholic, Tertullian had allowed the
laity the right to baptize and held to the general priesthood.

While Montanism caused Tertullian to become more rigorist, as we
have noted regarding his attitude to second marriages, this resulted in a
change only of tone, not substance. Montanism also caused him to
emphasize the power of the Spirit more, but there is no indication that
this affected any other than the tone of his opinion of the general
priesthood, as his Catholic references to the general priesthood
illustrate. There is no evidence, as we have repeatedly noted, that he
ever sought to remove the priesthood of the ordained or to supplant
them with the laity. Whilst all Christians are priests in virtue of their
baptismal anointing, and so are eligible for baptizing and offering the
eucharist, normally it is those selected for the special, priestly order who
do these things. The difference between their priesthoods originates in
the church's decision and consists in the usual exercise of these priestly
functions.

So much time has been spent on *Chastity* 7 because of its central
importance to the debate whether Tertullian's views on the general

---

[135] So ibid. For examples, see Le Saint, 140, n. 54 and Bévenot, 'Tertullian's thoughts' in de
Smedt et al., *Corona Gratiarum*, 134.

[136] Ryan, 'Patristic Teaching', *Irish Theological Quarterly* 29 (1962), 33.

[137] Bévenot, 'Tertullian's thoughts' in de Smedt et al., *Corona Gratiarum*, 133-6.

priesthood were changed by Montanism. Now we must consider some other references to that priesthood in his Montanist writings.

In *On Monogamy* 7:7-9, Tertullian is dealing with the problem of second marriages, as in *Chastity* 7. In both he states that the law 'forbids priests to remarry' (*Monogamy* 7:7; cf. *Chastity* 7:1) and adds, in *On Monogamy* 7:8, that 'Jesus the great High Priest of the Father, clothing us with his own garment – for "those who are baptized in Christ have put on Christ" – has made us priests to God His Father, as John declares.' He then connects Jesus' prohibition on a young man burying his father (Mt. 8:21 and Lk. 9:59) with the prohibition on the priest attending any corpse including his parent's in Leviticus 21:11 to show that, by the first, Jesus 'has appointed us priests'. In *On Monogamy* 7:9 he denies, inconsistently and speciously, that Leviticus 21:11 applies to Christians, but asserts, 'We are priests in very truth and our vocation is from Christ. So also we are obliged to practice monogamy, since this is according to the ancient law of God which in those days prophesied of us in the priests who were its ministers.'[138]

Tertullian here draws a closer connection than ever between Christ's priesthood and Christians', referring to Jesus as high priest clothing Christians with himself, and, by implication, with his priesthood,[139] through baptism and so making them priests. This connection is very like that made in *On Baptism* 7:1-2 between Christ's anointing and that of the faithful after baptism (cf. *Against Marcion* 5:9:9 also), providing evidence of significant continuity in Tertullian's understanding of the general priesthood between his Catholic and Montanist periods.[140] Further, the Levitical model is used in both.

The same is true in *On Monogamy* 12:2, another passage which we considered in section 4.3.2 because of its bearing on the priesthood of the clergy. Tertullian argues, against those maintaining that Paul denies only the clergy remarriage, that it must be prohibited to all, since the bishops and clergy are taken from all the Christians (12:1). He continues,

> Indeed, whenever we are minded to exalt ourselves with swelling pride at the
> expense of the clergy, then "we are all one", then we are all priests, for "He
> hath made us priests to God and His Father"! But when we are called upon to
> be the peers of priests in discipline, we lay aside our fillets – and pair off! The
> question under consideration concerned the qualities required in men who

---

[138] Le Saint, 84-5.

[139] So Bévenot, 'Tertullian's thoughts' in de Smedt et al., *Corona Gratiarum*, 127.

[140] So Otranto, 'Nonne et laici', *Vetera Christianorum* 8 (1971), 43.

were to receive orders in the Church. (12:2)[141]

This has a special interest in the light of accusations that, as a
Montanist, Tertullian sought to break down the distinction between
clergy and laity, since he implicitly rejects the views of those who use
the claim to be all one and all priests to exalt themselves against the
clergy. Whilst willing himself to use the argument that all are priests to
press home his opinion that the prohibition of second marriages is
binding on all Christians, he takes issue with such. He accepts the
necessity of bishops and clergy in arguing from the need to take them
from amongst the laity to the need for all therefore to be married only
once (12:1) and in pointing out that 'the question under consideration
concerned the qualities required in men who were to receive orders in
the Church.' He clearly accepts the distinction between clergy and
laity.[142]

This passage is also significant in that it is the only one which
intimates a possible discontent with the special priesthood amongst the
general priesthood. Although it could be the result of Tertullian's
sarcasm, the 'whenever we are minded to exalt ourselves with swelling
pride at the expense of the clergy, then "we are all one", then we are all
priests, etc.' reads as if Tertullian is quoting some who were dissatisfied
with the clergy claiming special priesthood and reminded them of the
general priesthood taught in Scripture.

A final, possible reference to the general priesthood comes in *On
Fasting* 11:4. Here Tertullian states, 'For, indubitably, both heresy and
pseudo-prophecy will, in the eyes of us who are all priests (*antistites*) of
one only God the Creator and of His Christ, be judged by diversity of
divinity: ....'[143] The uncertainty over whether *antistes* always connotes
priesthood has been noted earlier and applies here also, but it remains a
strong possibility.

Summing up, it has been shown that Tertullian maintained belief in
the general priesthood throughout his literary career alongside his
acceptance of the special priesthood of the clergy. There is no evidence
that he sought to remove that distinction. Whilst his conversion to
Montanism caused him to emphasize the need for only one marriage
more than earlier, and to be more intransigent in his insistence on it, he

---

[141] Le Saint, 99.

[142] Bardy, 'Le sacerdoce', *La Vie spirituelle* 58 (1939), 123, interprets this passage as
showing that Tertullian agreed with those who rejected the privileges of the ordained
priesthood but wanted them to accept its obligations as well. The context, however,
demonstrates that he did not agree with them in rejecting the clergy-laity distinction.

[143] Roberts, Donaldson and Coxe, vol. 4, 225.

had already, in *On Prayer* 28, taught the need for one's life to measure up to one's priestliness for prayer to be accepted and answered. Hanson rightly points to other examples of teaching the general priesthood, e.g., in Clement of Alexandria and Origen, to show that Tertullian's emphasis 'was not merely indulging a Montanist quirk'.[144]

Tertullian did not define the relationship between the two priesthoods. Faivre says that for him 'the hierarchy appeared only as an expression of the dignity and the duties of the whole Christian people.'[145] This fits what Tertullian maintains and may have been his view. His lack of explanation of this relationship, his reminders of the general priesthood, and his possible reference to some protesting against the special priesthood raise the possibility that the general priesthood was receiving less emphasis now that that of the clergy was achieving some prominence and that Tertullian, and perhaps others, had not yet been able to reconcile the two. The evidence could be interpreted that way and would fit with what we have already noted concerning the newness of the clerical priesthood and the well-established nature of the general priesthood.

It is likely that, if Tertullian was not himself one of the clergy, and the internal evidence points in that direction as we noted in section 4.3.1, this played a part in his promotion of the general priesthood. This is psychologically likely and suggested by the way in which it is precisely in two of his mentions of the general priesthood that he identifies himself with the laity, viz., in *Chastity* 7:3 ('For are not we lay people also priests?') and *On Monogamy* 12:2 ('we ... exalt ourselves', etc.). Although both have been explained in ways that do not necessitate Tertullian's identification of himself with the laity, both fit most easily with his having been lay. This does not mean that his was a purely personal belief in the general priesthood, held only to bolster his own self-esteem. His use of it so many times in somewhat diverse ways and different writings intended to influence behaviour in the churches shows that it was a generally held belief that he could adduce.

Otranto pertinently points out that, in contrast to almost all the authors of the first two centuries, Tertullian often emphasizes the priesthood of the individual Christian. A proof of this is found in the fact that, although its echo is there, he does not quote 1 Peter 2:5 and 9 but refers to Revelation 1:6 and 5:10.[146] The individualism which we noted in some second-century authors' use of the temple metaphor is

---

[144] Hanson, R.P.C., *Christian Priesthood Examined*, 30.

[145] Faivre, *Emergence*, 46.

[146] Otranto, 'Nonne et laici', *Vetera Christianorum* 8 (1971), 44-5.

found in Tertullian in his use of the priestly metaphor.

Tertullian has a theologically rich understanding of the general priesthood, richer than any before him. In *On Baptism* 7:1-2, he links its inception with baptismal unction and Christ's anointing, hinting that Christians thus share Christ's anointing and priesthood. In *Against Marcion* 5:9:9, Jesus is called the 'pontifex of the uncircumcised priesthood', again implying a close relationship between the general circumcision and Christ's. And in *On Monogamy* 7:7-9, Jesus as high priest is said to clothe us with himself, calling us priests. This presents thought-out connections between Christ's and the general priesthood unlike any such connections between Christ's and the special priesthood. This too suggests a longer established tradition behind the general than behind the special priesthood.

More frequently than any before him, Tertullian also takes Levitical laws as models for the general priesthood, mixing Law and gospel in a way characteristic of his general hermeneutics. Although on two of these occasions he applies these laws to the clerical priesthood as well, he has the general priesthood mainly in mind, and he never takes Levitical models for the clerical priesthood on other occasions. This suggests that the later use of the Levitical model for the clerical priesthood may have been influenced by its earlier use for the general priesthood. The use of these Levitical models relates above all to complete consecration and dedication to God. This is in the background of the allusions to priestly anointing in *On Baptism* 7:1-2, to the sacrifice of prayer issuing from total devotion to God in *On Prayer* 28:3-4, to priestly devotion in *Against Marcion* 4:23:10-11, to the prohibition of remarriage in *Chastity* 7:2-5, *On Monogamy* 7:7-9 and 12:2, and it lies behind the more metaphorical usages of 'priest' in the sense of 'dedicated servant'.

Although the influence of Montanism may be seen in Tertullian's increasing emphasis on the connotations of the general priesthood concerning second marriages, there is no evidence that he ever went back on his earlier view that an expression of this priesthood is the sacrifice of prayer issuing from a pure and whole-hearted devotion to God. He thus demonstrates that he stands in the mainstream of second-century understanding of this priesthood, continuing an emphasis we have noted in Justin in particular. He also related the general priesthood to enjoyment of eschatological salvation in *Against Marcion* 3:7:7, as did Irenaeus in *Against Heresies* 5:34:3. He went outside the mainstream in deducing from it the right to baptize and offer the eucharist in case of necessity. It may be that this deduction had not been made previously because there had been no special priesthood to connect their right to do both with their priesthood.

5.3.2 Use of the temple-metaphor

Tertullian uses temple-imagery of Christ in *Against Marcion* 3:20:9: 'it was Christ rather than Solomon who was to build up the temple of God, that holy manhood in which, as in a better temple, the Spirit of God was to dwell ....' In 3:21:3, he is called 'the catholic temple of God, in whom God is worshipped'. And in 3:24:10, he is identified with the eschatological temple of heaven: Jacob 'had seen Christ the Lord, who is the temple of God and also the gate, for by him we enter heaven.'[147] Most often, however, Tertullian uses temple-imagery of the church or the individual Christian, suggesting the close links we have already noted between these and Christ.

The communal application of this metaphor is found in *On Women's Apparel* 2:1:1 in his Catholic period where he calls Christians 'the temple of God' in virtue of the Spirit's indwelling, with echoes of 1 Corinthians 3:16 and 2 Corinthians 6:16. *Against Marcion* 3:7:7, as noted in section 5.3.1 above, may be from Tertullian's Catholic period. In it he calls Christians 'the priests of the spiritual temple, which is the Church'.[148] Further, in *Against Marcion* 3:23:2, he writes of '"the wise master-builder", namely, the Holy Spirit, who is building the Church, which is the temple and home and city of God.'[149]

He continues to apply this metaphor in a communal way in his Montanist period. In *Against Marcion* 5:6:12, 1 Corinthians 3:16-17 are referred to the Christian community as that which Christians have built on the foundation of Christ to show that the Spirit of the same God who created the church dwells in it.[150] In *On Monogamy* 8:3 Anna is presented as showing 'what manner of persons should be adherents of the spiritual temple, that is, the Church.'[151] The metaphor is, not surprisingly, used several times in *On Modesty* to bring out the holiness of the church: in 1:9, it is called 'the earthly temple of God' in the context of its true holiness; in 19:25 Tertullian gives a list of vices ending 'and every other profanation of God's temple'; and in 20:1 all

---

[147] Evans, E., *Against Marcion*, 235 and 237.

[148] Ibid., 191.

[149] Ibid., 243. This is very like a passage in *Against the Jews* 13.25, omitted here because the latter chapters of that book are regarded as possibly not by Tertullian.

[150] Ibid., 547.

[151] Le Saint, 86.

immodesty is to be removed from the 'temple of God'.[152] There is nothing unusual about any of these references, Tertullian here adhering to the mainstream of what had been taught before.

This is true also of the application of this metaphor to the individual Christian. This only occurs once in Tertullian's Catholic period, but this is enough, together with the passages we have noted concerning the collective or communal application, to show that it was an active part of his thought-world. This reference comes in *To His Wife* 2:3:1 where, proving that Christians should not marry pagans, Tertullian quotes 1 Corinthians 3:16, 6:15 and 6:19-20 as applying to such marriages.[153] There are several applications of the temple-metaphor to bring out the holiness of the Christian in his Montanist writings: one in *Against Marcion* and four in *On Modesty*.[154] Twice in *On the Resurrection of the Dead* he refers to individual Christians' bodies as temples in the context of the resurrection of the flesh.[155] And he actually uses the plural in *The Chaplet* 9:2 where he is arguing that the Jerusalem temple was not crowned so we should not be, 'for we are ... temples of God.'[156]

In both applications of the temple-metaphor, therefore, Tertullian shows that he is in the mainstream of second-century Christian belief on the subject without striking out in any new directions. Naturally, he uses them in ways which suit his own particular concerns.

5.4 Hippolytus

We noted in section 4.4 above that Hippolytus had a strong understanding of the priesthood of the clergy and of material offerings as sacrifices. Not only the eucharist and its elements, but also oil, cheese, olives, milk and honey, and water are described as sacrificial offerings. Although brought by Christians in general, the clergy offer them in a way different from others, as evinced in the denial of ordination by the imposition of hands to the widow 'because she does not offer the offering nor has she a liturgical duty.'[157] We also noted the few instances of non-material offerings mentioned by Hippolytus. One was in the ordination-prayer for the bishop where God is asked to grant him 'to please you in gentleness and a pure heart, offering to you a

---

[152] Micaelli and Munier, 147-9 and 260-263.
[153] Le Saint, 28.
[154] *Against Marcion* 5:7:4; *On Modesty* 6:17, 15:7, 16:1-3 and 21:2.
[155] *On the Resurrection of the Dead* 10:4-5 and 44:4.
[156] Kroymann, in Dekkers et al., 1052.
[157] *Apostolic Tradition* 10: Botte, 30-31.

sweet-smelling savour',[158] and the others were in interpretations of incense as Christians' self-offering.

We shall now examine Hippolytus' statements relating to the general priesthood, and Christians being a temple.

5.4.1 The general priesthood

Garrett finds 'no evidence of his teaching the priesthood of all Christians' in Hippolytus' extant writings. Lécuyer, Ryan and Eastwood imply this by either not mentioning him at all, or by quoting him only about Christians' sacrifices. Dabin cites only a passage in *Commentary on Daniel* 4:34 in which Hippolytus quotes Revelation 5:10.[159] This is not relevant to this study as he here quotes the whole of Revelation 5:1-10 to make a point which has nothing to do with Revelation 5:10 or the general priesthood.

Lietzmann, Hanson and Young, however, note a passage in the *Apostolic Tradition* 4 referred to in section 4.4 earlier as describing Christians in general as priestly.[160] It is in the context of the new bishop's prayer over the eucharist at his ordination. After a reminder of Christ's words at the last supper, the Latin version reads, 'Remembering therefore his death and resurrection, we offer to you the bread and the cup, giving you thanks because you have considered us worthy to stand before you and minister to you.' The Latin translation of the Ethiopic has much the same except that, instead of 'and minister to you', it ends, 'and to practise the priesthood.' In Botte's view, the Ethiopic and the *Testamentum Domini* support *hierateuein* ('to be a priest' or 'to exercise the priesthood'), which is the verb given in the parallel chapter of the *Apostolic Constitutions*.[161] In any case, the Latin version has strong priestly connotations.

Hanson argues that the first person plurals here show that the bishop is referring to more than just himself.[162] However, he gives no reasons why they should not refer to the bishop and the presbyters, who also have their hands on the elements during his prayer. In favour of this is the restriction of the priesthood to the bishops and presbyters in the

---

[158] *Apostolic Tradition* 3: Botte, 10-11.

[159] Garrett, 'Pre-Cyprianic Doctrine' in Church and George, *Continuity and Discontinuity*, 61; Lécuyer, 'Essai', *La Maison-Dieu* 27 (1951), 21; Ryan, 'Patristic Teaching', *Irish Theological Quarterly* 29 (1962); Eastwood, 1963; and Dabin, *Le sacerdoce royal des fidèles*, 517.

[160] Lietzmann, 176; Young, 264; Hanson, R.P.C., *Christian Priesthood Examined*, 30 and *Studies*, 96.

[161] Botte, 16-7 for the text and note (3) for the textual comment.

[162] Hanson, R.P.C., *Christian Priesthood Examined*, 30.

Apostolic Tradition 8. On the other hand, the context gives the impression that the bishop is praying on behalf of the whole church. Although the eucharistic liturgy begins with the bishop addressing those present and being addressed by them, this part ends with the invitation, 'Let us give thanks to the Lord', to which the people reply, 'It is fitting and right', and the bishop begins a prayer which is in the first person plural throughout. Further, God is thanked through Christ, 'whom in the last times you sent to us as saviour and redeemer and angel of your will, ...' It is unlikely that the bishop was speaking only for himself and the presbyters, since all Christians have been the objects of Christ's work of salvation. Moreover, our passage is preceded by references to Christ's words at the last supper, '"this is my body that is broken for you"' and '"this is my blood that is poured out for you"', which again include all Christians rather than only the bishop and presbyters; and they are separated from the passage quoted earlier only by the words, '"when you do this, do it in memory of me"', which must again include all. Also, all present would have been 'remembering therefore his death and resurrection', and our passage is followed by the request for the Holy Spirit to be sent 'upon the offering of the holy church' and for all participants to be filled with the Spirit.[163] Finally, Young points out that this interpretation 'is supported by references to the Church as the priesthood of God in Justin and Irenaeus, ...'[164]

Scholars have questioned whether all the prayer was originally as given now, Stevenson arguing that the 'remembering therefore ...' 'reads rather like a car changing gears'. Even so, he acknowledges that the present text 'implies a definite logic'.[165] Certainly, the Latin and the Ethiopic agree on this text and the internal evidence suits it.

How significant is this reference to the general priesthood? The fact that it is the only one extant in Hippolytus' writings suggests that it was not an important doctrine for him, but he was aware of it, as he was of other Christian uses of cultic language. He thus stands in the line of Justin, Irenaeus and Tertullian. It also shows, as does Tertullian's work, that acceptance of the clergy's peculiar priesthood did not rule out holding the general priesthood, although there is no attempt to relate the two. That the bishop represents the community in praying is clear, but that his and the clergy's priesthood represented the community's, whilst fitting the available evidence, is not clearly explained by Hippolytus. Further, it shows that, although offering the sacrifice of the eucharist

---

[163] Botte, 12-7.
[164] Young, 264.
[165] Stevenson, 21.

was an important part of what made the clergy priestly (cf. the prayer for the bishop in the *Apostolic Tradition* 3, in which 'the gifts' must have included the eucharist, and the instruction noted above in the *Apostolic Tradition* 10 regarding a widow not being ordained 'because she does not offer the offering', of which the same must be true), it was also part of what made the whole church priestly. Even so, Hippolytus' emphasis lies far more on the priesthood of the clergy in his use of priestly language. Also, it cannot be assumed that he viewed the Christian community as priestly only in offering the eucharist, since he uses sacrificial language of other matters as well.

5.4.2 The temple-metaphor

In Daly's view, 'the temple theme is not even mentioned in any place where [Hippolytus] is explaining his own thought.'[166] Strictly speaking, this is true. However, he refers to the church as God's sanctuary three times, twice in the ordination-prayer for the bishop in the *Apostolic Tradition* 3. God is addressed as having 'instituted leaders and priests [of Israel] and you did not leave your sanctuary without a ministry.' This is soon followed by a reference to the apostles 'who established the church in every place as your sanctuary, ...'[167] Clearly the church is in the author's mind here. Moreover, the allusion to priests ensures that he is thinking, not of just any sanctuary, but of the temple.

The third such reference is less well-attested textually since the actual allusion is given in the later Ethiopic version and the *Testamentum Domini*, but not in the earlier Latin or Sahidic. It is noted here, therefore, as only possibly in the original of the *Apostolic Tradition* 8, in the prayer for a deacon. The Latin text reads, 'give the Spirit of grace and caring to your servant [the deacon] whom you have chosen to serve your Church and to present', the Ethiopic continuing 'in your sanctuary what is offered to you by him who is established as your high priest, ...' and the *Testamentum Domini* contributing, 'in holiness at your sanctuary ....'[168] Although a reference to the area in the church-building known as a sanctuary was possible by the time the Ethiopic version and the *Testamentum Domini* were written, if this passage was in the early third-century original, then the church is most likely to have been meant.

These references are very little to base any conclusions on. They

---

[166] Daly, *Christian Sacrifice*, 361.

[167] Botte, 6-9.

[168] Botte, 26-7.

emphasize the corporate aspect of the temple-metaphor, but Hippolytus is fully aware that God indwells each Christian by his Spirit.[169] They do, however, show again that he stands in the same tradition as the other second- to third-century Christian authors examined.

5.4.3 Conclusion

Hippolytus is the first author we have studied in whose writings the priesthood of the clergy receives more attention than that of the whole church. It could be argued that this is mainly due to the nature of his extant writings, in particular that of the *Apostolic Tradition* as a liturgical treatise. The possibility remains that another factor is the increasing attention and significance being given to the priesthood of the ordained. However, more evidence from other writers is needed if such a possibility is to be any more than that.

Although the paucity of references is a problem in drawing conclusions about Hippolytus' use of cultic metaphors, in his extant works he has used sacrificial, priestly and temple ideas more of the church than the individual Christian and of the church's public worship as led by the clergy than the ordinary Christian's personal worship. Again, this impression may be due mainly or solely to the nature of Hippolytus' extant works, but it could also reflect a development in general Christian thinking, particularly that of church leaders. This too will need confirmation by evidence from other writers.

On the other hand, we have noted several similarities between his use of cultic metaphors and those of Justin, Irenaeus and Tertullian, including the connection of the general priesthood with the offering of sacrifice, the eucharist in particular.

5.5 Clement of Alexandria[170]

In section 4.5 above we noted that, for Clement, the true priest is the gnostic Christian and his sacrifices comprise the gnostic's worship. Further, Clement never calls the ordained 'priests' although he was probably aware of the practice, and uses 'sacrifice' to describe the eucharist understood as praise and prayer which are offered by the church as a whole. We are now going to examine his understanding of the general priesthood, how he viewed the relationship between ordinary

---

[169] See the *Apostolic Tradition* 16 (Botte, 38-9): 'for we all have the Spirit of God'; 42 (ibid., 100): '… put to flight by the Spirit in you.' See also the interpretations of Song 2:4-5, 3:9-10 and 4:4 in Bonwetsch and Achelis, 363, 368 and 370.

[170] As in section 4.5, 'Clement' will mean Clement of Alexandria in this section.

Christians and the priestly gnostic Christian, and how he used the temple-metaphor.

5.5.1 The general priesthood

Also noted in section 4.5 was a long passage which presented both the gnostic and ordinary Christians as priests. It begins in *Stromateis* 5:6:39:4 where the high priest is interpreted of both Christ and the gnostic Christian, the latter being depicted as 'above the other priests' and as one 'who hastens, passing the other priests'.[171] These other priests are described as having been 'washed by water, clothed in faith alone and receive the dwelling appropriate to them, ...' They are thus ordinary Christians compared as priests to the gnostic Christian as high priest. This contrast continues in 40:1 in which the gnostic Christian as high priest is said to have surpassed the ordinary priest in knowledge and holiness, and in 40:4 where Clement states that, 'in the image of the Lord, the better tried in the consecrated tribe were chosen as high priests; ....' Moreover, in 40:3, he interprets the high priest's putting off the robe he had put on to enter the holy place and washing his body of Christ's descent and of 'the one who has believed through him', probably referring to the Christian's baptism. This suggests he saw both priesthoods as beginning at baptism which is connected with the ordinary priesthood several times in this passage.[172]

Scholars commonly adduce three other passages to show that Clement taught the general priesthood,[173] although most make no distinction between the gnostic and the ordinary Christian in Clement's works and so do not consider the possibility that it is the gnostic rather than all Christians who are being referred to.[174] One passage is found in *Protreptikos* 4:59:2-3 where Clement quotes 1 Peter 2:9 whilst explaining why Christians should not pollute their ears with talk of the Greek gods' adultery. He states, 'we were consecrated as an offering to God on Christ's behalf: "we are the chosen race, the royal priesthood, a

---

[171] This and the following quotations from *Strom.* 5:6:39:4 and 40:1 are from Le Boulluec and Voulet, 88-91.

[172] Daly, *Christian Sacrifice*, 463, wrongly sees only the Levitical high priest, Christ, and 'the Christian himself (the Gnostic)' as referred to in this passage.

[173] All three are mentioned by Dabin, *Le sacerdoce royal des fidèles*, 513 and Otranto, 'Il sacerdozio', *Vetera Christianorum* 7 (1970), 242-4; two by Palmer, 'Lay Priesthood', *Th St* 8 (1947), 590-591 and Ryan, 'Patristic Teaching', *Irish Theological Quarterly* 29 (1962), 28-9; and one by Lécuyer, 'Essai', *La Maison-Dieu* 27 (1951), 45 and Daly, *Christian Sacrifice*, 473. It is surprising to find none of them mentioned in Eastwood, 73 or in Garrett, 'Pre-Cyprianic Doctrine' in Church and George, *Continuity and Discontinuity*, 53-5.

[174] An exception to this is Dabin, *Le sacerdoce royal des fidèles*, 514.

holy nation, a special people, those once not a people, who are now the people of God.'"[175] There is nothing in the context to suggest that he is thinking only of the gnostic Christian. Indeed, it involves a strong contrast between the pagan Greeks and the holy Christians. This is perhaps Clement's clearest reference to the general priesthood.

Clement's train of thought seems to be that, as bearers of the image of God which is Christ, Christians are consecrated as an offering to God for him. As bearers of Christ, they no longer belong to themselves and so are an offering on his behalf.

While 1 Peter 2:9 is quoted, and the whole section is set in the first person plural, a strong, underlying individualism is evident in the depiction of Christians as carrying around the image of God. Clement's main point in quoting 1 Peter 2:9 is to support what he has written about Christians being dedicated as an offering to God, the link being between 'consecrated' and 'priesthood'. He is aware, then, of Christians' dedication to God as both priesthood and offering.

Another passage showing that Clement knew of the general priesthood is found in a fragment from his *Adumbrationes in epistulas canonicas* which are well-attested as his,[176] but are extant mostly in fragments in Latin. The relevant section is a very brief comment on '"but you are a chosen people, a royal priesthood"'. It consists of 'priesthood on account of the oblation which is made by prayers and instructions, by which are gained the souls which are offered to God.'[177] Daly views this as referring to the gnostic Christian,[178] but the main reason for this is that he does not differentiate between the gnostic and the ordinary Christian in Clement's thought. The one indication that Clement may have meant the gnostic Christian is the expression 'by teachings', since he views the gnostic as supremely suited to teaching. However, he probably meant only the teaching by word and example which any Christian did before non-Christians or the teachings which formed the minds of all Christians.

The other passage taken to refer to the general priesthood is another fragment, also well-attested,[179] from his work *Against Judaizers*. It begins by alluding to Solomon's question in 1 Kings 8:27 as showing

---

[175] Mondésert and Plassart, 124.

[176] See the witnesses, etc. in Stählin, O., Früchtel, L. and Treu, U. (eds.), *Clemens Alexandrinus, Stromata Buch VII und VIII, Excerpta ex Theodoto, Eclogae Propheticae, Quis Dives Salvetur, Fragments* (Berlin, 1970²), XVIII-XX. Geerard, vol. 1, 138, accepts them as by Clement.

[177] Roberts, Donaldson and Coxe, vol. 2, 1161.

[178] Daly, *Christian Sacrifice*, 473.

[179] Stählin et al., XXI-XXII; Geerard, vol.1, 138.

that he understood that the true temple was celestial and spiritual, but also referred to Christ's physical body and the church. Christ dwells with men

> by the conjunction and harmony which obtains among the righteous, and which build and rear a new temple. For the righteous are the earth, being still encompassed with the earth; and earth, too, in comparison with the greatness of the Lord. Thus also the blessed Peter hesitates not to say, "Ye also, as living stones, are built up, a spiritual house, a holy temple, to offer up spiritual sacrifices, acceptable to God by Jesus Christ."[180]

Clearly all Christians, not only gnostic ones, are referred to here. The main point is not priesthood or sacrifice, nothing being made of either in the context, but being living stones which are built into a spiritual house, identified with the temple, God's dwelling-place on earth. This is, therefore, only an indirect and incidental reference to the general priesthood. It does, however, attest Clement's willingness to use the temple-metaphor corporately of the church, an idea we shall be looking at again below, and his awareness of 1 Peter 2:5.

As well as these three, other passages have been presented by individual scholars as proof of Clement's belief in the general priesthood. Dabin adduces his statement, in *Stromateis* 6:17:153:4, that the unction runs down from Christ the high priest to all his own,[181] but Clement is not relating this to the common priesthood in the context.[182] Further, Otranto points to Clement's use of the expression 'a priestly race' in *Stromateis* 7:7:36:2 as like Justin's reference to Christians as 'the true high-priestly race' in *Dialogue* 116:3 and relating to 1 Peter 2:9.[183] However, the whole context deals with the gnostic Christian and it is he of whom Clement writes, 'yes, there truly is the royal man, there is the pious priest of God.'[184] Clement is 'gnosticising' the concept of 'priestly race' here.

Clement, then, demonstrates an explicit awareness of the general priesthood which he does not of the clerical priesthood. In *Protreptikos* 4:59:2-3, it undergirds his understanding of the Christian as dedicated as an offering to God and so holy. He links it with offering sacrifice by prayer and teaching in the fragment commenting on 1 Peter 2:9, and it is mentioned indirectly and incidentally in the fragment from *Against*

---

[180] Roberts, Donaldson and Coxe, vol. 2, 1191.

[181] Dabin, *Le sacerdoce royal des fidèles*, 514.

[182] See text in Stählin , O. (ed.), *Clemens Alexandrinus, Stromata Butch I-VI* (Leipzig, 1906), 510.

[183] Otranto, 'Il sacerdozio', *Vetera Christianorum* 7 (1970), 243.

[184] Le Boulluec, 133

Judaizers. It is implied in *Stromateis* 5:6:39-40 but with emphasis on its inferiority to the high priesthood of the gnostic. Even so, it is connected with baptism and an inferior holiness and knowledge of God. In the light of the evidence adduced in section 4.5.2 earlier, Garrett's comment that 'one may ... aptly ask to what extent Clement has narrowed or constricted gnostically rather than clerically the apostolic doctrine of the priesthood of all Christians'[185] is apposite. Clement has done this, but not to the total exclusion of the general priesthood, as Garrett implies by his failure to consider any examples of him referring to it at all.

5.5.2 The gnostic and the ordinary Christian

We shall not investigate this subject fully here, but make only a survey to throw light on what we have just noted concerning Clement's constriction of the general priesthood. Because of this, it is Clement's theological understanding of their relationship more than the historical situation in the Alexandrian church[186] that we are concerned with.

Clement regards the gnostic Christian as the ideal Christian with the result that he is fully what the ordinary Christian is only partially. This means that they have many characteristics in common, but the gnostic has them to a far greater extent. In a sense they are all perfect since they are part of the church whose head is Christ.[187] They are all spiritual once they believe and have received baptism.[188] All are children of God[189] and have been regenerated and illuminated; they know what is perfect, viz., God.[190] Baptism allows them to contemplate the divine because the Holy Spirit flows into them.[191] Faith is the only means of salvation for all and God communicates himself equally and in the same way to all, with the result that there are no 'gnostics' and 'psychics' in the Logos, but all are equal and spiritual in God's eyes.[192] Clearly, Clement is combatting the views of heretical Gnostics in Alexandria, but his statements and arguments spring from personal conviction and are not just *ad hominem*. Further, Clement depicts all Christians as members of

---

[185] Garrett, 'Pre-Cyprianic Doctrine' in Church and George, *Continuity and Discontinuity*, 54-5.
[186] On this see Neymeyr, 86-93. His points about Clement's involvement in a Christian community are valid.
[187] So Marrou in Marrou and Harl, 31, adducing *Paid.* 1:5:18:4 and 1:6:27:1. See too *Paid.* 1:6:26:1.
[188] *Paid.* 1:6:36:3
[189] Ibid., 1:5:12:1 and 1:5:15:1.
[190] Ibid., 1:6:25:1.
[191] Ibid., 1:6:28:1.
[192] Ibid., 1:6:30:2-31:2.

the church[193] and so of the bride and the body of Christ.[194] As will be noted below, all are indwelt by God.

Völker stresses the importance, for Clement, of baptismal grace as 'the basis for all ethical effort ... [and] the rise to perfection.'[195] He also notes that love for God and the brethren, avoidance of evil deeds, striving after knowledge, thanksgiving and cooperation with God are expected of all the faithful.[196]

In spite of having so much in common, however, Clement regards the gnostic Christian as having surpassed the ordinary Christian so much that he alone shows what true Christianity is.[197] So, although all Christians are to strive after knowledge, some knowledge is reserved for the gnostic alone;[198] although all Christians are to pray, the gnostic's whole life is prayer and converse with God;[199] although all are assimilated to God, spiritual, elect and perfect, it is the gnostic who is so *par excellence.*[200]

That all the quotations concerning what Christians have in common come from the *Protreptikos* and the *Paidagogos* and all those concerning the gnostic from the *Stromateis* could leave the impression that Clement contradicts himself in seeking to address and please different audiences. Although his audience clearly has a fundamental influence on Clement's treatment, Völker points out that Clement uses *teleios* ('perfect') of all Christians as well as of the gnostic in *Stromateis.*[201] He also points out that Clement says faith is common to all Christians in *Stromateis* 7:2:8:1.[202]

Some things, however, the gnostic does not share with the ordinary Christian. For example, only the gnostic understands the hidden, symbolic meaning of Scripture.[203] Further, as a result of the perfection he has attained, only the gnostic no longer needs angelic mediation and is 'equal to the angels' and placed alongside the angels as serving men.[204] Moreover, as Völker notes, 'as the beginner is characterized by

---

[193] *Prot.* 9:82:6-7; *Paid.* 1:5:18:4 and 19:4; 1:6:27:2; 2:8:74:2; 2:10:110:2.

[194] *Paid.* 1:5:18:2-4 and 22:2; 1:6:32:2; 2:10:101:1; 3:12:94:3 and 101:2.

[195] Völker, *Wahre Gnostiker*, 147. See 147-152 on the benefits of baptism.

[196] Völker, *Wahre Gnostiker*, 296, 299, 362, 416 and 458.

[197] *Strom.* 7:1:1:1.

[198] Ibid., 6:9:78:5.

[199] Ibid., 7:12:73:1.

[200] Ibid., 4:26:168:2 and 7:11:68:3-5.

[201] Völker, *Wahre Gnostiker*, 450, pointing to *Strom.* 7:2:8:5: 'those made perfect through faith' (Le Boulluec, 55).

[202] Le Boulluec, 57.

[203] *Strom.* 6:15:131:3, cf. 5:9:57:1.

[204] So Völker, *Wahre Gnostiker*, 462, pointing to *Strom.* 4:12:104:1, 7:1:3:4 and 7:12:78:5-6.

faith and work produced by fear, so the gnostic is characterized by love and deeds conforming to it that lead to righteousness.'[205]

These differences mean that only the gnostic is qualified for leadership. He alone is likened to the apostles as well as the angels. As such, he is a real church leader and minister, whether recognized here on earth as such or not and he will be so regarded in heaven.[206] He is thus suited to be a teacher and spiritual guide.[207] He teaches others by word and deed, thus mediating contact and fellowship with God.[208]

The above demonstrates that there is, in Clement's thought, an organic unity between gnostic and ordinary Christians. All may strive after and achieve perfection, none is ruled out on the grounds of age, sex or social status. The gnostic grows out from amongst ordinary Christians as a flower from among the leaves of a plant. This picture fits well with the view that Clement did at times depict all Christians as priestly, but regarded the gnostic Christian as the (high) priest on the model of Christ. The ambiguities we perceive today result from his unawareness of the need to spell out this relationship as we have here.

5.5.3 The temple-image

Daly summarizes as follows: 'Clement sees both the Church and the individual Christian as the true temple, and the soul of the Christian, both collectively and individually, as the true altar. Behind this view stands a long and rich tradition .... Clement's temple theology introduces little that is specifically new, ...'[209]

Points at which Clement goes beyond the tradition are his connecting of the temple-cleansing theme with that of divine indwelling, his application of the concept of firstfruits directly to the individual Christian, and his making the reception of Christ in the eucharist almost equivalent to enshrining him as within a temple.[210] He can speak of the temple being in heaven and as including the whole church both in heaven and on earth,[211] and, betraying Hellenistic influence, he sometimes sees man as man rather than as Christian as the temple of God since man is indwelt by the Logos as Reason.[212] However, he

---

[205] Völker, *Wahre Gnostiker*, 467. See *Strom.* 4:22:135:1-4.
[206] *Strom.* 6:13:105:1-107:3.
[207] On this see Völker, *Wahre Gnostiker*, 550ff.
[208] *Strom.* 7:9:52:1.
[209] Daly, *Christian Sacrifice*, 481.
[210] On this see Daly, *Christian Sacrifice*, 482-4.
[211] Daly, *Christian Sacrifice*, 484, citing *Strom.* 5:1:13:4 and 6:14:114:1-2.
[212] In *Prot.* 1:5:3-4 and 1:11:117:4.

mainly interprets the temple as meaning the church, the individual Christian, and the gnostic Christian, at times leaving uncertainty over who exactly he is referring to.[213]

This tends to confirm what we have already noted about the relationship between gnostic and ordinary Christians and the general priesthood. Clement sees the whole church as God's temple, including ordinary Christians, but his aim is always that all should become as fully indwelt by God as the gnostic.

5.5.4 Conclusion

Clement has taken up what he has found in the church's teaching concerning the general priesthood, spiritual sacrifice and the temple, and developed it to encompass his view of the gnostic Christian as the Christian *par excellence*. It is an interesting thought that, had only his *Protreptikos* and *Paidagogos* been preserved, we would have had little awareness of his great emphasis on the gnostic Christian, whereas if only his *Stromateis* had survived, his appreciation of the whole church and the ordinary Christian would not have been known. This illustrates the dangers of assuming lack of knowledge from lack of documents. The readership at which he was aiming strongly influenced Clement in his writing, and his very strong upholding of the sacred character of all Christian people in the *Paidagogos* was partly due to apologetic purposes. Nonetheless, there is sufficient evidence to show that he was never using arguments in a purely *ad hominem* way.

Even so, it is apparent that it was the gnostic Christian who really mattered for him, and that he had some difficulty, at least at times, in appreciating ordinary Christians. This is true of the general priesthood which, in Garrett's words referred to earlier, 'Clement has narrowed or constricted gnostically'.[214] Major reasons for this were probably Clement's conception of the gnostic Christian, influenced by the educational practices of his day, their Greek philosophical bases, and heretical Gnostic views, and the state of the Christian community in Alexandria. Marrou argues from evidence in the *Paidagogos* that the general spiritual level there was mediocre, many acting as Christians within the church and as pagans without, and that a number belonged to the aristocracy with all the difficulties and temptations that raised for

---

[213] Of the church: *Strom.* 6:14:114:1-2; 7:5:29:3-5; 7:13:82:4; of the Christian: *Paid.* 2:10:110:1; *Strom.* 2:20:116:4-117:4; 3:7:62:3; 3:11:73:2; *QDS* 18:2; of the gnostic Christian: *Strom.* 4:21:131:4; 4:22:161:2; 6:7:60:2; 6:9:75:3; 7:11:64:7; 7:13:82:2-3; uncertain: *Strom.* 2.7.35.5 and 3.7.59.4.

[214] Garrett, 'Pre-Cyprianic Doctrine' in Church and George, *Continuity and Discontinuity*, 55.

genuine spirituality.[215] Faivre notes this last point particularly with reference to *Quis dives salvetur?* 36, in which Clement writes 'All the faithful, then, are good and godlike, ... There are, besides, some, the elect of the elect, ...'[216]

A credible reason suggested by Wright for Clement's emphasis on the priesthood of the gnostic to the detriment of the general priesthood is that the former may well have been viewed by Clement as devolved from Christ as the priestly mediator between the spiritual and physical orders to the gnostic Christian as such a mediator. This would not apply to the ordinary Christian who is not a mediator or at least not one in the same way.[217]

5.6 Origen

In section 4.6 we noted that the priestly figure *par excellence* for Origen is the 'perfect' or 'spiritual' Christian, as the gnostic is for Clement. We also noted that, unlike Clement, Origen does use priestly language of the ordained, but that his view of priestliness is largely determined by his view of the perfect Christian. The priestly functions which predominate, therefore, are studying, preaching and teaching God's word, and exercising church discipline, since the qualities of the perfect Christian make him ideally suited for these. It is no surprise, moreover, to find that Origen's understanding of sacrifice, whilst including the eucharist, is stronger on ideas of holy living, self-denial, prayer and understanding God's word. We shall now examine occasions on which he mentions the general priesthood, his view of the relationship between perfect and ordinary Christians, and his use of temple-imagery.

5.6.1 The general priesthood

Of Origen's early works only the *Peri Archon* and *Commentary on John* 1-2 have survived.[218] The former contains nothing relevant to this study and the latter contains just one relevant passage, but this relates only to the priesthood of the perfect.[219] As a result there are not adequate data

---

[215] Marrou in Marrou and Harl, 62-3.

[216] Faivre, *Emergence*, 56-7; Roberts, Donaldson and Coxe, vol. 2, 1218.

[217] Wright, D.F., in a personal communication as my supervisor. See *Strom.* 7:9:52:1 in particular.

[218] Nautin, 368-386 and Crouzel, *Origène*, 66-7, were consulted concerning the dates of Origen's works.

[219] *C. Jn.* 1:2(3-4): Origen likens the Levites, priests and high priests to those who devote themselves fully to study of the word and God's service, distinguishing such from the majority who attend to the things of this life and so are like the ordinary Israelites.

on which to base any conclusions regarding developments in Origen's thought concerning the general priesthood.

Vogt describes Origen's very nuanced approach to the general priesthood. He points out that Origen deals with this subject mainly in his homilies on the historical books of the OT, which contain God's demands on his covenant people. He continues,

> Origen explains them in a far-reachingly moral way, i.e., he takes up from them directions for the Christian life and spiritual progress. So also the concept of the common priesthood of believers emerges here not primarily as a statement about the special worth of the baptized, even if this also is meant, but as the embodiment of the duties or works to which Christians see themselves called. Origen impresses on his audience that they are said to be a "chosen people, a royal priesthood, a people belonging to God." But, although this is said in Scripture, it does not at all hold true of all believers. To be sure it does not rest with them, but the statement is at the same time an obligation that only becomes true through believers' own wills. ... Faith alone, without penetration into the deeper meaning, does not yet make a person into a priest; anyone who only believes occupies a lower rank and seems therefore to possess the common priesthood at most potentially.[220]

Taken as they stand, Origen makes contradictory statements about the general priesthood. On the one hand, he states or implies that all Christians are priests. For example, in *Homilies on Joshua* 7:2 Origen comments on the priests' blowing of the trumpets at Jericho,

> each of us must accomplish these things in himself. You have Jesus within you to lead you by faith, so make yourself "hammered out trumpets" if you are a priest; indeed, because you are a priest – "for" you have been made "a royal people" and you are called "a holy priesthood" – make yourself hammered out trumpets from the holy Scriptures. From them draw out thoughts and words for that is why they are called "hammered out trumpets". Sound them, that is, sound them "in psalms, hymns and spiritual songs", in prophetic symbols, in the mysteries of the law, in apostolic teachings.[221]

The 'each of us', the quotation of 1 Peter 2:9, and above all the 'because you are a priest' can only mean that he views each of his Christian hearers as a priest. They are to do such things because they are already priests, not in order to be priests. Nonetheless, his emphasis is on their activity as priests in living out what the Scriptures teach and in worship,

---

[220] Vogt, 112; cf. Lécuyer, 'Sacerdoce', *Vetera Christianorum* 7 (1970), 257: 'all the baptized have been anointed with a priestly unction. But there are conditions for this priesthood to become worthy of the name and be truly effective ....'

[221] Jaubert, 200. Vogt, 112, cites this in support of the statement quoted above. Schäfer, 49, also sees a reference to the general priesthood here.

and the 'if you are a priest' conveys a degree of doubt at the same time as he makes the assertion 'because you are a priest'.

In a number of other passages too, as we shall see below, Origen writes as if all Christians are priests. On the other hand, he sometimes states or implies that they are not all priests. In *Homilies on Numbers* 22:1 he says that,

> It often happens that there are not a few of our brothers who do not have a high or profound intelligence .... Such a man does not understand anything, he is dead to spiritual intelligence, but if he has produced ... works of service and obedience to God's commands, he will receive an inheritance of land with God's people. Doubtless he will not be able to be counted among those whose "portion is the Lord", he will not be able to be taken in the number of the ministers and priests, but in his humble order he will receive an inheritance in the Promised Land ....[222]

Méhat holds that deacons and bishops as well as the perfect are meant by 'ministers and priests' here,[223] and a degree of ambiguity has to be admitted, but the qualities expected are all those of the perfect for Origen. If they are the true priests, then not all Christians are priests, although they will still get to heaven.

Other passages too, as we shall find, imply that not all Christians are priests. Is Vogt right then? Did Origen really believe in the general priesthood? Or did he see all Christians only as potential priests, needing to actualize their priestliness through their own efforts? We are going to consider the rest of his texts relating to this priesthood in order to attain as full as possible a picture before we draw final conclusions.

Origen alludes to 1 Peter 2:5 and 9 more frequently than any other we shall consider. However, at times he uses them to refer to matters other than the general priesthood. On one occasion he quotes 1 Peter 2:9 when explaining the Jews' value to God and their desire to avoid moral contamination by those around them.[224] Twice he quotes it to illustrate the kingship of the apostles and of all believers.[225] He also twice quotes 1 Peter 2:5 of the church when explaining Jesus' statement in John 2:19-21 about raising the temple in three days.[226] Nothing is made of the concept of priesthood so that it is almost incidental. These passages

---

[222] Méhat, 425-6.

[223] Ibid., n. 4.

[224] *CC* 4:32.

[225] *H. Num.* 12:2 and *H. Judg.* 6:3:

[226] *C. Jn.* 10:35(20) and 39(23). Ryan, 'Patristic Teaching', *Irish Theological Quarterly* 29 (1962), 29 and Garrett, 'Pre-Cyprianic Doctrine' in Church and George, *Continuity and Discontinuity*, 57, cite the latter as one of Origen's references to the general priesthood.

show, however, that Origen could interpret the temple of the whole church and that he could link this with the idea of the 'holy priesthood' in the same way as the author of 1 Peter.

In *Homilies on Numbers* 4:3, 1 Peter 2:9 is cited in a context which deals solely with the priesthood of the perfect.[227] Having explained that priests have had 'the secrets of the mysteries of wisdom' vouchsafed to them, he exhorts them not to divulge these secrets 'to inferiors, that is, to the ignorant' plainly and fully for their own good. He concludes with an exhortation that 'we must show ourselves such that we are proved worthy of the order of priesthood', reminding his hearers of 1 Peter 2:9.[228] He wants what he is saying to apply to all his hearers, who are potentially perfect, and so he exhorts them to become such. This usage constricts the general priesthood to the perfect.

Interestingly, after developing the ideas of the priesthood of the perfect in *Homilies on Numbers* 5:1-3, he adds, 'But for fear that these excessive precautions to conceal and veil should discourage and overwhelm our hearers, we are going to try to uncover some of these things out of those that there is no danger for us to reveal and no sacrilege for you to see, since, as we said above, we are called "a royal race and a priesthood, a holy nation and a people belonging to God".'[229] He then interprets the furniture of the tabernacle in terms of the degrees of merit and grace of different Christians. This brings out the ambivalence of Origen's view of priesthood. On the one hand, only the perfect are true priests; on the other, all Christians are priests. Because of his multi-layered hermeneutic, he can interpret Scripture of either or both. It also brings out his pastoral and hortatory preoccupations in these homilies and his desire that all Christians should ultimately be perfect priests.

That all Christians are priests is again clear in *Homilies on Leviticus* 6:2, as is Origen's denial that this is true of all in the church. He exhorts his hearers to listen to his exposition of the priest's or high priest's consecration 'because, according to the promises of God, you also are priests of the Lord. "For you are a holy race and a priesthood."'[230] As Moses had to wash the priests before clothing them, so each of his hearers has to be washed in baptism before being clothed with Christ. Likening baptism, therefore, to the anointing and consecration of the

---

[227] It is so understood by Crouzel, *Origène et la 'connaissance mystique'*, 157, 409 and 492; see too Méhat, 106, n. 1. Dabin, *Le sacerdoce royal des fidèles*, 522-3 and Schäfer, 56, n. 35, find references to the ordained here but the context tells against this.
[228] Doutreleau, 112-3.
[229] Ibid., 130-131.
[230] Barkley, 118.

priests, he writes, 'For there are many priests but there are those whom the Law has not washed and the Word of God has not made pure and the divine Word has not cleansed from the filthiness of sins.' The context does not mention church leaders so he still has the common priesthood in mind.[231] He is, then, accusing many who claim to be Christians and so priests of not being true Christians or priests because, although they have received baptism outwardly, they have not changed inwardly.

This need for internal holiness is an important connotation of priestliness for Origen. It is again evinced in *Homilies on Leviticus* 9:6 where Origen interprets the high priest's expulsion of the scapegoat on the Day of Atonement in terms of the Christian expelling 'evil thoughts, evil desires', assimilating such to Christ.[232] Similarly, in *Homilies on Leviticus* 13:5, commenting on the fact that God has given Aaron and his sons the privilege of eating the bread in the holy place, Origen describes them as '"an elect race, a priestly race", to whom God gave this portion of holy things which all we who believe in Christ now are.'[233] He locates the holy place in the pure heart or rational mind where the word of God is to be received, the last words quoted showing that he views all Christians as having such.

Another general reference to Christians as priests is found in *Homilies on Joshua* 1:5. Expounding the meaning of the stalks of flax in which Rahab had hidden the spies in Jericho, Origen says, 'The linen is the priestly clothing, which means, either the priestly summit handed over to those who were to be invited – as the Apostle Peter says: "You are a holy nation, a kingdom of priests" – or certainly, where it is a question of priests in the symbolism of the law, there was hidden the secret vocation of this people that comes "from among the Gentiles".'[234] Both sides of the alternative given here seem to involve the general priesthood, and its calling by God.

The need for priestly holiness as expressed in giving glory to Christ comes out in *Homilies on Leviticus* 9:2. Having interpreted the high priestly ornaments as referring to Christ, Origen concludes, 'each of us also ought to adorn his head with priestly ornaments. ... And whoever acts so that he brings glory to Christ out of his deeds, he has adorned his "head who is Christ."'[235]

---

[231] So Dabin, *Le sacerdoce royal des fidèles*, 520; Vogt, 112; and Schäfer, 48 and 92.

[232] Barkley, 188. Schäfer, 48, sees this as a reference to the general priesthood.

[233] Barkley, 243. Only Ryan, 'Patristic Teaching', *Irish Theological Quarterly* 29 (1962), 29-30, cites this passage of the general priesthood.

[234] Jaubert, 104-6. Only Dabin, *Le sacerdoce royal des fidèles*, 523, cites this of the general priesthood.

[235] Barkley, 180. Only Dabin, *Le sacerdoce royal des fidèles*, 518, cites this as a reference to

Holiness in the sense of dedication to, and reliance on, God is connoted by priestliness in *Homilies on Genesis* 16:5. Contrasting Pharaoh's provision of land for his priests with the Lord's failure to so provide, Origen exhorts, 'observe all the priests of the Lord and notice what difference there is between the priests, ...' He then quotes Christ's words about renouncing all to follow him and exhorts his hearers, 'let us hasten to pass over from the priests of Pharao ... to the priests of the Lord, who have no portion in the earth, whose "portion" is "the Lord."'[236] This is more likely to refer to believers in general than to the ordained.[237] The difference between them is that some cultivate the soil, not the mind, and attend to the fields and not the Law, whereas others give up everything to follow Christ and rely on God alone. Origen seems not to have had a clearly thought-out understanding of the general priesthood here, with the 'priests of the Lord' perfect Christians and the 'priests of Pharao' ordinary ones, but rather to be responding to the text in a homily. It shows that he could question whether all Christians are living the way priests should and exhort them to do so.

Other important qualities of priestliness for Origen include faith and knowledge, especially the understanding of Scripture, as was apparent earlier in *Homilies on Joshua* 7:2. Whilst this is especially true of the perfect, it is also true of Christians in general. So, in *Homilies on Leviticus* 4:6, Origen comments on the fact that there was always to be fire on the altar by exhorting his hearers, 'And you, if you want to be a priest of God, as it is written, "For every one of you will be priests of the Lord", hear that there is always to be "fire on the altar." For it is said that you are "an elect race, a royal priesthood, an acquired people." ... Therefore, let the "fire" of faith and the "light" of knowledge be kindled in you.'[238] The main purpose of the 'if you want to be a priest of God' is again hortatory and again illustrates Origen's desire for all Christians to live out their God-given priesthood.[239]

Similarly, in *Homilies on Leviticus* 9:8, Origen interprets the composition of the fine incense to be burnt on the altar of justice, piety, continence, prudence and all such virtues. He adds, 'But also we do not think it useless that it added "fine." For it does not want him who strives toward perfection to understand the word of God crassly or carnally but to examine the fine and subtle sense in these, ...' Although he is

---

the general priesthood.

[236] Heine, 222.

[237] So Vogt, 45, against Vilela, 89 and Schäfer, 85-7.

[238] Barkley, 78.

[239] Dabin, *Le sacerdoce royal des fidèles*, 520; Vogt,112; and Schäfer, 46 and 48, view this as a reference to the general priesthood.

thinking of the perfect here, three sentences later he continues, 'For it is necessary for each of us to offer something in the tabernacle of God, something even with priestly clothing, but something also that ascends by the hand of the high priest to God himself ....'[240] Again, while he has a special place in the church and in God's plans for the perfect, he wants all Christians to tend toward that perfection.

This connection of virtues and the knowledge of God and Scripture with priestliness relates also to Origen's depiction of the mind as the temple or priest. So, commenting on the high priest's garments in *Homilies on Leviticus* 6:5, he states, '... you too can function as a high priest ... if you would prepare your garments with zeal and vigilance; ....'[241] It continues with a series of such conditions, before concluding, 'even if you are hidden and unknown by men, with God you exercise the priesthood within the temple of your mind.'[242] Although this exposition makes it clear that Origen views the perfect as the true high priests, he both holds out the possibility of all becoming such and implies that all can act in a high priestly fashion in so far as they persevere in the paths of virtue and study of God's word.[243] One of these paths is that the grace of baptism should endure uncontaminated.

In *Homilies on Leviticus* 1:5, Origen states, 'The priest, and his sons, is in you the mind which is also its understanding in you who are rightly called a priest and "sons of a priest," for they are the only ones who perceive God and are capable of the knowledge of God. Therefore, the divine word desires that you offer your flesh to God in purity with reasonable understanding, as the Apostle says, ...' and he quotes from Romans 12:1. He goes on to differentiate these from 'others who offer their flesh as a whole burnt offering but not through the ministry of the priest.'[244] These possess only outward chastity of body, not inward chastity of spirit, being stained by vices such as pride and greed. Such are excluded from the kingdom so that Origen's readers are encouraged to be chaste in both body and spirit like Christ.

Schäfer sees Origen as referring to church leaders as priests here,[245] but Origen quotes Romans 12:1 and addresses in the singular each

---

[240] Barkley, 193.

[241] Ibid., 125.

[242] This is a literal translation of the Latin which is found in Borret, M. (ed.), *Origène: Homélies sur le Lévitique* (Paris, 1981), 290.

[243] Vogt, 32, sees this passage as an allusion to the general priesthood, while Trigg, *Origen*, 141-2 sees it as alluding to the priesthood of 'the inspired exegete.' They are commenting on different parts of the passage.

[244] Barkley, 37.

[245] Schäfer, 91-2; cf. 46, where he cites this verse regarding the believer's sacrifice.

member of a congregation which is unlikely to have consisted of only the ordained. Nor is he distinguishing between perfect and ordinary Christians, it would appear, since the 'others' are excluded from the kingdom. Rather, all Christians are to offer themselves to God and have a priestly mind capable of knowing and understanding God.

In *Homilies on Exodus* 9:4,[246] Origen likens the tabernacle to the church and states that we can each build a tabernacle by developing virtues and responding to God's word, with an altar on which to offer sacrifices of prayers, good deeds and vices. He then interprets the furniture of the tabernacle in terms of spiritual virtues, culminating in the high priest's adornments:

> For that part which is the most precious in man can hold the office of high priest. Some call it the overseer of the heart, others, rational understanding, or intellectual substance, but whatever it is called, it is that part of us in which we can have a capacity for God. Let that part in us, therefore, as a kind of high priest, be adorned with garments and costly jewels, with a long linen priestly garment.[247]

These 'garments and costly jewels' include chastity, good works, the truth of the gospel and the trinity, holiness, and speaking out about the last times. 'In this manner, therefore, our inner man is adorned as high priest to God that he may be able to enter not only the sanctuary, but also the Holy of Holies; .... The sanctuary can be those things which a holy way of life can have in the present world. But the Holy of Holies ... is, I think, the passage to heaven ....' Origen clearly wants all his hearers to be or have such tabernacles (he sums up 'that each of us also might be zealous to make a tabernacle for God within himself'), adorned as such high priests. He is not concerned with a distinction between perfect and ordinary Christians, although he tends to imply that only those who attain to these virtues are high priests. This was not his intention which was rather to exhort all Christians to become such.

In *Contra Celsum* 8:17-19, we find a similar linkage of altar, sacrifice and priestliness with the mind in a passage already noted in section 4.6.4. Replying to Celsus' reproaches that Christians have no altars, Origen states, 'our altars are the mind of each righteous man, from which true and intelligible incense with a sweet savour is sent up,

---

[246] Vogt, 112, cites, 'Let that part in us, therefore, as a kind of high priest' in support of his assertion, noted earlier, that for Origen, the priesthood of all Christians 'does not rest with them, but the statement is at the same time an obligation that only becomes true through believers' own wills.'

[247] Heine, 343-4.

prayers from a pure conscience' (8:17). In the following chapter he
adds, 'all Christians try to set up such altars as we have mentioned ...'
and in 8:19 he quotes 1 Peter 2:5 to argue that Christians do not build
lifeless temples but the temple of the body looking to its future
resurrection.[248] As in two passages noted earlier, Origen is mentioning
the general priesthood only in passing and because 1 Peter 2:5 comes
into his mind when he is dealing with the idea of the temple. However,
the use of cultic vocabulary is more extensive here, since the ideas of
altar and sacrifice are so developed, and the similarities to other
passages noted suggest he had the general priesthood in mind.[249]

As noted in several references above, another major connotation of
the general priesthood for Origen is the offering of spiritual sacrifices
such as prayer, good deeds, vices, and ourselves in holiness. This theme
is taken up more fully in other passages. In *Homilies on Leviticus* 9:9,
Origen interprets the room in the tabernacle or temple accessible to all
the priests as the church, 'For all who have been anointed with the
chrism of the sacred anointing have become priests, just as Peter also
says to all the Church, "But you are an elect race, a royal priesthood, a
holy people." Therefore, you are "a priestly race," and because of this
you approach the sanctuary.'[250] This is an unequivocal statement,
similar to that in *Homilies on Joshua* 7:2 noted near the beginning of
this section, that all who have been baptized are priests.[251] Origen
continues, 'But each one of us also has in himself his whole burnt
offering and he himself lights the altar of his whole burnt offering that it
may always burn.' As examples of these sacrifices he mentions
renouncing all to follow Christ, martyrdom, dying for brethren, justice
or truth, and dying to the world. If I offer any of these, 'I ... myself
become the priest of my offering.' This list makes us think of what
Origen expected of the perfect and again illustrates that he wants all
priests ideally to become such. This is made clear by his further
comment, 'Blessed is he whose coals of his whole burnt offering he
finds ... living and ... fiery .... Blessed is he in whose heart he finds so
subtle, so fine, and so spiritual an understanding and so composed with
a diverse sweetness of virtues ....'

---

[248] Chadwick, 464-6.
[249] Dabin, *Le sacerdoce royal des fidèles*, 520, lists this as a reference to the general priesthood.
[250] Barkley, 196.
[251] So Dabin, *Le sacerdoce royal des fidèles*, 518; Daniélou, 57; Ryan, 'Patristic Teaching', *Irish Theological Quarterly* 29 (1962), 28; Eastwood, 77; Vilela, 62; Lies, 201; Schäfer, 46; and Garrett, 'Pre-Cyprianic Doctrine' in Church and George, *Continuity and Discontinuity*, 57.

This development is again clear in *Homilies on Joshua* 9:1, where, commenting on Joshua's construction of an altar for sacrifice after the destruction of Ai, Origen says, 'All we who believe in Christ Jesus are said to be "living stones" according to what Scripture announces' and then quotes 1 Peter 2.5.[252] Having explained that the strongest stones, i.e., Christ and the apostles and prophets, make up the foundations, he adds, 'But in this building of the church there must also be an altar. And so I think that all those among you "living stones" who are capable of this and ready to make time for prayer to offer entreaties to God night and day and to sacrifice the victims of their supplications, are those from whom Jesus builds an altar.' While seeing all Christians as 'living stones', Origen implies a differentiation between them, only those devoted to prayer night and day being used for the altar. He achieves a delicate balance here between the priestly dignity of all Christians and the enhanced priesthood of those who merit it.

Origen also quotes 1 Peter 2:5 in *Commentary on John* 13:13 where he is commenting on the true Jerusalem which he identifies as 'the Church that is built of living stones. This is the place of the holy priesthood, the place where spiritual sacrifices are offered to God by people who are spiritual ....'[253] The references to the church and the spiritual leave us with an ambiguity which is probably to be resolved by assuming that, on this occasion, Origen was viewing all Christians as spiritual.

There is less ambiguity when he quotes 1 Peter 2:9 in *Homilies on Leviticus* 9:1. Origen says that the law concerning the high priest's preparation for entering the Holy of Holies concerns and applies to all Christians,

> For it commands that we know how we ought to approach the altar of God. For it is upon the altar that we offer our prayers to God that we may know how we ought to offer, certainly that we lay aside "sordid clothes" which are the uncleanness of the flesh, the vices of habits, the stains of passion. Or are you ignorant that to you also, that is, to all of the church of God and to the people of believers, the priesthood was given? Hear what Peter says about the faithful: "You are an elect race, royal, priestly, a holy nation, a chosen people." Therefore, you have a priesthood because you are "a priestly nation," and for this reason "you ought to offer an offering of praise to God," an offering of prayers, an offering of mercy, an offering of purity, an offering of justice, an offering of holiness.[254]

---

[252] Jaubert, 244.

[253] Heine, 85.

[254] Barkley, 177.

There can be no doubt that Origen has the general priesthood in mind here,[255] the 'because you are "a priestly nation"' reminding us of the 'because you are a priest' in *Homilies on Joshua* 7:2. Moreover, the 'Or are you ignorant that to you also ...' shows that his hearers were thoroughly familiar with this idea.[256] Even so, he is clearly concerned that they should offer sacrifices in a worthy manner.

Finally,[257] in *Contra Celsum* 8:73-74 Origen defends Christians against Celsus' accusation that they are unwilling to take up arms and fight for the Emperor. He points out that even non-Christians do not make priests fight so that they can continue to offer sacrifice and continues, 'If, then, this is reasonable, how much more reasonable is it that, while others fight, Christians also should be fighting as priests and worshippers of God keeping their right hands pure and by their prayers to God striving for those who fight in a righteous cause and for the emperor who reigns righteously, ...' Moreover, Christians do not do this for show; rather, 'our prayers are made in secret in the mind itself, and are sent up as from priests ....'[258] Here, for the first time, we meet the idea of the Christian priesthood as interceding for the Roman Empire,[259] though alongside other ideas which are familiar to us from elsewhere in Origen's writings.

We could examine a large number of other passages in Origen's works in which priesthood is dealt with or mentioned but which bear on the priesthood of the perfect.[260] However, considerations of time and space prevent us from doing this, which brings the danger of giving an unbalanced impression of Origen's view of priesthood. As we have mentioned before, and as has become apparent even through the passages studied here and in section 4.6.3, the true priest for Origen is the Christian who is like Christ and so is perfect. Nonetheless, he unambiguously believes in the general priesthood, as is clear from the passages studied above from *Homilies on Joshua* 7:2, *Homilies on*

---

[255] So Dabin, *Le sacerdoce royal des fidèles*, 518; Daniélou, 48; Ryan, 'Patristic Teaching', *Irish Theological Quarterly* 29 (1962), 28; Eastwood, 79; Vilela, 62; Schäfer, 45; and Garrett, 'Pre-Cyprianic Doctrine' in Church and George, *Continuity and Discontinuity*, 57.

[256] A point made by Palmer, 'Lay Priesthood', *Th St* 8 (1947), 580, although he refers, in n. 16, to homily 8 instead of 9.

[257] Vogt, 86 and Lies, 200, rightly view a passage in *H. Lev.* 15:3 as indicating the priesthood of the perfect, although Schäfer, 48, sees it as referring to the general priesthood. Vilela, 62, n. 11, and Schäfer, 48, find a reference to the common priesthood in *H. Num.* 24:2, but it is not clearly implied there.

[258] Chadwick, 509.

[259] Pointed out to me by Wright, D.F., in a personal communication as my supervisor.

[260] See *C. Jn.* 1:2(3-4), 13:13, *H. Lev.* 1:4, 4:9, 6:3, 6:5, 6:6, 13:3, 13:6, *H. Num.* 1:3, 3:3, 4:3, 5:1, 6:1, 10:1, 10:3, 11:6, 23:4, 27:4, *H. Josh.* 2:1, 9:5, 17:2-3, *PE* 28:8-10 and *EM* 30. There is some ambiguity in some of these, but they seem to me to refer to the perfect.

Leviticus 9:1 and 9:9 in particular. However, he teaches that priesthood in overwhelmingly hortatory contexts, and, in most cases, with the aim of persuading his hearers and readers to so live out their priesthood that they become the perfect. Vogt, therefore, is very near the truth in the passage we quoted at the beginning of this section. His one fault is that he does not allow adequately for Origen's genuine acceptance of the general priesthood. This in turn may be because he does not allow sufficiently for Origen's multi-layered hermeneutic which allows him to interpret the Scriptures concerning priesthood in so many ways that complete consistency is not to be expected.[261]

As a result, Origen can write of the ordained, the perfect and all Christians as priests without attempting to relate them to each other. However, it is the perfect who are priests *par excellence* because they are most like the high priest, Christ. This means that he wants both the ordained and Christians in general to approximate as closely as possible to this ideal of priesthood,[262] so that, when he begins by interpreting a passage in terms of the general priesthood, he often develops his interpretation towards the priesthood of the perfect which he wants all to attain. His overall picture of priesthood is thus like Clement's in the tendency to constrict it to the perfect, who are Clement's gnostics, without abandonment of the general priesthood.

The major connotations of the general priesthood for Origen, then, relate closely to those of the priesthood of the perfect: holiness, expressed in the eradication of vices and the cultivation of virtues and dedication to God; the offering of spiritual sacrifices, expressed in the same terms plus devotion to prayer, good deeds, and the spiritual understanding of God and his word; and the mind as that by which we can receive God and his mysteries.

In the last Origen betrays philosophical Hellenistic[263] as well as biblical influence. At times, however, the influence of church tradition is allied to that of the Bible as he traces the general priesthood to baptism and the reformation meant to precede it (*Homilies on Leviticus* 6:2, 6:5 and 9:9).[264] As far as the Bible is concerned, it is evident from our study above that 1 Peter 2:9 and, to a lesser extent, 2:5 were often in his mind when he commented on passages from the Bible which

---

[261] So Lécuyer, 'Sacerdoce', *Vetera Christianorum* 7 (1970), 264: 'it is obvious that Origen never intended to write a treatise on priesthood; it would therefore be futile to attempt to make a perfectly coherent synthesis.'

[262] On this see Vogt, 117.

[263] Méhat, 198, n. 1 sees Stoic influence here.

[264] On this see Palmer, 'Lay Priesthood', *Th St* 8 (1947), 585; Ryan, 'Patristic Teaching', *Irish Theological Quarterly* 29 (1962), 39-40; Daniélou, 57; and Schäfer, 51.

referred to priesthood and temple.[265] Very important too was the Levitical priesthood which, as we have seen, he could interpret in terms of the perfect, Christians in general, the ordained, and Christ himself.

There is ambiguity in Origen's treatment of the relationship between Christ's and Christians' priesthoods produced by his freedom to interpret in different ways for different purposes. He often interprets the Levitical priesthood in terms of both, thereby suggesting a close relationship between the two, but in *Commentary on John* 1:2(3), 'Christ is a priest according to the order of Melchisedech, whereas Christians are priests ... according to that of Aaron.'[266] However, Origen makes this distinction out of the desire not to elevate men as high priests to the level of Christ as high priest. This is the only time he makes this distinction, as far as I am aware. Whilst the Christian priesthood is clearly inferior to Christ's and dependent on Christ's in that Christians' offerings reach God through Christ, according to *Homilies on Leviticus* 9:8, and Christians as priests are washed and clothed with Christ, according to *Homilies on Leviticus* 6:2, Ryan goes too far when he states that 'beyond this relation of dependence Origen sees nothing common in Christ's priesthood and that of the faithful.'[267] This is because Origen clearly depicts Christ's fulfilment of the priesthood as an example for Christians in *Homilies on Leviticus* 4:6 and he often interprets the Levitical priesthood in terms of both Christ and Christians.

Origen, then, has a complex and ample understanding of Christian priesthood which undoubtedly has its closest similarities in Clement, but has links with others too.

5.6.2 The perfect and the ordinary Christian

It has already become apparent that Origen's view of the relationship between the perfect and the ordinary Christian was basically the same as Clement's, viz., an organic one. They are both priestly, only the perfect are more so, indeed, much more so. Further, the potential for all Christians to become perfect, as we have so often seen Origen exhort them to do in the texts we have studied,[268] suggests a strong element of continuity between them, as do the ways in which Origen depicts their becoming perfect.

Another confirmation of this organic unity between the perfect and

---

[265] So Ryan, 'Patristic Teaching', *Irish Theological Quarterly* 29 (1962), 28.
[266] Ibid., 30.
[267] Ibid.
[268] And as Crouzel, *Origène et la 'connaissance mystique'*, 475-6, emphasizes.

the ordinary Christian for Origen lies in the area of spiritual gifts. As Hällstrom points out,[269] in *Commentary on John* 13:53(52) Origen contrasts walking by faith with walking by sight: 'It is better indeed to walk by sight than by faith.' Both involve spiritual gifts, walking by sight those of the 'word of wisdom' and the 'word of knowledge' and walking by faith that of faith, although those with the latter are 'inferior to the former in rank.'[270]

Similarly, in *Contra Celsum* 6:79, Origen argues that, if someone wishes to see many bodies filled with the divine Spirit and imitating Christ, 'let him realize that those who in many places teach the doctrine of Jesus rightly and live an upright life are themselves also called Christs by the divine scriptures ....'[271] That he means the perfect is shown both by the fact that he viewed them as teachers and by his reference further on in the same chapter to Aaron's beard as symbolizing the perfect man. This reference, however, comes in the middle of a passage in which he states that Christ has received an anointing and 'his fellows, each one as he had the capacity, shared in his anointing', continuing by pointing out that Christ is the head of the church so that they form one body and the ointment descended from Aaron's head to his beard and to the skirt of his garment. The clear implication is that the whole church is anointed with Christ's anointing according to each Christian's capacity, although the perfect have and display that anointing most fully.

5.6.3 Temple-imagery

Origen uses temple-imagery of the church, but his emphasis lies far more on its application to the individual Christian. One example of the former is found in *Commentary on Matthew* 16:25, in which Origen likens the Jerusalem temple in Jesus' day to the church. Other examples are found in *Commentary on John* 10:35(20) and 10:39(23), passages considered in section 5.6.1 as two in which Christians are likened to the stones which make up the temple of the church and to the members which make up the body of Christ, thus emphasising the roles of individual Christians even as collective images are being used. A third is in *Homilies on Leviticus* 4:8, in which Origen likens those who tear churches apart and introduce strange and corrupt doctrines to priests

---

[269] Hällstrom, G. af, *'Fides simpliciorum' according to Origen of Alexandria* (Helsinki, 1984), 42.
[270] Heine, 144.
[271] Chadwick, 392.

who think they can eat holy flesh outside the temple of God. A fourth is in *Homilies on Leviticus* 9:9, another passage noted in section 5.6.1, where the holy place in the temple is likened to the church in which Christians are priests, the individualistic interpretation again being made. A fifth is in *Homilies on Joshua* 26:3, where Origen claims that Christ as high priest makes the true spiritual sacrifices 'among us where is built "the temple of God from living stones" that is "the church of the living God"...',[272] the individual stones again being mentioned. Although the word 'temple' is not used, the same image is highly developed in *Homilies on Joshua* 9:1, as we noted earlier.

More often than not, then, when Origen uses the temple-image collectively, he develops it in terms of individual Christians. However, it would be unwise to over-emphasize this, as he clearly sees a need for all Christians to be involved in the church. He is not individualistic in the modern sense, but, like Clement, he stresses the individual Christian's role, possibly more than is done in the NT.

Several times Origen uses the temple-image of the individual Christian also. There are Hellenistic as well as biblical influences here, however, as we have noted before. In *Commentary on Romans* 1:18 he states that when the soul adheres to the Spirit then the body becomes a temple. In *Homilies on Leviticus* 6:5 he ends his exposition, 'even if you are hidden and unknown by men, with God you exercise the priesthood within the temple of your mind',[273] developing the image as the NT does not. Describing divine joy over those who are converted in *Homilies on Numbers* 23:2, he writes, 'The Holy Spirit also celebrates feasts in seeing himself being multiplied in those who are converted to God, temples prepared for him.'[274] Likening cities conquered by the Israelites to individual souls in *Homilies on Joshua* 13:1, Origen says that Jesus wants to drive out bad rulers from them and to make them '"the habitation of God" and "the temple of the Spirit", ...'[275] Further, in *Contra Celsum* 4:26, while lauding Christians' piety, Origen takes up the argument from 1 Corinthians 6:15, pointing out that Christians have learnt that 'the body of the rational being that is devoted to the God of the universe is a temple of the God whom they worship.'[276] Again, in

[272] Jaubert, 500.
[273] This is a literal translation of the Latin found in Borret, 290.
[274] Méhat, 436.
[275] Jaubert, 304-6. Although Origen uses the singular 'habitation' and 'temple' here, suggesting that they are to become one temple, he has likened each soul to a city just before this and stated that Christ fulfils what Joshua did 'for every one of the souls of believers' so that the emphasis still falls on the individual.
[276] Chadwick, 202.

Contra Celsum 6:63, he says that the body of one who has a soul indwelt by God is a temple of God, whilst in 7:22 he calls the just man's soul the temple of God, and in 8:19, as we noted in section 5.6.1, he quotes 1 Peter 2:5 to illustrate that Christians do not build lifeless temples but the temple of the body looking to its future resurrection.

We have also noted a number of passages in which the church and, above all, the individual Christian are likened to the tabernacle or to parts of it. One example of this is in *Homilies on Exodus* 9:3-4, the tabernacle being identified with the church in 9:3 and with the individual Christian in 9:4. The Christian is also likened to the holy place (*Homilies on Leviticus* 9:9 and 13:5) and the altar (*Homilies on Leviticus* 9:1 and 9:9).

There is plenty of evidence, then, that Origen liked cultic imagery to describe the church and the individual, especially the perfect, Christian. This was clearly more congenial to him than the practice of describing the ordained in priestly terms, although, as we saw in section 4.6.3, he was willing to do this too. Nor was this due only to the fact that many of his extant works consist of expositions of biblical material relating to the cult, since he used it in the *Contra Celsum* as well. His liking for it clearly owed a great deal to the way in which he could interpret it to fit his picture of the ideal Christian.

5.7 Cyprian and the Western Church in the mid-third century

In section 4.7 we noted that Cyprian marks a watershed in the use of priestly language. One item of evidence for this is that he is the first to use 'priest' as the regular way of describing the bishop; another is the way that he links this with the sacrifice of the eucharist in particular. In this section we will investigate whether there is anything novel about his approach to the general priesthood and his other uses of cultic imagery. Before we do so, evidence will be examined from two other significant Western authors of the third century, Minucius Felix and Novatian.

5.7.1 Minucius Felix' use of cultic imagery

Noted in section 4.7 was the possible allusion to Christians' use of priestly language for their leader in *Octavius* 9:4. This was placed in the mouth of a pagan, Caecilius, as being found in reports from pagans. Similarly placed in Caecilius' mouth is the expression, *antistites veritatis* concerning a Christian in *Octavius* 6:1.[277] However, not only is

---

[277] Halm, *CSEL* 2, 1867, 9.

there the question, which we have met before, of whether *antistes* means 'priest', but it is placed in a pagan's mouth, and 'priests of truth',[278] if an accurate translation, would involve a metaphorical use of the term 'priest', and possibly a use of irony.[279] It is therefore unreliable as a witness to Minucius Felix' awareness of the general priesthood.

Minucius Felix may well be reporting a widely held, pagan view in *Octavius* 10:2 when he puts in Caecilius' mouth a complaint about Christians' secrecy over their worship, asking, 'Why do they have no altars, no temples, no publicly-known images?' He follows this up in 10:4 with the comment, 'The only other group to have worshiped one god is the wretched tribe of the Jews, but they did so in the open, with temples and altars, with sacrifice and ceremonial.'[280] This suggests that Christian communities in North Africa at some time between 175 and 225, depending on when the *Octavius* is dated, had nothing that pagans could identify as cultic worship involving temples, altars, images, sacrifices and ceremonials. The lack of priests is not mentioned. It is difficult to know how to interpret this omission: is it because church leaders were beginning to be known as priests? or does the lack of Christian temples, altars and sacrifices imply a lack of Christian priests? It is also possible that the omission does not imply anything with regard to priesthood.[281] Clearly it would be unwise to build anything on it.

The same is true of Octavius' refutation of Caecilius' accusation in *Octavius* 32:1-3. However, he clearly accepts its validity as far as Christians not having temples, etc. goes, arguing, like Solomon and others,[282] that a temple is inappropriate since the universe cannot contain God: 'It is a better course, you must agree, that He should be dedicated in our minds, or rather consecrated in our hearts.' He next argues that offering sacrifices is throwing God's gifts back at him:

> That would show ingratitude, seeing that an honest heart, a pure mind, and a clear conscience make acceptable offerings. And, therefore, to cherish innocence is to make supplication to God; to practise justice is to pour libation to God; to refrain from wickedness is to offer propitiation to God; to rescue another from peril is to slay a perfect victim. These are our sacrifices, these are our acts of homage to God.'[283]

We have met these ideas before, and, as we argued concerning

---

[278] Clarke, *Octavius*, 59, translates 'you hierophants of truth'.

[279] Ibid., 189, n. 63, makes this last suggestion.

[280] Ibid., 66.

[281] See the comments from Clarke on *Oct* 32:1-3 below.

[282] Ibid., 343, n. 533, points to both biblical and extra-biblical, especially Stoic, parallels.

[283] Ibid., 111.

Caecilius' accusation in *Octavius* 10:2, they may well not imply anything with regard to priestliness. As Clarke argues, 'observe that Octavius denies *templa* and *arae*, terms closely associated with pagan ritual and worship - they do not exclude *coetus, ecclesiae* etc., and *altaria*. The lines of the present argument ... do give the misleading impression that the Christian community engaged in no liturgical action at all.'[284] Clarke is mostly right, but he does not sufficiently draw out what Minucius is implying here. His denial of *templa* and *arae* may not be due only to their association with pagan ritual and worship. It could also be due to Christians' lack of such material objects, as was clearly the case for sacrifices and images. Indeed, their use alongside these suggests that it did. If so, then it is likely that Minucius was writing at a time when Christians did not erect special buildings dedicated to their God, but used whatever buildings were available to them for worship, and did not have special tables regarded as altars, on which their sacrifices were offered. Definitely implied, in any case, is that worship inspired by the Spirit and affecting the whole of the Christian's life and conduct is of paramount importance.

The *Octavius*, then, continues the anti-cultic lines of argument we have noted earlier in the writings of the second-century Apologists, including that of 'spiritual sacrifices', though without using that expression. Although this is clearly compatible with the general priesthood, and, in view of the general prevalence of belief in this in Tertullian's work in particular, Minucius may well have been aware of it, there is nothing in the *Octavius* to show this for certain.[285]

5.7.2 Novatian's use of cultic imagery

Novatian rarely uses cultic imagery in his extant work. He never refers to the general priesthood but he does allude to himself and other confessors in Rome as 'those destined to be sacrificial victims ... [who] now make their petition for help of such a high-priest [Latin: 'priest']' in a passage noted earlier as attesting the bishop's priesthood.[286] It is interesting to note that Novatian depicts the bishop as the priest in a context in which second-century authors might have depicted the

---

[284] Ibid., 342, n. 531.

[285] Minucius Felix is omitted from some treatments of the general priesthood in the early period, viz., from Eastwood, Ryan, 'Patristic Teaching', *Irish Theological Quarterly* 29 (1962), and Garrett, 'Pre-Cyprianic Doctrine' in Church and George, *Continuity and Discontinuity*. In Dabin, *Le sacerdoce royal des fidèles*, 69 and Lécuyer, 'Essai', *La Maison-Dieu* 27 (1951), 23, some of the passages dealt with here are mentioned.

[286] *Ep.* 31:5:2 in the Cyprianic corpus: Clarke, *Epistles*, vol. 2, 36.

confessors themselves as priests.

Other than this, Novatian has only two references to Christians as temples, in *De Trinitate* 29:16 and *De Bono Pudicitiae* 2:1. These do not deviate from earlier Christian writing, Christ being said to have made us the temple and dwelling place of God in the former, and Christians being reminded that they know they are 'the temple of the Lord, the members of Christ, the dwelling place of the Holy Spirit, ...'[287] in the latter. Only the consciously trinitarian cast of this is unusual.

5.7.3 Cyprian and the general priesthood

Scholars are unanimous that Cyprian did not call the laity priests.[288] However, there is one passage none of them have considered. In *De habitu virginum* 2, while extolling discipline, Cyprian reminds Christians that 'our members are the temples of God, cleansed from all impurity of the old corruption by the sanctifying waters of life, and that we are under obligation not to dishonor nor to defile them, since he who dishonors the body is himself dishonored. Of these temples we are the keepers and the high priests [*antistites*].'[289] That his mind is full of Paul's teaching in 1 Corinthians 6 here is shown by the way in which he continues by quoting 1 Corinthians 6:19 and developing further the idea of the Christian as a temple.

The wider context of a treatise addressed to the general Christian public, and the immediate context of the reference to purging through baptism leave no doubt that Cyprian is describing Christians in general.[290] Although we have already noted that *antistes* does not necessarily mean 'priest',[291] there are two facts which make it more likely than not that it does here. A vital one is the context, in which the cultic idea of the parts of the Christian's body as temples predominates, the concept of Christians as their keepers and *antistites* being part of this picture. The second is the fact that Cyprian often uses *antistes* as a synonym for *sacerdos*.[292] Pontius does the same.[293]

---

[287] De Simone, R.J. (ed.), *Novatian: The Trinity, The Spectacles, Jewish Foods, In Praise of Purity, Letters* (Washington, 1974), 166.
[288] Goetz, 89; Eastwood, 87; Walker, G.S.M., 36; Bévenot, '"Sacerdos"', *J Th St* 30 (1979), 416; Faivre, *Emergence*, 114; and Garrett, 'Pre-Cyprianic Doctrine' in Church and George, *Continuity and Discontinuity*, 24.
[289] Keenan in Deferrari, 32.
[290] Against Goetz, 86, who views this passage as referring to the people's leaders as priests.
[291] Cf. Clarke, *Epistles*, vol. 1, 325, n. 24: '*antistes* ... is an already acceptable Christian word, being the etymological equivalent of Justin's [*proestôs*] .... Like the word *minister*, *antistes* can also be used in a more general sense (= "patron," "protector," etc.)'
[292] So, ibid. For examples of this use, see *Epp.* 59:18:3, 61:2:3, 66:5:1-2. Clarke, *Epistles*, vol.

How significant is this reference, however? It suggests that Cyprian was aware of the practice of calling ordinary Christians 'priests' and was not totally averse to doing so himself. This conclusion is reinforced by what we have already seen in section 4.7.6 of Cyprian's willingness to call 'sacrifice' prayer, praise, justice, a humbled heart, martyrdom, peace, concord and unity between Christians, giving to the poor, offering oneself and bringing materials for the eucharist, the maintenance of the clergy or the poor.[294] Whilst the eucharist, above all, is the Christian sacrifice, his willingness to call these other matters 'sacrifice' illustrates his links with earlier Christian thought and practice. So does what we have just seen and what we shall see below concerning his use of temple-imagery. We may rightly conclude, then, with Benson, that the 'universal Lay-priesthood is not dwelt upon in Cyprian, but there is no sufficient reason to question his belief in it.'[295]

Bévenot, however, points out that Cyprian does not quote any of the scriptural texts referring to the general priesthood except Revelation 5:10, and that only incidentally as part of Revelation 5:6-10 concerning the glorification of the Lamb.[296] He also argues,

> that Cyprian's avoidance of the title "sacerdotes" for all the baptized was quite deliberate is shown by the way in which he uses I Pet. ii. ... Not that Cyprian was unacquainted with this chapter: he seems to be echoing its first verse in *Zel. et Liv.* 17, and quotes the verses following (11-12) three times (*Quir.* iii. 11; *ep.* 13. 3. 2; cf. *Mort.* 26.1). We can only conclude that he must have had some good reason for skipping the verses about the "priesthood of the people".[297]

This reason was Tertullian and the ways in which Cyprian agreed and disagreed with him. Most relevant of the latter is Cyprian's rejection of Tertullian's use, in *Chastity* 7:3 and *On Flight in Persecution* 14:1, of Christ's promise to be with two or three gathered in his name (Mt.

3, 86, 93 and 119, translates *antistes* in these passages 'priestly minister', 'a priest', 'priest' and 'the priest'.

[293] *Vita* 1, 6, 12 and 13.

[294] Garrett, 'Pre-Cyprianic Doctrine' in Church and George, *Continuity and Discontinuity*, 24, notes that 'Cyprian ... clearly retains two essential aspects of the pre-Cyprianic doctrine of the priesthood of all Christians, namely, prayer and Christian deeds of mercy as sacrifices to God.' See also Dabin, *Le sacerdoce royal des fidèles*, 72; Lécuyer, 'Essai', *La Maison-Dieu* 27 (1951), 35; and Ryan, 'Patristic Teaching', *Irish Theological Quarterly* 29 (1962), 45, 48-9.

[295] Benson, 38-9. See too a similar comment by Bernard noted in Garrett, 'Pre-Cyprianic Doctrine' in Church and George, *Continuity and Discontinuity*, 24, n. 40.

[296] In *Test* 2:15.

[297] Bévenot, '"Sacerdos"', *J Th St* 30 (1979), 423-4.

18:20) to assure such a group of the guidance of the Spirit and to dispense them from the authority of the bishops. Cyprian refutes this interpretation in the *De ecclesiae unitate*, explicitly in chapter 12. 'Christ's words were addressed to his followers within the Church, not those who were in revolt against it.'[298]

For Bévenot, then, Cyprian's avoidance of 1 Peter 2:5 and 9, and, presumably, of any reference to the common priesthood was deliberate, based on his view of the church as centred on the bishop, and his consequent rejection of Tertullian's view of the common priesthood and its independence of bishops.

There is a degree of plausibility about this argument. For example, in *De ecclesiae unitate* 12 Cyprian clearly is attacking the kind of view which Bévenot depicts as the result of Tertullian's arguments in *Chastity* 7:3 and *On Flight in Persecution* 14:1; and if you grant that Cyprian was reacting against that view, then it follows logically and psychologically that he could well have reacted against Tertullian's use of the concept of the general priesthood. However, there are some assumptions in this argument which are less than convincing. One is that Tertullian was teaching the independence of the laity from the bishops in the passages mentioned. As we noted when dealing with those passages, Tertullian envisages the possibility of the laity acting as priests in the same way as the ordained only when the ordained are not available. He never seeks to justify schism or the rejection of episcopal authority on this basis. Bévenot's interpretation of what Tertullian was saying goes beyond what Tertullian actually says or clearly implies. Although it is still possible that Cyprian understood Tertullian as Bévenot suggests, this is unlikely if Tertullian did not clearly mean that. On the whole, therefore, Bévenot's case remains unproven.

More likely as an explanation of the undoubted facts that the 'universal Lay-priesthood is not dwelt upon in Cyprian',[299] and that he does not use 'priest' of the ordinary Christian, is the equally undoubted fact that this was his preferred designation for the bishop. Allied to this is his exalted conception of the bishop's priesthood which we noted in sections 4.7.2 and 4.7.4. Although the evidence falls short of definite proof, the likeliest explanation of the relative eclipse of the general priesthood for Cyprian is his desire to reserve 'priest', with all that that now connoted in the way of sacral authority, etc. for the bishop and his delegates.

Eastwood goes too far when he writes of 'the eclipse of the idea of

---

[298] Ibid., 426.
[299] Benson, 38-9.

the universal priesthood ... [which] vanished at the first Council of Carthage and was not revived by the Church until the appearance of Martin Luther ....'[300] The idea is not totally eclipsed, even in Cyprian's work, and the studies of Ryan and especially of Garrett,[301] show that it continued in both East and West after Cyprian. Ryan's comments on the superiority of Western teaching on this subject,[302] however, seem very partisan in the light of Cyprian's lack of emphasis on it. Garrett's conclusion is the most balanced and brings out the watershed which Cyprian's writings marked for the general priesthood: 'prior to Cyprian the concept had a place in patristic thought despite and alongside the emergence of the concept of the clerical priesthood. After Cyprian's delineation of a doctrine of the clerical priesthood, the latter attained to dominance in patristic usage even though the general priesthood continued to appear in patristic literature.'[303]

5.7.4 Cyprian's use of temple-imagery

Cyprian uses the temple to describe the individual Christian moderately often,[304] in line with what we have noted of earlier Christian usage, but, as far as I have been able to ascertain, never to describe the church as a whole.[305] This is somewhat strange since he and others imply that the church is endued with the Spirit in *Epistles* 70:3:1 and 74:4:2, he calls the church 'the house of God' in *De ecclesiae unitate* 8,[306] and he uses the collective image of the body for the church, albeit in a more institutional way than Paul, in a number of passages.[307] Was it because *templum* connoted a building for pagan worship and so was inappropriate for a church now using buildings for worship? or because *ecclesia* now possessed connotations which made *templum* inappropriate?

Finally, Cyprian's use of 'altar' is in line with his main use of 'sacrifice', connoting public Christian worship as the business of the

---

[300] Eastwood, 87.
[301] Ryan, 'Patristic Teaching', *Irish Theological Quarterly* 29 (1962); Garrett, 'Pre-Cyprianic Doctrine', in Church and George, *Continuity and Discontinuity*.
[302] Ryan, 'Patristic Teaching', *Irish Theological Quarterly* 29 (1962), 33.
[303] Garrett, 'Pre-Cyprianic Doctrine' in Church and George, *Continuity and Discontinuity*, 22.
[304] In *Epp.* 6:1:2, 13:5:1, 55:26:1; 55:27:2; 58:4:1; 62:2:1; 69:11:3; 73:12:2; 74:5:2; 76:2:3; *Lap.* 10 and 35; *Don.* 15; *Zel.* 14; *Dom.* 11; *Pat.* 14; and *Hab. Virg.* 2.
[305] Clarke, *Epistles*, vol. 1, 193, n. 9, on the first use of 'temple' in Cyprian's letters, notes that 'Cyprian insists frequently on the baptized Christian being a *templum Dei*' but mentions nothing about the phrase being used of the church.
[306] Bévenot in Weber et al., 255.
[307] *Epp.* 36:4:1, 44:3:1, 45:1:1, 46:1:2, 62:1:2, *Un.* 4, 5 and 12.

ordained as 'priests', as, for example, in *Epistle* 1:1:1.[308] Some of the
passages in which it is used, especially *Epistles* 45:2:2 and 59:18:1,
suggest 'some temporarily placed structure - Christian altars at this stage
often being tables and made of wood ....'[309] This development may well
have been linked with the increasing tendency to view the eucharist as
the Christian sacrifice *par excellence*. Cyprian never uses 'altar' of the
individual Christian or his mind, as some earlier writers had.

He thus uses cultic imagery in many ways similarly to earlier
Christians, but his overall emphasis has clearly shifted from application
to the individual Christian and the church as a whole to application to
the clergy in particular and their leadership of worship, especially their
celebration of the eucharist.

5.8 Other third-century material

The most significant bodies of material relevant to this study other than
those already dealt with are found in the *Didascalia* and the writings of
Methodius of Olympus. These will therefore be studied in turn before
the remaining relevant material from the third century is brought
together.

5.8.1 The Didascalia Apostolorum

Already noted in section 4.8.2 was the one passage in this document in
which the general priesthood is mentioned. This is in chapter 9 of the
Syriac and 25 of the Latin versions. The laymen are called the 'Catholic
Church, the holy and perfect, "a royal priesthood, a holy multitude, a
people for inheritance", the great Church, the bride adorned for the Lord
God.' Thus far the emphasis lies on the church's election and holiness,
but the way the document continues suggests that the mention of
priesthood is also to the fore:

> Those things then which were said beforetime, hear thou also now. Set by
> part-offerings and tithes and firstfruits to Christ, the true High Priest, and to
> his ministers, even tithes of salvation .... Instead of the sacrifices which then
> were, offer now prayers and petitions and thanksgivings. Then were firstfruits
> and tithes and part-offerings and gifts; but today the oblations which are
> offered through the bishops to the Lord God.[310]

---

[308] See too *Epp.* 1:2:2, 3:3:2, 43:5:2, 45:2:2, 59:18:1, 61:2:3, 67:1:2, 69:1:4 and 73:2:3.
[309] Clarke, *Epistles*, vol. 2, 239-240, n. 18.
[310] Connolly, 84-7.

The author is thus following an interpretation of the general priesthood in terms of sacrifices which we have found before. Significantly, however, it is considerably devalued by its juxtaposition with the priesthood of the bishop, in particular. The likening of him to the high priest as the one through whom these gifts are offered in the following sentence, and the likening of the presbyters, deacons, orphans and widows to the priests and Levites as those who benefit from these gifts, leaves the ordinary Christian in the position of the ordinary Israelite as the one who supplies the gifts. This is clear soon afterwards in the words, 'And as it was not lawful ... for one who was not a Levite to draw near to the altar or to offer aught without the high priest, so you also shall do nothing without the bishop.'[311] The ordinary Christian is no longer depicted as a priest. Although alluded to,[312] the general priesthood has lost most of its value in comparison with the priesthood of the bishop.

Further, the likening of widows and orphans to priests and Levites in this passage is not a reference to the general priesthood. For one thing, they are so likened over against the rest of the laity who are to supply the gifts for their support, and, for another, as noted in section 4.8.3, they are only likened to priests and Levites in that they benefit from the laity's gifts. The author likens the OT anointing of priests and kings to the anointing of those who receive baptism in chapter 16, but his main point is how and by whom the baptism and anointing are to be performed. No reference to the general priesthood is implied.[313]

Such an implication could be deduced from a passage in chapter 7, but it is doubtful whether it was so meant. The bishop is being instructed in his duties which include the burden of the people's sinful tendencies. In this context, he is reminded that 'it is written: "The Lord said unto Moses: Thou and Aaron shall take upon you the sins of the priesthood."' The author continues, 'for as thou art to render an account for many, so be careful of all; ....'[314] Logically, the 'priesthood' in the quotation from Numbers 18:1 are all the Christians under the bishop's charge. However, nothing is made of this priesthood and the quotation could well have been chosen purely on the basis of the allusion to leaders bearing others' sins without any desire to identify the rest of the church

[311] Ibid., 89.
[312] Dabin, *Le sacerdoce royal des fidèles*, 524; Lanne, E. 'Le laïc dans l'Église ancienne', *Verbum Caro* 18 (1964), 112; and Vilela, 198, find a reference to the common priesthood here but without noting its devaluation.
[313] Against Ryan, 'Patristic Teaching', *Irish Theological Quarterly* 29 (1962), 40 and n. 3, if this is the passage he is referring to, as seems likely.
[314] Connolly, 56.

as priests. This seems much the more likely.

Both in section 4.8.2 and above we have noted that some sacrifices are referred to in the *Didascalia* which all Christians can offer, and that these are closely connected to the quotation including a reference to the general priesthood in chapter 9 (25). As with this reference to the general priesthood, however, the force of these offerings as implying that priesthood is much diminished by the author's view that they have to be offered through the bishop as high priest. Certainly with regard to the material offerings, though possibly not with regard to the prayers and thanksgivings, the ordinary Christian is like the ordinary, non-priestly Israelite, and it is the bishop who, like the priest or high priest, makes the sacrifice.[315]

The same is true of the ways in which 'altar' and 'temple' or 'tabernacle' are used. 'Altar' is never used of the individual Christian or of Christians in general, but always of widows and orphans, in a way going back to Ignatius at least. In 9 (25-26), the orphans and widows are likened to priests and Levites and to the altar as those who benefit from the people's gifts, but this is immediately followed by a passage already quoted: 'And as it was not lawful ... for one who was not a Levite to draw near to the altar or to offer aught without the high priest, so you also shall do nothing without the bishop.'[316] The image of the altar is used as something at which the bishop, not the ordinary Christian, acts as priest. Although this is not stated in the other references to the widow as altar in 15 ('but let a widow know that she is the altar of God' and 'for you are the holy altar of God'), and in 18 (38) ('Do you the bishops and deacons be constant therefore in the ministry of the altar of Christ – we mean the widows and the orphans'),[317] the same is likely to be true of them.

One passage in chapter 9 has an implied reference to the church as 'sanctuary' and/or 'temple'. It comes after an instruction that the laity are to make known anything they want to do to the bishop through the deacons, 'for neither formerly in the temple of the sanctuary was anything offered or done without the priest. And moreover, even the idol-temples of the impure and abhorred and reprobate heathen to this day imitate the sanctuary. Far indeed in comparison be the house of abomination from the sanctuary: nevertheless, even in their absurd rites they neither offer nor do anything without their unclean priest ....'[318] The

---

[315] This point is made, as noted above, in 9 (25), but also in 9 (28): Connolly, 98-100.

[316] Ibid., 89.

[317] Ibid., 133, 143 and 156-7.

[318] Ibid., 90-92.

parallel is clear, but its main point is that nothing should be done in the church as temple without the bishop as priest.

Similarly, in chapter 8 the church is likened to the OT tabernacle, but again with reference to the priesthood of the bishop: 'you also then to-day, O bishops, are priests to your people, and the Levites who minister to the tabernacle of God, the holy Catholic Church, ...'[319]

Thus nearly all the cultic references used in the *Didascalia* are employed concerning the bishop as priest. The allusion to 1 Peter 2:9 and the references to the sacrifices which the laity can offer testify to the author's links with traditional early Christian teaching, but, as with Cyprian, his emphasis is vastly more on the priesthood of the bishop than on the general priesthood, which is almost emptied of meaning.

5.8.2 Methodius

Musurillo sums up what can be known of Methodius as follows: 'the most one can say is that the author of the *Banquet* was definitely a Christian teacher, that he was perhaps also a bishop and a martyr who was active in certain parts of Lycia ... during the second half of the third century.'[320]

His only work to be entirely preserved is *The Symposium (or Banquet): A Treatise on Chastity*, written around 260-290 according to Musurillo.[321] It contains no reference to the general priesthood but does use cultic language. In 1:1, the soul which has been purified through Christ's words is likened to the OT sacrifice sprinkled with salt in the context of instructions on virginity. Apart from the last, this reminds us of Origen's emphasis on the soul as sacrifice and on studying the word of God, which is not surprising in view of Methodius' other affinities with Platonism and 'Philonian alexandrinism.'[322] In 5:1, virginity is depicted as 'the greatest and most illustrious offering and gift'. This picture is developed in 5:2, the one who offers himself completely being called 'complete and not deficient', reminding us of the perfect Christian who is the true priest in Origen; and in 5:3 perfect self-offering is spoken of again.[323] In 5:6, the same theme is apparent when 'the community of those who are chaste' is called 'God's unbloody

---

[319] Ibid., 80.

[320] Musurillo in Musurillo, H. and Debidour, V.-H. (eds.), *Méthode d'Olympe: Le Banquet* (Paris, 1963), 11. Geerard, vol. 1, 248, dates his death to 312.

[321] In Musurillo and Debidour, 13.

[322] On this see Musurillo in ibid., 14-6

[323] Musurillo, H. (ed.), *St. Methodius: The Symposium: A Treatise on Chastity* (London, 1958), 81-8.

altar' and immaculate virginity is said to stand in the holy of holies as
the altar of incense.

This last image is used again in 5:8 in the context of a fuller
exposition of the tabernacle which is called the 'symbol of the Church,
as the Church is a symbol of heaven' in a hermeneutical scheme similar
to Origen's. Then the bronze altar is likened to the widows as that to
which the sacrifices are brought, before the golden altar of incense is
likened to those living in virginity, the incense being their prayers.[324]
The heavenly application of the temple-image is taken up in 6:2 and 6:4,
again describing the destiny of those preserving virginity. In 8:5 the
church is likened to both the temple and the tabernacle but as an
eschatological entity into which the church's children will come after
the resurrection. Another application of the tabernacle-image is to the
resurrection-body in 9:2 and 9:5, although the use of the image in the
former implies that the body is already a tabernacle in this life. This
usage is found in the extant portions of the *Discourse on the
Resurrection* 1:5, 1:12 and 1:14. In the Epilogue to the *Symposium* the
perfectly chaste are again likened to temples in which the Holy Spirit
dwells.

The similarities of the above to Clement's and especially Origen's
usage of cultic imagery are obvious. Although they do not exalt
virginity as does Methodius, and allow more reference to ordinary
believers when using this imagery, they too tend to constrict their use of
that imagery to the gnostic or the perfect Christian. Like them,
Methodius does not abandon the ordinary Christian completely. He is
depicted as regenerated through baptism, receiving the Holy Spirit and
becoming a member of Christ in *Symposium* 3:8 and 8:6 and as not
finally condemned in 7:3. In 3:8, however, the author reveals his very
strong bias towards the perfect by writing, 'For in fact frequently the
Scriptures … refer to the Church as the actual multitude and assembly
of the faithful taken as a whole, while they also conceive of those who
are more perfect in spiritual progress as the one person and body of the
Church.'[325] He goes on to describe the 'more perfect' again as becoming
the church and identifies them as those who form and give birth to the
imperfect until they become the church and themselves give birth to and
train up other children. As with Clement and Origen there is an organic
unity between the imperfect and the perfect Christian, the perfect being
meant to help the imperfect become perfect, but Methodius implies that
only the perfect form the church and so the temple or tabernacle in

---

[324] Ibid., 89.
[325] Ibid., 66.

heaven. On the other hand, he is unable to present a consistent picture and, in *Symposium* 7:3, points out strongly that it is not only virgins who will reach heaven, but that they will have the best places there. Even so, we may well imagine that if Methodius ever, in some lost work, used priestly language of Christians, it was of perfect Christians living in virginity.

5.8.3 Other relevant material

There is one other quotation of 1 Peter 2:9 in what is probably third-century material, in the *Epistola 1 ad virgines*, pseudonymously ascribed to Clement of Rome.[326] In chapter 9 of this document what is involved in being indwelt by the Holy Spirit is dealt with. The description bears many similarities to Methodius' description of the perfect, including the expectation of virginity and the use of the temple-image. Near the end, such people are addressed in highly laudatory terms which include 'a chosen race, a royal priesthood, a holy nation, a people belonging to God, ...'[327] We cannot tell whether the author would have included all Christians in such a description, but it does help to show that a number of third-century authors were viewing what they defined as perfect Christians as those who really made up the general priesthood and were the true temples of God.

Similar teaching is given in the apocryphal *Acts of Thomas*, in section 12 of which a character is urged to recognize that, if he refrains from sexual intercourse even with his wife, he becomes a holy temple. More teaching on the need to refrain from sexual intercourse in the context of becoming a temple through baptism and holiness is given in sections 86-88, 94 and 156.

The problems concerning the source-criticism of the Pseudo-Clementine literature are legion.[328] Accepting the view of Strecker and others that the *Grundschrift* comes from the third century, and accepting Strecker's delineation of that,[329] the only thing in it relevant to this thesis is a considerable amount of anti-sacrificial polemic[330] but without

---

[326] Geerard, vol 1, 7, writes of the two such epistles, 'they were not written before the third century.'

[327] Migne, J.-P. (ed.), *Patrologiae cursus completus, series graeca* (Paris, 1857), vol. 1, 398-9.

[328] See Jones, F.S., 'The Pseudo-Clementines: A History of Research', *The Second Century* 2 (1982), 1-33 and 63-96.

[329] Strecker, G., *Das Judenchristentum in den Pseudoklementinen* (Berlin, 1981²), 267, for the date of the 'Grundschrift' and 92-6 for its delineation. For others' views see Jones, 'The Pseudo-Clementines', *The Second Century* 2 (1982), 8-16.

[330] On this see Strecker, 179-183.

any positive teaching regarding Christian sacrifice.

5.8.4 Summary and conclusion

It is significant that in almost all the documents dealt with in this section cultic imagery in general and the common priesthood in particular are constricted. In the *Didascalia* this is by the priesthood of the bishop, as in Cyprian's writings, and in Minucius' *Octavius*, the *Epistola I ad virgines* and the *Acts of Thomas*, it is by the priesthood of the perfect, as in the works of Clement of Alexandria and Origen. It is time now to look back over all that we have discovered in this examination of Christian teaching of the general priesthood and the use of cultic imagery in the first three centuries.

5.9 Summary and conclusion

This chapter set out to examine if belief in the general priesthood was maintained over the first three centuries of the church, and, if so, how strongly and with which meanings and connotations. Special attention was to be paid to any correlation between the increasing emphasis on the priesthood of the ordained later in the period and a lack of emphasis on the priesthood of Christians in general. The time has now come to draw our findings together and to answer these questions.

5.9.1 Maintenance of belief in the general priesthood

Although there is no mention of this priesthood in the works of the Apostolic Fathers, we noted that there is no reason to assume that they were unaware of it. Its presence in the works of Justin and Irenaeus, and the presence of ideas linked to it in the NT in the works of the Apostolic Fathers themselves make it more likely than not that they were acquainted with it. This assertion is best supported by the clear evidence that the majority were acquainted with the concept of individual Christians and the church as a whole offering sacrifices of praise, prayer, humility and themselves. It is also supported by Ignatius' use of the theme of Christians as living stones being built into a temple, which demonstrates his awareness of 1 Peter 2:5.

Justin, Irenaeus and Melito explicitly allude to the general priesthood. There are also possible allusions to it in the *Odes of Solomon*, the Gnostic *Gospel of Philip* and the *Teaching of Silvanus*. Although not a concept as frequently mentioned as spiritual sacrifices or even Christians individually and corporately as temples, these allusions render it certain that many Christians were aware that it was appropriate, as in the NT, to use of the church and individual Christians cultic concepts which in the OT had related mainly or solely to the priestly tribe. Bévenot denies this. While it is unlikely, as he points out, that, 'for all their "spiritual sacrifices", the Christians called each other "priests"', they were probably aware that it was appropriate to think of themselves in that way. Even less certain is his argument that although,

> in technical language, "priesthood" is a correlative of "sacrifice", ... we ourselves have, in common parlance, lost hold of that connection. A man may be prepared to sacrifice a fortune rather than betray a trust: we do not call him a priest on that account. ... So, it is likely that, even in the first two centuries when the good Christian was very conscious of the "sacrifices" which in a pagan environment the gospel demanded of him, he did not think of himself as "a priest" even at the eucharist.[331]

To an extent, this argument depends on an analogy between a present situation in Western culture, in which the idea of sacrifice has been largely secularized and transferred to mean whatever costs us something, and an ancient culture in which sacrifice normally connoted priesthood and was part of everyday experience. It is more likely that, in this ancient culture, sacrifice did normally connote priesthood. On the other hand, it is true, as we have noted, that the idea of immaterial sacrifices was widespread by the second century AD, and that they may not always have connoted priesthood in the way that the offering of material sacrifices did. Bévenot, however, states that 'in the first two centuries the title of "priest" was avoided among Christians save for Christ himself', and implies that Tertullian was the first to use it of Christians.[332] This is not true to the evidence we have examined which demonstrates that at least one prominent and representative church leader, Irenaeus, and one eminent teacher, Justin, were aware that all Christians could be described as priests, and saw no need to justify this, whilst Justin shows that he could link this idea with the offering of Christian sacrifice, arguing that, 'God receives sacrifices from no one, except through his priests'[333] and so demonstrating that he saw a correlation between sacrifice and priesthood. If you add to this the other evidence we have adduced, then it is certain that some leaders and

---

[331] Bévenot, '"Sacerdos"', *J Th St* 30 (1979), 416. He does add, 'later on, no doubt, pastors and others would appeal to the scriptural phrases, when exhorting their people to live up to their Christian responsibilities, but rarely, if ever, did they address them as "priests".'
[332] Ibid., 416-7.
[333] *Dial.* 116:3: Falls, 328.

teachers, and so, some ordinary Christians, before Tertullian viewed some or all Christians as priests. Although they did not call each other 'priests' or frequently think of themselves as such, some did at times, at least when they were reminded of it.

Undoubtedly the teaching of the general priesthood achieves greater significance in the writings of Tertullian and Clement of Alexandria than in any documents before them. As we shall note below, they not only give it greater prominence, but also add meanings and connotations. This is especially true in the work of Origen who has the richest teaching of all in the first three centuries on it. Even the three authors who most emphasize the priesthood of the bishop, Hippolytus, Cyprian and the author of the *Didascalia*, demonstrate that they know of the general priesthood. The silence of Minucius Felix, Novatian and Methodius regarding it is, therefore, insignificant, in view of the paucity of their extant works. A further third-century witness to awareness of 1 Peter 2:9 is found in the pseudonymous *Epistola 1 ad virgines*.

In addition, there is Origen's rhetorical question, in *Homilies on Leviticus* 9:1, 'Or are you ignorant that to you also, that is, to all of the Church of God and to the people of believers, the priesthood was given?' which is immediately followed by the quotation of 1 Peter 2:9.[334] Although his frequent reminders of this verse and the fact to which it testifies, and his other exhortations to his hearers and readers could suggest Origen felt they were ignorant of it, he was probably using irony and/or sarcasm and implying that they were well aware of it. He certainly implies that they should be and did his best to make sure that they were. As we noted concerning the second-century evidence, therefore, although we cannot tell how many Christians were aware of it, those at least who heard or read the teaching we have noted must have been and this makes it likely that many others were also, since it is probable that not only those whose works are extant taught it.

5.9.2 Significance and derivation of the general priesthood

We cannot know for certain what, if anything, the idea of Christians in general being priests meant to the Apostolic Fathers because they do not mention it. Clearly, however, the idea of Christians being able to offer sacrifices, of prayer, praise, their gifts and themselves, to God was familiar to most of them. A major reason for this was the teaching of both Old and New Testaments as, for example, Clement of Rome's quotations from the OT and echoes of Pauline teaching testify. Another

---

[334] Barkley, 177.

was intertestamental Jewish teaching, as Young argues concerning Ignatius' understanding of martyrdom as sacrifice.[335] Clement also views Christians' offerings as being made through their high priest, Christ, in passages dependent on Hebrews. Other cultic ideas deriving mainly from NT teaching were those of the church and the Christian as temple. A new development, doubtless related to these, is the likening of the Christian widow and the church to an altar on which offerings are made.

For Justin the teaching that all Christians are a 'high-priestly race' is not very important, since he mentions it only once. Even so, it has a certain significance related to the fulfilment of OT types and prophecies of priesthood and sacrifice in Christ and his work of salvation, and in Christians' offering of pure sacrifices in the eucharist. That it is mentioned in the context of the correct interpretation of the OT, albeit Zechariah 3, in the light of Christ, demonstrates the importance of OT ideas for the general priesthood which has already been noted in the NT. In the latter, however, it was Exodus 19:5-6 which was most important, whereas here it is a Levitical high priest. Further, Christ's high priesthood and purification of Christians to be high priests and offer pure sacrifices are mentioned in the immediate context and imply that Christians' high priesthood derives from Christ's.

The teaching that all Christ's disciples are priests is similarly not a highly significant one for Irenaeus. As with Justin, it is linked with the fulfilment of the OT by Christ, only now, for the first time, with specifically Levitical ordinances. These concern relying on God alone for sustenance and serving him continually. Other connotations are being blameless and rejoicing eschatologically. Although offering sacrifice is not mentioned in connection with this priesthood because irrelevant to the contexts, serving the altar is. Service in the temple of the body is related to working righteousness in *Demonstration of the Apostolic Preaching* 96. As for Justin, Irenaeus' treatment comes in an apologetic and polemical context, though against Gnosticism rather than Judaism.

In Melito's *Peri Pascha* 68, 'a new priesthood and an eternal people personal to him' is one of a number of ways in which the salvation achieved and provided by Christ is described.[336] It is also the earliest clear allusion to 1 Peter 2:5 and/or 9. *Odes of Solomon* 20, like Justin and Irenaeus, depicts an active priesthood in that the author writes of serving as a priest. There is, however, no explicitly christological

---

[335] Young, 108-9.
[336] Hall, 37.

allusion present, unlike the other texts noted so far, a link being made with the offering of sacrifice, as in Justin, albeit the offering of God's thought, of righteousness and purity rather than the eucharist, and with priestly service, as in Irenaeus. Purity is the condition of being a priest and a Levite in the *Teaching of Silvanus*, illustrating the frequent connotation of holiness when priestliness is mentioned. It is the result of allowing Christ to dwell in the temple of the soul and cast out the evil merchants, and it is maintained in performing his service. Another passage depicts understanding as 'a high priestly garment',[337] while the Gnostic *Gospel of Philip* is the first to connect priesthood with entering the holy of holies which means knowing the secret of the truth, but this appears to be the priesthood of only the spiritual or perfect.

The general priesthood is of more significance to Tertullian than to any writer before him. He mentions it more frequently, gives it more connotations and not only adduces it whilst dealing with other, more significant matters, as do Justin and Irenaeus, but makes it an important part of his argument against remarriage in *Chastity* 7 and *On Monogamy* 7. He does not allude to 1 Peter 2:5 or 9, but takes the Levitical priesthood and the regulations for it as his model in *On Baptism* 7, *Against Marcion* 3:7:7, 4:23:10-11, *Chastity* 7 and *On Monogamy* 7, also using Revelation 1:6 and/or 5:10 in *Chastity* 7 and in *On Monogamy* 7 and 12. Like Justin, Irenaeus and Melito, Tertullian links the general priesthood with the enjoyment of the benefits of salvation, connecting it clearly, as none before him had, with the events surrounding baptism. So in *On Baptism* 7 it connotes forgiveness and reception of the Spirit, the latter being related to Christ's anointing with the Spirit, and, in *On Monogamy* 7, Christ the high priest clothing us with himself. It is also connected with the enjoyment of salvation as the benefit of Christ's self-sacrifice, in *Against Marcion* 3:7:7, in which he further links priesthood with belonging to the spiritual temple, the church. The same enjoyment of Christ and his salvation is the main connotation of the Christian priesthood of which Christ is described as the *pontifex* in *Against Marcion* 5:9:9. The main connotation is dedication to God and his service in *Against Marcion* 4:23:10-11 whilst Tertullian links general priesthood and the sacrifice of prayer in *On Prayer* 28, in which wholehearted devotion, faith, truth, purity, love, good works, and praise are also involved. He is the first and only person in the first three centuries to link the general priesthood with the administration of baptism and the offering of the eucharist in case of necessity in *Chastity* 7, in which the priestly discipline of only one

---

[337] Section 89: Peel and Zandee in Robinson, 349.

marriage is the main point, as in *On Monogamy* 7 and 12.

He thus shows that he is aware of the connection of the general priesthood with spiritual sacrifices, as was Justin, of its link with a life of service and purity, as was Irenaeus, and of its connection with holiness, as in the *Teaching of Silvanus*. He uses the Levitical regulations for the general priesthood more frequently than any before him, and is even stronger than earlier writers on the relationship between the general priesthood and the enjoyment of salvation. He is the first to link this priesthood with Revelation 1:6 and/or 5:10, the prohibition on remarriage, and administering baptism and the eucharist when necessary. His is therefore a highly significant contribution to the understanding of the general priesthood. We cannot pursue here the interesting question of why he never refers to 1 Peter 2:5 or 9.

In contrast, Hippolytus implies the general priesthood only once. As for Justin this is in relation to the eucharist, of which sacrificial language is used in the same sentence, and which is viewed as the whole church's priestly offering. Apart from his use of the incense-analogy, his application of cultic imagery is to the church as an institution, and to public worship as led by the clergy, rather than to the individual or to the church as a community.

With Clement of Alexandria we find a strong belief in the priesthood of only 'gnostic' Christians, similar to the Gnostic *Gospel of Philip*, although he shows awareness of the general priesthood. A clear example of this is found in *Stromateis* 5:6:39:4-40:4, where he compares the gnostic as the chief priest to other Christians as ordinary priests, but with a strong emphasis on the superiority of the gnostic to the others. The connotations of being one of the ordinary priests are being baptized, having faith and hoping for heaven, but these are determined as much by what it means to be an ordinary Christian for Clement as by what it means to be a priest. Nonetheless, Clement thus connects entry into the general priesthood with baptism and faith as does Tertullian. The allusion to the general priesthood in the passage in which 1 Peter 2:9-10 is quoted in *Protreptikos* 4:59:2-3 is only incidental, involving consecration to God and so holiness; and the comment on 1 Peter 2:9 in the *Adumbrationes* involves the Christian's mind making offerings in prayers and teachings, in a way reminiscent of the idea of the temple of the mind in the *Teaching of Silvanus*. Generally, Clement's idea of Christian priesthood is determined much more by his view of the qualities and duties of the gnostic Christian than by the statements about the general priesthood in the NT, connoting spiritual perfection, self-denial and holiness, knowing and contemplating God and the secret things of his word and teaching those things, and being assimilated to the Logos. Although aware of the concept of the general priesthood prevalent in the contemporary church, influences peculiar to Alexandria and related circles caused him to emphasize the priesthood of the perfect far more.

More or less the same is true of Origen, although he refers to both the perfect and ordinary Christians as priests much more often than does Clement. The priesthood of the perfect connotes much the same for him as does the priesthood of the gnostic for Clement. He also brings out the continuity between the perfect and the ordinary Christian more, repeatedly exhorting all to become perfect as priests and holding that all could do so. His overwhelming concern in mentioning the general priesthood so often is pastoral: he clearly expected the fact of it and his use of it to play a part in awakening ordinary Christians to their responsibilities and possibilities. It was also important exegetically in that it enabled him to make the OT Levitical legislation relevant to all his hearers and readers. It thus had considerable significance for him, probably more than for anyone else in the period under consideration, with the possible exception of Tertullian. Further evidence of its significance for him is provided by the relative frequency with which he quotes 1 Peter 2:5 or 9.

The general priesthood has many connotations for Origen. These include the offering of spiritual sacrifices but less those involving the eucharist, as for Justin and Hippolytus, than those of prayer, as for Tertullian, and of good works. Purity and holiness of life are very important concomitants of priesthood for Origen, as for Tertullian. Dedication to, and complete dependence on, God are also, as for Irenaeus. Similarly to Clement, he at times depicts as priest the Christian's mind as that by which he can comprehend and receive God and his word, and emphasizes the cultivation of virtues and the abnegation of vices as sacrifices offered up by the Christian as priest far more than anyone before him. He links the general priesthood with baptism and the anointing and self-consecration connected with it, as did Tertullian. Often, however, his interpretation of priesthood and application of 1 Peter 2:9 develop into expositions of perfection, connoting self-denial and complete devotion, the cultivation of virtues, study of the word, and understanding it spiritually not carnally, thus knowing the mysteries and secret wisdom of God, and imparting them wisely to those with the capacity to receive them.

With Tertullian, then, Origen has the richest appreciation and understanding of the general priesthood, even though he tends to constict it to the perfect as Tertullian does not. The two of them appreciated the possibilities of this teaching far more than anyone else in the first three hundred years. This fact is almost certainly connected with the church's growth in the final decades of the second century and the first decades of the third. Characteristically, Tertullian's use of it is at times for more outwardly disciplinary reasons than Origen, but they both use it with doctrinal and above all pastoral concerns, none excelling Origen in the latter. Their appreciation and development of this teaching owes much to their own genius and ability to relate it to some of their main concerns.

The general priesthood is not at all significant for Cyprian, with only one possible mention of it in the whole of his corpus. In that, it connotes the need for holiness after the cleansing and sanctification involved in baptism, emphases we have noted in Tertullian especially, though also in Origen, and the need to obey and serve God, emphases noted in several earlier writers. This suggests that Cyprian was aware of the general priesthood through the teaching around him, but that he made little of it himself.

The quotation of 1 Peter 2:9 in the *Didascalia* involves Christians' election and holiness and the sacrifices of prayer, thanksgiving and material gifts, again emphases we have noted earlier. As with Cyprian, this teaching seems likely to have been received via church tradition but to have not meant much to the author. The only other allusion to 1 Peter 2:9 probably from the third century, that in the *Epistola 1 ad virgines*, makes nothing of the general priesthood.

This survey makes it clear that the teaching that all Christians are priests was of varying significance to, and was given varying connotations and meanings by, the Christian writers of the first three centuries whose writings are extant. While most were aware of it, it is only Tertullian and Origen for whom it attains some considerable significance. We have noted the likely reasons for this. That the link between priesthood and sacrifice was normal and frequently made is shown by the fact that the general priesthood connotes spiritual sacrifices for several authors, particularly the sacrifices of the eucharist, and of prayer, praise and the self in devotion and holy living, as in the Bible. A clearer link was made between baptism and priesthood by Tertullian and Origen than is apparent in the NT, the baptismal anointing being the central point of the analogy with the OT priesthood. Although holiness is a freqent connotation of priesthood for these early writers, this is developed much further by Clement of Alexandria and Origen under influences common to them and to Gnosticism and because of the deterioration, as Origen especially perceived it, in the quality of Christian living. Tertullian too develops the teaching of the general priesthood in ways particularly conducive to his concerns, above all that of prohibiting second marriages. Whilst not very significant for many of the writers considered, the evidence suggests that belief in the general priesthood was fairly constant and general in the whole church of this period, and that it could be considerably significant for any motivated to make it so.

Several writers link the origins of this priesthood with baptism and the purifying work of Christ involved in it. Tertullian and Justin imply a link between Christ's and the general priesthood, the latter resulting from Christ's work in the former. Origen and Clement of Rome view Christian sacrifices as being offered through Christ as high priest.

5.9.3 Correlation with the growth in the special priesthood

There is no simple correlation between the growth in importance of the priesthood of the ordained, the bishop in particular, and the decline in importance of the general priesthood. The general priesthood does not achieve considerable significance until Tertullian and Origen, both of whom accept the special priesthood of the ordained, and belief in the general priesthood clearly did not die out with the prominence of the priesthood of the ordained. Even so, it seems likely that such a correlation took place.

None of the writers considered explicitly links the general and special priesthoods, except Tertullian, who seems to see the latter as an ecclesiastical derivation from the divinely ordained former, implying a deep continuity between them confirmed by his application of some Levitical legislation to both and his allowance of the major priestly functions for him to both. Further, it was argued in section 5.3 that one of the reasons for Tertullian's more frequent allusions to the general priesthood was the increasing prominence being given in his day to the priesthood of the ordained, which is likely to have been a fairly recent development itself. This is probably shown in his statements in *Chastity* 7 regarding the common priesthood. Although he does not object to the use of 'priests' for the ordained, he stresses very strongly that the laity are priests also, as if this was a truth now in danger of being forgotten by some, particularly concerning second marriages. He seems to make a contrast between the 'It is written: "He hath made us also a kingdom, and priests to God and His father"' and the 'It is ecclesiastical authority which distinguishes clergy and laity',[338] as if some needed reminding that God had ordained the general priesthood, whereas the difference between those in the clergy and the rest depended only on the church's authority. He further has to argue that Christians are called priests in *On Monogamy* 7, whilst 12 suggests that some Christians in Carthage were resentful of the clergy's power and so insisting on equality, particularly concerning priesthood, on the basis of Scripture. Although his main concern in all these passages is the prohibition of remarriage, they also show Tertullian trying to hold a mediating position between those insisting on the power and authority of the ordained as priests and those insisting on the equal priesthood of all Christians. And the fact that he has to provide arguments to buttress his maintenance of the general priesthood but not concerning the priesthood of the ordained suggests that it was the latter which had the power and prominence and the former which was in danger of being forgotten by some.

These suggestions are, if anything, reinforced by what we find in Cyprian's works some forty to fifty years later. As we have noted, he emphasizes the sacral authority of the bishop as priest in the context of challenges to his authority. These challenges were so acute that they were probably an important reason why he reserved *sacerdos* for bishops and never commented on any of the NT texts which teach the general priesthood. *Sacerdos* had such connotations of sacral authority for him that it is unlikely that he could ever have seen it as appropriate for the laity. It is possible that his unwillingness to refer to the general priesthood, except on one isolated occasion, arose partly from the fact that there were still those, as there had been in Tertullian's day, who were insisting on the equal priesthood of all Christians in Carthage, although this is the only indication of this possibility and so the evidence is weak. Tertullian's and Cyprian's evidence together, however, suggests that the connotations of sacral authority and power attached by such as Cyprian to the title of *sacerdos* as used of the bishop in particular were having an adverse influence on the teaching of the general priesthood, at least in Cyprian's case and probably for others also.

Hippolytus implies continuity between the general and special priesthoods by his depiction of the eucharist as the whole church's priestly offering. However, he also implies a great difference between them, one which goes beyond Tertullian's picture, by presenting ordination to the priesthood as involving God-given powers vitally important to the church which were not open to Christians in general.

---

[338] Le Saint, 53.

Such a picture of ordination is taken for granted in Cyprian's and the *Didascalia*'s depiction of the bishop's priestly powers. It is surely highly significant that, in Hippolytus and Cyprian, the general priesthood is only implied once, Cyprian is unwilling to use *sacerdos* of ordinary Christians, and the *Didascalia* completely devalues that priesthood in favour of the special priesthood. Clearly what separates these two priesthoods is far more significant than what they have in common, a picture so unlike Tertullian's.

In Alexandria the evolution was different, though with a similar result as far as the general priesthood was concerned. Various influences combined to produce a view of the true priest as the perfect Christian. Although both Clement and Origen were aware of the teaching that all Christians were priests, and Origen in particular used it as a means of persuading Christians to live up to what priesthood required, their constriction of true priesthood to the gnostic or perfect Christian tended in the same direction as did Cyprian's constriction of priesthood to the ordained. Either way, the general priesthood as understood of all Christians equally and without distinction in the NT was being narrowed and restricted to certain Christians in particular.

In their different ways, Tertullian and Origen sought to maintain a balance between the different types of priesthood with which they dealt. Tertullian sought to emphasize the continuity between the priesthood of the ordained and the common priesthood by pointing out that those who made up the former had to be chosen from those who made up the latter so that prohibitions relating to the former related also to the latter. Origen sought to emphasize the continuity between the priesthood of the perfect and the general priesthood by depicting their relationship as an organic one such that any in the latter could become a participant in the former, those in the former all having to pass through the latter, whilst he emphasized the continuity between the priesthood of the ordained and that of the perfect by similarly stressing that any in the former could become a participant in the latter. Where this continuity was not maintained, as in Cyprian's works and the *Didascalia*, then one priesthood won out at the expense of the other, a danger that is clear in the works of Clement and Origen as well.

There are, therefore, two lines of evidence that the introduction of other kinds of priesthoods than those of Christ and all the faithful tended to undermine the significance and value attributed to the general priesthood. The main aim in the next chapter will be to examine whether this tendency was related to other developments in the first three centuries of the church.

CHAPTER 6

Developments Bearing on the Relationship between the General and Special Priesthoods

This chapter will trace developments in the first three centuries of the church which bear on the relationship between the general and special priesthoods. The 'special priesthood' means that of the ordained because that was to prove of continuing significance in the life of the church to the present day, whereas the priesthood of the perfect did not so prove. This last priesthood will only be referred to where developments related to it provide parallels with those concerning the priesthood of the ordained and its influences on the general priesthood.

Since the general priesthood covered all Christians, whereas the special priesthood included only the designated leaders of the church, the most significant developments concerned the relationship between leaders and other Christians. Because the general priesthood embraced leaders not as leaders but as Christians, it covered all Christians, ordained and unordained. This must be remembered as this study follows Tertullian and Origen, in particular, in relating it mainly to the unordained.

In our look at the NT we noted the Pauline picture of God distributing many gifts (*charismata*) to individual Christians, at least one to each, all of which were to be used to build up the church, a picture which in some ways paralleled the Petrine picture of all Christians being living stones built together to form a spiritual house and a holy priesthood offering spiritual sacrifices. Some of the gifts mentioned by Paul were abilities which related to leadership. We also noted that leaders were part of the church from its inception, and that other Christians were exhorted to respect and obey them. Even so, the underlying sense of community, fellowship, equality, and the dignity and privileges of each Christian and all Christians together before God was far stronger than the sense of what set certain Christians apart from others. We further noted that, as a result of the gifts which Christians in general received, they were all, both collectively and individually, considered to have ministries. As priesthood in the Bible related to dignity and service, so do the gifts. Our study will therefore examine developments in the areas of power and ministry in the church, seeking to show that, as the ordained increasingly captured both, and as both were related to their priesthood, so other Christians increasingly lost both and their priesthood was devalued.

6.1 The Apostolic Fathers

6.1.1 Attempts to subordinate the rest to the leadership

In the NT exhortations and instructions to Christians to submit themselves to the leadership are found (1 Thess. 5:12-13, Heb. 13:17 and 1 Pet. 5:5), but these are few and do not emphasize the rights of the leaders who are themselves exhorted concerning their duties and the way they are to perform them (1 Pet. 5:1-4). The change in tone and content is marked in some of the Apostolic Fathers, in Ignatius' letters especially.

There is, for example, no equivalent in the NT to the instructions in *Smyrnaeans* 8:

> You must all follow the bishop, as Jesus Christ followed the Father, and follow the presbytery as you would the apostles; respect the deacons as the commandment of God. Let no one do anything that has to do with the church without the bishop. Only that Eucharist which is under the authority of the bishop (or whomever he himself designates) is to be considered valid. Wherever the bishop appears, there let the congregation be; just as wherever Jesus Christ is, there is the catholic church. It is not permissible either to baptize or to hold a love feast without the bishop. But whatever he approves is also pleasing to God, in order that everything you do may be trustworthy and valid.[1]

This illustrates the kind of power which one bishop felt bishops should have over the church, its meetings and its main means of grace. Ignatius' several mentions of this subject[2] and the stress some others also laid on it, as we shall see, suggest that there was widespread unwillingness to yield such all-encompassing and utter submission to the bishop and his delegates. The struggle with heresy and his own evaluation of the fundamental value of Christian unity and harmony also contributed greatly to Ignatius' emphasis on the oneness of the church around the bishop.[3]

---

[1] Lightfoot, Harmer and Holmes, 189, 191.
[2] Note also *Smyrn.* 9:1, *Magn.* 6:1, *Trall.* 3:1, and *Philad.* 4 (cf. Hein, 211-3).
[3] So von Campenhausen, *Ecclesiastical Authority*, 99-100.

This tendency, whilst not carried to the same extremes, is apparent in *1 Clement* also. This is not surprising since it was written to a church in which some had rebelled against the presbyters. Clement's tone is far less peremptory than Ignatius', but he deploys several arguments to illustrate the necessity of order in the church, not least of which is the one we noted in section 4.1 where he argues that, just as God appointed a certain order in OT times, so God has appointed one for the church (40-44). It is in this context that Clement is the first to introduce the concept of the layman to extant Christian literature (40:5). Whatever the precise significance of this word to Clement,[4] it comes at the end of a hierarchical list of OT offices and corresponds to the ordinary, non-priestly Israelite. Further, the order established for and in the church is presented as ordained by God, a theory of 'apostolic succession' being suggested, and an OT text slightly altered to provide a divine prophecy of the appointment of bishops and deacons (42-43). This order is made into a leading principle of the church's life. As von Campenhausen comments,

> that everything should be done "decently and in order" is, indeed, an idea which Paul himself could express at the appropriate moment. In Paul, however, it occurs only as a peripheral comment, an obvious truth which ought not to be forgotten. For Clement it has turned into a piece of sacred knowledge which touches the essence of the Church, a fundamental, exalted truth, which he makes the content of his whole sermon.[5]

One result is that this order becomes something over against Christians into which they must fit (40:5-41:1), a concept quite foreign to Paul and the NT. Another is that it involves superior and inferior positions, a concept largely foreign to Paul and the NT.[6] Moreover, God is made its protector (45:7), giving it ultimate value and sanction, so that to break it is to sin against God (41:3).

There is a danger of overstating the situation, however, and it is noteworthy that *1 Clement* warns only against overthrowing those presbyters who exercise their oversight blamelessly (44:3-4), illustrating that conformity with God-given order had its limits. Moreover, 'the decision whether they have in fact done so plainly belongs to the

---

[4] On this, see especially Faivre, *Emergence*, 15-24. See also Williams G.H, 'The Ancient Church, AD 30-313' in Neill, S.C. and Weber, H.-R. (eds.), *The Layman in Christian History* (London, 1963), 30, and Lanne, 'Le laïc', *Verbum Caro* 18 (1964), 108.

[5] Von Campenhausen, *Ecclesiastical Authority*, 87.

[6] Largely foreign to Paul because he acknowledges something of a hierarchy of gifts - but of gifts and not offices - in 1 Cor. 12:28 and Eph. 4:11; and largely foreign to the NT because the office of bishop is regarded as 'a noble task' in 1 Tim. 3:1.

congregation',[7] since the leaders of the rebellion are urged to 'do whatever is ordered by the people.'[8] Further, Clement writes in the name of the church in Rome to that in Corinth, addressing them all and not just the leaders (see the salutation and 1:1). Neither does Ignatius ignore ordinary Christians, viewing them, as we have noted before, as 'carrying your God and your shrine, your Christ and your holy things, ...'[9] Nonetheless, the tendency to subordinate other Christians to their leaders is apparent.

There is little mention of church officials in *The Shepherd*, because the author is not one himself, the book deals with general moral problems, and there seems to have been no friction, at least concerning the subjects treated, between the officials and the author.[10] Presbyters are mentioned in *Visions* 2:4:2-3 (or 8:2-3) as those through whom the author should make his message known to other churches, the author reading it himself in his own church in the elders' presence. Given a vital place in the tower which is the church in *Visions* 3:5:1 (or 13:1) are 'the apostles and bishops and teachers and deacons' who have lived and served to God's glory.[11] Such bishops are protected by God, according to *Similitudes* 9:27:2-3 (104:2-3). The leaders are called shepherds in *Similitudes* 9:31:5-6 (108:5-6) and are held responsible by God for the right behaviour of their flock. They are the 'occupants of the seats of honour', according to *Visions* 3:9:7 (17:7).[12]. In spite of saying so little about church officials, then, *The Shepherd* still demonstrates their important positions, albeit with none of the emphasis or the subjection of other Christians to them evidenced in *1 Clement* and Ignatius' letters.

That a church leader could be deposed legitimately, though not how, is shown by Polycarp's approval of the deposition of a presbyter at Philippi in *Philippians* 11:1, 4 for having given in to greed. On the other hand, Polycarp finds it necessary (in 5:3) to warn the younger men to 'be obedient to the presbyters and deacons as to God and Christ.'[13]

There is, then, considerable evidence that, in the early second century, church leaders were feeling the need to stress their God-given right to expect both respect and obedience from the rest of the congregation because of their position as well as the quality of their life and service. For Ignatius, the congregation, though filled with the Spirit, is to be in

---

[7] Von Campenhausen, *Ecclesiastical Authority*, 93.
[8] *1 Clem.* 54:2: Lightfoot, Harmer and Holmes, 89
[9] *Eph.* 9:2: ibid., 143.
[10] On this, see von Campenhausen, *Ecclesiastical Authority*, 95.
[11] Lightfoot, Harmer and Holmes, 355.
[12] Ibid., 363.
[13] Ibid., 213.

total subjection to the bishop who has oversight of everything connected with the church, and for Clement, the order which prescribes some as leaders and others as led is elevated to the status of a God-given principle of the church. The other documents do not share these strong emphases, which suggests that they arose mainly where there were problems over leadership. Even so, these other documents also demonstrate leaders' importance and oversight.

6.1.2 The gifts, ministry and leadership

Most significant concerning the relationship within the Christian community between those with certain gifts and leadership is the *Didache*. It has many more contacts with the Pauline picture of the gifts than the other Apostolic Fathers. It knows of itinerant apostles, teachers and prophets, and urges the congregation to test any such, 'for you will have insight [into] what is true and what is false' (cf. 1 Cor. 14:29, 1 Jn. 4:1 and 2:18-27).[14] However, not all churches now have prophets (cf. 13:4) and the instruction is given to 'therefore appoint for yourselves bishops and deacons ..., for they too carry out for you the ministry of the prophets and teachers.' That bishops and deacons were not yet as greatly respected as the presumably settled prophets and teachers is suggested by the following, 'You must not, therefore, despise them, for they are your honoured men, along with the prophets and teachers' (15:1-2).[15] Whether or not chapter 15 was a later addition to the rest,[16] the document as it now stands witnesses to a transition in at least one church in the early second century from a leadership dominated by those recognized as having the requisite gifts, to a leadership consisting of those appointed as bishops and deacons who are now considered to have the same ministry, implying the same gifts.[17] According to 15:1-2, both existed together for a time. The emphasis, however, is no longer on the gifts, but on the qualities of life necessary for leaders (see 15:1). This reversal of emphasis is already seen in the Pastoral Epistles in the NT, which is one reason why their Pauline and early origin has been questioned.

---

[14] *Did.* 12:1: ibid., 265. Note, however, the change implied by *Did.* 11:7, on which see Ash, J.L., 'The Decline of Ecstatic Prophecy in the Early Church', *Theological Studies* 37.2 (1976), 232-3.

[15] Lightfoot, Harmer and Holmes, 267.

[16] See discussion in Kydd, R.A.N., *Charismata to 320 A.D. A Study of the Overt Pneumatic Experience of the Early Church* (unpublished thesis, 1973), 118-9.

[17] So Grant, *Introduction*, 160; Kydd, 117-120; and Ash, 'Decline', *Th St* 37.2 (1976), 235. In contrast note Lawson, 99.

The main ministry of the apostles, prophets and teachers is to bring messages from God, the teacher didactically,[18] and the prophet and apostle possibly ecstatically (cf. 11:7 and 5). Prophets are also to be allowed to give thanks as they will (10:7).[19] All are to be accorded the highest honour (4:1; 11:2, 4, cf. 7). The exhortation not to despise bishops and deacons but to honour them alongside the prophets and teachers (15:1-2) suggests that the same respect was to be afforded to them also. Finally, the fact that the qualities to be sought for bishops and deacons relate to worthy leadership and oversight of money, plus the fact that they are said to minister the same ministry as the prophets and teachers (15:1-2), suggests that all four had administrative and other duties of oversight of the congregation. Even so, the congregation, as we have already noted, is given instruction in how to discern true prophets and teachers from false,[20] and is told to appoint bishops and deacons, demonstrating that it still had considerable power. Yet the gifts are now apparently restricted to certain individuals rather than distributed throughout the congregation, as in the churches Paul depicted in Corinth, Rome and Ephesus.

The only mention of a gift in *1 Clement* comes in 38:1. Its context is an exhortation to 'let the whole body be saved in Christ Jesus, and let each man be subject to his neighbor, to the degree determined by his spiritual gift.'[21] It was suggested to Clement by his use of the body-metaphor in 37:5 in a way very similar to Paul's in 1 Corinthians 12:12-25 in his treatment of the gifts in chapters 12-14. Yet Clement juxtaposes this with submission to others, and with the strong caring for the weak and the weak honouring the strong, not with building up the body, as Paul does. There is no suggestion that the gift is to result in ministry in the meetings of the church, as in 1 Corinthians 12-14. It is true that each of the brethren has a ministry (*leitourgia*) according to *1 Clement* 41:1, but this is in the context of the exhortation, 'Let each ... in his proper order give thanks to God, ... not overstepping the designated rule of his ministry, but acting with reverence', followed by further warnings in 41:2-4.[22] This service is severely restricted by the

---

[18] See Neymeyr, 140-155 on teachers in the *Didache*.

[19] Bârlea, O., *Die Weihe der Bischöfe, Presbyter und Diakone in vornicänischer Zeit* (Munich, 1969), 95-6 and Hein, 203, see the *eucharistein* (literally, 'give thanks') as referring to presiding at or celebrating the eucharist, but, although it would include at the eucharist, it is not necessarily restricted to that occasion.

[20] Note von Campenhausen, *Ecclesiastical Authority*, 72-3 and Ash, 'Decline', *Th St* 37.2 (1976), 232, on the changes from Paul's day in the kinds of test applied.

[21] Lightfoot, Harmer and Holmes, 71.

[22] Ibid., 73, 75.

hierarchical order which we noted in section 6.1.1.

We noted in section 4.1.1 that Clement depicts the presbyters as 'those who have offered the gifts [of the episcopacy] ...',[23] which probably involved presidency at church services that included the eucharist, at which they were the spokesmen of the people's praise and thanksgiving. Furthermore, his emphasis on order and exercising ministries only as permitted to one's order suggests that the leaders were to have the most important ministries.

Although Ignatius greets the Smyrnaean church as 'mercifully endowed with every spiritual gift, ...[and] not lacking in any spiritual gift',[24] he makes no further reference to this, suggesting that it is only flattery consciously based on 1 Corinthians 1:7. In *Philadelphians* 7 he describes an example of his own exercise of prophecy. Significantly, however, it is to command the people, '"Pay attention to the bishop and to the presbytery and deacons"', and '"Do nothing without the bishop."'[25] His only other mention of prophecy is in *Polycarp* 2:2 where Polycarp is exhorted, 'ask, in order that the unseen things may be revealed to you, that you may be lacking in nothing and abound in every spiritual gift.'[26] Ash may be right that Ignatius viewed the bishop alone as possessing the prophetic gift.[27] Further, Polycarp is described as having received a prophecy of his death in *Martyrdom of Polycarp* 5:2 and as 'an apostolic and prophetic teacher' in 16:2.[28]

We have already noted that, as far as Ignatius is concerned, all important functions are in principle in the bishop's hands, including public worship, administration of the sacraments, marriages, and instruction.[29] In spite of his view of all Christians as bearers of God, etc. (*Eph.* 9:2), the public ministry of the church is not to be in their hands and they have little part to play.

We noted in 6.1.1 that the author of *The Shepherd* is a prophet. Although he never calls himself this, he claims visions which suggest it.[30] Since he is instructed to read out what he has received in front of the elders,[31] we have a situation, like that in the *Didache*, in which others than the official church leaders could bring messages to the

---

[23] *1 Clem.* 44:4: ibid., 79.

[24] Ibid., 185.

[25] Ibid., 181.

[26] Ibid., 197.

[27] Ash, 'Decline', *Th St* 37.2 (1976), 234.

[28] Lightfoot, Harmer and Holmes, 239, 241.

[29] Von Campenhausen, *Ecclesiastical Authority*, 101.

[30] So Kydd, 185-6.

[31] *Vis.* 2:4:2-3 (8:2-3).

congregation, under the leaders' oversight. That the congregation was also responsible to evaluate such messages is implied in *Mandates* 11, which is a long warning to all Christians against false prophecy, with instructions, in some ways similar to those in the *Didache*, on how to distinguish true from false.

There are several allusions to teachers in the *Didache*.[32] Their mention alongside apostles, bishops and deacons in *Visions* 3:5:1 suggests that they were viewed as a third category of leaders alongside the bishops and deacons. Neymeyr also argues that the author of *The Epistle of Barnabas* wanted to be recognized as a teacher,[33] but our paucity of knowledge about him precludes speculation over him exercising leadership. *2 Clement* 17:3 and 5, however, depict the elders as exhorting and teaching the congregation.[34]

In contrast with the NT, then, ministry, especially that in the churches' meetings, is mainly, in some cases solely, the responsibility of those recognized as leaders. Those with the gifts of prophecy and teaching continued to exist in some places alongside bishops and deacons, but there are indications that bishops in particular were viewed as endowed with the gift of prophecy and that they and presbyters taught the congregation regularly. *Didache* 13:4 shows that prophets were not found everywhere. This and the instruction to appoint bishops and deacons arouses the suspicion that there were no longer so many recognized as possessing the gifts of prophecy and teaching and a solution was to appoint in their stead worthy leaders who were not as conspicuously gifted. The probable attestation to the office of teacher in *The Shepherd*, on the other hand, suggests that this gift was more widespread and continued for longer in some places. The most extreme case of all ministry being in the purview of the bishop is found in Ignatius.

6.1.3 The whole church's involvement in discipline

Von Campenhausen points out that the forgiveness of sins plays a surprisingly small role in the early development of church order.[35] Reasons for this include the fact that all are forgiven by God and are to forgive one another. Both the sayings concerning binding and loosing in Matthew (16:19 and 18:18) are given in the context of references to the

---
[32] See Neymeyr, 10-15.
[33] Neymeyr, 169-180, especially 179-180.
[34] So Hanson, R.P.C., *Studies*, 123.
[35] Von Campenhausen, *Ecclesiastical Authority*, 124.

church. In the latter,

> plainly the assembly of the congregation here plays the part of a final and
> definitive court of appeal. ... That the direction may have been in the hands of
> elders or of an "apostle" cannot be ruled out, but there is not a single word to
> suggest it, and it cannot therefore have played any very decisive role. It is the
> Church as a whole in which this great power is vested. Her essentially
> spiritual character, grounded in the presence of Christ, is taken as axiomatic:
> [Mt. 18:20][36]

While this power is connected specifically with Peter in Matthew 16:19
and Acts 5:1-11 and 8:9-24, it is with Peter as one enlightened by the
Spirit or the Father and having an authority based on that. In the rest of
the NT it is either the individual Christian or the church as a whole who
are to exercise discipline in its broadest sense. The forgiveness of a sick
man's sins appears to be a minor aspect of the elders' prayers for his
healing in James 5:15, whilst sin is to be confessed 'to one another' and
Christians are to 'pray for one another, that you may be healed' in James
5:16, suggesting that the elders represent the whole congregation in this.
Paul's attitude is summed up in Galatians 6:1: 'brethren, if a man is
overtaken in any trespass, you who are spiritual should restore him in a
spirit of gentleness.' In the extreme case mentioned in 1 Corinthians
5:1-5 Paul tells the Corinthian Christians what to do, but it is they,
assembled together, who are to make the judgment (cf. 5:12 and 6:2).

The writings of the Apostolic Fathers, where they give relevant
information, do not contradict this picture but confirm that it continued.
Christians in general are exhorted to intercede 'for those who are
involved in some transgression', and are reminded that, 'The reproof
which we give one to another is good and exceedingly useful' in *1
Clement* 56:1-2; they are urged to help one another 'to restore those who
are weak with respect to goodness, so that we may all be saved, and let
us admonish and turn back one another' in *2 Clement* 17:2; the
individual Christian is told, 'You shall not show partiality when
reproving someone for a transgression' in *Barnabas* 19:4, a similar
expression being used in *Didache* 4:3: 'You shall judge righteously; you
shall not show partiality when reproving transgressions'; and Christians
in general are told, 'correct one another, not in anger but in peace, ...' in
Didache 15:3.[37] Moreover, *The Shepherd*, which deals at great length
with different sins and how they are to be expiated, leaves repentance to

---

[36] Ibid., 128.
[37] Lightfoot, Harmer and Holmes, 91, 123, 125, 321, 255, 267. This list of references is given
in von Campenhausen, *Ecclesiastical Authority*, 133, n. 39.

the individual. Von Campenhausen makes the valid point that, 'even Ignatius has nothing to say about the readmission of penitents or about excommunication; and in view of the completeness with which he expresses himself on all the other duties of a bishop his silence on the matter of penitential discipline simply cannot be accidental.'[38] He makes a general reference to the bishop bringing troublesome disciples to subjection by his gentleness in *Polycarp* 2:1, but gives no information about readmission or excommunication. Similarly, Polycarp urges presbyters to be busy in 'turning back those who have gone astray' in *Philippians* 6:1, but says nothing about excommunication or readmission even in the case of Valens in chapter 11.[39] He does, however, tell the Philippians in general not to consider Valens and his wife as enemies, 'but, as sick and straying members, restore them, in order that you may save your body in its entirety.'[40]

It is evident in what we have just examined that the onus in dealing with sinners lay on every Christian and not just the leaders. If there were formal procedures for excommunication and readmission, nothing is said about them, probably because they did not exist, in view of Ignatius' interest in the bishops' powers. This forms, at least, a contrast with what we find in the mid-third century.

6.1.4 Conclusion

There is evidence here of a fluid situation from place to place, from time to time, and from subject to subject covered. Whilst there is strong emphasis on the subordination of the Christian community to its leaders in Ignatius' and Clement's letters, and a tendency to vest public ministry in leaders recognized either for their *charismata* or, increasingly, for their quality of life, there is also recognition of the continuing spiritual authority of ordinary Christians, or the whole congregation, particularly in dealing with sinners.

---

[38] Ibid., 142. So too Hanson, R.P.C., *Christian Priesthood Examined*, 21 and *Studies*, 123.

[39] Williams G.H., 'Ancient Church' in Neill and Weber, *The Layman in Christian History*, 38, calls this passage 'a clear indication that the whole church and more specifically the laity with their presbyters had the right to depose and excommunicate one of their presbyters, ...' Although *Phil.* 11 implies that Valens has left the church, there is no indication as to how he left. It was argued above that a deposition is implied, the only alternative being voluntary resignation, but excommunication goes beyond the evidence.

[40] Lightfoot, Harmer and Holmes, 217, 219.

6.2 The period of the second-century Apologists

6.2.1 Justin Martyr

There is little emphasis on church leaders' authority in Justin's writings. Two major reasons for this are Justin's status as a layman and, above all, the apologetic and polemic nature of his extant writings. Unlike Ignatius he has no leadership status to defend, and unlike Clement he is not addressing a situation in which leaders have been removed. His silence must therefore be interpreted in the light of what he does say.

A leader is mentioned by Justin, but he is called *ho proestôs*, the president. This raises the possibility that he was not an official leader but just one of the Christians who presided on that occasion. The lack of any other example of this in extant literature, together with the attestation of the leadership of the bishop or the presbyter in Christian worship elsewhere, plus Justin's witness to his functions, make it likely that an officially recognized leader was meant, as argued in section 4.2.1. The main function of this figure presented by Justin is presidency at the eucharist, which involves receiving bread and a cup of wine mixed with water, praising God and thanking him for all his gifts, thereupon allowing the deacons to distribute the bread and cup. This happens both after a baptism (*Apol.* 1:65) and every Sunday (*Apol.* 1:67), when the *proestôs* also rebukes and exhorts those present, and receives their gifts, being responsible for their distribution to the needy. Faivre points out that the president's distribution of gifts to the needy implies 'management ability ... and sufficient authority to be able to resolve the conflicts that might result from the redistribution of those goods.'[41] It also suggests knowledge of those who are needy. Overall, the *proestôs* is presented as having a caring authority which fits well what we know elsewhere concerning the bishop.

Justin's apologetic intentions must have affected the picture he gives of a Christian community in which behaviour is exemplary and there are few, if any, problems (see, e.g., *Apol.* 1:14:2-3). They are less likely to have influenced the prominence he gives to the participation of all in worship, since his description must have depicted reality fairly accurately if his *Apology* was to be convincing to outsiders. Twice mentioned is their sharing with the needy (1:14:2 and 67:1), aid which is provided as part of their Sunday worship-services (1:67:6-7). Everyone's involvement in a baptismal service is stressed: they all help to prepare the candidate (1:61:2), accompany him to hear his assent to

---

[41] Faivre, *Emergence*, 33.

the faith, pray for him and others, greet each other with the kiss of peace; after the president's praise over the bread and cup, they all say, 'Amen' and participate in the eucharist (1:65). The same is true of the Sunday service (1:67), and we saw in sections 4.2.1 and 5.2.1 the way in which the eucharist is depicted as the sacrifice of all Christians who are 'the true high-priestly race of God' in *Dialogue* 41:2-3 and 116-117.

Justin also emphasizes the unity and communion of Christians with one another by his use of the body-metaphor in *Dialogue* 42:3, the vine-metaphor in *Dialogue* 110:3-4, the house-metaphor in *Dialogue* 86:6, and the ideas of Christians as the people of God in *Dialogue* 119:2-4, the true sons of God in *Dialogue* 123:9, and the house of Jacob by faith and the Spirit in *Dialogue* 135:6. Those who believe in Christ are 'of one soul and one synagogue and one church ... for we all are called Christians' (*Dial.* 63:5).[42] Further, he defines Christians above all as 'disciples' and, for him, 'there was no division between Christians, no antinomy between clergy and laity and not even a difference between the priest and the Christian.'[43] This shines through in his repeated descriptions of what Christians share because of their faith. He also expects all Christians' lives to convert others.[44]

Justin has a lively sense of all Christians being helped by the Spirit, especially in knowledge of the truth,[45] and is aware of the *charismata*. These are received by each Christian, as Paul had said, according to Justin's statement in *Dialogue* 39:2 about Jews who become Christians.[46] In *Dialogue* 82:1 Justin argues, 'From the fact that even to this day the gifts of prophecy exist among us Christians, you should realize that the gifts which had resided among your people have now been transferred to us.'[47] He then speaks of the existence of false teachers amongst Christians, identifying Christian teaching with prophecy. He returns to the same argument in *Dialogue* 87:5-88:1, and

---

[42] Falls, 248.

[43] Faivre, *Emergence*, 31.

[44] On these last two points see Faivre, *Emergence*, 34-5, Eastwood, 65-6 and Williams G.H., 'Ancient Church' in Neill and Weber, *The Layman in Christian History*, 46. They point to *Apol.* 1:23, 31 and 39.

[45] Having pointed to some of Plato's teachings as borrowed from Moses, he says in *Apol.* 1:60:11, 'Among us this teaching can be heard and learnt from those who do not even know the form of the letters of Scripture, people who are ignorant and barbarous in language, ... so that one comes to understand that it is not the work of a human wisdom, but the teaching of a power of God' (Wartelle, 181).

[46] '... this same name of Christ enlightens you to receive all the graces and gifts according to your merits. One receives the spirit of wisdom, another of counsel, another of fortitude, another of healing, another of foreknowledge, another of teaching, and another of the fear of God' (Falls, 207).

[47] Ibid., 278.

claims, 'you can see among us Christians both men and women endowed with gifts from the Spirit of God.'[48] Kydd argues that scholars generally feel that Justin's reports are trustworthy and that there is evidence of *charismata* at Rome before and after him from Clement and Hippolytus,[49] although this evidence is not as strong as in Justin. The only information he gives on the part played by those who had these gifts in Christian meetings or otherwise in the community concerns himself as a teacher, though this may not be significant.

While Justin does not mention the office of prophet,[50] he does mention teachers, and acted as one himself. He claims the assistance of God's grace in his teaching (*Dial.* 9:1 and 58:1), and mentions the spirit of teaching among the *charismata* in *Dialogue* 39:2.[51] *Acta Justini* 3:3 indicates that he taught from his home. He probably taught catechumens as well as non-Christians who formed his main audience.[52] Neymeyr convincingly argues that he did not form a school with a curriculum but that people came to him sporadically. He further argues that there is no evidence that Justin was appointed by the church to teach, but what we have already noted of his knowledge of practices concerning baptism, the eucharist and Sunday services demonstrates he participated in its life.[53] Justin is thus an important witness to the gift of teaching being exercised by one outside church leadership, though not in church meetings, in the middle of the second century.

His evidence is frustratingly limited in scope, however. As far as it goes, it suggests a church-situation more like that depicted by Paul in 1 Corinthans than does any other evidence outside the NT with the exception of the *Didache*. But its limited, apologetic and polemical nature makes its silence on the handling of discipline and other internal problems involving authority, and its depiction of church-life as harmonious understandable without recourse to any theories based on them. It is fair to conclude, however, that the *charismata* were exercised, that all Christians were viewed as having great dignity, privileges and responsibilities in God's sight, and that there was a

---

[48] Ibid., 288.

[49] Kydd, 318-9.

[50] Ash, 'Decline', *Th St* 37.2 (1976), 235-6, points out that the office of prophet was unknown after Ignatius as part of his argument that episcopacy took over this gift and was mainly responsible for its demise in the church. This holds only if the relevant parts of the *Didache* are dated before Ignatius and the evidence of the gift elsewhere is rejected. Whilst episcopacy certainly contributed to the demise of the office of prophet, other factors also were at work.

[51] On the first point, see von Campenhausen, *Ecclesiastical Authority*, 193 and Neymeyr, 34. On the second, see ibid., 34.

[52] So ibid., 26-7.

[53] Ibid., 29-30.

considerable degree of involvement of non-leaders in church-life, although whether and how far that meant in public ministry is not clear; also that there were recognized leaders who presided at worship-services and exercised important ministries.

6.2.2 *Irenaeus*

Irenaeus has much more to say about the importance of church leaders than did Justin, but again the major reason lies in the nature of his main extant work. Many Gnostics stressed that their leaders had received their major teachings from the apostles secretly and orally. In reply, Irenaeus emphasized that the true Christian tradition has come down from the apostles and 'through the succession of presbyters is kept in the Churches'. Moreover, 'we could enumerate the bishops[54] who were established by the apostles in the Church and their successors down to us. Now they have not taught or known anything that resembles the delirious imaginings of those people.' To these the apostles handed on 'their own mission of teaching ...' (*AH* 3:2:2-3:3:1). Irenaeus then gives Rome and its succession-list as an example (*AH* 3:3:2-3).[55] These leaders are the repositories and custodians of the truth and the guarantors of its reliability.

Irenaeus returns to this theme in *Against Heresies* 4:26:2. Having dealt with the importance of the correct interpretation of Scripture in 4:26:1, he continues, 'That is why we must listen to the presbyters who are in the Church: they are the successors of the apostles, as we have shown, and, with the episcopal succession, they have received the certain charism of the truth according to the Father's good pleasure. As for all the others, who separate themselves from the original succession ....'[56] This implies that *charisma* enabling them to understand and preserve the truth is received, probably at their ordination or elevation to leadership. Hanson denies this,[57] but the juxtaposition of 'with the

---

[54] For similar treatments of why Irenaeus used *prebyteros*' and *episkopos* in this way, see Harvey, 'Elders', *J Th St* 25 (1974), 328-332 and Powell, 'Ordo Presbyterii', *Journal of Theological Studies* 26 (1975), 291-327.

[55] Rousseau et al., 26-31.

[56] Rousseau et al., 718.

[57] Hanson, R.P.C., *Christian Priesthood Examined*, 68-9: 'that would be an altogether modern idea .... He probably means that the church chooses and ordains as bishops those whom it perceives to have been endowed by the Holy Spirit with the charisma of seeing truth better ... than others'. See also Hanson, R.P.C., *Studies*, 140-141, where he recognises that his view implies that Irenaeus sees the charismatic gifts 'as to a large extent channelled into the official ministry.' Whether his view is adopted or the one I have espoused, the distance is increased between the leaders of the church and the rest of its members.

episcopal succession' with 'they have received the ... charism of truth' suggests the reception of the gift at the same time as the episcopal succession is received. Von Campenhausen's view that by 'the charism of truth' is meant 'not any special official "charisma" but the traditional doctrine itself'[58] does not carry conviction because of the way Irenaeus describes the *charismata* elsewhere (see below), and in *Against Heresies* 4:26:5, where, having quoted part of 1 Corinthians 12:28, he says, 'It is in fact where the charisms of God were placed that one must be instructed in the truth, that is, from those in whom are found united the succession in the Church since the apostles.'[59] He thus demonstrates that he viewed the gift of teachers as pertaining to the church's leaders, as was implied in 4:26:2. They are also identified with the 'perfect disciple' mentioned at the end of 4:26:1 as the one who understands Scripture rightly, further suggesting that a gift, not only a tradition, was involved. Moreover, any Christians who meet separately from the official leadership are to be regarded as suspect since they are heretics or schismatics or hypocrites.[60]

Whilst the main reason for this emphasis was an excellent one, a result was a theoretical increase in the importance of the church's leaders as compared with the rest of its members. Instead of each member being viewed as able to discern truth from error because anointed by God, as in 1 John 2:18-27, they are to agree with their leaders' teaching, thus rendering them essentially passive and the leaders alone active in this vital area of church life. The difference between some leaders and the rest was further stressed, albeit unintentionally and only by implication, through the idea that a special charism of truth was received probably when such leaders were appointed, and through the idea that succession to those whose appointment could ultimately be traced to the apostles was vital to the conservation of the Christian faith.[61] That this involved the exercise of power is implied through the dismissal of those who meet apart from the officially designated church leaders as heretics or schismatics or

---

[58] Von Campenhausen, *Ecclesiastical Authority*, 171-2.

[59] Rousseau et al., 728.

[60] Irenaeus mentions the apostolic succession of bishops again in *AH* 4:33:8.

[61] Hanson, R.P.C., *Studies*, 125, rightly points out that 'the succession invoked here is not a succession of ordination but a succession of witness to tradition' and that 'the claim that a line of valid ordination of bishops guaranteed either the purity of the faith or the authenticity of the Church did not enter the head of any of the writers.' However, von Campenhausen, *Ecclesiastical Authority*, 164, gauges the burden of Irenaeus' emphasis correctly when he argues with regard to Hegesippus, before Irenaeus, that 'the intellectual continuity of a teaching succession becomes something like succession to the highest teaching office in the Church, ...'

hypocrites and through the statement that any dispute should be settled by recourse to the oldest churches in which the apostles had lived (*AH* 3:4:1). Agreement in doctrine with such church leaders was thus made a condition of entrance into eternal life (*AH* 3:4:1[62]) and power over salvation was therefore very much in the hands of the leaders, in theory at least.

However, von Campenhausen seems right to argue that there is in Irenaeus' work no evidence of excommunication by church leaders as later understood,[63] nor of 'the authority of the bishops as opposed to that of the laity, ...'[64] Hein holds that Irenaeus does 'give evidence that he knows of a real excommunication formally pronounced by the Church acting through the bishop' in *Against Hereses* 4:32:1 and 3:4:3,[65] but these passages do not provide such evidence unequivocally, neither excommunication nor the bishop being mentioned or clearly implied in either.[66]

The impression that Irenaeus did not intend to emphasize the distinction between the church's leaders and the rest of the congregation, whatever the results of his theories concerning the importance of those leaders, is reinforced by an examination of his understanding of the *charismata* and of the Spirit's work in each Christian. This is most extensively shown in *Against Heresies* 5:6-10. In 5:6:1, having quoted 1 Corinthians 2:6, '"We speak wisdom among the perfect"', he interprets Paul as meaning by the perfect 'those who have received God's Spirit and speak every language thanks to this Spirit ....' The following is preserved by Eusebius in Greek: '... as we also hear many of the brethren in the church who have prophetic gifts and speak in all sorts of languages through the Spirit and reveal people's secrets for their profit and tell the mysteries of God.' The Latin continues, 'whom the apostle calls spiritual, which they are by a participation in the Spirit, ...'[67] With the use of the present tense in 'we hear', the presumption must be that Irenaeus was aware of such events and had quite possibly witnessed them himself.[68] Moreover, his exposition of being 'psychic ... and carnal' clarifies the fact that he understands all

---

[62] Just before the passage referred to concerning recourse to the oldest churches, Irenaeus defines the church, being the repository of the truth, as the 'the way of access to life; all the others are thieves and robbers' (Rousseau et al., 44-5).

[63] Implied in von Campenhausen, *Ecclesiastical Authority*, 144-5 and especially n. 122.

[64] Von Campenhausen, *Ecclesiastical Authority*, 172.

[65] Hein, 257-8.

[66] On the first, see the textual criticism and interpretation by Rousseau in Rousseau et al., 266-7. On the second, see von Campenhausen, *Ecclesiastical Authority*, 145, n. 123.

[67] Rousseau et al., 74-5.

[68] So Kydd, 341-3, who also points out that Eusebius trusted Irenaeus' testimony on this.

devout Christians as 'spiritual' and 'perfect', not just an élite. Progress in spirituality is expected (5:10:1), but there is no indication that complete perfection must be achieved before Christians can be considered to be spiritual. The same emphasis is found in Irenaeus' *Demonstration of the Apostolic Preaching* 5, 7, 42 and 96.

Returning to Irenaeus' treatment of the *charismata*, we note that in *Against Heresies* 2:32:4, he claims that in Christ's name

> his true disciples, after receiving grace from him, work for the benefit of others according to the gift that each has received from him. Some drive out demons in all certainty and truth, ...; others have knowledge of the future and visions and prophetic words; others still lay hands on the sick and restore them to health; and even, as we have said,[69] some of the dead have been raised and stayed with us a good number of years. ... It is not possible to tell the number of charisms that, in the whole world, the church has received from God ....[70]

The similarities to Romans 12 and 1 Corinthians 12 include the kinds of gifts mentioned,[71] (exorcism and resurrection being viewed as miracles,) and the fact that each true disciple has received a gift.[72]

This and the passage noted earlier from *Against Heresies* 5:6:1 are the only ones which clearly depict the *charismata* as exercised in Irenaeus' day.[73] Nonetheless, they are used in apologetic and polemic arguments intended to convince believers and heretics; the 'we hear' of 5:6:1 suggests a present reality, as does the description of the raising of the dead in 2:31:2; Eusebius thought these two passages worth preserving; and Irenaeus has been shown to be reliable in other matters, especially his depiction of Gnosticism.[74] His evidence here is therefore likely to be reliable and to point to the continued exercise of the *charismata* in the church, not only by the leaders.

Finally, Faivre rightly notes that Irenaeus 'refused to classify Christians in different categories.'[75] He does not divide them into clergy and laity, he depicts all Christians as priests, and he rejects the Valentinian distinction between the simple and the perfect.[76]

Moreover, although Irenaeus enhanced the importance of church

---

[69] In 2:31:2, in which the cooperation of the whole church is stressed.

[70] Rousseau et al., 340-343.

[71] So Kydd, 341.

[72] Emphasized by Eastwood, 67 and 70 and by Faivre, *Emergence*, 40.

[73] The mentions of the gift of prophecy in *AH* 3:11:9 and in *DAP* 99 probably relate only to the time of Paul.

[74] This last point is argued by Kydd, 336-8.

[75] Faivre, *Emergence*, 37. For the points made below, see ibid., 35-7.

[76] See *AH* 1:6:4 and 3:15:2.

leaders in the way we earlier outlined, he mentions, in *Against Heresies* 4:26:3, 'Those who are indeed considered presbyters by many, but who are slaves of their passions and do not put the fear of God before everything in their hearts but abuse others and are inflated with pride because of their place of leadership and do evil in a hidden way and say, "No-one sees us", ...'[77]

Whilst retaining much of the emphasis found in the NT on the value of each individual Christian, then, because of the Gnostic menace, Irenaeus enhanced the importance of church leaders.

6.2.3 Other evidence from the second century

This all relates to the place of those who were not leaders in the church, reflecting the fact that much of it was written by those who were not leaders themselves and on subjects for which leadership was irrelevant. Three main areas are touched on: the use of the gifts, the existence of teachers who were not church leaders, and the active involvement of all Christians in the life of the church.

Kydd follows others in viewing the author of the *Odes of Solomon* as a prophet.[78] The most convincing proof that this is correct is found in Ode 12:1-2: '[God] hath filled me with words of truth; that I may speak the same; and like the flow of waters flows truth from my mouth, ...'; and in Ode 42, which develops from verse 4 into a message *ex ore Christi*' ('out of the mouth of Christ').[79] This is, then, evidence that prophecy existed in the second century in Syria, and probably, as Kydd claims, that prophets did. However, we have no evidence as to the author's status in the church.

Further, Eusebius states that a certain Quadratus 'was, like Philip's daughters, eminent from a prophetic gift.'[80] We know only that this was before the rise of Montanism,[81] and this Quadratus could be the same as the Apologist of the same name.[82] Unless he is to be identified with a bishop of the same name also mentioned by Eusebius, a possibility which Williamson and Louth consider unlikely,[83] he was probably not a church leader.

Ash argues that Eusebius, in his *Historia ecclesiastica* 5:24, depicts

---

[77] Rousseau et al., 720.
[78] For this and what follows, see Kydd, 178-184.
[79] Harris, 105 and 136-7. The author also claims divine inspiration in Ode 36.
[80] *HE* 3:37:1: Williamson and Louth, 100.
[81] This is made clear in *HE* 5:17:2-4.
[82] So Williamson and Louth, 411.
[83] Ibid.

Melito of Sardis as having prophesied c.167-168, and that Melito's *Peri Pascha* 101-103 are in ecstatic language.[84] Eusebius describes Melito as 'the eunuch, who lived entirely in the Holy Spirit'.[85] His exercise of one of the gifts is the likeliest reason for such a comment, and prophecy would be a gift easily recognized. Moreover, *Peri Pascha* 101-103 are presented as spoken by Christ through Melito and so increase the probability that Melito, a bishop, prophesied. There is, on the other hand, no evidence that he was able to prophesy precisely because he was a bishop, as Ash seems to suggest.[86]

Kydd considers it likely that Celsus' references to prophecy in Phoenicia and Palestine, mentioned by Origen in his *Contra Celsum* 7:9-11 but made c.178, are to Christian prophecy and glossolalia, since these were not foreign to the second-century church and Celsus knew Christianity well enough to have met them.[87] Moreover, it is Celsus' criticisms of Christianity which Origen is combatting and Origen states that Celsus spoke of it 'as though he had heard it and had a thorough first-hand knowledge of it.' His quotation of Celsus as calling them 'nameless'[88] suggests that they are unlikely to have been church leaders, although it could be explained in other ways.

There are many events which fit the exercise of gifts in the apocryphal Acts of various Apostles.[89] However, as Kydd notes, this must be regarded as uncertain evidence because they could well be explained as the use of traditional language about the period when the gifts were regarded as having been commonly exercised by such people.[90]

We noted in section 6.1 above the references in the *Martyrdom of Polycarp* to Polycarp experiencing a vision which revealed the future to him, and to him being called prophetic. Other than this, in the second-century *Acts* of the martyrs, there is one reference to a gift. This is found in the *Letter of the Churches of Lyon and Vienne* 1:49 where a physician named Alexander is said to have possessed 'a share in the charism of the apostles' because of his outspokenness in preaching the word.[91] He does not seem to have been a church leader but beyond this we cannot go.

---

[84] Ash, 'Decline', *Th St* 37.2 (1976), 235.

[85] *HE* 5:24:5: Williamson and Louth, 172.

[86] Ash, 'Decline', *Th St* 37.2 (1976), 234-6.

[87] Kydd, 229-239.

[88] *CC* 7:9: Chadwick, 402.

[89] For a list, see Kydd, 245-254.

[90] Kydd, 255; but cf. 244, where he gives a 'qualified yes' to the question whether there is any indication that the communities from which they arose were familiar with the *charismata*.

[91] Musurillo, 77.

There are also signs that the *charismata* were known amongst the Gnostics. In his *Excerpta ex Theodoto* 24:1-2, Clement of Alexandria describes the beliefs of eastern Valentinians who were active c.160-170.[92] In 24:1 he reports that they believe the Holy Spirit has been poured out on all those in the church, 'that is why the "signs" of the Spirit, - healings and prophecies, are carried out by the Church.'[93] The use of the present 'are carried out' may well indicate that healings and prophecies were known among these Gnostics.

Another more developed Gnostic reference to spiritual gifts is found in *The Interpretation of Knowledge*. No date is given for this in *The Nag Hammadi Library in English*, a second- or third-century date being suggested only by the assignment of others of the tractates to this period.[94] A major reason for writing this document was to argue that 'it is fitting for [each] of us to [enjoy] the gift that he has received from [God, and] that we be not jealous. ... Does someone have a prophetic gift? Share it without hesitation. ... [If] you [love] the Head who possesses them, you also possess the one from whom it is that these outpourings of gifts exist among your brethren.'[95] The author goes on to develop the same kind of analogy regarding the body and its members as Paul in 1 Corinthians 12. The only gifts he mentions are prophecy and the public teaching of the Word, but the fact that he is combatting jealousy concerning them demonstrates that they were a present experience, whilst his statement that each should enjoy his gift shows that they were not the province of official leaders alone.

We have, then, found enough evidence to warrant the assertion that the gifts continued to be exercised in some Christian communities, both of Gnostic and of orthodox faith, up to the late second century. Further, those who exercised them were not only officially recognized church leaders and the gift most frequently instanced was prophecy, although healing and preaching are mentioned too.

There is also evidence that Christian teaching continued to be given by others than recognized church leaders up to the late second century, at least in some places.[96] Neymeyr argues that the Pseudo-Clementine

---

[92] So Kydd, 344-7.
[93] Sagnard, 109-111. Kydd, 346-7, follows Sagnard in holding the Valentinian church was meant here.
[94] Pagels in Robinson, 427. The preceding tractate is dated 'probably in the early third century' (Pearson in ibid., 417), whilst a later one is believed to have reached its final form 'around or shortly after 200 C.E.' (Turner in ibid., 461).
[95] Sections 15-16: Turner in ibid., 432.
[96] Von Campenhausen, *Ecclesiastical Authority*, 196, overstates the case when he writes that 'when we come down to it, ... there is only one man left, Clement of Alexandria.'

writings 'testify to the disappearance of an independent office of catechist',[97] with the earliest, second-century layer knowing a leadership consisting of catechists as well as bishops, presbyters and deacons, and the later, third-century *Grundschrift* and fourth-century reworking betraying that this office had by then disappeared. If this view is correct, and the authorities cited by Neymeyr are impressive, as are his arguments, then these writings are important testimony to the situation in the second-century, Syrian church. They suggest a transitional phase between the situation in the *Didache* and that in the third century,[98] a phase in which the leaders were bringing the gift and function of teaching under their control, but had not yet fully assimilated it to their own gifts and functions.

Neymeyr considers the Syrian Bardaisan an example of a teacher, but, after considering the evidence, holds it likely that, although a Christian and influenced by Christian ideas, Bardaisan taught and discussed general, philosophical questions on the basis of knowledge not derived from the biblical revelation.[99] This renders him irrelevant to this discussion.

Tatian, however, is relevant. From Syria, he heard Justin in Rome, left the church after Justin's martyrdom, considered himself a teacher (being 'elated and inflated by the presumption that he was a teacher'), and taught some Gnostic ideas, according to Irenaeus.[100] That Tatian worked in Rome as a teacher is confirmed by Eusebius' report of an opponent of Marcion called Rhodo whose testimony to being a disciple of Tatian Eusebius had read.[101] It is further confirmed by the existence and contents of his *Oratio ad Graecos*. This evidence also suggests that he taught both pagans and Christians who were interested,[102] whilst there is no evidence that he was a recognized church leader. He is thus an example of what would later be regarded as a layman whose interests and education led to him, like Justin, becoming a Christian teacher of any who sought him out. If, and if so, how far, he exercised this function within the church is impossible to say.

If Athenagoras was a recognized church leader, then the available records say nothing about it. However, the complete lack of early

---

[97] Neymeyr, 155. For detailed argumentation on which this view is based, see 155-7.

[98] Implied by ibid., 156-7. Note also other scholars cited as sharing his view in n. 95.

[99] Ibid., 158-168. See especially his conclusion on 168.

[100] *AH* 1:28:1: Rousseau et al., 356. See Neymeyr, 183-5 for a consideration of this information and what actually happened.

[101] *EH* 5:13:1 and 8.

[102] So Neymeyr, 194.

information about him[103] renders it dangerous to base any conclusions on this silence. Although his *Supplicatio* is evidence of his teaching activity, nothing can be deduced from it for the purposes of this study.

We have already, in section 4.5.1, outlined the way in which the reliability of Eusebius' reports of the early Alexandrian 'school' has been questioned and the likely reality behind them understood. Neymeyr doubts his report that Pantaenus 'ended up as principal of the academy in Alexandria, where both orally and in writing he revealed the treasures of the divine doctrine',[104] but accepts that he exercised some teaching activity in Alexandria.[105] This conclusion is based on the references to Pantaenus in Clement's *Eclogae* 56:2, in which his rule on the use of time in the prophetic writings of the OT is cited as of 'our Pantaenus',[106] and Eusebius' reports that Clement mentioned him as his teacher in his lost *Hypotyposeis*.[107] Although he probably belonged to the 'presbyters' mentioned by Clement in *Eclogae* 27:1, Neymeyr is right to point out that this does not mean a church official, but a '"biblical scholar and theologian ...."'[108] He is, then, another example, like Justin and Tatian, of what would later be called laymen who were suited to at least personal teaching of both Christians and pagans who were interested in Christianity. Although there are indications of their involvement in church-life, there are no suggestions as to how they related to the church's leaders, nor whether they ever taught within church-meetings or outside them with the approval of those leaders.

In a consideration of Gnostic teachers, Neymeyr notes several passages in the Nag Hammadi Codices in which they polemicize against church officials' claims to authority which are based on their office. In contrast, theirs depend on their possession of knowledge and of gifts.[109] In his comparison of Christian and Gnostic teachers, however, Neymeyr argues that there are similarities and differences between them, in particular, between Clement of Alexandria and the Gnostics. They are similar in that 'authority can only be based on gnostic perfection, not on church office alone. But while the Gnostics polemicized against church officials who grounded their authority on their office without possessing Gnosis, Clement did not allow himself to be carried away to polemicize

---

[103] On what is available, see ibid., 195-200.
[104] *HE* 5:10:4: Williamson and Louth, 157.
[105] Neymeyr, 45, cf. 41. Wilken, 'Alexandria' in Henry, *Schools of Thought*, 17-18, agrees on the last point.
[106] Stählin et al., 152-3.
[107] *HE* 5:11:1-2 and 6:13:2.
[108] Neymeyr, 40, quoting from Hornschuh.
[109] Ibid., 202-4.

against such officials, but promised the true gnostic a celestial place of honour.'[110] There is less evidence of Christian teachers viewing their authority as based on gifting than he suggests, but otherwise this is a fair conclusion and again shows that the teaching function had not yet been totally assimilated by the official leaders of the church.

Finally, we note evidence of the continued involvement of all Christians in the church's life. Tatian stresses the lack of pride and the unity among Christians, adding that even the poor received instruction freely, both young and old being treated with respect.[111] Athenagoras makes the same point in his *Supplicatio* 11:4, where he writes, 'In our ranks ... you could find common men, artisans, and old women'; even if they cannot explain their beliefs in words, they show their understanding of them in good deeds.[112] Aristides gives a beautiful picture of the simple beliefs, morally and ethically pure lives, and especially the care for others exhibited by Christians in his *Apology* 15. He also points out that when they persuade any, including their servants and children, to become Christians, they call them brothers. That this was normal Christian practice is amply borne out in the early *Acts* of the martyrs and in the apocryphal *Acts* of various apostles, in which 'brothers' is frequently used.[113] Even when due allowance is made for the idealistic picture of Christians understandably presented in Apologies, the basic equality and involvement of all Christians in the church's life is reflected in these statements.

6.2.4 Conclusion

In the areas just examined, the writings used in this section reflect the picture given of the church in the NT better than the writings of the Apostolic Fathers. Further, with their lack of emphasis on subordination to church leaders, they contrast strongly with Clement of Rome and Ignatius. Moreover, the fact that this is so not only in the writings of a non-leader like Justin but in those of a bishop like Irenaeus suggests that not all leaders felt threatened as did Ignatius. The limited extent and the polemical nature of Irenaeus' writings, however, tell against drawing any strong conclusions from his silence on this, except that his accounts

---

[110] Ibid., 214.

[111] *Oratio* 32: Whittaker, 59.

[112] Schoedel, 25.

[113] In *Mart Poly* 1:2; *The Letter of the Church of Lyon and Vienne* 1:3, 2:3, 2:4, 2:5 and 2:8; *Acts of John* 18, 19, 27, etc.; *Acts of Paul* 5, 9, 10, 11; *Acts of Peter* 2:1:1, 2:1:2, etc. Whatever unorthodox influences may be discerned in these apocryphal *Acts*, they are likely to reflect general Christian practice in this regard.

of the essentials of Christian belief do not include reference to obedience to the bishop other than as a bulwark against the dangers of Gnosticism. On the whole, then, the writings studied in this section depict a church in which leadership existed without becoming in any way oppressive to the rest and without inciting insurrection from them. Even so, the arguments which Irenaeus used in his defence of the church against Gnosticism left the door open to those who would later want to strengthen the powers of leaders against the rest.

6.3 Tertullian and the North African church c.195-215

6.3.1 The demarcation between church leaders and the rest

With the possible exceptions of *1 Clement* and the letters of Ignatius, the main emphasis of Christian writers up to Tertullian has been on the basic equality and unity of Christians. Even in *1 Clement* and Ignatius' letters, this emphasis is not lacking, though significantly modified by other concerns. There has been no impression of a divide appearing between church leaders and the rest. Prepared by the stress we have noted in *1 Clement*, Ignatius' letters, and Irenaeus' writings, this divide becomes apparent in the writings of Tertullian. As Faivre writes,

> his works are among the first Christian writings in which we are given a structure of the church as organized in two groups – clergy and laity. He identifies the laity with the *plebs* or ordinary people, who are distinguished from the "priestly" or "ecclesiastical order" of bishops, presbyters and deacons and, in a very general way, from the clergy, who are regarded as "leaders" (*duces*) and pastors.[114]

This divide appears both in the words used to distinguish between them and in the way that Tertullian writes about them.

Powell's study of *ordo* and *clerus*, and their Greek equivalents, shows that they were used first in extant literature by Tertullian to mean a body of men set apart from the rest in a church for particular, very significant purposes.[115] That this happens in the writings of the one who is also the first to use 'priest' of church leaders seems more than a coincidence and suggests a close connection between these developments. This is borne

[114] Faivre, *Emergence*, 46.
[115] Powell, 'Ordo Presbyterii', *J Th St* 26 (1975), 292ff. See also Gy, 'Remarques' in *Études sur le sacrement de l'ordre*, 126-7, Lanne, 'Le laïc', *Verbum Caro* 18 (1964), 110, Vilela, 228-231, and Hanson, R.P.C., *Christian Priesthood Examined*, 29, who points out that Tertullian recognises the distinction between clergy and laity throughout his writings.

out by Tertullian's argument, noted before, in *On Monogamy* 12:2:

> Indeed, whenever we are minded to exalt ourselves with swelling pride at the
> expense of the clergy, then "we are all one", then we are all priests, for "He
> hath made us priests to God and His Father"! But when we are called upon to
> be the peers of priests in discipline, we lay aside our fillets – and pair off! The
> question under consideration concerned the qualities required in men who
> were to receive orders in the Church.[116]

It is likely that the beginning of this would not have entered his mind
had there not been some resentment against the clergy on the part of the
rest. Moreover, this passage suggests that calling the clergy 'priests' was
a reason for this resentment, although the laity were not averse to using
it to their own advantage if they could. The main point we are noting
here, however, is that the issue of who is called 'priest' is closely linked
with the division between the 'clergy' and the rest.

A similar connection is apparent in another passage noted before,
Chastity 7:3. After the rhetorical question, 'For are not we lay people
also priests?', and a reference to Revelation 1:6 and/or 5:10, Tertullian
continues, 'It is ecclesiastical authority which distinguishes clergy and
laity, this and the dignity which sets a man apart by reason of
membership in the hierarchy. Hence, where there is no such hierarchy,
you yourself offer sacrifice, you baptize, and you are your own priest.
Obviously, where there are three gathered together, even though they
are lay persons, there is a Church.'[117] As we argued in section 5.3.1
against Powell, there is a probable contrast here between Christ's
making all Christians priests and the church's authority making the
difference between the 'clergy' and the 'laity'. The first has priority, for
Tertullian and many others, although the place of the second is
recognized. That this debate did not arise only out of Tertullian's
Montanism is rightly recognized by Powell when he accepts that 'a
Catholic basis for *De Exhort*. vii can be found in *De Baptismo* xvii. 1-
2',[118] in which Tertullian allows the laity the right of baptism in case of
necessity.

Further evidence of the close link between the rise of the concepts of
'order' and 'clergy' and the rise of the use of 'priest' for the ordained is
the expression 'priestly order' which appears in *Chastity* 7:2. Other

---

[116] Le Saint, 99.

[117] Ibid., 53.

[118] Powell, 'Ordo Presbyterii', *J Th St* 26 (1975), 293. Powell does, however, see the 'you …
offer' of *Chastity* 7:3 as a Montanist extension of the layman's right to baptize into a right to
all sacerdotal functions, not recognising that all or both are only in case of necessity.

adjectives can be used with 'order', e.g., we have seen 'ecclesiastical' above, so that priestliness is only one aspect of the 'order', but clearly a significant one.

All this is not to deny that there was an important differentiation in the church between its leaders and the rest before Tertullian. What is new is the implication that the differentiation was becoming as important as the deep and basic unity and equality between Christians, although Tertullian and others were resisting it. This is one reason why Tertullian emphasizes that Christ has made all Christians priests, and that, in case of necessity, they all have the right to do what the leaders normally do as priests. He accepts, however, the leaders' right to be called 'priests' in a special sense and to normally perform significant activities. The division of the community into two has taken place, and the use of 'priests' in a special sense is an important part of this, but he seeks to minimize their inequality.

Before we leave this issue, we must note the question of whether Tertullian included women amongst the priestly laity. Faivre has argued that he did not since, in *On the Veiling of Virgins* 9:1, he denies the right of women to speak in church, baptize, offer, and to perform any function proper to men or the priesthood, and, in *On Baptism* 17:4, he condemns a heretical woman for teaching and fears some women might even baptize, whereas, in *Chastity* 7, he allows the laity as priests to baptize and offer and so be priests.[119] Juxtaposing these passages, Faivre's case is logical. On the other hand, it is unlikely that Tertullian would have excluded women from the priestly laity if he had addressed the question directly, since he quotes Revelation 1:6 in *Chastity* 7:3 as support for his contention that all Christians are priests and, not only does he not exclude women from this, but it is doubtful that he would have viewed its author as doing so. Faivre is more systematic than Tertullian and his logical conclusion wrong. Tertullian probably saw all non-clergy as forming the priestly laity but assumed the rightness of only males ever performing publicly priestly tasks on the twin bases of OT teaching concerning priests and NT teaching concerning the place of women in the church.

---

[119] Faivre, *Emergence*, 51 and 'The Laity in the First Centuries: Issues Revealed by Historical Research' *Lumen Vitae* 42 (1987), 137-8. In ibid., 136-7, he further argues that, as well as referring to the 'Christian community in general', the laity 'could designate an elite composed of mature, worthy men, married only once, contributing to the financial upkeep of the ministers of the altar and consituting a "clerical reserve" from which the Church could draw when it wished to ordain someone.' This is unlikely since it is based on what Tertullian depicted as an ideal rather than a reality.

6.3.2 The power of the clergy

We noted a number of passages in section 4.3.1 which demonstrated that the clergy, and especially the bishop, were in control of certain important matters, and normally performed them. It is significant that so many of them involve the use of priestly ideas. So, in *On Baptism* 17, it is the bishop as high priest who has the supreme right to give baptism, followed by the presbyters and deacons, though only with the bishop's authority. Tertullian goes on to uphold the laity's right to baptize, but has to argue that this is correct, suggesting that it was disputed. He also warns against arrogating the bishop's office, and stresses that this right should only be used 'in emergencies' and not by women.[120] He is not attacking the bishop or clergy here, but defending the laity's rights.

Further, in *Prescription* 41:8, Tertullian criticizes some heretics because 'they charge even laymen with priestly functions.'[121] What these were is not specified, but they clearly belong to the bishop, deacon and presbyter, who have just been mentioned.

The above come from Tertullian's pre-Montanist period. When under the influence of Montanism he declares that women are not permitted to exercise the priestly office, nor to speak, teach, baptize and offer in church,[122] and identifies the essence of priesthood as involving baptizing and offering in *Chastity* 7:3, implying that, although in case of necessity any Christian may perform these as priest, normally it is the ordained who do so as such. That this is so in the case of offering is confirmed by a reference to offering 'through the ministry of a priest whose monogamy is a necessary condition for his ordination' in *Chastity* 11:2.[123] In *On Modesty* 1:6, Tertullian refers sarcastically to a 'sovereign pontiff, the bishop of bishops' who has decreed that he forgives those who have committed adultery and fornication and demonstrated their repentance.[124] Finally, his declaration that 'the church will forgive sins, but the church of the Spirit, through a spiritual man, not the church constituted by many bishops. For it is a right and decision that belongs to the Lord and not to the servant, to God himself and not to the priest'[125] also demonstrates that some bishops were claiming to forgive serious sin as priests.

This evidence, then, suggests that claims of the bishop's and clergy's

---

[120] Ibid., 37.
[121] Refoulé and de Labriolle, 148.
[122] *On the Veiling of Virgins* 9:1.
[123] Le Saint, 60.
[124] Micaelli and Munier, 146-7.
[125] *On Modesty* 21:17: ibid., 274-5.

exclusive right of baptizing, offering and forgiving sin, and Tertullian's acceptance of their normal right to alone do these things were, to some extent at least, linked to the concept of their exclusive priesthood. Further, Tertullian's attempt to preserve the laity's right to baptize and offer in exceptional circumstances was, on one occasion, linked to their general priesthood. The issue of priesthood was not peripheral here. Whilst its precise relationship to these activities is never clarified by or in Tertullian's works, that they were appropriate to priesthood and, in the case of baptizing and offering, were vital constituents of it, is implied. Any attempts to restrict them to leaders viewed as priests were, therefore, attempts to diminish the general priesthood for the benefit of the ordained priesthood.

On the other hand, that these activities were not viewed as performed by anyone precisely or solely because he was a priest is suggested by their ascription to leaders without any mention of priesthood. These same passages, of course, witness further to the leadership's exercise of these activities. So *On Repentance* 6:10, from Tertullian's Catholic period, describes the baptizer as 'in charge of this matter', and *The Chaplet* 3:2, from his Montanist period, calls him the *antistes*, the 'presider' or 'priest', whilst *The Chaplet* 3:3 mentions the taking of the eucharist 'from no other hand than that of those presiding', and *On Modesty* 18:18 the obtaining of pardon from the bishop for lighter sins.[126] Our earlier discoveries about the general restriction of these functions to the clergy renders it probable that the clergy and/or the bishop are referred to in these passages.

Further, *On Monogamy* 11:1-2 and *On the Soul* 51:6 indicate that the clergy perform marriages and burials, and 'to preside' is used of church leaders several times. No indication of what this involved is given in *To His Wife* 1:7:4 or *On Fasting* 17:4 but *The Chaplet* 3:3 involves dispensing the eucharist, *On Modesty* 14:16 excommunication,[127] *On Monogamy* 12:3-4, presiding over Scripture being read, and *Apology* 39:1-5 presiding over meetings including prayer, readings, exhortations, rebukes and judging. Moreover, the bishop is responsible for the assignment of women to the order of widows,[128] he is described as issuing an edict regarding church discipline in *On Modesty* 1:6, and *On Fasting* 13:3 states that 'bishops are accustomed to order all the

---

[126] Dekkers et al., 330, 1042-3 and 1319.

[127] So Bévenot, 'Tertullian's thoughts' in de Smedt et al., *Corona Gratiarum*, 132. In view of *Chastity* 7:3 Bévenot ('but not even here did he give them the title of *sacerdotes*') sees too much significance in Tertullian's lack of reference to the president at the eucharist as priest in *The Chaplet* 3:3.

[128] *On the Veiling of Virgins* 9:2.

ordinary people to fast'.[129] The latter is not disapproved by Tertullian, even as a Montanist, whilst the former demonstrates his abhorrence at the edict's contents rather than at the practice of bishops making edicts.

These allusions, then, suggest that important powers of decision-making, as well as the exclusive right to perform certain functions vital to the community's welfare, were being claimed by church leaders, and particularly the bishop. The possibility of consultation with others preceding those decisions will be considered below, as will whether others than the clergy could teach.

6.3.3 The power and ministries of the laity

Tertullian's view of the power and ministries of the laity is undergirded by his view of what the laity are in and through Christ. His rich understanding of the general priesthood and his application of the temple-metaphor to Christians both corporately and individually were noted in sections 5.3.1 and 2. He also utilizes the Pauline metaphor of the body and its head and members for Christians corporately and individually.[130] He links it with the *charismata* in *Against Marcion* 5:8:9, but develops it especially graphically in his pre-Montanist *On Repentance* 10:6. Dealing with the reception of a penitent he argues, 'where one or two believers are, there is the church, but the church is Christ. And so, when you stretch out your hands to your brothers' knees, it is Christ you are touching, it is Christ you are beseeching. Similarly, when they shed tears over you, it is Christ who suffers, it is Christ who intercedes.'

This passage follows on from another in 9:1-6 in which the process of public confession is described. Part of this is 'to throw oneself down before the elders, to kneel at the altars of God, to urge all the brethren to be the ambassadors of your request.'[131] The practice of the penitent seeking the intercession of all the brethren is confirmed in *On Modesty* 13:7.

It was probably, therefore, the general practice in North Africa for the penitent to seek the aid of all Christians in asking forgiveness from God. These passages also imply that 'forgiveness results from the

---

[129] Dekkers et al., 1281-2 and 1272.

[130] Twice he describes the Christian man's head as Christ (*Chaplet* 14:1 and 3); thrice he likens the church to Christ or Christ's body (*Penitence* 10:5-6, *Against Marcion* 5:8:9 and 5:19:6), and several times he depicts individual Christians as members of Christ (*Wife* 2:3:1, *Against Marcion* 5:7:4, *Resurrection* 10:4-5, *Modesty* 6:17 and 16:8ff.).

[131] Munier, C. (ed.), *Tertullien: La Pénitence* (Paris, 1984), 180-181.

exomologesis itself'.[132] Von Campenhausen goes beyond the available evidence in suggesting that 'the congregation carries out the readmission whenever it is convinced that the penitent has done enough, ...' We have already noted that, in his Montanist writings, Tertullian mentions the bishop as the one by whom forgiveness is granted, a practice which 'cannot possibly be a Montanist innovation.'[133] This is confirmed in *Apology* 39:4-5 where, having described excommunication, Tertullian adds, 'certain approved elders [*seniores*] preside, ...'[134] These were probably the bishop and the presbyters,[135] suggesting their leading involvement in excommunication and implying the same for readmission. Even so, the laity's presence and prayers were significant.

Even before he became a Montanist, Tertullian held that 'confessors', i.e., those who had suffered for their faith without yet being martyred, could grant 'peace', meaning forgiveness and reconciliation to the church. So in *To the Martyrs* 1:6 he states, without any disapproval, that, 'Some, not able to find this peace in the Church, are accustomed to seek it from the martyrs in prison.'[136] The preceding, '"do not grieve the Holy Spirit" who has entered prison with you' (1:3), suggests that they could grant peace because filled with the Spirit.[137] Tertullian also states approvingly that confessors have the keys of the church given to Peter in *Scorpiace* 10:8. This demonstrates that non-church-leaders were commonly viewed as able to communicate God's forgiveness on the basis of their being filled with the Spirit.

This belief was probably one reason for Tertullian's acceptance in his Montanist period of the view that only the truly spiritual could forgive sins, other reasons being Montanism's emphases on prophetic power and moral rigour. We have already noted this in *On Modesty* 21:17, but he argues it throughout that chapter. It is impossible to know whether, and if so, how many of, those who remained in the Catholic church would have shared Tertullian's perception, but it is quite possible that some sympathized with it. In any case, this, like the information concerning the general perception that confessors could forgive sin,

---

[132] Le Saint, W.P. (ed.), *Tertullian: Treatises on Penance* (London, 1959), 176, n. 164.
[133] Von Campenhausen, *Ecclesiastical Authority*, 227, although he acknowledges that 'the question, which particular individuals have the task of speaking for the "Church", and of carrying out its sentence, is not discussed.'
[134] R. Arbesmann, E.J. Daly and E.A. Quain, *Tertullian: Apologetical Works and Minucius Felix: Octavius* (Washington, 1950), 98.
[135] So von Campenhausen, *Ecclesiastical Authority*, 227, and see below on *seniores laici*.
[136] Arbesmann et al., 18-9.
[137] So Evans, R.F., *One and Holy*, 17.

demonstrates that the forgiveness of sin was not yet viewed as the sole prerogative of church officials.

Furthermore, the laity were involved in the choice of church officials. As evidence of this Vilela points first to *Apology* 39.5 and the statement, 'Certain approved elders [*seniores*] preside, men who have obtained this honor, not by money, but by the evidence of good character', and second to *Prescription* 43:5, in which Tertullian contrasts with the heretics the 'careful choice ... and deserved advancement' of his own church.[138] Vilela argues that *honor* 'was used especially for the civil magistrates chosen through popular consultation' and that *adlectio* involved 'a nomination made by the leader alone and considered by the people', rendering it likely that the clergy chose ordinands who were then presented to the people for their approval or rejection. Faivre sees the laity's involvement in this process referred to also in the statement in *Chastity* 7:3 that 'it is ecclesiastical authority which distinguishes clergy and laity, this and the dignity which sets a man apart by reason of membership in the hierarchy.'[139] As he argues, this is the more likely since the next sentence indicates that the laity form the church where there are no ordained. Although none of these passages states unambiguously that the laity were actively involved in the choice of church officials, what we shall see later from Cyprian's writings indicating such an involvement renders this very likely.

Turning to evidence of the *charismata* in the Carthaginian church in Tertullian's day we strike the problem of assessing just what the situation was there in this regard and the relevance to this of the *Passio Perpetuae et Felicitatis*.[140] Robeck cogently argues that the latter reflects the situation of the church generally at Carthage and contains nothing unique to Montanism, while Barnes postulates a time in the church's history there when Montanistic tendencies, such as those he finds in the *Passio Perpetuae*, were tolerated in it.[141] These views, together with evidence we are going to examine from Tertullian's writings, suggest that the *charismata* were not confined to Montanist meetings, but experienced in the Catholic church also. Kydd[142] argues

---

[138] Vilela, 246-9. Quotations from Arbesmann et al, 98 and Refoulé and de Labriolle, 150. Bardy, 'Le sacerdoce', *La Vie spirituelle* 58 (1939), 117, also views *Apology* 39:4 as showing that 'the bishops and the priests were chosen according to the community's witness.'

[139] Faivre, *Emergence*, 47.

[140] Abbreviated to *Passio Perpetuae* below.

[141] Robeck, C.M., *The Role and Function of Prophetic Gifts for the Church at Carthage, AD 202-258* (Ann Arbor, 1985), 26-34 and Barnes, 77-9. Robeck, 260-262, agrees with Barnes' interpretation of the main passage on which Barnes' view is based.

[142] For this and other references to Kydd below see Kydd, 260-270. Robeck, 192-7, agrees, although he finds a more specialized concern with prophetic gifts in Tertullian's Montanist

that Tertullian believed it was right to experience and use the
charismata throughout his life and had a similar attitude to them both
before and after he became a Montanist, concluding that both Catholics
and Montanists in Carthage were familiar with them at this time. Kydd
points to evidence of this in writings generally accepted as from both
Tertullian's pre-Montanist and Montanist periods.

Probably the first chronologically is found in *Prescription* 29:3, but
this refers only to 'so many charisms' in a list of things Gnostics
considered done wrongly in the church.[143] The second is found in *On
Baptism* 20:5 where Tertullian exhorts the newly baptized, 'ask of your
Lord that special grants of grace and apportionments of spiritual gifts be
yours.'[144] This shows that Tertullian did not view spiritual gifts as
optional but as important for every Christian, nor did he regard them as
only for an élite.[145] Only approval of the seeking and exercise of these
gifts can be found, then, in his pre-Montanist period. This impression is
reinforced by a pre-Montanist allusion to a revelation given to an
individual in *The Shows* 26:3.

In *Against Marcion* 5:8:4-12, Tertullian, like Justin, argues that the
charismata have been removed from the Jews that Christ should give
them to the apostles (5:8:5). After commenting on aspects of 1
Corinthians 12:12-30, he challenges,

> … let Marcion put in evidence any gifts there are of his god, any prophets,
> provided they have spoken not by human emotion but by God's spirit, who
> have foretold things to come, and also made manifest the secrets of the heart:
> let him produce some psalm, some vision, some prayer, so long as it is a
> spiritual one, in ecstasy, which means abeyance of mind, if there is added also
> an interpretation of the tongue …. If all such proofs are more readily put in
> evidence by me, … without doubt both Christ and the Spirit and the apostle
> will belong to my God.[146]

The 'if all such proofs are more readily put in evidence by me' clearly
implies that he can produce those who have these gifts since otherwise
his whole argument falls. He issues a similar challenge in 5:15:5-6.

In *On the Soul* 9:3-4, after mentioning spiritual gifts, Tertullian
describes a sister who receives visions during the regular church
services and, after the service, reports them to the leaders who examine

---

period.
[143] Refoulé and de Labriolle, 125.
[144] Evans, E., *Baptism*, 43.
[145] So Robeck, 192-3.
[146] Evans, E., *Against Marcion*, 561-3.

them.[147] *Charismata* are mentioned again in 58:8. Finally, in *On Monogamy* 1:2-3, Tertullian claims, 'We ... are deservedly called the Spiritual because of the spiritual charisms which acknowledgedly are ours, ... But the Sensualists, not receiving the Spirit, take no pleasure in such things as are of the Spirit.'[148] This does not imply that the Catholics reject the *charismata* but, in view of what we have already seen, probably refers to their rejection of particular teachings which the Montanists claim to have received via the gifts.

If Robeck's and/or Barnes' views of the situation in the Carthaginian church when the *Passio Perpetuae* was written be accepted, then it too witnesses to the general acceptance of the *charismata* in that church. The author states in his preface (1:5) that 'we ... know and honour prophecies as well as new visions as effects of the same promise, and ... consider all the other powerful manifestations of the Holy Spirit as destined for the church's instruction – for this same Spirit was sent to it to distribute all its gifts among us in the measure that the Lord allocates them to each one ....'[149] Further, even before she became a confessor, indeed apparently at her baptism, we are told by Perpetua that 'the Spirit told me to ask at the water only the strength to endure the suffering of the flesh' (3:5).[150] This and Tertullian's exhortation to seek spiritual gifts right after baptism suggests such seeking was common in Tertullian's day. It is likely that she received the gift of prophecy since several visions were given to her. So, on her imprisonment, she seeks and receives a vision which she interprets as meaning martyrdom for her (4:3-10). Somewhat later she receives two more visions concerning her dead brother (7:4-8:4) and, later still, another assuring her of victory over the Devil in her suffering (10:1-14). After this a vision granted to Saturus, a fellow-sufferer, is recounted (11:1-13:8). Part of this depicts a bishop and an 'elder teacher' casting themselves at the feet of the glorified Saturus and Perpetua and asking them to reconcile them to each other. The martyrs protest, calling the bishop '"our father"',[151] and are trying to help them when angels drive the church officials away warning the bishop to rebuke his people for factiousness (13:1-6). Robeck plausibly suggests that the bishop may have asked for such help

---

[147] Dekkers et al., 792. Barnes, 89, postulates that this happened in a Catholic church, the Montanists remaining behind after the services to hear the revelations. Robeck, 260-262, agrees.

[148] Le Saint, 70.

[149] Amat, J. (ed.), *Passion de Perpétue et de Félicite suivi des Actes* (Paris, 1996), 102-3.

[150] Ibid., 108-9.

[151] Ibid., 150-151.

and the angels' words in the vision provide the instruction he needs.[152]

These visions probably illustrate both the kinds of *charismata* which some ordinary Christians, and confessors in particular, received, whilst the last episode noted suggests that some church officials recognized the confessors' special gifts and sought their help. Moreover, Tertullian 'does not associate these gifts specifically with ordination or with clergy',[153] as is true of the *Passio Perpetuae* also.

Evidence that the clergy had not yet completely taken over the ministry of teaching comes in the self-understanding and function of Tertullian, if he was never ordained as was argued in section 4.3.1. In spite of his opposition to philosophy, he argues for the rightness of wearing the philosopher's *pallium* and implies that he wore it himself (*Concerning the Pallium* 1:5-6). His writings are a clear indication of his teaching activity, whilst Barnes argues that several are in the form of sermons, and four were probably actually delivered: *On Prayer*, *On Baptism*, *On Patience*, and *On Penitence*.[154] Neymeyr[155] views only *On Women's Apparel* 2 as based on an address but also finds evidence of Tertullian's oral teaching activity in *On the Soul* 9:4 in which, as we noted, a sister is described as receiving a revelation while 'we had discoursed ... about the soul'.[156] This shows that Tertullian taught in a Catholic or Montanist Sunday service as a layman.[157] Neymeyr also points to Tertullian's reply, in *On Flight in Persecution* 1:1, to a request for advice from a Catholic Christian as attesting that, even as a Montanist, his advice could be sought by a Catholic because of his recognized qualities. Neymeyr argues that this picture is like that of the 'teacher' in *Prescription* 14:2, suggesting that Tertullian was one.

In *Prescription* 3:5 Tertullian names the teacher alongside the bishop, deacon, widow, virgin and martyr as important members of the congregation, but this cannot tell us whether the teacher belonged to the clergy or held a special office.[158] Neither can the second, 14:2, in which Tertullian tells his readers that, other than the rule of faith, they may discuss as they please: if something is unclear or doubtful, 'there is ... some learned brother endowed with the gift of knowledge ....'[159] The

---

[152] Robeck, 166-7. See also Robeck's interesting analyses of the contents of the other visions.
[153] Hanson, R.P.C., *Studies*, 141.
[154] Barnes, 117.
[155] For the arguments below see Neymeyr, 124-133.
[156] Roberts, Donaldson and Coxe, vol. 4, 336.
[157] Neymeyr, 130-131, argues for a Montanist service; Barnes, 77-9 and Robeck, 26-34, argue for a Catholic service.
[158] See Neymeyr, 114-8 on these two passages in *Prescription*.
[159] Refoulé and de Labriolle, 107.

reference to 'brother' here may suggest that this is not a church official, but this is uncertain.

Another relevant passage is that in *Passio Perpetuae* already noted in which, in Saturus' vision, he and Perpetua meet a bishop and an 'elder teacher' (13:1). Clearly this was one who combined being a presbyter with a recognized teaching gift. Neymeyr argues plausibly that this, together with the fact that, as we shall see, in Cyprian's day the task of teaching had been taken over by the presbyters, plus Tertullian's presentation of himself as a 'teacher', all makes it plausible that his omission of 'elder' and insertion of 'teacher' in the list of important people in *Prescription* 3:5 was due to his desire to protect his position as a lay teacher when this function was being taken over by presbyters.[160]

Frend and Quispel have argued for the existence of 'lay elders' in the African church in Tertullian's day. These are definitely attested later,[161] but the only reference to them in Tertullian's work is *Apology* 39:4, according to Frend and Quispel.[162] Apart from the significantly later external evidence, however, there is only the fact that in *Apology* 39:4 Tertullian refers to *seniores* and not presbyters or bishops.[163] It is as likely, moreover, that Tertullian uses it as a common Latin word for the benefit of those outside the church to refer to those normally known within the church as presbyters.[164] While possible, the existence of 'lay elders' in Tertullian's day has not been proved.

Finally, we must note the important place Tertullian assigns to all believers in the services which he describes in *Apology* 39. Even when due allowance has been made for the fact that he is putting the best gloss on the facts for outsiders, his descriptions must bear a close relationship to reality. He depicts the Christians as 'one body because of our religious convictions, and because of the divine origin of our way of life and the bond of common hope. We come together for a meeting and a congregation, in order to besiege God with prayers, like an army in battle formation .... We assemble for the consideration of the Holy Scriptures ....' (39:1-3).[165] His mention of the 'approved elders' (5) who

---

[160] So Neymeyr, 124 and 138. See also Faivre, *Emergence*, 53.

[161] See the evidence in Frend, W.H.C, 'The *seniores laici* and the origins of the church in North Africa', *J Th St New Series* 12 (1961), 280-282.

[162] Ibid., 282; also 'The Church of the Roman Empire 313-600' in Neill. S.C. and Weber, H.-R. (eds.), *The Layman in Christian History* (London, 1963), 62-3; 'Jews and Christians' in *Paganisme, Judaïsme, Christianisme*, 191; and Quispel, 'African Christianity' in den Boeff and Kessels, *Actus*, 276.

[163] Dekkers et al, 150.

[164] So Williams, G.H., 'The Ancient Church' in Neill and Weber, *The Layman in Christian History*, 38-9 and Vilela, 236-7.

[165] For these quotations from and references to *Apology* 39 see Arbesmann et al., 98-101.

preside gives no indication of a separation in the community but only of those who preside appropriately on account of their proven characters. Giving as each is able for the support of their needy is then described (5-6) as are their love for one another and calling one another 'brethren' because of all they have in common (7-11). After pointing out that Christians have all things in common except their wives (12-13), Tertullian compares the excesses of others' feasts with the Christians' agape-suppers which benefit the needy and are characterized by modesty and moderation (14-17). When each has finished, 'the hands are washed and lamps are lit, and each one, according to his ability to do so, reads the Holy Scriptures or is invited into the center to sing a hymn to God' (18). The precise meaning of this is unclear but it suggests a situation of freedom and informality in which each Christian could speak either on scripture or from his own mind.[166] Indeed, the whole picture Tertullian gives of the church in this chapter is of a united community of brothers who care for and minister to each other, a picture confirmed by other passages[167] but needing to be modified in the light of what we have already noted concerning the increasing division between the clergy and the laity, a picture which would not have served Tertullian's apologetic purposes in *Apology* 39.

6.3.4 Conclusion

In Tertullian's writings there is, then, evidence both of the continuing vitality, ministry and importance of all Christians in church life and of their increasing domination by the leadership. There is also evidence of resistance to this domination in objections to them arrogating to themselves the name and functions of 'priest' (*On Monogamy* 12:2 and *Chastity* 7:3), teaching and, amongst Montanists at least, the forgiveness of mortal sins. This was, then, a period of transition in the church in Carthage and, probably, in the church throughout North Africa, from a time when the basic equality of all Christians was foremost to one when it was being challenged by the deepening division of the Christian community into clergy and laity in which the ascription of 'priest' to the former in a way different from the latter was a significant element.

---

[166] Cf. Barnes, 112: 'after the meal, the scriptures are discussed, everyone present being called upon to say what he can'; and 117: 'after their common meal Christians were invited to speak, either to recite something from the scriptures or according to each man's capabilities.'
[167] On the unity of the church, its communion, mutual care and brotherhood, see *Prescription* 20:18, *To the Martyrs* 1:1, *On Women's Apparel* 2:1:1, *To His Wife* 2:4:2-3 and 2:8:7, *On the Veiling of Virgins* 14:2 and *Chastity* 12:3. On Christians praying together see *On Prayer* 18:1 and 27:1.

6.4 Hippolytus and the Roman church c.220-235

Dating from the period just after Tertullian but connected with the Roman church, Hippolytus confirms some of the developments noted from Tertullian's works and adds details which fill them out for us. He thus shows that these developments were not confined to North Africa but were happening more generally in the Western church.

6.4.1 The clergy-laity divide

Hippolytus not only attests the presence of this divide but provides additional information concerning where it is made. As we noted in section 4.4.2, in the *Apostolic Tradition* 8 he denies that the deacon shares 'in the counsel of the clergy' but in chapter 10 he implies that the deacon is of the clergy when rejecting the ordination of a widow 'because she does not offer the offering nor has she a liturgical duty (*liturgia*). Ordination is done with the clergy on account of their liturgical duties.'[168] At least part of the explanation for this confusion is fluidity and uncertainty over the boundary between the clergy and the laity at this time, pointing to a transition-period.[169] The passage in the *Apostolic Tradition* 10 further shows that attempts were being made to develop a different nomenclature for the ordination of the clergy and the recognition of non-clergy with a special ministry.[170] The distinction was being made increasingly clear probably because, as Faivre suggests, ordination was becoming more and more important as a frontier between the clergy and the laity, and others than the bishop, presbyters and deacons were seeking it.[171]

One reason for the increasing importance of ordination as such a frontier may well have been the view that it conveyed a special gift or enduement of the Spirit for the functions involved. We noted in section 4.4.2 that Hippolytus describes himself in the preface to *Refutation of All Heresies* 6 as of those who are 'partakers of the same grace of high priesthood and of teaching',[172] whilst the ordination-prayer for a new

---

[168] Botte, 24-5 and 30-31.

[169] Powell, 'Ordo Presbyterii', *J Th St* 26 (1975), 310-311, suggests that 'the prayer for the *principalis spiritus* ['sovereign' or 'princely spirit'] is a late second-century innovation, shaped by a closer following of the typology of Numbers ... [which] stressed those called presbyters.' He also argues that this 'is the most probable source of the exclusion of the deacon from the *sacerdotium*'. This may be another part of the explanation.

[170] So Faivre, *Emergence*, 80-81, noting that *cheirotonia* ('ordination') is used of the bishop and implied for the presbyter whilst both *kathistemi* ('appoint') and *cheirotonia* are used of the deacon.

[171] Faivre, *Naissance*, 50-51.

[172] Legge, vol. 1, 34.

bishop in the *Apostolic Tradition* 3 requests God to grant him 'by the spirit of high priesthood, to have the power to forgive sins' and the following section describes him as 'made worthy' through the prayer and imposition of hands.[173] The ordination-prayers for the presbyter and deacon similarly ask God to impart the spirit of grace necessary.[174] Although we shall note later hints that Hippolytus does not see spiritual gifts as restricted to the clergy, we have here indications that attempts were being made to channel these through the clergy.[175]

As in Tertullian, the demarcation between clergy and laity is related to the use of 'priest' for the clergy in a way different from the laity. This is apparent when what we have seen regarding the ways in which the frontier between the clergy and the laity was being reinforced is compared with the way in which, as we noted in section 4.4.2, Hippolytus describes the bishop in high priestly language and implies the priesthood of the presbyter but not the deacon in the *Apostolic Tradition* 8. In that passage he explains that only the bishop should lay hands on the deacon to ordain him. The first reason he gives is 'because he is not being ordained to the priesthood', and the second is, 'for he does not share in the counsel of the clergy'. Clearly being ordained to the priesthood and being part of the counsel of the clergy are identical.

6.4.2 The power of the clergy

Hippolytus confirms Tertullian's depiction of the clergy as those who normally administer baptism in the *Apostolic Tradition* 21, making it clear that bishop, presbyters and deacons were all involved in different ways. He does not, in contrast to Tertullian, affirm the laity's right to baptize in emergencies. Although this might be because this right was not contested and did not form an appropriate subject for his writings, what we shall now note concerning the eucharist means that this silence could be significant.

Hippolytus also confirms Tertullian's presentation of the clergy as the usual presidents at eucharists. He does this first, in the *Apostolic Tradition* 3, by his description of the prayer of consecration of a bishop as containing a request for him to present the church's gifts, which, as we argued in section 4.4.2, included the bread and the wine. Moreover,

---

[173] Botte, 8-11. Von Campenhausen, *Ecclesiastical Authority*, 176, Vilela, 347-8, and Faivre, *Naissance*, 56, so interpret these passages. Faivre holds that, in the *Apostolic Tradition*, 'the meaning of the laying on of hands has passed from "recognition of a gift of the Spirit" to "a gift of the Spirit through those who have already received it."'

[174] *Apostolic Tradition* 7 and 8. So again von Campenhausen, *Ecclesiastical Authority*, 177.

[175] So Faivre, *Naissance*, 51.

this follows the requests for the bishop 'to exercise the high priesthood ..., serving night and day; to propitiate you ...', suggesting that presenting the church's gifts was part of acting as high priest. Then, in the *Apostolic Tradition* 4, it is the deacons who present the eucharistic offering, the bishop and the presbyters who lay hands on it and the bishop who prays over it. In chapter 8 the ordination-prayer for a deacon alludes to him presenting what is offered by the high priest, clearly the bishop, whilst chapter 10 identifies the clergy with those who are ordained, offer sacrifice and have a 'liturgical duty ', which is a service connected with this offering. The clergy are thus delimited in terms of the offering of sacrifice and ordination with a view to this service. The deacons' presentation of the eucharistic offering to the bishop and the bishop's prayer over it are again mentioned in the *Apostolic Tradition* 21, in which the bishop presents the elements to the communicants with the presbyters and deacons holding the chalices of water, milk and wine. And chapter 22 depicts the bishop and presbyters as distributing the elements while the deacons and presbyters break the bread. Similar arrangements pertain to the presentation of offerings such as oil, cheese, olives and fruits.[176]

Hippolytus' omission of the laity's right to offer the eucharistic elements in case of necessity may be significant, mainly because he makes a close connection between the bishop as high priest and his offering the church's gifts which include the eucharist in the *Apostolic Tradition* 3,[177] and because he delimits the clergy in chapter 10 in terms of ordination, offering sacrifice and service connected with this sacrifice. In all his descriptions, the laity's only activities are to bring the materials for sacrifice, say 'Amen' to the prayers, and receive the elements. This suggests that, in some circles at least, the laity's right to offer the church's gifts even in emergencies was being discounted. A remnant of it may be found in the passage in the *Apostolic Tradition* 4, discussed in section 5.4.1, in which the laity are depicted as priestly during the bishop's offering of the bread and chalice, and this offering is made by the whole congregation through the bishop, but this is not necessarily so. This evidence also indicates that priesthood was closely related to the offering of sacrifice so that this issue was vital to the eclipse of the general by the particular priesthood.

As in Tertullian, so in Hippolytus the forgiving of sin by the bishop is

---

[176] *Apostolic Tradition* 5, 6, 31.

[177] Hein, 302-3, states that 'in the absence of the bishop, apparently no Eucharist can be held', although he recognizes exceptions between the death of one bishop and the election of another and for weekday celebrations by presbyters and deacons in the bishop's absence and with his approval.

linked with his priesthood. We have noted earlier that, in the *Apostolic Tradition* 3, the episcopal authority to forgive sins is given 'by the spirit of high priesthood'. Again like Tertullian, Hippolytus disapproves of some uses of this power, as is seen in *Refutation of All Heresies* 9:12:20 where he accuses Bishop Callistus of encouraging men in their pleasures by saying he forgives their sins. Although deploring Callistus' laxness, he never attacks his right to forgive sin.[178] Further, in *Contra Noetum* 1:4-7 Hippolytus relates that the presbyters of the Roman church summoned, questioned, condemned and expelled Noetus. We can only speculate over why it was the presbyters, but this again demonstrates the disciplinary power vested in the clergy.

In view of the importance which ordination was assuming, the right to ordain was attaining great significance for ministry. Hippolytus makes it clear that the right to ordain lay exclusively with the clergy, indeed with the bishop. In the bishop's ordination it is bishops who are to lay hands on the candidate, one of their number praying the consecratory prayer, while 'the presbytery shall stand by doing nothing.'[179] For a presbyter it is the bishop and presbyters who lay hands on him and the bishop who prays, and for a deacon the bishop alone lays hands on him and prays.[180] Indeed, in the *Apostolic Tradition* 8 it is made clear that the bishop alone has the power to ordain. The accompanying denial of this power to the presbyters arouses the suspicion that they had claimed it but it was now being restricted to the bishop.

Regarding teaching, a similar situation in Rome to that in North Africa is disclosed in Hippolytus' writings. Not only is the bishop's pastoral responsibility referred to in the *Apostolic Tradition* 3[181] very likely to have included teaching, but the passage in the preface to *Refutation of All Heresies* 6 referred to earlier has Hippolytus claiming that bishops are 'partakers of the same grace of high priesthood and of teaching ....'[182] The context is one of combatting heresies and probably involves a claim to a special grace vouchsafed to bishops as successors of the Apostles to refute these heresies.[183] The bishop's duty to teach the faithful is confirmed by the statement in the *Apostolic Tradition* 21 that 'if it is appropriate to recall anything else, the bishop will say it in secret to those who receive baptism.'[184]

---

[178] So Faivre, *Emergence*, 85.
[179] *Apostolic Tradition* 2: Botte, 4-5.
[180] *Apostolic Tradition* 7 and 8.
[181] '... to feed your holy flock': Botte, 8-9.
[182] Legge, vol. 1, 34.
[183] So von Campenhausen, *Ecclesiastical Authority*, 175-6.
[184] Botte, 58-9.

There were clearly others who taught in the church, however. In the *Apostolic Tradition* 39 the presbyters and deacons are told to meet daily where the bishop prescribes. It continues, 'And the deacons will not neglect to gather at all times, unless illness prevents them. When all have gathered, they will teach those who are in the church, and so, after having prayed, let them each go to the work that falls to him.'[185] The antecedent to 'they will teach' has to be 'the deacons', although the presbyters may also have been involved. The same situation seems to be referred to in the *Apostolic Tradition* 41 in which each Christian is told, when he or she arises, to pray and go to work, but 'if there is some instruction in the word, each will prefer to go there, considering in his heart that it is God that he hears in the one who instructs' and 'you will profit from what the Holy Spirit will give you through the instructor.' There is a possible mention of a teacher (*doctor*), but it is textually uncertain[186] and probably refers to a deacon or presbyter anyway. The same situation is referred to in the *Apostolic Tradition* 35.[187]

Hippolytus' only clear reference to the possibility of a lay teacher is in the *Apostolic Tradition* 19. After describing the involvement of *doctores* in the preparation of those to be baptized in chapters 15-18, he writes, 'whether the teacher is a cleric or a layman, let him act thus.'[188] Faivre plausibly suggests that this text 'has to be situated ... at a time when there was a strong tendency to demand that the doctor should be a member of the clergy. It is significant, however, that the author of the *Apostolic Tradition* was discreetly opposed to this tendency. This is clear from his observation that the doctor could be "either a member of the clergy or a layman."'[189] He also notes that the teaching function depicted here is catechetical and so more modest than the teaching activity exercised by such as Origen. Neymeyr rightly points out that these catechists were probably officially appointed by the Christian community for their task and stood in close relationship to its ordained officials, making it all the more understandable that the latter should at times shoulder this task.[190]

Finally, there is the clergy's, and especially the bishop's, power to

---

[185] Ibid., 86-7.

[186] Ibid., 89 note (4).

[187] Kydd, 279-280, notes this as an indication of the *charisma* of teaching continuing in the church, but, even if it is, it is probably restricted to the clergy in the light of the *Apostolic Tradition* 39.

[188] Botte, 40-41.

[189] Faivre, *Emergence*, 78-9.

[190] Neymeyr, 38-9. He agrees that the *Apostolic Tradition* attests 'the assumption of baptismal instruction by the clergy.'

rule and direct the affairs of the church, similar to that noted in Tertullian. This power is symbolized in a reference to the bishop's throne in *Refutation of All Heresies* 9:11:1. It is expressed in the uses of the words *diepo*, 'conduct, manage, administer', for Zephyrinus' relationship to the church in *Refutation of All Heresies* 9:7:1, and *katastasis*, 'control, direction', for his relationship to his clergy in *Refutation of All Heresies* 9:12:14.[191] It is also expressed in the ordination-prayer for the bishop in the *Apostolic Tradition* 3 where God is said to have instituted 'leaders (*principes*) and priests', he is requested to give the 'power ... of the princely (*principalis*) spirit', and the bishop's purpose is 'to distribute church responsibilities'.[192] That some of this government was shared with the prebyters is implied by the plea, in their ordination-prayer, for the 'the Spirit of grace and counsel of the presbytery, that he (the presbyter) may help and govern your people' on the model of the elders God filled with his Spirit to help Moses.[193] Since this Spirit differentiates between the presbyters and deacons and between being ordained to the priesthood and not being so ordained, according to the *Apostolic Tradition* 8, priesthood is linked with leadership.

We have already noted examples of the bishop's control extending to all church affairs. He controlled the clergy and appointed people to their responsibilities; he alone ordained the clergy and was the normal president at all church meetings and services; his was the main responsibility for church discipline. Although he shared some of these responsibilities, it was only with the presbyters or the presbyters and deacons. The *Apostolic Tradition* 28 brings out the respect owed him by ordinary Christians in instructions concerning certain communal meals: 'During the meal those invited will eat in silence, not contending with words, but as the bishop allows; and if he asks anything, they will reply. And when the bishop says a word, let all be modestly silent and approving, until he asks another question.'[194] Although the 'not contending with words' implies there had been some dissension at such meals, which was the main occasion for these instructions, the danger of excessive respect being given to the bishop's words is evident too. Another aspect of the differentiation between the clergy and laity is given at the end of section 28 where it is stated, 'For a layman cannot make a blessing ', although there is uncertainty whether this refers to a

---

[191] Legge, vol. 2, 118 and 128. For the meanings of the Greek words, see Lampe.
[192] Botte, 6-11.
[193] *Apostolic Tradition* 7: Botte, 20-21.
[194] Ibid., 70-73.

prayer or the meal.[195]

6.4.3 Increasing development of the hierarchy

These were fertile grounds for future developments in which the distance between the clergy and the laity was to be emphasized and increased to the detriment of the status and ministry of the laity.

The pre-eminent position of the bishop has already been made clear, as has the differentiation between the presbyters and the deacons. Something not noted thus far is the attainment, for the first time, of lectors and subdeacons to official positions within the church. Faivre views the lector as a relic of the ministry of prophets and doctors that has lost its earlier prestige. The lector is placed amongst the laity, the denial of ordination suggesting that

> the readers ... were also anxious to be included among the ministers of the altar. This indicates how dominant the clergy had become by that time and how all those who fulfilled any service in the community were drawn to the clerical status. The readers must have tried to come closer to those involved in the liturgy rather than to the doctors because the place occupied by the former seemed to them to be more prestigious.[196]

Similarly, the subdeacon is not to be ordained, but only nominated.[197]

Faivre further argues that there is a hint of the beginnings of a *cursus honorum* ('course of honours') in the ordination-prayer for a deacon which asks that the deacon may serve and present the offerings 'that ... he may attain the rank of a higher order', according to the Ethopic version of the *Apostolic Tradition*. The *Testamentum Domini* gives only 'that ... he may be worthy of this high and lofty rank',[198] so that there is the danger of later reworking, but Faivre may be right.[199]

6.4.4 The laity's responsibilities and powers

Noted in section 5.4 were the passage in which Hippolytus probably refers to the general priesthood in the context of offering the eucharist, passages in which he depicts Christians generally as able to offer spiritual sacrifices, and references to the church as God's sanctuary and

---

[195] In the *Apostolic Tradition* 26 (Botte, 66-7), a communal meal is also called a *eulogia*.

[196] Faivre, *Emergence*, 80; see also *Naissance*, 58-62.

[197] *Apostolic Tradition* 13.

[198] Ibid., 8: Botte, 26-7.

[199] Faivre, *Naissance*, 117. Note also von Campenhausen, *Ecclesiastical Authority*, 177, n. 171.

to all Christians being indwelt by the Spirit. He also follows earlier writers in viewing all the faithful as part of Christ's body, albeit only in *Commentary on Daniel* 4:37:2.[200]

In contrast to Tertullian's, Hippolytus' writings provide no evidence that the laity were involved in the process of church discipline, but they do evince awareness of the confessor's privileged position, though not in the arena of granting forgiveness, as in Tertullian. It is likely, however, that the same notion of the confessor as filled with the Spirit, on the basis of which he was seen as able to forgive sin, underlies what we find in Hippolytus. This is that, 'if a confessor was in chains for the name of the Lord, he shall not have hands laid on him for the diaconate or the presbyterate. For he has the honour of the presbyterate by his confession. But if he is appointed bishop, hands shall be laid on him.'[201] Since the ordinations of presbyter and deacon involve prayers for the relevant endowment of the Spirit, the confessor was probably regarded as having received that endowment.[202] That he received it through his suffering is shown by the ensuing qualification that he should be ordained normally if he had been punished in lesser fashion than by imprisonment. Further, it implies continuity with an earlier time when office depended on gifting not necessarily conveyed through ordination.[203]

That *charismata* were still prevalent and recognized in Rome, as in North Africa, is indicated in several ways in Hippolytus' works. One is the instruction in the *Apostolic Tradition* 14: 'But if anyone says, "I have received a gift of healing by a revelation", hands shall not be laid on him. For the facts themselves will show if he has told the truth.'[204] This probably means that a claim to a gift of healing should not be followed by ordination but its truth will be borne out by events.[205] If correct, this demonstrates that not all the spiritual gifts had yet been channelled through the clergy.

---

[200] Bardy, G. and Lefèvre, M. (eds.), *Hippolyte: Commentaire sur Daniel* (Paris, 1947), 338: 'For he hmself was the perfect body, and we his members, who are one with his perfect body ....'

[201] *Apostolic Tradition* 9: Botte, 28-9.

[202] Vilela, 358-360, considers the possibility that what is involved is only the right to sit amongst the presbyters without the exercise of presbyteral rights, rather than endowment with the Spirit. Based on one word and a possible parallel in a later letter of Cornelius concerning bishops, this possibility is less secure than the one adopted here.

[203] Cf. von Campenhausen, *Ecclesiastical Authority*, 177: 'the pneumatic-charismatic and the official-sacramental conceptions are here still co-existing without difficulty.'

[204] Botte, 32-3.

[205] So Faivre, *Naissance*, 93 against Hanson, R.P.C., *Studies*, 141, who argues that it means that 'it must first become clear through experience whether the man really has this charisma' and then he can be ordained.

Further possible evidence that the *charismata* were prevalent and recognized is found at the beginning of the *Apostolic Tradition* 1 and in *Commentary on Daniel* 4:36:6. On the other hand, the first makes only a general reference to gifts, and the second interprets Christ's priestly tunic in terms of the varied *charismata* with which the nations awaiting Christ's coming could be clothed. Neither passage clarifies what it means by *charismata*.[206]

Ash argues that Hippolytus rejected the validity of contemporary prophecy and upheld the canon of Scripture in its place on the basis of *Refutation of All Heresies* 8:19, *Contra Noetum* 9 and *Commentary on Daniel* 4:21:1, while von Campenhausen argues similarly on the basis of *The Antichrist* 31.[207] In the first Hippolytus roundly condemns Montanists for imagining that they learn more through contemporary prophets 'than from the Law, the Prophets, and the Gospels. They glorify these [women] above Apostles and every grace, since some of them dare to say that there are those among them who have become greater than Christ.'[208] Although consistent with the view noted, this is also consistent with the view that he was rejecting these particular contemporary prophecies because the Montanists were claiming to learn more from them than from Scripture, and were exalting these prophetesses above the Apostles, every *charisma*, and even Christ. There is nothing to necessitate Ash's interpretation, and the 'every grace [*charisma*]', which Ash acknowledges could show Hippolytus upheld the propriety of claiming such gifts, in such a context suggests that he did not reject contemporary gifts, including prophecy. Further, in a passage just before this, he criticizes the Montanists, not for believing in prophecy, but for not judging the prophecy by reason and not heeding those able to judge.

In *Contra Noetum* 9 Hippolytus begins setting out his method of establishing the truth: 'There is one God, and we acquire knowledge of him from no other source ... than the Holy Scriptures.'[209] However, it is unwise to take this as ruling out knowledge of God via creation or via prophecy. It is simply the only sure way of establishing the truth as against Noetus' views.

In *Commentary on Daniel* 4:21:1 Hippolytus states, 'the words of the

---

[206] Kydd, 277, argues that Hippolytus contains only hints of the *charismata* because he may already have written a book about them as suggested in the reference in the *Apostolic Tradition* 1.

[207] Ash, 'Decline', *Th St* 37.2 (1976), 244-5; and von Campenhausen, *Ecclesiastical Authority*, 191-2.

[208] Legge, vol. 2, 114.

[209] Butterworth, 67.

Lord are true but, as the Scriptures say, "every man is false", ...'[210] in
the context of condemning a church leader who believed more in his
own visions than in the Scriptures and predicted wrongly 'as a prophet.'
All that this passage requires is that Hippolytus held that all such visions
and prophecies should not be valued above Scripture and needed to be
judged in the light of Scripture.

Finally, in *The Antichrist* 31 Hippolytus addresses the prophets
Jeremiah, Daniel and John, 'you proclaimed to all generations the words
of God', but nowhere denies that later prophets were able to do so.[211]
There is, then, no statement in Hippolytus' writings requiring that he
rejected all contemporary prophecy, although what we noted earlier
concerning teaching being assimilated by the clergy and what we have
just noted concerning a church leader speaking as a prophet supports
Faivre's view that both of these charismatic functions were being taken
over by the clergy.[212]

As compared with Tertullian, there are few references to the
charismata in Hippolytus' writings with more than one suggestion that
they, especially prophecy and teaching, are becoming the province of
the clergy. The only gift probably attested as possessed by a lay person
is that of healing, although teaching has not yet become the exclusive
province of the clergy, either.

In our examination of Tertullian's writings in section 6.3.3 we noted
possible evidence that the laity were involved in the choice of church
officials. This is attested at Rome in the *Apostolic Tradition* 2 which
begins, 'Let him be ordained bishop who has been chosen by all the
people and is blameless. When he has been named and accepted by all,
let the people gather with the presbytery and the bishops who are
present, on the Lord's day. All consenting, they shall lay hands on him
and the presbytery shall stand by doing nothing.'[213] Gryson depicts the
situation plausibly as, 'the candidate's name must be announced
publicly so that it can be ascertained whether he is approved by
everyone.'[214] The statement in the *Apostolic Tradition* 8, 'And when a
deacon is ordained, let him be chosen according to what was said
above'[215] probably means he is to be chosen in the same way as the
bishop.[216]

---

[210] Bardy and Lefèvre, 302.
[211] Bonwetsch and Achelis, 20. On this see Ash, 'Decline', *Th St* 37.2 (1976), 246-7.
[212] Faivre, *Naissance*, 56.
[213] Botte, 4-5.
[214] Gryson, 'Les élections', *R Hist Eccl* 68 (1973), 356. So too Bârlea, 162.
[215] Botte, 22-3.
[216] So Bârlea, 164.

6.4.5 Conclusion

Whilst Hippolytus' writings confirm many points in Tertullian's, they also evince some significant developments, all in the direction of greater differentiation between clergy and laity and greater control over the affairs and ministry of the church by the clergy with the laity's role diminishing.

For example, Hippolytus presents greater evidence than Tertullian concerning the increasing importance of ordination as the line of demarcation between the clergy and the laity, together with hints that others besides the bishop, presbyter and deacons desired it because of its prestige. He also presents more evidence than Tertullian that ordination was regarded as a vehicle of special endowments of the Spirit and that only the bishop had the power to ordain, although the presbyters probably desired it. Other ways in which Hippolytus implies the clergy's greater powers over church life and ministry than does Tertullian consist in his lack of affirmation of the laity's rights to baptize and offer the church's gifts, his strong emphasis on the bishop as the usual president at the Eucharist, and his delimitation of the clergy in terms of service connected with the offering of sacrifice. Further, Hippolytus does not, like Tertullian, suggest any involvement of the laity in church discipline, but connects it strongly with the bishop, although presbyters can be involved too. Moreover, his evidence implies more strongly than Tertullian's that teaching is being brought under the clergy's control and it may show that spiritual gifts are too. He also marks a development beyond Tertullian in his awareness of the official positions of lector and subdeacon who may have taken up aspects of earlier 'charismatic' functions and are under clerical control.

In other ways Hippolytus only confirms what Tertullian made clear. For example, he shows that direction of the church's affairs lies firmly in the clergy's hands, that the laity are involved in the choice of church officials, that the whole church offers its sacrifices through the bishop, that Christians in general can offer spiritual sacrifices, are indwelt by the Spirit, and are part of Christ's body, and that the confessor is viewed as especially endowed by the Spirit.

Hippolytus is also like Tertullian and earlier writers in being aware of the general priesthood, while emphasising it far less than Tertullian, and he is like Tertullian in attesting the clergy's specialized priesthood. He does this regarding the bishop as offering the church's gifts, especially the eucharist, and regarding the clergy as those serving in connection with offering sacrifice. He also does it, like Tertullian, concerning the forgiving of sin, and, probably, government of the church.

We note, then, a continuing awareness of the clergy's priesthood and a diminished emphasis on the laity's coinciding with an increased emphasis on the position of the clergy, its demarcation from the laity, and the diminished role of the laity in the church's life and service. We also find that the clergy's priesthood is a significant aspect of its difference from the laity. All this demonstrates that the issue of the two human priesthoods was an important part of the larger development of the enhancement of the clergy's role in church life and ministry at the expense of the laity's.

6.5 Clement and the Alexandrian church c.180-c.200

With Clement[217] we turn to the Eastern church and go back 20 years or more from Hippolytus' time to one more contemporaneous with Tertullian. We also turn to one whose literary remains, though substantial, do not contain any equivalent to Hippolytus' *Apostolic Tradition*, from which so much of our information in the last section was drawn, nor any evidence of a dispute with the orthodox church such as that which occasioned some of Tertullian's writings relating to the subject at hand.

6.5.1 The clergy-laity divide

We noted, when considering Tertullian in section 6.3.1, Faivre's controversial and, in some ways at least, mistaken views concerning the meaning of 'lay person' at this period. He points out, rightly, that Clement of Alexandria is the first to use it since Clement of Rome and the first ever to use it 'to designate explicitly a category of Christians.'[218] Less certain are his conclusions that 'the layman represented an elite', deduced from the fact that, 'like the bishop, the presbyter and the deacon, he had to be monogamous', and that 'women remained outside the lay group.'[219] Elsewhere he argues that, like Tertullian, Clement faced the problem of where the clergy could be recruited from if Christians were not restricted to one marriage. Faivre is not certain 'whether laymen were all the "non-ordained" male members of the community – in which case all the men had to try to remain "husbands of only one woman" – or whether they really formed that reserve of future possible members of the clergy about whom the ascetic

---

[217] For this section 'Clement' will refer to Clement of Alexandria unless otherwise indicated.

[218] Faivre, 'The Laity', *Lumen Vitae* 42 (1987), 129 and 132.

[219] Ibid., 132 and 137.

and hot-headed Tertullian did not want to hear.'[220] The first alternative seems more likely since there is no other evidence of such a 'reserve of future possible members of the clergy' ever having existed. Moreover, as was argued in section 6.3.1, whilst Faivre's conclusion that the laity consisted only of men at this period is logically plausible from the texts considered, there is no statement by Tertullian or Clement requiring that women were not part of the laity.

The sole text on which Faivre bases his arguments from Clement, and the only one in which Clement uses *laikos* as a noun, is *Stromateis* 3:12:90:1, where Clement writes that Paul 'entirely approves of the man who is husband of one wife, whether he be presbyter, deacon, or layman, if he conducts his marriage unblameably.'[221] Faivre points out that the Greek *laikos* here has to mean a lay*man*[222] but this was required by the context of the discussion of being the husband of one wife, not by the laity comprising only men. Corroborative evidence is needed to prove Faivre's point.

This passage demonstrates that Clement is aware of a differentiation between the laity and the presbyter and deacon. Faivre argues that 'Clement is not contrasting the laity and the clergy here, but is associating the layman with presbyters and deacons within the same discipline.'[223] This is correct as far as the discipline goes but it does not remove the differentiation involved.

Clement's only use of *kléros* to mean 'clergy'[224] is in *Quis dives salvetur?* 42:2 where he writes that the Apostle John went to areas around Ephesus, 'here to appoint bishops, ... there to ordain [as clergy] such as were marked out by the Spirit.'[225] Hanson views this as reproducing 'the view which we have attributed to Irenaeus' which is that 'the Church guided by the Spirit chooses and ordains for its ministry men who have a God-given gift for perceiving and teaching Christian truth', and so that the charismatic gifts are 'to a large extent channelled into the official ministry.'[226] We questioned this interpretation of Irenaeus in section 6.2.2. It is more clearly true of this passage, but it is possible that Clement is referring back to a state of

---

[220] Faivre, *Emergence*, 56.

[221] Oulton, J.E.L. and Chadwick, H. (eds.), *Alexandrian Christianity* (London, 1954).

[222] Faivre, *Emergence*, 55.

[223] Ibid.

[224] He uses it three times, in *Strom* 4:26:163:5, 6:14:110:2 and 114:1, to mean 'lot' or 'inheritance.'

[225] Roberts, Donaldson and Coxe, vol. 2, 1221 with 'as clergy' added because it is there in the Greek.

[226] Hanson, R.P.C., *Studies*, 140-141.

affairs which he believed had pertained in the time of John but had changed in his own. It certainly demonstrates awareness of the practice of having a *kléros* who were ordained. These seem to have been in addition to the bishop.

There is, then, evidence in Clement's writings of the awareness of the categories of clergy and laity in his time in Alexandria, confirming what we have noted in Tertullian and Hippolytus, and showing that this was a widespread development by the end of the second century.

6.5.2 The position and ministries of the clergy

In section 4.5.3 we noted reasons to believe that the hierarchy had real value in Clement's eyes. One is Clement's comparisons, in *Stromateis* 6:13:105:1-107:3, of the gnostic Christian valued by God and exalted in heaven with presbyters and deacons ordained by men. Although he implies that the gnostic's value is a true one not necessarily matched by the church's estimation of him, he does not denigrate the hierarchy's worth and, as an imitation of heaven's hierarchy, it has an indeterminate value of its own. Similarly, in *Stromateis* 7:1:3:3-4 Clement compares the gnostic's ministry to God with the presbyters' and deacons' ministries. He evinces the need to defend and support the worth of the gnostic Christian and his ministry, whereas he seems to take that of the church's hierarchy for granted.

Further, in *Paidagogos* 1:6:37:3, he calls 'the leaders of the churches' shepherds on the model of Jesus, the good shepherd, who rightly care for the flock.[227] A similar reference, in *Stromateis* 6:17:158:1-2, may allude to gnostic teachers,[228] but, if we remember that for Clement church leaders will ideally be gnostics, the 'those fit to lead and teach' here[229] may well mean the hierarchy, since he adds that God wants to use them in instruction, government and administration. If so, he presents church leaders, qualified by the power of divine providence, an idea similar to that in *Quis dives salvetur?* 42:2 of John ordaining on the basis of the Spirit's manifestation, as rightly ruling and teaching God's people.

The presbyter is mentioned in passing in *Paidagogos* 3:11:63:1. Arguing against the use of wigs, Clement writes, 'On whose head, indeed, will the presbyter lay his hands? Whom will he bless?'[230] All

---

[227] Marrou and Harl, 179.

[228] So von Campenhausen, *Ecclesiastical Authority*, 199, n. 138.

[229] Roberts, Donaldson and Coxe, vol.2, 1047-8.

[230] Mondésert, et al., 128.

three clerical grades, plus widows, are mentioned in *Paidagogos* 3:12:97:2 as those concerning whom many commands are found in the Bible,[231] and without widows in *Stromateis* 6:13:106-107, a passage already discussed in section 4.5.3. Another passage discussed there is *Stromateis* 7:1:3:3-4, in which presbyters and deacons are alluded to. *Stromateis* 3:12:90:1 was examined in section 6.5.1 as referring to the presbyter and deacon alongside the layman.

In *Stromateis* 3:6:53:4 Clement refers to women deacons as taught about by Paul in 1 Timothy 5:9-10. Whilst this does not necessarily mean there were women deacons in Alexandria in Clement's day, it makes their existence more likely than not. If they did exist, this would tell against Faivre's view discussed above that the laity consisted only of men at this time.

Presbyters and leaders are mentioned in an exhortation to respect and revere them quoted from *1 Clement* in *Stromateis* 4:17:108:1. Clement is dealing with the gnostic Christian, but, as we have noted before, he sees such as the most fitted to be the church's leaders. Similarly, in *Stromateis* 7:7:42:7, whilst treating the gnostic, Clement writes of God's care for us, 'it is as the shepherds care for their flock or as the king cares for his subjects; we too behave obediently towards our superiors, who take the management of us, as appointed, in accordance with the commission from God with which they are invested.'[232] This indicates that Clement viewed at least gnostic, and probably all, church leaders as commissioned by God.

As well as the reference to the John's appointment of bishops noted earlier, there are two other mentions of bishops alone. In both, *Stromateis* 3:12:79:6 and 3:18:108:2, Clement alludes to Paul's instruction, in 1 Timothy 3:4-5, concerning bishops ruling their own households and the church well.

All this serves to confirm what was noted in section 4.5.3 with the addition that ordinary Christians were expected to honour their leaders, the bishops, presbyters and deacons, who were appointed by God. It also suggests that Clement saw their main functions as government, administration and teaching. Although it would be unwise to make anything of his omission of other functions, like church discipline and offering the church's gifts, which we have found in Tertullian and Hippolytus, it is fair to conclude that these are not as important for Clement as the functions just mentioned.

---

[231] Ibid., 182.
[232] Roberts, Donaldson and Coxe, vol. 2, p. 1085.

6.5.3 The position and ministries of the laity

We noted in section 6.5.1 that Clement is not interested in the laity as such, and, in section 5.5.2, that his main focus is on the gnostic Christian, although the gnostic is in many ways fully what the ordinary Christian is partially. All Christians are members of the church which is Christ's bride and body and indwelt by God, but only the gnostic is fit for teaching and leadership. Even so, as we noted in section 4.5.3, the gnostic may not be part of the church's leadership on earth, though he will be so valued in heaven. He may, then, be part of the laity. Given what we shall note concerning Origen, there were probably teachers in Alexandria during Clement's time who were not bishops, presbyters or deacons.[233] Further, the lay could aspire to become gnostics.[234]

Apart from this, there is little evidence to go on in Clement's writings. There is nothing about the part of the laity in elections,[235] and the only likely mention of the *charismata*[236] is found in *Excerpta ex Theodoto* 24:1 with reference to the Valentinians.

6.5.4 Conclusion

We have reaped a very meagre harvest from Clement concerning developments in the ministries of the clergy and the laity, a harvest to some extent commensurate with what we harvested earlier concerning the priesthoods of the ordained and the faithful. The major reason for this is Clement's overwhelming interest in the importance of the gnostic Christian and his ministry (and his priesthood). Some of the possible reasons for this were mentioned in sections 4.5.6 and 5.5.4. If one was a need to promote the gnostic teacher's vital importance in view of the taking over of teaching by clergy not fitted for the task, it has left no impression on Clement's treatment of the clergy and is therefore uncertain.

How widely Clement's views in this area were held is unclear, but it must be assumed that some in Alexandria shared them, especially if, as Neymeyr cogently argues,[237] the *Stromateis* were written for those who

---

[233] So Faivre, *Emergence*, 53-4, on Pantaenus. Neymeyr, 93, concludes that 'Clement needed no official authorisation for his educational work', although whether he was ordained or not is unclear.

[234] So Williams G. H., 'The Ancient Church' in Neill and Weber, *The Layman in Christian History*, 32.

[235] Gryson, 'Les élections', *R Hist Eccl* 68 (1973), does not mention anything about elections from Clement's writings.

[236] So Kydd, 344-7.

[237] Neymeyr, 76-9.

aspired to become gnostic Christians and teachers. The evidence for a kind of school, noted in section 4.5.1, implies that there may have been many such. Von Campenhausen holds that Clement's attitude was, 'with individual variations, widespread among other teachers in the East.'[238] Origen goes a considerable way towards confirming this for Alexandria and Caesarea, but otherwise there is too little evidence to be sure.

Clement's evidence confirms the existence of a division between clergy and laity at this period in Alexandria as well as in Carthage and Rome. It does not confirm a link between this division and the use of priestly language for the clergy. It also introduces an emphasis on the all-important function of teaching different from that of all others we have considered and locates the qualifications for this not in ordination but in moral, intellectual and spiritual striving resulting in divine enduement. Whilst this stress is not completely absent elsewhere, it nowhere reaches the pitch of importance assigned to it by Clement. He thus witnesses to the development of a view concerning ministry which overlaps with what we have seen elsewhere mainly at points which are not very important to Clement himself, and which places at centre-stage a function which is only one amongst a number of important functions for the other writers we have examined. That he ties this function so closely to priesthood is therefore all the more significant, demonstrating the importance which this category had assumed in different places and ways in the church's thinking concerning ministry. He also shows that it had not yet been tied down either to the ordained or to the faithful.

6.6 Origen and the Alexandrian and Caesarean churches c.200-c.250

6.6.1 The clergy-laity divide

Origen confirms what we have noted concerning the existence of this divide in the Alexandrian church in Clement's writings.[239] Commenting in *Homilies on Jeremiah* 11:3 on an interpretation he has found, Origen writes,

> ... this word will help both you and us. Some of us suppose there to be by virtue of office some who preside over you, such that some want to reach for this office. But know that the *office* does not altogether save. For even many presbyters will be damned; even many laity will be proven blessed. Since

---

[238] Von Campenhausen, *Ecclesiastical Authority*, 211.
[239] The following quotation comes from his time in Caesarea but probably reflects the situation in Alexandria too in view of all else we have seen.

there are some in the *office* who do not live in a way that they profit and honour the *office*, ...[240]

Origen here contrasts the clergy with the laity and includes in the clergy the presbyters, deacons and bishops. This is apparent in the rest of the passage in which the presbyterium, the deacon and the one 'who has undertaken the chief ecclesiastical office' are mentioned alongside the layman in an ascending order of responsibility to live virtuously in accordance with each rank. This shows that Origen is aware of the clergy's superior dignity.[241]

This is further demonstrated in *Homilies on Ezekiel* 5:4 where Origen is commenting on the degrees of punishment each Christian should expect for his sin: 'Compared with the deacons, is the lay person not more worthy of pardon, and in turn, compared with the presbyter, does the deacon not deserve pardon more? ... What does it profit me, the title-holder occupying the seat with my head high, to receive greater honour, if I cannot have deeds appropriate to my dignity?'[242]

Origen also depicts a gradation between the laity, the Levite, the priest, and the high priest in the power to deal with sin in *Homilies on Numbers* 10:1. We shall see in section 6.6.3 that Origen never depicts others than the clergy as dealing with sin, although he also sees the perfect alone as able to do so. Certainly the reference to the *laicus* here suggests that the clergy are referred to. This is probably true of two other passages Faivre refers to in *Homilies on Leviticus* 5:7 and 5:3 in which he finds a hierarchy of knowledge and perfection between priests and laity.[243]

These last references raise the question of the relationship between the clergy and priesthood. This was investigated in section 4.6.3 where we found that Origen describes the ordained as priests unambiguously at times. Also relevant, as Vilela and Schäfer show, is Jerome's translation of –'*apo klérou*' in *Homilies on Jeremiah* 11:3 as '*in clericatus ... ordine*'.[244] This identifies *kléros* with *ordo*, which Origen's Latin translators usually use for *taksis* and which is used more often than *kléros* in Origen's works but for the same group of people. Another point about Origen's use of *ordo* is that he often qualifies it by *sacerdotalis* or links it in some other way with priesthood,[245] confirming

---

[240] Smith, 104-5. The *kleroi* and the *laikoi* are contrasted in *Sel. Jer.* 12.13 too.

[241] See on this Faivre, *Emergence*, 61.

[242] Borret, M. (ed.), *Origène: Homélies sur Ézéchiel* (Paris, 1989), 200-202.

[243] Faivre, *Emergence*, 60.

[244] Vilela, 108 and Schäfer, 55-6.

[245] *Ordo* sacerdotalis is used in *H. Lev.* 13:4 and 15:1, of the priestly tribe of Levi and, in *H.*

what we noted earlier in Hippolytus' and Tertullian's writings about the close link between the clergy-laity divide and the rise in the use of priestly language for the clergy.

6.6.2 The composition of the laity

Faivre follows up what we noted in section 6.5.1 about the putative evidence of the laity' consisting of only monogamous male Christians by pointing out that Origen 'made a distinction between those who called on the Lord and Chist's true disciples' in *Commentary on John* 6:59 (38), and makes it even more explicit in *Homilies on Luke* 17:10-11. In the last Origen affirms that the monogamous belong to the church but denies that the twice-married do; rather they are of those who call on the Lord and are saved in his name but not crowned by him.[246] Faivre concludes that the laity are only the monogamous, although this may have been no more than an ideal by the time of Origen, having been a reality briefly in the time of Clement.[247]

On the other hand, in the passage noted from *Homelies on Ezekiel* 5:4 in the last section, Origen identifies the *laicus* with the *fidelis* ('faithful one') and encompasses the whole church by mentioning the catechumen, the lay person, the deacon, the presbyter and the bishop. Similarly in *Dialogue with Heraclides* 5 he mentions the bishop, the presbyter, the deacon and the layman as participants in the church's meetings. Possibly he would have distinguished the laity from the non-monogamous faithful if pressed, but probably not.

Another doubt concerning the composition of the laity for Origen is raised by Hällström's point that Origen does not use *laikos* for the *simpliciores*. Since Hällström also rightly argues that Origen viewed the majority in the church as *simpliciores*,[248] and since, as we have just noted, Origen views the non-church officials as the laity, it is most likely that the *simpliciores* made up the majority of the laity.

Lev. 6:3, *ordinatio* is used of ordination to the priesthood in Origen's times; in *H. Num.* 2:1, Origen relates the *'sacerdotalem vel Leviticum ordinem'* to the actions of bishop, presbyter and deacon; in *H. Josh.* 4:1, he identifies the same with the 'ministers of God'; in *H. Judg.* 3:2, he contrasts implicitly the *'sacerdotalem et leviticum ordinem'* with the 'poor of the people'; in *H. Ezek.* 9:2, he links *'sacerdotalis ordo et leviticus gradus'* with *'ecclesiasticam dignitatem'* and being presbyters; and, in *H. Josh.* 3:3, he identifies the ordinary Israelite with the *'laicus'* who is to supply the priests' and Levites' material needs.

[246] Crouzel, H. et al (eds.), *Origène: Homélies sur Saint Luc* (Paris, 1962), 262.

[247] Faivre, *Emergence*, 61-3.

[248] Hällström, 18-19.

6.6.3 The powers and ministries of the clergy

Three passages were noted in section 4.6.3 which indicated that Origen viewed the priestly clergy as presiding over God's people. In *Homilies on Exodus* 11:6 he also accuses them of being unwilling to accept advice from inferior priests, a lay person or a pagan, describes the qualities appropriate to the 'leaders of the people', and calls on the 'leaders of the people and the presbyters of the people', probably the bishops and presbyters,[249] to hear what Jethro told Moses about leaders judging the people, which Origen interprets as reconciling them.[250]

In *Homilies on Leviticus* 5:4 Origen cites the 'the priests of the Lord who preside in the churches' and likens to the Levitical offering of propitiatory sacrifice the process of leading a sinner to repentance.[251] In *Homilies on Joshua* 7:6 he refers to 'the priests who preside over the people' in the context of the need to be severe with sinners, going on to again mention 'those who preside in the churches' and call the leader the body's eye.[252] In these three passages, leadership is linked with priestliness and returning individuals to right relationships with other Christians and with God.

The clergy's status as leaders is further expressed through intimations of their places of honour in church meetings,[253] indications of the respect normally accorded them,[254] suggestions that some boast of belonging to the priesthood and designate their relatives as their successors,[255] mentions of an elevated rank and priestly honour,[256] and descriptions of the clergy as 'leaders' sitting 'in the priestly assembly'.[257] More references intimating the clergy's leadership and criticising their exercise of it could be cited.[258] Even allowing for Origen's resentment over his treatment by Bishop Demetrius, the power involved in leadership was clearly corrupting many wielding it. Often, though not always,[259] these indications of leadership are bound up with

---

[249] So Vogt, 37.
[250] Heine, 362.
[251] Barkley, 98.
[252] Jaubert, 208-211.
[253] *C. Mt.* 15:26 and *H. Jer.* 11:3.
[254] *H. Josh.* 10:3.
[255] *H. Num.* 2:1 and 22:4; *H. Jdg.* 3:2.
[256] *H. Num.* 2:1 and 10:3.
[257] *H. Num.* 22:4 and *H. Josh.* 9:5.
[258] See Daniélou, 44; Trigg, *Origen*, 14; etc.
[259] As well as the passages in *H. Jer.* 11:3, *H. Ex.* 11:6, *C. Mt.* 15:26, *H. Num.* 22:4 noted earlier in sections 6.6.1 and 6.6.3, *see H. Ezek.* 2:1 where leaders are referred to as 'heads of the churches', and *H. Num.* 12:2 where they are called kings and said to reign. Vogt, 4 and Schäfer, 67-80, give fuller lists of Origen's designations of bishops, many implying their power and authority. Vilela, 94, points out the presbyters shared in this to some extent as part

priestliness.

Vogt argues that *Homilies on Numbers* 22:1 shows that the presbyters were chosen by the bishop on the basis that, while Origen criticizes the choice of the bishop by the people's acclamation because Moses did not choose his successor that way, he says that God told Moses to choose elders and intends this as a model to follow.[260] The use of *'presbyteri'* and the likening of Moses to the bishop render this likely.

The references to the bishop's and presbyters' seats of honour already noted intimate that they presided over the church's meetings for worship, including, presumably, the eucharist. The few passages alluding to the clergy's special role in worship and, possibly, the eucharist, were examined in section 4.6.4. A clear indication of the clergy's presidency at baptism is given in *Homilies on Joshua* 4:1 where Origen describes baptism 'in the presence of the priestly and Levitical order' and likens it to crossing the Jordan to the promised land 'thanks to the priests' ministry'.[261]

There has been debate over whether Origen viewed others than the clergy as able to administer church discipline.[262] On the one hand, he saw perfection as required in order to bind and loose; on the other, he regarded the clergy as those who did so. The former is demonstrated, above all, by *Commentary on Matthew* 12:10, 11 and 14 in which, commenting on Matthew 16:16-19, Origen explains that Jesus' promise of the power to bind and loose was not given to Peter alone but also to those who are perfect like him, and that when bishops apply this promise to themselves, they are right if perfect but not if not. The same kind of point is made in *On Prayer* 28:8-10, only there the truly spiritual are likened to priests and apostles.

That Origen regarded the clergy as those who normally exercised church discipline is evinced in several passages. One is in *Homilies on Judges* 2:5 where Origen writes, '... not only by his apostles has God "delivered" those who have sinned "into the hands of their enemies" but also by those who preside over the Church and have the power not only to loose but also to bind, sinners "are handed over for the loss of the

---

of the *consessus*.

[260] Vogt, 11.

[261] Jaubert, 148.

[262] This debate has been fuelled by Trigg, 'The Charismatic Intellectual', *Ch H* 50 (1981), 15-18 and *Origen*, 196, who holds that Origen views only the spiritual as having the power to bind and loose, and attacks the exclusive claims of bishops to do so. See Völker, *Vollkommenheitsideal*, 172, n. 6, for earlier debate between Roman Catholics and Protestants on this. Others (Daniélou, 71-2; von Campenhausen, *Ecclesiastical Authority*, 257-263; Vogt, 123 and 130-132; Schäfer, 163-5; and Crouzel, *Origène*, 298-302) argue that it was only if the spiritual were bishops that they could excommunicate, according to Origen.

flesh" when, because of their faults, they are separated from the body of Christ', going on to describe these leaders as 'priests' just after.[263]

A second is in *Homilies on Leviticus* 2:4 in which Origen describes the remission of sins by penitence, when the sinner confesses his sins to the Lord's priest seeking a remedy, thus fulfilling what James 5:14-15 says about calling the church's presbyters to, among other things, pray for the forgiveness of sins.[264] Third, in *Homilies on Judges* 3:3, Origen writes of the 'leaders and judges of the Church', adding 'to whom judgment was given not only over actions but also over souls.' Sadly, 'I do not know if any judge in the Church is such that "God" makes worthy "of being filled with his Spirit", ...'[265] These must be church officials since Origen would never have doubted that the perfect were filled with the Spirit.[266] Fourth, in *Homilies on Leviticus* 14:2, Origen describes how, if 'someone of the faithful has sinned, although this one is not yet cast out by the judgment of the bishop, nevertheless he was already cast out by the sin itself which he committed.' He repeats this in 14:3.[267]

The one passage in which Trigg[268] has grounds for arguing that Origen presents someone unordained as to be sought out for help by the sinner is in *Homilies on Psalm* 37, 2:6. Here Origen urges his hearers to seek out one to whom they should confess their sins on the basis of his spiritual gifts in this area. However, the exact circumstances are not clear and Vogt may be right to argue that the fact that the person's qualification for this work must be generally known renders it unlikely that Origen is thinking of someone outside the hierarchy.[269] Further, it may be that only private advice is meant.

On the whole, then, it seems most plausible that Origen viewed the clergy as those who exercised public church discipline, although that discipline was confirmed in heaven only in so far as the clergy exercising it conformed to his view of perfection. There is no clear evidence in his writings of anyone outside the clergy exercising such public discipline. Moreover, he often links this function with priesthood,[270] as well as with leadership, judging and apostleship.

The clearest evidence that Origen lived during a transitional period

---

[263] Messié et al., 90-91.

[264] Vogt, 134 and 177-8, finds a reference to official reconciliation to the church here.

[265] Messié et al., 104-7.

[266] Vogt, 135, so interprets this passage, though without using this argument.

[267] Barkley, 246 and 250.

[268] Trigg, The Charismatic Intellectual', *Ch H* 50 (1981), 17-18.

[269] Vogt, 178-9.

[270] In section 4.6.3 we noted this link also in *H. Lev.* 5:3 and *H. Num.* 10:1.

regarding the transfer of the most important functions and ministries exclusively to the clergy concerns his experience in teaching and preaching. Noted in section 4.6.3 was evidence that Origen viewed the study and teaching of God's word as the greatest priestly task. Here we are examining whether this ministry was confined to the clergy in Alexandria, Caesarea and more widely in Origen's day.

Much relevant evidence derives from reports of Origen's experiences, although there has been debate over many details of what happened.[271] We shall trace the broad outlines as reflected on in some recent scholarship. First, whilst still a layman, Origen was recognized as a teacher of catechumens by Bishop Demetrius.[272] This recognition probably continued when Origen handed the teaching over to Heraclas in order to dedicate himself to higher Christian instruction to Christians, heretics and pagans.[273] As noted in section 4.6.1, scholars disagree over precisely which factors were significant in Origen's problems with Bishop Demetrius and resulted in his departure from Alexandria for Caesarea.[274] Most significant for us is the fact that, during a first visit to Palestine, bishops allowed Origen to preach, though a layman, in the church's meeting, presumably before the eucharist was celebrated. Demetrius protested that lay people preaching with bishops present had never been heard of. Bishops Alexander of Jerusalem and Theoctistos of Caesarea replied that, "'In cases where persons are found duly qualified to assist the clergy, they are called on by the holy bishops to preach to the laity'", and gave three examples of this, adding, "'Probably there are other places too where this happens, unknown to us.'"[275] Later Origen was ordained in Caesarea,[276] probably by the same two bishops. After Demetrius' protests and death, he moved to Caesarea permanently and taught there as a presbyter.

These events, and especially the controversy between Demetrius,

---

[271] Compare Nautin, 413-441; Trigg, *Origen*; and Crouzel, *Origène*, 17-61, three important recent studies.
[272] Exactly when is disputed: Neymeyr, 99, and Trigg, *Origen*, 35, agree with Nautin, 417, that it was in 211 rather than, as Eusebius states, in *HE* 6:3:3, when Origen was eighteen. Crouzel, *Origène*, 26, accepts Eusebius' report as correct.
[273] So Neymeyr, 99. Neymeyr thinks Origen was probably supported by the church at this time.
[274] Eusebius, in *HE* 6:8:4, depicts Demetrius as jealous of Origen's success and fame; Nautin, 423-6, argues that Origen's teachings had made him suspect and Demetrius' ordination of Heraclas instead of Origen decided him to leave; Trigg, *Origen*, 130-132, traces the tension ultimately to the differences between an organizer and an intellectual, as well as noting the factors suggested by Eusebius and Nautin; and Crouzel, *Origène*, 44-5, follows Eusebius closely.
[275] Eusebius, *HE* 6:19:16-19 (Williamson and Louth, 197).
[276] Ibid., 6:23:4.

Alexander and Theoctistos over whether it was customary for laymen to preach in the church's Sunday services, make it clear that the practice was becoming rarer in Asia Minor, Palestine and Egypt,[277] although it had not entirely died out. Neymeyr also cites Socrates' *Historia Ecclesiastica* 5:22 as reporting meetings of the Alexandrian church on Wednesday and Friday during which the teachers, including Origen, interpreted the Scriptures. It was, then, probably because it involved the eucharistic Sunday service, with the bishop(s) present, that Demetrius objected so strongly.[278] Further, Demetrius' ordination of Heraclas and Dionysius' succession to Heraclas as head of the catechetical school and then as bishop suggests that the teaching of catechumens and others outside church services was also being brought more closely under the control and into the ministry of the clergy.[279]

This transition is also reflected in Origen's writings. Although von Campenhausen asserts that 'Origen nowhere envisages an independent "teaching profession" distinct from the clergy', Vogt and Schäfer point to a passage in *Homilies on Ezekiel* 3:7 as suggesting this.[280] Interpreting Ezekiel 14:1 in which elders are mentioned, Origen states that the word of God 'touches all and does not spare any kind of the orders established in the Church, ... here, for example, its speaks to the presbyters. Indeed, what precedes concerns teachers.'[281] Presbyters and teachers are depicted as two 'orders'. Vogt also cites a passage in *Analecta sacra* 3:151 in which Origen divides the leaders in meetings into teachers and priests.[282] On the other hand, Origen sometimes identifies teachers with the church's leaders. Vogt cites passages in *Homilies on Leviticus* 6:6 and *Homilies on Numbers* 2:1 as indicating this.[283] This confirms that teaching in the church's services was becoming increasingly the province of the ordained, although lay teachers still existed but were becoming ever fewer. Origen's ordination shows at least that he was bowing to the inevitable.[284]

---

[277] The places cited by Alexander and Theoctistos were Laranda, Iconium and Synnada (see *HE* 6:19:18).

[278] Neymeyr, 101; see the text in n. 490.

[279] So Faivre, *Emergence*, 63-4, who views Origen as 'the last of the great lay *didaskaloi* or catechetical teachers.'

[280] Von Campenhausen, *Ecclesiastical Authority*, 250; Vogt, 60; and Schäfer, 218. Trigg, *Origen*, 29, holds that Demetrius restricted the teaching function to the clergy during his episcopate, a view similar to that taken below.

[281] Borret, 138-141.

[282] Vogt, 60.

[283] Ibid., 61.

[284] As the tenor of Trigg, The Charismatic Intellectual', *Ch H* 50 (1981), and *Origen* suggests. The is more likely than the view of Schäfer, 228, that Origen agreed that teachers should be ordained.

Origen's writings and experiences thus disclose a situation in which the clergy's powers and ministries were continuing to increase at the expense of the laity's.

6.6.4 The powers and ministries of the laity

Origen's teaching on the priesthood of all the faithful and the sacrifices they should offer was examined in section 5.6.1 above. They involve active purity of life, good works, prayer, worship, self-denial, and study of God's word resulting in teaching, all of which culminate in the perfect. In section 5.6.2 we found an organic unity between the ordinary and perfect Christian for Origen demonstrated in a common participation, but at different depths, in priesthood, spiritual gifts, and anointing by Christ. And in section 5.6.3 we discovered Origen's use of temple-imagery for the church, as well as for individual Christians.

On the other hand, we have also uncovered evidence of an ambiguous attitude towards ordinary Christians based on Origen's disappointment with their standard of Christian living. In section 5.6.1 we noticed how he repeatedly uses the common priesthood to exhort them to live out that priesthood and tend toward perfection. At times he implies that some were not doing so. This attitude is also discerned in his allusions to the *simpliciores*. As Hällström shows, Origen depicts them as forming the majority of the church and as, above all, intellectually deficient and spiritually immature.[285] Origen further criticizes his hearers for making worldly matters a greater priority than attendance at church to hear God's word, not paying attention when they are present, leaving before the sermon or inattention during it, not studying the Bible, living sinfully, despising new converts or those of lower status or wealth, and for many sins.[286] These criticisms are largely based on his perception that spirituality has declined greatly since earlier times, a perception poignantly expressed in *Homilies on Jeremiah* 4:3.

Origen thus held an exalted view of the true Christian who was tending towards perfection but a low view of the majority of the faithful who were not. This is reflected in some of the rest of what we find in his writings about the laity's powers and ministries and forms the background to all of it.

Daniélou is right to argue that Origen's picture of the church in *Contra Celsum* is idealized for the purpose of apologetics,[287] but its

---

[285] Hällström, especially 7, 24-7 and 38-41.
[286] Taken from Daniélou, 41-3, where he gives quotations from Origen's writings.
[287] Ibid., 40.

apologetic nature also makes it likely that there is truth in it. In 3:9 Origen depicts Christians as diffusing their teaching throughout the world, travelling around towns and villages to win others. This may well have still been done by laymen in Origen's days.[288] We noted in section 6.6.3 that laymen's active involvement in official church discipline in Origen's days was unlikely, although they were probably important witnesses to what occurred.[289]

What we have noted concerning teaching is relevant to Origen's depiction of spiritual gifts too. Although he clearly viewed the perfect as the only appropriate teachers, one reason for which was their enduement with the necessary gifts, the opportunities for the public exercise of those gifts within church services were becoming increasingly limited. Nonetheless, Origen was clearly aware of their continuing existence and that they were not confined to the clergy. He interprets some of them in a way which Paul did not mean. For example, he interprets the word of wisdom and the word of knowledge, the gifts he most often mentions, in terms of right understanding of Scripture and wise teaching rather than as direct revelations from God.[290] Similarly, he views prophecy as helping in the interpretation of Scripture, and discernment as enabling to detect which teaching is of God and which is not.[291] Indeed, his explicit mentions of the *charismata* are focused mainly on gifts necessary for understanding and teaching God's word.[292] Further, he depicts these gifts as earnt and merited rather than given by God out of pure grace,[293] and divides gifts into two classes, greater and smaller, the former involving prophecy, words of wisdom and knowledge, and possibly discernment, the latter faith, miraculous healing, and exorcism, the two types corresponding to perfect and simple Christians.[294]

On the other hand, he says of Christians in general, in *Contra Celsum* 1:46, 'They charm daemons away and perform many cures and perceive

---

[288] So Williams G. H., 'The Ancient Church' in Neill and Weber, *The Layman in Christian History*, 41.

[289] Note Rahner, 'La doctrine' in *Recher Sci Rel* 37 (1950), 275, on church discipline as part of the church's function as a community. *CC* 3:51 suggests this although the details are unclear.

[290] This is clearest in *CC* 1:44, 3:18 and 46, and *H. Josh.* 26:2.

[291] See *H. Ex.* 4:5 and 3:2.

[292] The main exception to this concerns marriage and celibacy, which Origen views as involving gifts, though not a spiritual gift as far as marriage is concerned (so Hällström, 80, n. 37). On this, see Crouzel, *Origène*, 191 and 194.

[293] See *PA* 2:7:3 and 3:3:3.

[294] On this, see Hällström, 79-80. In n. 34, he quotes Grau, on a similar view in Clement, as speaking of '"an intellectualisation of the understanding of the charisma that is completely foreign to Paul"' and as attributing the change to the influence of Greek thought.

certain things about the future according to the will of the Logos',[295] which is much nearer to NT descriptions. In *Contra Celsum* 1:2 and 2:8, he writes of traces of the miracles of NT times in his own, stating in 2:8 that they are important and he has seen some.[296] Further, in 7:8, he indicates that the signs given by the Holy Spirit during Christ's ministry and after his ascension have diminished, 'nevertheless, even to this day there are traces of him in a few people whose souls have been purified by the Logos and by the actions which follow his teaching.'[297] Origen's status as a highly regarded churchman, familiar with the contemporary church, having visited Rome, Arabia, Antioch, Greece, and Cappadocia, and the incidental nature of his references to spiritual gifts, provide grounds for believing what he says.[298]

None of these passages includes explicit allusions to the *charismata*, suggesting that for Origen and those like him, they were understood above all as involving gifts necessary for understanding and teaching God's word, a function which was being increasingly restricted to the clergy. Moreover, although he knew of some of the effects of what were known as spiritual gifts in NT times continuing, he was aware that they were manifested less often than earlier. Thus the major source of the laity's ministry was diminishing in people's experiences and being increasingly dominated by the clergy.

An area of church life in which the laity retained some of its ancient power and privileges is the election of bishops, as we noted in Tertullian and Hippolytus. We noted in section 4.6.3 a passage in *Homilies on Leviticus* 6:3 where Origen says, 'For in ordaining a priest, the presence of the people is also required that all may know and be certain that from all the people one is chosen for the priesthood who is more excellent, who is more wise, who is more holy, who is more eminent in every virtue, ...'[299] Scholars are right to see a reference to contemporary practice here.[300] Further, in *Homilies on Numbers* 22:4, Origen describes the people as giving their favour under the influence of clamour or perhaps money, while, in *Homilies on Genesis* 3:3, he asks why the Lord tells Moses alone to choose elders whom he knows to be elders, not those whom the ignorant multitude recognized.[301]

---

[295] Chadwick, 42.

[296] Ibid., 8 and 72.

[297] Ibid., 402.

[298] Kydd, 370-373.

[299] Barkley, 120.

[300] Bârlea, 158; Vilela, 64; and Gryson, 'Les élections', *R Hist Eccl* 68 (1973), 391-2.

[301] On these passages, see Vilela, 63-4 and Gryson, 'Les élections', *R Hist Eccl* 68 (1973), 389-394.

We noted in section 6.6.3 likely evidence of the bishops' special role in choosing presbyters. There is also a passage in *Commentary on Matthew* 16:22 in which Origen criticizes the bishops and presbyters for handing the church over to those unsuitable as leaders, and, in *Homilies on Numbers* 22:4, one in which some princes of the church are said to have willed their episcopates to their relatives. Probably, then, the whole church was involved in approving the candidate selected by the presbyters, if the bishop had died,[302] or in approving some or all of the candidates presented by the bishop and presbyters if new presbyters were needed.[303]

In addition, Origen's writings and reports concerning his life make it clear that lay people were present at some synods and public meetings. He reports that many were present during a public disputation and that he spoke with Heraclides before the people, while the whole community listened to him during a synod in Arabia, according to Eusebius, and Origen reports that bishops sign decisions in front of the faithful.[304] No indication is given of their participation so that we cannot gauge the significance of this beyond the fact that the laity were still present. In view of what we have noted of their involvement in elections, they probably voiced approval or disapproval of what they heard.

Further, Origen believed that the laity should support the clergy financially, as we noted in section 4.6.3. In *Homilies on Joshua* 17:3, in particular, Origen relates this duty directly to the laws concerning the priests and Levites.[305]

Again, then, we note the increasing subordination of the laity to the clergy, not least in the areas of spiritual gifts and support of the clergy. Even so, they are not totally ignored, not least in elections and ordinations. They also have their part to play in the eucharistic meetings in prayer.[306]

6.6.5 Summary and conclusion

Origen reinforces what Clement tells us regarding the existence of the clergy-laity divide in Alexandria and establishes its existence in

---

[302] Note Lécuyer, 'Sacerdoce', *Vetera Christianorum* 7 (1970), 263-4; Vilela, 176-8; and Gryson, 'Les élections', *R Hist Eccl* 68 (1973), 395-9 on evidence that the bishop of Alexandria was elected and enthroned by the presbyters without ordination by another bishop.

[303] Something like this seems to be envisaged by Vilela, 64; Gryson, 'Les élections', *R Hist Eccl* 68 (1973), 392; and Schäfer, 84.

[304] See evidence in Vilela, 65.

[305] So Faivre, A., 'Aux origines du laïcat', *L'Année canonique* 29 (1985/86), 49.

[306] On this see Faivre, *Emergence*, 62.

Caesarea too. He provides more indications of a link between this and the clergy's special priesthood than does Clement, being more like Tertullian and Hippolytus in this. On the other hand, Origen follows Clement regarding the spiritual Christian's importance in the church and the centrality of teaching, both being closely tied to priesthood. Tertullian has a similar emphasis on the spiritual Christian in his Montanist period, but does not link it with teaching or priesthood as do Clement and Origen. What we have noted suggests that the, for them, central priestly function of teaching had become more restricted to the clergy in Origen's than in Clement's time. This contributes to the impression that the clergy-laity divide had become clearer and better established by the time of Origen. Contributing to the same is the lack of implications of the laity's resentment against the clergy in Origen's writings[307] as compared with Tertullian's, and the presence of clerical resentment against a layman in the case of Bishop Demetrius and Origen.

Their emphasis on the significance of the gnostic or perfect Christian means that Clement and Origen do not bring out the basic unity of the clergy and laity as much as Tertullian, for whom both can, in cases of necessity, do most of the same things. It is still present, though, in that both clergy and laity are criticized and urged to become gnostic or perfect. This, as we have noted, is often linked to the understanding of the perfect as priests and with the use of the concept of the general priesthood. Origen and Tertullian, at least in the latter's Montanist period, are alike in viewing the spiritual as alone able to forgive sin.

Largely because of their stress on the gnostic or perfect Christian's significance, Clement and Origen are not as interested in the laity's power and ministries as Tertullian is. The laity's part in elections of clergy is mentioned in all three and Hippolytus, as are the *charismata*, but these appear more common in Carthage, whether because of Montanist influence or as a characteristic of the North African church or for some other reason. There is also an awareness in Origen not found elsewhere so far that they occur less often than earlier in the church's life and there is much more interest in those viewed as relating to understanding and teaching God's word. As in Hippolytus, there are indications in Origen that they are becoming restricted to the clergy.

Origen's stress on the need to be perfect probably goes a long way towards explaining why he never indicates that ordination conveys a

---

[307] We have noted the likelihood that Origen's resentment at his treatment by Demetrius was a factor in some of his criticisms of the clergy but there is no indication that the general laity shared this, and he criticized the laity as much as the clergy.

special enduement of the Spirit, such as we saw in Hippolytus, but he does suggest that the clergy have a greater responsibility to live virtuously and a greater liability to punishment for sin. Any greater ability to deal with sin they may have is also more likely to derive from perfection than from ordination. What information Origen provides corroborates that from Tertullian and Hippolytus concerning the clergy's leading part in the church's decision-making and services, and the link between leadership and priesthood. Origen evinces more awareness of the general abuses of clerical privilege than any before him, but he is even-handed in that he criticizes the laity equally. He is more aware of generally declining standards. He is also more emphatic than any before on the need for the laity to support the clergy financially.

In brief, Origen provides evidence that he lived at a time when the division between the clergy and the laity was more established and developed than when Tertullian and Clement were active. On the other hand, he also demonstrates that the laity could and, in his view, should be as interested in what really counts, viz., progression in holiness and understanding of God's word, as the clergy. The basic unity within the church has thus not been lost sight of. Though not as central as in Tertullian, priesthood is important to both the distinction between clergy and laity and to what is expected of them both in Origen.

6.7 Cyprian and the Western church in the mid-third century

6.7.1 Minucius Felix

Being concerned mainly with apologetics and polemics, Minucius Felix' *Octavius* contains little or nothing relevant to the relationship between the clergy and the laity. At the beginning of section 4.7 we noted 9:4, in which Christians are said to "'worship the genitals of their pontiff and priest, adoring, it appears, the sex of their 'father'.'"[308] This may involve a reference to the revering of the bishop and, possibly, presbyters.[309] This would fit what we shall note concerning the church in North Africa from Cyprian's writings.

---

[308] Clarke, *Octavius*, 64.
[309] So ibid., 219, n. 119.

6.7.2 Novatian and Cornelius

Eusebius' report of the dispute between Novatian and Cornelius over the treatment of the lapsed describes a synod at Rome which included sixty bishops and even more presbyters and deacons.[310] He does not mention the laity which suggests that the clergy had taken over this important decision. Eusebius then narrates how Cornelius reported the decisions to Bishop Fabius of Antioch, showing that the bishops disseminated them to other churches to encourage a united stand. Eusebius quotes Cornelius' letter, in which the importance of the confessors' initial support for Novatian and later repudiation of him is made clear. This repudiation was made in the presence of many people, bishops, presbyters and laymen. In *Epistle* 49 of the Cyprianic corpus Cornelius says the confessors first reported to the presbyters who examined and reproached them. When Cornelius was informed, he called a meeting of the presbyters and five visiting bishops who heard and accepted the confessors' repentance. Thereupon the faithful were consulted and welcomed the penitents. Cornelius[311] directed one to resume his position as presbyter and remitted the actions of the others. The laity were involved, 'but only by way of assent (not deliberation) and at the very conclusion of the process.'[312]

Cornelius also describes Novatian's machinations to attain consecration by three bishops, confirming the need of this; the later repentance and restoration of one bishop as a layman at the people's intercession, demonstrating the part the people could play in discipline and that being a layman was a demotion; and the replacement of these bishops by successors apparently ordained and sent by Cornelius, showing the increasing power of bishops in some central sees. He then accuses Novatian of being unaware that there can be only one bishop in each church and enumerates the presbyters, deacons, sub-deacons, acolytes, exorcists, lectors and doorkeepers, widows and poor supported by the church. The people are mentioned separately. Probably all except the widows and poor form the clergy, showing how the clergy in Rome has grown since Hippolytus.

Next Cornelius depicts exorcists as having helped a Novatian into whom Satan had entered, and his baptism in bed without sealing by the bishop, without which he could not receive the Spirit. Cornelius further mentions Novatian's ordination to the presbyteral order by the bishop on

---

[310] For the references to Eusebius here and immediately below, see *EH* 6:43:2-6: Williamson and Louth, 214-6.

[311] So Clarke, *Epistles*, vol. 2, 273, n. 18, interpreting Cornelius' use of the first person plural.

[312] Ibid., 270, n. 11. See also Vilela, 383-6.

the bishop's specific request against the opposition of the clergy and many of the laity.[313]

Whatever the accuracy of Cornelius' depiction of Novatian, the details of church life given here can be relied on, since Cornelius would have wanted to lend verisimilitude to any inventions. They indicate the subordinate role which the laity could still play at times in discipline and the choice of clergy. They also show that the numbers of clergy had grown along with their power, especially the bishops', over the most important functions and decisions in the church.

Novatian mentions the *charismata* in *De Trinitate* 29:10 in the present tense, but the list is largely derived from 1 Corinthians 12:8-11 and he may be enumerating them only because Paul did so. In *De Spectaculis* 4:2-3, however, he implies that a faithful Christian can exorcize demons.

In *Epistles* 30:5:3 and 31:6:2 of the Cyprianic corpus Novatian denominates as to be consulted regarding the case of the lapsed the bishops, presbyters, deacons, confessors and 'faithful laity',[314] presumably as together making up the church. In *Epistle* 30:8:1, he indicates that, during an interregnum, the Roman church took advice from neighbouring and visiting bishops over the lapsed. He uses 'we' of the church,[315] probably meaning the presbyters and deacons sending the letter, in view of the size of the church noted above. He also gives their decision on what should be done until God gives them a bishop. A similar situation is reflected in *Epistle* 8 of the Cyprianic corpus which is from the Roman church, especially its confessors and presbyters.[316] Its tone is 'notably imperative, authoritative, indeed episcopal', more so indeed than *Epistle* 30.[317] Its authors see themselves as 'church leaders and … to keep watch over the flock, acting in the place of our shepherds' during the interregnum.

The laity, then, are consulted but final decisions are in the clergy's hands. Further, the bishop's position as ultimate arbiter is brought out in *Epistle* 36:2:3 where the confessors are reported to have sent the lapsed to him and the lapsed are urged to submit to him.

6.7.3 The clergy-laity divide in Cyprian

In sections 4.7.2-3 and 5.7.3 we noted the division created by 'priest'

---

[313] *EH* 6:43:8-17: Williamson and Louth, 216-7.
[314] Clarke, *Epistles*, vol. 2, 37.
[315] ibid., 32-3.
[316] *Ep.* 8:1:1: Clarke, *Epistles*, vol. 1, 68.
[317] ibid., 203. On the relationship between *Epp.* 8 and 30, see ibid., 204.

being Cyprian's preferred designation for the bishop, with whose priesthood he at times associates the presbyters, and by his lack of explicit reference to the general priesthood and use of *sacerdos* for Christians in general. We also found, in sections 4.7.4-6, that 'priest' for him connotes sacral authority, discipline, and offering eucharistic sacrifice, all functions which Cyprian regards as central to church life and, as we shall note in section 6.7.4, restricts mainly to the bishop. Here we are examining the constituents of the clergy and laity for Cyprian and the nature of the division between them.

Faivre notes a difference between Tertullian's, Hippolytus' and Origen's understandings of the composition of the clergy, on the one hand, and Cyprian's, on the other: for the former it consists of the bishop, presbyters and deacons only, but for the latter, it consists of 'all that can be described as "function" in the Church: bishop, presbyters deacon, subdeacon, lector, acolyte, exorcist, ...' Further, the clergy receive a monthly payment,[318] so that, not only liturgical service, but reception of this payment forms the frontier between the clergy and the laity.[319] Faivre also notes that Cyprian uses *kléros* most often of the presbyters and deacons, sometimes of the bishop and presbyters, and sometimes to include all the lesser ministries.[320]

Cyprian uses *laici* ('laymen'), but prefers *fideles* ('the faithful') and *plebs* ('the people'), with *fraternitas* ('brotherhood') and *populus* ('people') as possible variants.[321] More important is the question of who made up the laity, which is related to the nature of the distinction between them and the clergy, since Cyprian does not address it directly. He tends to oppose those with priestly functions to the laity, in a way similar to Cornelius. So, in *Epistle* 1, he writes, 'everyone honoured with the sacred priesthood and appointed to clerical office ought to dedicate himself exclusively to altar and sacrifices and devote himself entirely to prayer and supplication',[322] justifying it mainly on the basis of the Levitical law, according to which they are to be supported by the brethren. Further, in *Epistle* 65:3:3, he contrasts those who serve the

---

[318] See *Ep.* 34:4.

[319] Faivre, A., 'Clerc/laïc: histoire d'une frontière', *Revue des sciences religieuses* 57.3 (1983), 201.

[320] Faivre, *Emergence*, 108-9, which see for evidence.

[321] See Clarke, *Epistles*, vol. 1, 149; and Faivre, *Emergence*, 111.

[322] Clarke, *Epistles*, vol. 1, 51. Clarke in ibid., 154-5, especially n. 11, argues that 'priests' in *Ep.* 1:1 refers to the bishop's high-priesthood with 'clerical office' referring to the rest of the clergy. This may be so, but we noted, in section 4.7.3, that Cyprian at least associated the presbyters with the bishop's priesthood, and the justification based on OT priestly law refers to all.

altar and have lapsed with the brethren and the 'fallen laity'.[323] Faivre points out that 'the connection between the clergy and the altar becomes the symbol of all kinds of "religious and spiritual occupations" performed by the clergy.'[324] He also concludes that 'the idea of the clergy as such, then, began to be determined almost exclusively by the concept of "sacerdotalization"' and that, 'Laymen could be defined either positively as those who fed and sustained the ministers of the altar, symbolized by the levitical hierarchy, or negatively as those who were not priests.'[325] This implies that Cyprian views all Christians in good standing as composing the laity.

The clergy's superiority to the laity is evinced, above all, in that laicization of the clergy is a definite demotion.[326] As a corollary, becoming a member of the clergy is depicted as a promotion and an honour.[327] Although Cyprian does not indicate explicitly what happens in ordination, he mentions it,[328] and implies the differences which ordination makes. He clearly believes in bishops' apostolic succession, and, since this is 'so that the Church is founded upon the bishops and every act of the Church is governed through those same appointed leaders', and, 'this establishment has been founded ... in this way by law of God',[329] the correct ordination of bishops is vital to the church's life. We shall examine the following ministries in more detail below, but von Campenhausen summarizes the differences resulting from ordination: 'henceforward [the priest] can pass on special spiritual gifts by the laying on of his hands in baptism or penance, and as bishop he can by himself ordain new clergy. He can consecrate the baptismal water, offer the eucharistic sacrifice, and make especially effectual intercession for others. No layman is competent to do anything of the sort.'[330]

Further, Cyrpian appoints confessors as lectors, with the intention of making them presbyters later,[331] in contrast to the situation we noted in

---

[323] Ibid., vol. 3, 115.

[324] Faivre, 'Clerc/laïc', *R Sci Rel* 57.3 (1983), 217.

[325] Faivre, *Emergence*, 114.

[326] For this, see *Epp.* 55:11:1-3, 67:6:2 and 72:2:1.

[327] See, e.g., *Ep.* 1:1: 'everyone honoured with the sacred priesthood' and 'those who are advanced in the Church of God by clerical appointment' (Clarke, *Epistles*, vol. 1, 51-2).

[328] He mentions the laying on of hands on bishops in *Ep.* 67:5, and uses 'ordination' of presbyters and deacons in *Ep.* 72:2, of deacons in *Ep.* 67:4, and of a lector in *Ep.* 38:2. See Clarke, *Epistles*, vol. 2, 184, n. 16.

[329] *Ep.* 33:1: Clarke, *Epistles*, vol. 2, 40. Ibid., 146, n. 4, gives a list of passages in Cyprian's correspondence reflecting his views on this.

[330] Von Campenhausen, *Ecclesiastical Authority*, 270-271.

[331] *Ep.* 39:5.

Hippolytus' *Apostolic Tradition* 9. Moreover, as noted in section 4.7.3, in *Epistle* 40 we probably find a confessor who had been a presbyter elsewhere being enlisted amongst the Carthaginian clergy,[332] demonstrating that official recognition was needed even for one who had been a presbyter elsewhere as well as being a confessor. Enduement by the Spirit resulting from suffering is no longer enough.[333]

Finally, the distance between the higher clergy and the laity is increased by the importance Cyprian ascribes to the lower clergy, and the elevation in status and honour evinced by the reference to 'higher grades to which one can rise in the Church' in *Epistle* 39:4:2, and the description of Bishop Cornelius in *Epistle* 55:8:2 as, 'having advanced through all the successive ecclesiastical offices …, he reached the lofty pinnacle of the priesthood by climbing up through every grade in the Church's ministry.'[334]

6.7.4 The clergy's powers and ministries in Cyprian

In sections 4.7.4-6 we explored the main connotations of priesthood, especially that of the bishop, for Cyprian. The first is sacral authority which is divine in origin and nature. This is apparent in *Epistle* 59:5 where Cyprian denies that a bishop can be made without God's choice, knowledge or permission, and calls the bishop 'priest and judge who acts in Christ's stead for the time being'.[335] This authority comes and is guaranteed by the apostolic succession noted in section 6.7.3. That this was generally held in the North African church is demonstrated by Clarus of Mascula's statement at the council in 256 that, 'The meaning of our Lord Jesus Christ is clear when he sends his apostles and gives up to them alone the power given to him by the Father. To them we succeed, with the same power governing the church of the Lord and baptizing the faith of those who believe.'[336] Further, Firmilian of Cappadocian Caesarea writes that Christ gave power to forgive sins to the bishops who succeeded the apostles.[337]

As a result, absolutely everything in the church on earth comes under the authority of the bishops, as we noted in *Epistle* 33:1 where Cyprian states that every action of the church is governed through the bishops,

---

[332] Clarke, *Epistles*, vol. 2, 58.
[333] See on this subject, von Campenhausen, *Ecclesiastical Authority*, 271 and Faivre, *Emergence*, 118-120.
[334] Clarke, *Epistles*, vol. 2, 56 and vol. 3, 37.
[335] Ibid., vol. 3, 72.
[336] Hartel, W. (ed.), *Cyprianus: Opera omnia* (Vienna, 1871), 459.
[337] *Ep.* 75:16.

and the church in each city is founded on the bishops. The bishop is therefore the incarnation of the church and its unity.[338] He has authority over the presbyters and deacons as well as everyone else,[339] and he has overall charge of the dispensing of the church's charity.[340]

Although the bishop's authority is in theory absolute, since none can judge him except God,[341] in practice there are checks on it. One derives from the presbyters' involvement in government, suggested by Cyprian's practice of calling them *conpresbyteri*, their being seated with the bishop during services while others remained standing, their formation of a *consessus* ('assembly') with the bishop, their possession of a *locus* ('place') and *honor* relating to his, and their ability to take the bishop's place when he is absent or the episcopate is vacant.[342] Doubtless the extent to which they were consulted and the power they exercised depended on the bishop under whom they served, but they normally had a say in decisions and a more important say than anyone else in the church. Next to them came the deacons, whose inclusion in the church's government is suggested mainly by Cyprian's addressing of his letters to the presbyters and deacons.[343] In addition, Cyprian normally consulted the laity on important decisions, as we shall see below. Even so, ultimate earthly authority in the church lay with the bishop, the higher clergy having more opportunity to influence him and exercise his delegated power[344] than anyone else.

The bishop's authority and power over the clergy included the ability to appoint, ordain, and discipline. Although he would normally consult the church, on occasion Cyprian would appoint someone to the clergy on his own, always taking care to explain what he had done.[345] Further, neighbouring bishops were necessary to a bishop's consecration.[346]

Administering baptism was normally the bishop's prerogative. We noted above Clarus of Mascula's statement that bishops have the power to govern and baptize. In *Epistle* 69:8 Cyprian condemns those who 'arrogate to themselves … a bishop's powers, claiming the lawful right to sacrifice and to baptize',[347] suggesting that these are the bishop's two main powers. In *Epistle* 70:1:3 he writes that, 'if it is possible for water

---

[338] *Epp.* 55:24 and 66:8.

[339] The presbyters: *Ep.* 16:1 and 17:2; and the deacons: *Ep.* 3:3.

[340] On this see d'Alès, 103-4, and the references cited there.

[341] See *Ep.* 59:5.

[342] On this see d'Alès, 313; Vilela, 279-281 and 285-7; and Clarke, *Epistles*, vol. 1, 150.

[343] So d'Alès, 315.

[344] See below in this section.

[345] See *Epp.* 38-40, and earlier comments on them.

[346] See *Epp.* 67:5, 55:8, and earlier comments on them.

[347] Clarke, *Epistles*, vol. 4, 38.

to clean away by its baptismal washing the sins of a man who is being baptized, then it is essential that that water should first be cleansed and sanctified by a priest',[348] which makes the priestly bishop absolutely necessary to grace-giving baptism. Similarly, he states in *Epistle* 73:7 that 'we perceive that only those leaders who are set in authority within the Church ... have the lawful power to baptize and to grant forgiveness of sins; ....' Only the leaders are permitted to baptize, then. This is confirmed in *Epistle* 73:9, where he adds that the baptized 'by our prayer and the imposition of our hands ... receive the Holy Spirit ....'[349] Firmilian shows that this was so in Asia Minor by stating, in *Epistle* 75:7, that, 'there the elders sit in authority – they are the ones who possess the powers of baptizing and laying-on of hands and of appointing to clerical office.'[350]

The only indications that the presbyters could baptize are the references to *praepositi* ('leaders who are set in authority') in *Epistle* 73:7 and 9, although they could refer only to bishops, and the allusion, just quoted from *Epistle* 75:7, to *maiores natu* ('elders'). Clarke argues that the use of *praesideo* ('to preside') and the reference to baptism, imposition of hands and ordination mean these must be bishops too.[351] There is, then, no proof that presbyters baptized, although they, and the deacons, must have helped, and one wonders what happened when the bishop was absent or there was an interregnum. This power involving forgiving sin and conveying the Spirit apparently belonged to the bishop alone.

In section 4.7.5 we found that Cyprian frequently used priestly language of the bishop in the context of the different stages of administering church discipline. Although in his earliest letters he wrote of the laying on of hands 'by the bishop and the clergy', later he spoke of it mainly as by the bishops. Even so, in section 4.7.3 we observed a passage in *Epistle* 18:1 in which Cyprian indicates that, when he was absent, those who wished to confess their sin could do so to a presbyter or a deacon and hands could be laid upon them in forgiveness. This suggests that normal practice was for the bishop and clergy to hear confession and restore to communion, although later Cyprian emphasized the place of the bishop alone. Firmilian viewed the remission of sin as the prerogative mainly of the bishop.[352] Like baptism, this involved an exercise of vital spiritual power.

---

[348] Ibid., 46.
[349] Ibid., 58-9.
[350] Ibid., 83.
[351] Ibid., 261, n. 32.
[352] *Ep.* 75:16.

The other exercise of spiritual power closely connected to the bishop as priest and examined in section 4.7.6 was the offering of sacrifice, especially eucharistic sacrifice. One passage studied was *Epistle* 76:3 where Cyprian writes that, in the mines, 'priests of God are allowed no opportunity for offering and celebrating the divine sacrifices',[353] implying that they alone could normally offer such sacrifices. This is confirmed by what we noted in *Epistle* 69:8 where Cyprian rebukes those who try to 'arrogate to themselves ... a bishop's powers, claiming the lawful right to sacrifice and to baptize'.[354] In section 4.7.3, however, we found that presbyters offered the eucharistic sacrifice and probably 'as a matter of course and not as a special privilege ... under emergency conditions.'[355] This privilege seems to have been limited to the bishop and presbyters. D'Alès points out some of the effects of receiving the eucharist, according to Cyprian: it purifies the conscience as part of the procedure of reconciliation, harms the unreconciled lapsed, incorporates into Christ's body and salvation, protects and fortifies for martyrdom.[356] It is spiritually powerful and only the clergy can provide it.

According to Cyprian, the above are the major tasks and ministries of the clergy and the bishop in particular, all closely associated with priestliness and the communication of God's grace and power. In contrast to Origen, teaching is not one of these, but it is one of the clergy's tasks. In *Epistle* 55:14, Cyprian depicts one of the lapsed as saying, '"I had previously read and I had learnt from my bishop's preaching ..."',[357] and in *Epistle* 58:4 he juxtaposes the people gathering and the bishop teaching in such a way as to imply that it was normally the bishop who taught the assembled congregation. Apart from these, there are a passing mention of the bishop teaching in *Epistle* 74:10, two references to the bishop's *cathedra* ('chair'), which probably symbolizes his teaching right and activity,[358] and an allusion to the bishop's warnings and teaching in *De lapsis* 23. None of these is closely linked to the bishop's priestliness.

Although the bishops were the main ones to teach at this time, Cyprian clearly expects his presbyters and deacons to inform, instruct and teach the confessors, according to *Epistle* 14:2, and to instruct all,

---

[353] Clarke, *Epistles*, vol. 4, 97.

[354] Ibid., 38.

[355] Ibid., vol. 1, 187.

[356] D'Alès, 258 and 264-6, referring to *Lap.* 16, 25-26, *Dom.* 18, and *Epp.* 57:2 and 58:1.

[357] Clarke, *Epistles*, vol. 3, 41; cf. 187, n. 62: 'a relatively rare direct allusion in Cyprian to the role of bishop as teacher ....'

[358] So Bardy, 'Le sacerdoce', *La Vie spirituelle* 58 (1939), 98, and d'Alès, 311, citing *Epp.* 3:1 and 17:2.

according to *Epistle* 16:2. He also mentions 'teacher-presbyters' and 'teachers of catechumens' in *Epistle* 29:1.[359] The context suggests they were involved in the teaching of catechumens and potential clerics.[360] In *Epistle* 73:3 Cyprian mentions teachers without identifying them as of the clergy. Clarke translates this 'catechists',[361] which is true to the context, and argues that they may have been the same as the 'teachers of catechumens' of *Epistle* 29:1, whose leaders were the 'teacher-presbyters' and who may have included laymen. The parallels he cites in Tertullian, Hippolytus and the *Passio Perpetuae* make this likely.[362] Neymeyr's conclusion is balanced and fair: 'Cyprian's writings, then, testify that the task of the teacher was taken over by the presbyters, but do not exclude the possibility that there were also teachers who did not belong to the clergy.'[363]

We noted earlier that von Campenhausen wrote of Cyprian's view of the bishop that the latter can 'make especially effectual intercession for others.'[364] Although Cyprian often mentions the priest-bishop's prayers together with the altar and sacrifice,[365] these probably involve 'the specialized use of *prex*, used technically for the solemn eucharistic canon, in which ... petition would be included.'[366] The special efficacy of Cyprian's prayers as a 'bishop who is covered in ... glory' is mentioned by the Roman confessors in *Epistle* 31:5.[367] Even if allowance be made for flattery, they probably did view his prayers as especially effective.

The clergy, and especially the bishop, thus monopolize the power and ministries of the church. There remains to see what was left for the laity.

6.7.5 The laity's powers and ministries in Cyprian

In section 5.7.3 we noted that Cyprian was aware of the practice of calling ordinary Christians 'priests', although he never used the word *sacerdotes* of them, and in section 4.7.6 we found that he called

---

[359] Clarke, *Epistles*, vol. 2, 25.

[360] So ibid., 111-3 and Neymeyr, 121-3.

[361] So Clarke, *Epistles*, vol. 4, 56.

[362] Ibid., vol. 2, 112-3. Vilela, 312, disagrees, pointing out that Cyprian himself was catechised by a presbyter according to *Vita* 4. Neymeyr, 123-4, leaves the question open.

[363] Neymeyr, 124.

[364] Von Campenhausen, *Ecclesiastical Authority*, 270-271. His justification of this on the basis of *Ep.* 18:2 and *Lap.* 36 seems unlikely since the former does not allude to intercession and it is uncertain that the latter does.

[365] See *Epp.* 1:2, 61:4, 62:4, 65:2 and 4, and 67:2.

[366] Clarke, *Epistles*, vol. 1, 160.

[367] Ibid., vol. 2, 36.

'sacrifice' prayer, praise, and a number of other things which all
Christians could and should do, including bringing materials for the
eucharist and maintaining the clergy and the poor. We also discovered
in section 5.7.4 that Cyprian used temple-imagery for the individual
Christian but not the church as a whole, although he did imply that the
church was indwelt by the Spirit. Cyprian thus continues earlier
emphases regarding Christians in general, many of which go back to NT
times, in spite of the signs of clericalization we have studied.

The same is true of his understanding of the church as one body in
which all the members are important and have a function. He retains
some of the Pauline understanding of an organic union in *Epistle* 62:1:2
in which he quotes 1 Corinthians 12:26 and adds, 'We must now ...
reckon the captivity of our brethren as our own captivity also, and we
must account the distress of those in peril as our own distress; for ... we
form but one body ....'[368] At times, however, he applies this metaphor to
the church as an institution rather than an organism, partly owing to
circumstances, but partly because he and others tended to think of the
church increasingly in this way. This is clear when, in several places, he
complains that schismatics 'are trying to drag asunder the members of
Christ into schismatic factions and to split apart and tear to pieces the
body, the Catholic Church.'[369] The Roman clergy confirm that this trend
is prevalent in the Western church by writing in *Epistle* 36:4:1, 'For it
does indeed befit us all to keep watchful vigil over the whole body of
the Church, the members of which are spread through all the various
provinces.'[370]

Turning to the ministries open to the laity, as well as those connected
with the offering of spiritual sacrifices and the possibility of lay teachers
of catechumens explored in the last section, it seems that laymen could
still function as lectors at times. Although normally denominating
lectors as clergy, in *Epistle* 29 Cyprian informs his presbyters and
deacons that he has made Saturus a lector and Optatus a subdeacon,
adding, 'Some time ago we all agreed together to place both of them in
a rank next to the clergy. In the case of Saturus, we gave him the
reading several times on Easter day; ....'[371] There was still fluidity in this
area.

Frend has argued that there were lay elders, *seniores laici*, in the
North African church in Cyprian's day.[372] However, all the explicit

---

[368] Ibid., vol. 3, 95.
[369] *Ep.* 44:3: Clarke, *Epistles*, vol. 2, 68. See also *Epp.* 45:1, 46:1, *Un.* 4, 5 and 12.
[370] Ibid., 48.
[371] Ibid., 25. See Faivre, *Emergence*, 114-6.
[372] Frend, 'The *seniores laici*', *J Th St* 12 (1961), 280-284. See also Quispel, 'African

evidence he gives derives from the fourth and fifth centuries, and the lack of explicit evidence from the third century makes any definite conclusion as to their existence precarious.

There is clear evidence of the *charismata* being exercised in the North African church in Cyprian's day. Cyprian himself received a number of revelations, was criticized for it,[373] and mentioned another bishop receiving one.[374] This has led several scholars to argue that he viewed bishops as inspired because they were bishops and priests and stood between God and the people.[375] This is supported by his statement in *Epistle* 48:4 that God protects bishops, 'inspiring them in their government'.[376] In spite of this, Cyprian knew of others than clergy who received revelations. It is uncertain to whom some revelations to which he refers were given, but the clearest illustration comes in *Epistle* 16:4 where he alludes to some boys who received them.[377] He also refers to exorcists who are part of the clergy,[378] but mentions of exorcism in *De dominica oratione* 5 and *Ad Demetrianum* 15 at least leave open the possibility that exorcism was performed by others.

However, the laity retained the right to participate in the election of bishops.[379] Their participation is important to Cyprian, as demonstrated by his lengthy justification of it in *Epistle* 67:4, and his statement that, 'an appointment may become right and lawful if it has been examined, judged, and voted upon by all.'[380] The people's role in his own election was clearly decisive,[381] and was so important to Cyprian that he refers to it in *Epistles* 43 and 59. He also noted it as part of what made Cornelius' election regular,[382] and upheld the laity's right to separate from a sinful bishop, though without making the mechanics of doing so explicit.[383]

This lay participation was probably 'acclamatory or confirmatory',

---

Christianity' in den Boeff and Kessels, *Actus*, 276-7.
[373] For visions, see *Epp.* 11:5, 16:4, 58:1, 63:1, 66:9, 78:2 and *Vita* 12. For criticism, see *Ep.* 66:10.
[374] *Mort.* 19.
[375] So Walker, G.S.M., 10 and 17; Clarke, *Epistles*, vol. 1, 288, n. 27; and Robeck, 300. Hinchliff, 105, questions this.
[376] Clarke, *Epistles*, vol. 2, 76.
[377] Ibid., vol. 1, 289-290, nn. 28-29, points out that 'boys below the age of puberty ... were highly valued for scrying by proxy' in contemporary non-Christian religion too.
[378] See especially *Ep.* 23; also *Epp.* 69:15 and 75:10 (Firmilian).
[379] For the fullest treatment of this in Cyprian, see Gryson, 'Les élections', *R Hist Eccl* 68 (1973), 360-388.
[380] Clarke, *Epistles*, vol. 4, 23.
[381] See *Vita* 5.
[382] *Ep.* 55:8.
[383] *Ep.* 67:3. On this see Clarke, *Epistles*, vol. 3, 147.

rather than involving voting,[384] although it was not a pure formality and could be the determining factor.[385] Cyprian certainly views it as universal,[386] although he may only have known the Western church.[387]

The laity's role in the choice of the clergy apart from the bishop is even more obscure,[388] but apparently equally important. In *Epistle* 38:1, Cyprian writes, 'it is our custom when we make appointments to clerical office to consult you beforehand, and in council together with you to weigh the character and qualities of each candidate',[389] and several of his letters deal with exceptions to this rule necessitated by his exile, but even then he explains and informs the laity about appointments.[390] Even so, the fact that he can make them without recourse to the people shows the bishop's determining role.

At least at first Cyprian also wanted to consult the laity on all matters of importance, as he writes in *Epistle* 14:4.[391] In the context he is concerned with treatment of the lapsed, concerning which, as we noted in section 4.7.5, several scholars discern a development towards not consulting the people. While the introduction to the *Sententiae* indicates that the *plebs* ('common people') were present at the vital council in Carthage in 256, it is only the bishops' opinions which are recorded from it. Although the consultations between local churches, which were increasing at this time, did not take anything away from the laity's rights in theory, in practice the laity could not participate in them directly and could only learn of their decisions afterwards, so that their participation was only symbolic.[392]

Cyprian certainly continued to consult the laity at a local level on the restoration of individuals who had lapsed.[393] In *Epistle* 17:3:1 he encourages the laity, 'you ... must guide the fallen individually and your restraining counsel must temper their attitudes to conform with God's

---

[384] Ibid., vol. 2, 178. So too Bardy, 'Le sacerdoce', *La Vie spirituelle* 58 (1939), 94; Gryson, 'Les élections', *R Hist Eccl* 68 (1973), 379-380; and Faivre, *Emergence*, 125, although the last views it as also possible that 'the people had to choose between different candidates who had already been selected and recognized as able and suitable ....'
[385] So ibid. and Gryson, 'Les élections', *R Hist Eccl* 68 (1973), 380-381.
[386] *Ep.* 67:5.
[387] So Gryson, 'Les élections', *R Hist Eccl* 68 (1973), 378-9.
[388] See discussions in Bardy, 'Le sacerdoce', *La Vie spirituelle* 58 (1939), 94-6 and Gryson, 'Les élections', *R Hist Eccl* 68 (1973), 386-8.
[389] Clarke, *Epistles*, vol. 2, 52.
[390] *Epp.* 38, 39, 40.
[391] On this subject, see Bardy, 'Le sacerdoce', *La Vie spirituelle* 58 (1939), 92-3; Eastwood, 87; Vilela, 288-303; Sage, 20; and Faivre, *Emergence*, 111 and 120-124.
[392] So Faivre, *Emergence*, 128.
[393] He also consults them over whether Cornelius or Novatian was the rightful bishop of Rome: see *Epp.* 44:2 and 45:2.

precepts',[394] and, in *Epistles* 16:4, 34:4, and 59:15:3, indicates that the lapsed should make their penitence known to, and their cases should be considered by, the bishop, the confessors and all the people. In the last passage, Cyprian presents himself as unable to persuade the laity to allow some to return to the church, saying that 'they put up noisy protest and resistance'.[395] We have already noted, in section 6.7.2, the laity's opposite reaction in Rome to several confessors' penitence. In this case, then, the people's wishes could prevail, although in other matters Clarke is probably right to state that 'the consultative roles of clergy and laity are distinctly different - the clergy may proffer counsel, the people may voice agreement, but the bishop decides.'[396]

6.7.6 Summary and conclusion

Cyprian's main ecclesiological emphases are quite clear: first and foremost the centrality of the episcopacy for the church's life. All depends on him and he is to be in control of everything under God and as God's representative. His most important designation, along with 'bishop', is 'priest', and it is as both that he rules, disciplines and offers the eucharistic sacrifice. These all involve great spiritual power and effects, as does baptism, which again is mainly, and possibly solely, the bishop's prerogative. He also teaches and his prayers are especially effective. Although the term is not used, he is the great mediator between God and man.

Second, there is the continuing clericalization of church life. This is evident in the way the higher clergy share in the bishop's rule, disciplinary powers, ability to offer the eucharistic sacrifice, and teaching. It is also apparent in the way that the lesser clergy have become clergy and taken their prerogatives with them into the clerical sphere. As Faivre argues, before Cyprian and Origen,

> there were still a number of functions which were exercised by the non-clerical Christians whom we now call "lay people". This was especially true of the cultural functions of the doctors or teachers, the catechists and the lectors. It is an historical fact that these non-clerical functions barely survived the generation that witnessed the institutionalization of the cleric/layman distinction. ... The historians (sic) is left with the inescapable impression that the existence of the clergy was, by definition, bound up with the religious

---

[394] Clarke, *Epistles*, vol. 1, 97.

[395] Ibid., vol. 3, 83.

[396] Ibid., vol. 1, 268. Note Faivre, *Emergence*, 124: 'In law, the bishop was always free not to heed their opinion or follow their advice, but, in general, the voice of the people counted for a great deal and the bishop would be reluctant to go against it.'

disqualification of the layman and involved the latter process.[397]

Third, as corollary to the last point, there is the increasing marginalization of the laity. Although retaining some of their earlier privileges in the areas of clerical elections, consultation on important issues, and church discipline, their power is decreasing even in these, and they no longer have any clear, regular opportunities for public ministry. Integral to this, at least as far as Cyprian is concerned, is the distinction between the ordained priesthood and the non-ordained laity.

Further, several developments related to these major points have been noted in the writings of Cornelius and Novatian, suggesting that they were prevalent in the Western church.

6.8 Other third-century material

6.8.1 The Didascalia Apostolorum

Section 4.8.2 noted the dominant ecclesiological characteristic of the *Didascalia*, viz., the centrality and divine authority of the bishop. Noted also was the likelihood that this was overdrawn because of threats to that authority. In spite of this, the fact that such a picture was presented suggests that it bore considerable resemblance to contemporary reality, since otherwise it would not have been taken seriously, and the fact that it was preserved suggests that it was a direction in which the church was moving.

So, although the bishop was not honoured as God,[398] he was usually highly honoured, though there were times when he was not and the author, and others like him, wanted to be. The same is probably true of the instructions 'you shall do nothing without the bishop' and 'it is not fitting that any man should do aught apart from the high priest.'[399] The threats against those who 'covet the primacy and dare to make a schism',[400] supported so similarly to Cyprian's defences of episcopal authority, imply that such people existed and were a problem to the author. Indeed, he is so concerned that his lack of reference to bishops' apostolic succession suggests that he was unaware of it.[401]

Similar conclusions can be arrived at concerning the author's exalted

---

[397] Faivre, 'The Laity', *Lumen Vitae* 42 (1987), 138.
[398] See the comments on 9 (25) in section 4.8.2 above.
[399] 9 (25): Connolly, 89. See comments in 4.8.2.
[400] 23: ibid., 194. See comments in 4.8.2.
[401] So von Campenhausen, *Ecclesiastical Authority*, 241.

view of the bishop's ministries and power. He was the normal, but perhaps not the sole, minister of the word and mediator. Certainly, as we have noted regarding the Western church, he is the main baptizer, although whether all would have considered him 'your father after God, who begot you through the water', may be doubted. Likewise he is the human ruler of the church, though not all would have agreed that he was 'your almighty king'.[402] Further, he was the main agent in church discipline, although some may have demurred from the statement that he is 'set in the likeness of God Almighty' and has 'authority to judge them that sin in the room of God Almighty.'[403] Indeed, his mediation of God's grace could hardly be more emphasized than when the Christian is told,

> but do you honour the bishops, who have loosed you from sins, who by the water regenerated you, who filled you with the Holy Spirit, who reared you with the word as with milk, who bred you up with doctrine, who confirmed you with admonition, and made you to partake of the holy Eucharist of God, and made you partakers and joint heirs of the promise of God. .... They have received from God the authority of life and death ...; the bishop reigns over soul and body, to bind and to loose on earth with heavenly power. For great power, heavenly, almighty, is given to him.[404]

Ruling, teaching and disciplining are the bishop's most important functions, then, with baptizing and offering the eucharistic sacrifice as significant too. Since, as we noted in section 4.8.2, the bishop's priestliness is mentioned in connection with authority, the reception, distribution and partaking of the people's material gifts, ministering God's word, caring for and disciplining the wayward, and holiness, we can gauge how central the bishop's priestliness was for this author.

The *Didascalia* also provides significant information about the 'clergy'. It does not use *kléros*,[405] but says the bishop takes for himself 'those whom he accounts and knows to be worthy of him and of his office, and appoints him presbyters as counsellors and assessors, and deacons and subdeacons, as many as he has need of in proportion to the ministry of the house.'[406] The bishop may not have had such absolute power as implied here, but he held the initiative in such appointments. As well as presbyters, deacons and subdeacons, lectors, deaconesses and widows are mentioned, although they are not as important where

[402] For these expressions, see again 9 (25) in Connolly, 87-9.
[403] 5: ibid., 40.
[404] 9: ibid., 94 and 96, cf. 97.
[405] Faivre, *Naissance*, 128.
[406] 9 (27): Connolly, 96.

functions are concerned.

The deacons' ministry is more frequently mentioned than the presbyters' and the former are at times ascribed more honour than the latter.[407] We can only speculate why this is so.[408] Though presented as totally subordinate to the bishop, the presbyters are called 'counsellors and assessors' to the bishop, they and the bishop are told to 'judge warily' and, with the deacons, they are to 'be ever present in all judgements with the bishops', the context being disputes between the faithful rather than their discipline.[409] They sit in a place of honour with the bishop amongst them, together being called 'the rulers', while the bishop is 'head among the presbytery in the Church in every congregation', and some widows are rebuked for claiming to know better 'even than the presbyters and the bishops.' Like the deacons, the presbyters could baptize when commanded by the bishop.[410]

The deacons could, then, baptize, join in judgment on cases between Christians and in excommunication,[411] and help the bishop in receiving and distributing alms and in visiting and helping the poor and needy.[412] Repeatedly, they are presented as intermediaries between the bishop and the laity,[413] and to be honoured only after the bishop.[414] They have disciplinary functions during the eucharist.[415] The honouring of the bishop, presbyters and deacons, and the lector, if there is one, with gifts suggests that they were at least partly supported by the congregation, the lack of gifts to the presbyter possibly implying that they had other work.[416]

As with Cyprian, then, the main power and public ministries in the church have been taken over by the bishop, presbyters and deacons. So the widows' duties consist mainly of intercessory prayer and visitation of the sick,[417] and the deaconesses are to minister only to women in visitation, anointing during baptism, and instruction after baptism.[418] Women are forbidden to baptize and the deaconess may anoint but not

---

[407] See, e.g., 9: Connolly, 89.
[408] See Vilela, 204 and 213-4; and Bârlea, 156, for possible explanations.
[409] 9 (27) and 11: Connolly, 97 and 111.
[410] 12, 4, 15 and 16: ibid., 119, 28, 140 and 146.
[411] See 5, 6 and 10: ibid., 40, 53, 102 and 105.
[412] See 9, 15, 16 and 18: ibid., 88, 143, 150, 156 and 160.
[413] See 9, 11, 15 and 16: ibid., 88, 90, 92, 108, 140, 148 and 150.
[414] See 9: ibid., 88, 92, and 90.
[415] See 11 and 12: ibid., 117 and 120.
[416] See 9: ibid., 90. On the last point, see Faivre, *Naissance*, 123.
[417] So 15 (31-34) and 18: Connolly, 132-140 and 158.
[418] 16: ibid., 146-7.

pronounce the invocation,[419] presumably the most significant aspect for the author. She is, however, to be honoured 'in the place of the Holy Spirit', after only the bishop and deacons and before the presbyters.[420] This suggests she may have been ordained like the presbyters and deacons.[421] The prohibition on women baptizing may well imply that they had sought this privilege.[422] Moreover, the author's lengthy justification of the deaconesses' existence[423] arouses the suspicion that this was a recent innovation.[424] Although these may be signs of an 'organisation that was being born',[425] and this could explain the perplexing relationship of the presbyters and deacons noted earlier, differentiation of function is under way, and public ministry belongs to the recognized officials.

The laity's subordinate role in the church can be inferred from what we have seen of the officials' prominence, although the laity were probably not as quiescent as the author wished. In section 5.8.1 we noted that the mention of the general priesthood and the associated sacrifices of prayer, praise and material gifts have been devalued by their juxtaposition with the high priesthood of the bishop and the priesthood of the presbyters, deacons, orphans and widows, which leave the ordinary Christian in the position of an ordinary Israelite. This is part of what von Campenhausen calls 'a strong anti-laical emphasis'. This is especially clear in the restatement of Ignatius' requirement to do nothing without the bishop, since 'it is explicitly stated that without the bishop [the laity's] actions at the altar are "null and void".'[426] This comes precisely in the passage on the general priesthood, and is justified by the fact that 'it is not fitting that any man should do aught apart from the high priest.' The general priesthood's devaluation is thus closely connected with the church's clericalization.

Further, the laity are repeatedly told to fear, honour and obey the bishop, and not to speak against or judge him.[427] They are not to trouble him, approaching him only through the deacon, and they are not to

---

[419] 15 and 16: ibid., 142 and 146.

[420] 9 (25): ibid., 88.

[421] So Bârlea, 287, who with Colson, *La fonction diaconale*, 135 and Faivre, *Naissance*, 135 and 137, points out that they are to be ordained according to the later *Apostolic Constitutions*.

[422] So Faivre, *Emergence*, 98.

[423] 16 (35): Connolly, 146-149.

[424] Faivre, *Naissance*, 137, argues that the author wanted the widows' institution and role to decline and the deaconesses to meet the needs of growing communities. See also Faivre, *Emergence*, 100.

[425] Faivre, *Naissance*, 138.

[426] Von Campenhausen, *Ecclesiastical Authority*, 242, referring to 9 (26): Connolly, 88-9.

[427] 7 (17), 9 (25), 9 (27) and 9: ibid., 60-61, 86-7, 92-3, 96-7 and 100-101.

require any account of his use of gifts the layman has brought.[428] They are forbidden to teach because they will 'speak without the knowledge of doctrine ... [and] bring blasphemy upon the word.'[429] Although they may pray over the penitent while the bishop restores him, neither the congregation nor the martyrs now have a right to intercede for his restoration.[430] The congregation is consulted over the choice of the bishop, but there is no indication that this is so concerning presbyters, deacons and deaconesses.[431]

As with other writings of this period, Faivre argues that the laity consisted of only the males.[432] He has more reason in the *Didascalia* than in some others since, in prescribing the order during meetings of the church, it specifies that, after the bishops and presbyters should sit 'the lay men and then the women'.[433] Faivre also points out that it never refers to lay women and argues that this is because they are to submit to their husbands and so cannot give the tithe, which is the laity's defining function.

The main problem with this theory is the position of the deaconesses. Although it is not certain that they were ordained, they did perform a public ministry during the baptism of women which the laity apparently did not. Moreover, although the layman is most frequently set over against the bishop, or the bishop and deacon, sometimes with the presbyter,[434] in one passage he is set over against the bishop, presbyters, deacons, widows and orphans, and even deaconesses, whom he is told to honour 'in the place of the Holy Spirit'.[435] These facts make it likely that the deaconesses were viewed as more important than the laity, and this lessens the likelihood that women were viewed as inadequate to belong to the laity.

Another problem with Faivre's theory is the view that the women are unable to give the tithe. In the passage in chapter 9 (25) which we have cited so often, the laity are called 'the Catholic Church' before this function is alluded to, the impression being given that all in the church are included. Further, the lay person is called one 'in whom Christ dwells' and 'in whom dwells the Holy Spirit of God', and a woman is

---

[428] 9: ibid., 90 and 98-100.
[429] 15: ibid., 132.
[430] See von Campenhausen, *Ecclesiastical Authority*, 243 and n.42, and *Didasc.* 7 and 10: Connolly, 56 and 104.
[431] See 4 (9): ibid., 30-31 and Gryson, 'Les élections', *R Hist Eccl* 68 (1973), 389.
[432] Faivre, *Emergence*, 92 and 101.
[433] 12: Connolly, 119.
[434] 6 (13), 7 (17), 9, and 15: ibid., 44-5, 60-61, 92-3, and 145.
[435] 9 (25): ibid., 85-9.

told that 'the Holy Spirit is always in thee'.[436] Again, Faivre's case is not proven and the laity probably included all Christians in good standing.

In conclusion we note that, although the laity are still able to perform vital functions in the church, these very functions emphasize their subordination to the bishop, above all, but also to the presbyters, deacons and even deaconesses. They have no public ministry at all and are being persuaded to give total power to the bishop. If the term 'clergy' is not used, there are definite leaders who exercise the power and public ministry in the church. And again, a significant element in this development is the devaluation of the general priesthood and its complete overshadowing by that of the bishop.

6.8.2 Other relevant material

There is little other relevant material definitely from the third century. In the *Epistula Clementis*,[437] recommendations concerning clerics 'are mixed in with exhortations to the simple faithful whose role could be summed up thus: to obey the bishop and respect him, not to bother him, to refer matters to the presbyters' arbitration, to practise chastity and charity, not to hesitate to ask when they have doubts concerning the faith.'[438] They are also to support the clergy and poor materially.[439] Similarities to the picture of the laity in the *Didascalia* are clear, especially their subordinate position.

Faivre argues that the function and position of the lector had a similar evolution to that of the catechist noted in section 6.2.3. Drawing on the *Canones ecclesiastici* or *apostolici*, he points to the way in which they mention the ordination of a lector who is, among other things, able to make discourses, between those of the presbyter and the deacon. Since it also mentions the possibility of the bishop being illiterate, Faivre concludes that the lector 'would also have interpreted the texts and preached the homily during the liturgy of the word, which may at that time still have been celebrated separately from the eucharistic synaxis.' However, in the Pseudo-Clementine literature, the bishop takes the books from the one who looked after them, presumably the lector, although he is not so called, for fear that they may be falsified or misinterpreted: 'The function of interpreting, then, was taken over by

---

[436] 9 and 26 (57): ibid., 93 and 244-5.
[437] Strecker, 90-92, assigns this to the third century.
[438] Faivre, *Naissance*, 155.
[439] Vilela, 186-7.

the bishop.'[440] This may well be correct.

More certain, and significant for us, is the fact that the laity are again told to submit 'to those who preside at the altar.'[441] Earlier in the document, as Faivre points out, the bishop and presbyter are associated with the altar and with keeping order among the people.[442] As in Cyprian, part of the definition of the laity here involves their subordination to those at the altar. We are now ready to summarize this chapter.

6.9 Summary and conclusion

We set out in this chapter to examine developments in the areas of power and ministry in the church, seeking to show that, as the ordained increasingly captured both, and as both were related to their priesthood, so other Christians increasingly lost both and their priesthood was devalued. We shall now summarize the major developments which demonstrate that this was so. Detailed documentation for these points will be found in the appropriate sections in this chapter.

For most of the second century the basic unity and equality of the church and its members come through in the literature more than any inequality and division. Although there were leaders, these were clearly at times, though not always, chosen and removed by the congregation. So, in the *Didache*, it is the congregation who are urged to test itinerant apostles, teachers and prophets, and to appoint bishops and deacons to replace prophets and teachers; in *The Shepherd*, the people are to evaluate prophecy as to whether it is true or false; even *1 Clement*, written to encourage the restoration by the congregation of presbyters wrongly removed, and expressing the view that these presbyters were appointed by the apostles or other eminent men, urges the rebels to obey the people's commands to leave; and Ignatius' insistence on all obeying the bishop suggests that some at times did not. Significant power rested with the congregation, not the leadership.

Further, Justin, a valuable witness because not addressing domestic church concerns, emphasizes the place of all in the church's worship, their unity, communion and equality, and their possession of gifts of the Spirit. Irenaeus sees all Christians as spiritual and as having spiritual gifts. Examples of these gifts are found in the itinerant apostles, prophets and teachers of the *Didache*, and the prophet outside the

---

[440] Faivre, *Emergence*, 68; cf. *Naissance*, 145-150.
[441] Tidner, 110.
[442] Faivre, *Naissance*, 147.

church's leadership in *The Shepherd*. Justin himself seems to have been a teacher outside church leadership, as do Tatian and, possibly, Pantaenus. Ministry was far from restricted to the leaders. Significantly, in view of later developments, all the faithful, or the individual believer, in *1 Clement* are encouraged to intercede for sinners and admonish one another, in *2 Clement* to bring back the weak and convert and exhort one another, in *Barnabas* to reprove transgression, and in the *Didache* to give righteous judgment in reproving transgression and to reprove one another.

As far as leadership is concerned, there is evidence of a variety of organisations and a marked lack of uniformity. The *Didache* shows that settled bishops and deacons, appointed by the church mainly because of their qualities of character, were replacing prophets and teachers marked out and recognized by their gifts. In *The Shepherd*, apostles, bishops, teachers, and deacons are mentioned, although the author is a prophet, apparently outside the leadership, who brings messages which the congregation are to evaluate under the leaders' oversight. Ignatius knows of bishops, presbyters, and deacons, the only pattern he recognizes, and one known to Irenaeus too, whereas Clement knows only of presbyters who have the oversight, and Justin mentions a *proestôs*, who may have been a bishop or presbyter, and deacons.

But, alongside this variety and the underlying unity of the church, there are repeated attempts to subordinate the rest to the leaders, most clearly in the writings of Ignatius and Clement. These provide definite evidence of power struggles in the church, Clement directly and Ignatius by inference. Further, the threats from false teaching outside the church and within cause both Ignatius and Irenaeus to stress the authoritative teaching which originates from the leaders alone. Moreover, Clement stresses God's provision of an order which is central and fundamental to the church and into which everyone must fit in their allotted places but with the leaders clearly superior to the led.

These emphases continue into the period from c.190 to 300, but with a marked increase in stress on the power and authority of the leaders as over against the led which coincides with the division of the church into clergy and laity and the use of priestly terminology for the clergy in a way different from the laity. So we find the congregation retains its right to be consulted in the choice of its leaders. On some occasions its will is clearly decisive but one bishop appoints a presbyter against the advice of other clergy and the laity, and another appoints lesser clergy himself and informs the congregation afterwards, albeit exceptionally. So too the congregation retains its right to be consulted on matters which affect it, but the clergy's advice is weightier, and the advent of councils of bishops is eroding this right's effectiveness. The *charismata* continue to be experienced and used by those who are not of the clergy, but there are indications that they are being increasingly seen as the province of the clergy, and of the bishop in particular.

Alongside these continuing intimations of the laity's activity and rights, there are many more of the increasing domination of church life by the clergy in both ministry and authority. The claims of the bishop to rule by God's authority and inspiration are particularly strong in Cyprian and the *Didascalia*, and their advocacy of them, together with the circumstances in which we know Cyprian to have made them, demonstrate that this authority was being disputed at times and by some. Nonetheless, authority was being increasingly vested in the bishop and the clergy. We have noted this in the choice of the clergy and the discussion of important matters. It was so too in the areas of ordination, baptism, offering the eucharist, teaching, and administering church discipline, particularly the exclusion of the impenitent and the reconciliation of the penitent. All these involve the exercise of spiritual, not just political, authority, and the *Didascalia* especially brings out the significance of the bishop as mediator of God's grace. And, whereas in Justin and the earlier second-century writers the leader appears to do these things on behalf of the congregation, in the *Didascalia* he does them as a go-between, representing God to man rather than man to God. Both authority and ministry are largely, if not solely, in the clergy's hands, although this was more in theory than in practice at times.

Alongside, and to some extent involved with, this division of the church into clergy and laity, we found the increasing use of priestly terminology and ideas for the former and, in Hippolytus, diminution, in Cyprian, avoidance, and in the *Didascalia*, dilution, of the general priesthood. Indeed, the priesthood of the ordained, and of the bishop in particular, seems to have been vitally linked to their God-given authority. This is apparent in North Africa with both Tertullian and Cyprian, in Rome with Hippolytus, and in Syria with the *Didascalia*. In Tertullian's *On Monogamy* 12:2 there is a likely intimation that priestly terminology and ideas were a bone of contention between the clergy and the laity. The laity were claiming an equal priesthood to the clergy's on occasion, but disavowing it on others. In view of Tertullian's 'definition' of priesthood in *Chastity* 7:3 in terms of offering the (eucharistic) sacrifice and baptizing, and his defence of the laity's right to perform these as priests in case of necessity, we can conclude that this equal priesthood encompassed at least this right which involved highly significant exercises of spiritual power and authority. In Cyprian, we noted repeated uses of OT stories concerning God's vindication of priests to warn of rebellion against bishops and their authority, and we found the same in the *Didascalia*. In Hippolytus, priestliness is involved in the ordination of the bishop and the conferring of him with various spiritual powers. The priestliness of bishops was clearly important for their spiritual authority, and that precisely in the writings of authors who avoid or devalue the general priesthood.

The picture is different for Alexandria, though with significant similarities. Here too the general priesthood is devalued, but this time in favour of that of the perfect Christian. Even so, this priesthood is integrally linked with spiritual ministry and power, as in North Africa, although this pertains more to study and teaching of God's word than to baptism, offering the eucharistic sacrifice, and rule. Further, Origen views the priestly, perfect Christian as the ideal church leader, so that he too connects priestliness with the exercise of what we might call both 'political' and spiritual power. On the other hand, he sees this spiritual power as available to all, not just the ordained, whereas Cyprian and the *Didascalia* do not.

This picture is considerably complicated by issues of different genres of literature and personal preferences of authors, but the general picture has become clear: in the period of continuing development of the church and its leadership in the second to third centuries the leadership was increasingly taking over all power and authority under God, and an integral part was played in its claims to do so by its pretensions to being priestly in a different and higher way from the faithful. Conversely, the laity's claims to some ministries in the church were sometimes linked to their pretensions to priestliness and the offering of spiritual sacrifices, and their exercise of the more public ones was being arrogated by the clergy, especially the bishop, and often by the bishop as priest.

CHAPTER 7

Summary and Conclusion

7.1 Summary and conclusion thus far

In chapter 2 we adduced the reasons why study of the subject of priesthood is considered important today and some issues raised by modern discussion of it. The reasons were, first, a shortage of clergy, and all the alleged causes for it – a 'crisis of identity', the requirement of celibacy, and the non-ordination of women – all of which relate in some way to the issue of priesthood; second, a rediscovery of the role of the laity, linked at times to its priesthood, and a desire to articulate and realize it more clearly; and, third, a desire to reunite the churches, an important obstacle to which is the non-recognition of each other's ministries, which is, in some ways, connected to the matter of priesthood. The issues raised were, first, the importance of the evidence of the first three centuries; second, whether the distinction between the clergy and the laity is essential, functional, or at all valid; third, the part that priesthood should play in the understanding of the ordained, whether it is central and defining, important but less comprehensive than other understandings, or unhelpful compared with other understandings; fourth, how the priesthood of the ordained should be understood and where it is derived from, i.e., whether it is essentially different from, and superior to, the general priesthood, and involving an ontological transformation into participation in Christ's priesthood and mediation, enabling the priest to bring about the eucharistic sacrifice and to rule, or derives solely from the church's participation in Christ's priesthood and concentrates that participation, or again derives from both Christ's and the church's priesthood and represents both; and, fifth, on what basis it is biblically and theologically justified, apostolic succession from Christ, Paul's use of cultic imagery for his apostolic mission, the sacrificial understanding of the eucharist, derivation from Christ's or the church's priesthood, its role in building up the church's priesthood, analogy with the Levitical priesthood, development guided by the Spirit, or universal need.

In chapter 3 we examined the attempts at justifying the ordained's special priesthood on the basis of the NT and found them unconvincing. There is no clear evidence of the succession of church leaders by ordination from the apostles and the high priesthood of Christ. Paul's use of cultic imagery does not require that he saw himself as more priestly than any other Christian. Although the eucharist was understood to have sacrificial connotations, no one person was considered more priestly than others because he presided at it. There were no priestly leaders for their priesthood to be derived from Christ's or the church's, or from building up the church's, and the Levitical priesthood is depicted as finished in Hebrews. Moreover, only Christ and Christians in general and individually are understood in priestly terms in the NT, and ideas are found there which undercut conceptions of a peculiarly priestly group within the church, except for the possibility of leaders representing the whole church's priestliness. Chief among these is the teaching that Christ has offered the only effective sacrifice for sin so that appropriate sacrifices consist of people's lives whether considered in whole or in aspects thereof, sacrifices which all Christians can offer. Fundamental too is the understanding that all Christians are to mediate Christ and his blessings through witness to non-Christians and use of the gift(s) received from Christ through the Spirit.

At the end of chapter 3 we noted that the major remaining justification was that the special priesthood of the ordained developed after the NT under the guidance and inspiration of the Spirit. We went on to note that, if this were so, then we would expect that the NT's emphases on the general priesthood and the dignity and ministry of all Christians in virtue of their gifting by the Spirit would not be diminished but rather enhanced by such a development. In chapters 4 to 6 we examined the relevant evidence from the first three centuries to see whether this was so. We found that use of cultic language for Christ, the church, and the individual Christian continued throughout, echoing and developing the NT's allusions to their priesthood, sacrifices, and likeness to the temple as God's dwelling-places, with increasing references to the OT sacrificial system. We also found that the priesthood of the church's leaders, above all of the bishop, but usually also the presbyters, and even, at times, the deacons, appeared fully established c.AD 200. Justin's silence, in particular, suggests that he was unaware of it, so that it arose between 150 and 200, possibly later in that period, if Clement of Alexandria's lack of explicit mention of it is significant in this way. Its earliest connotations were holiness, serving God, baptizing, offering the church's sacrifices, which included the eucharist, and forgiving sin. It is often related to the OT Levitical priesthood and regulations for it. Thus, the need to understand the OT's relevance for the church, forced on Christian thinkers by Gnosticism especially, was a major factor in this development, as was the leaders' presidency at worship, especially the eucharist, both of which were understood in sacrificial terms, and in discipline.

In Alexandria, priesthood generally was conceived in spiritual and intellectual terms as connoting dedication to, and dependence on, God, and access to and knowledge of him, resulting in fitness to teach, discipline, and lead. Origen summons both the leaders and Christians in general, of whose separate priesthoods he is aware, to attain this priestliness, which owes most to his view of perfection and his allegorical interpretation of the OT.

Cyprian marks a watershed in the priesthood of the ordained, being the first to make 'priest' his preferred designation of the bishop. It has highly important connotations for him, especially sacral authority, discipline, and presidency at the eucharist. He is also the first to view the bishop as acting on Christ's behalf in the eucharist, which he views as a true sacrifice consisting in Christ's passion. In this, and in ruling and discipline, the bishop is God's representative, not the church's, as he seems to be in Tertullian and Hippolytus. He is thus the mediator of God's grace, a term used of the bishop as priest in the *Didascalia*, where his priestliness is linked with authority, discipline, and teaching, and with holiness, dedication to God, and support by the laity.

We also noted that two writers who are aware of the special priesthood, Tertullian and Origen, are those who most develop the understanding of the general priesthood, demonstrating that the co-existence of the two priesthoods is possible. Tertullian links the two, apparently viewing the special as an ecclesiastical derivation from the divinely ordained general priesthood, and stressing the continuity between them by applying the same disciplinary regulations from the OT to both and by teaching that ordinary Christians could also baptize and offer in virtue of the general priesthood. His need to buttress the general priesthood with arguments to show its divine appointment, while taking the special priesthood as a given, and his report that some non-ordained are claiming to be as much priests as the ordained, suggest that he and others have to stress the general priesthood because of the special priesthood's increasing prominence. This indicates that, although the two co-existed, tensions appeared between them soon after the special priesthood surfaced. Hippolytus implies continuity between these priesthoods regarding the eucharist, but vital differences between them in the powers resulting from ordination. These are taken for granted in Cyprian and the *Didascalia*. Significantly, the general priesthood is scarcely mentioned in Hippolytus, only hinted at in Cyprian, who seems to deliberately avoid using the normal word for priest, *sacerdos*, for Christians in general, and completely devalued in the *Didascalia*. It is also constricted as we have outlined in Clement of Alexandria and Origen. There is, then, a clear correlation between an emphasis on the difference of special priesthoods (whether of the perfect or the ordained) from the general priesthood and a devaluation of the general priesthood. It is only Tertullian who seeks to balance them and even he attests to tensions between them.

Finally, we studied how, especially from c.200, the ordained increasingly took over the power and public ministry in the church at the same time as their priesthood was being taught and emphasized, while the laity lost power and opportunities for public ministry as their priesthood was being devalued and/or largely ignored. Moreover, the power and public ministry being taken over by the ordained were intimately linked to their special priesthood in the minds of the authors we have examined, whilst, in Origen and the *Didascalia*, the general priesthood was being linked with the laity's support of the ordained. The issue of priesthood was linked to that of the division between clergy, with which the special priesthood was linked in various ways, and laity which emerged at exactly the same period as the special priesthood. Further, the *charismata*, whilst still experienced by non-leaders as late as Cyprian, were increasingly being restricted to the ordained, particularly in the vital area of teaching which was regarded as a priestly ministry by several of those studied. Power, both spiritual and 'political', was becoming concentrated in those who claimed a special priesthood and authority from God, as was most, if not all, exercise of public ministry in the church.

It seems fair, then, to conclude that both the understanding of the general priesthood and the active participation of the laity in the church's life, and above all in its public life, ministry and mediation of God's grace, were significantly limited, diminished, and harmed by the rise in the clergy's specialized priesthood and the clergy's domination of the church's power and public ministry. The rise in the specialized, and the diminution and dilution of the general priesthood were integral to these developments. In so far as these developments involved limitations on the Spirit's use of the non-ordained in public ministry and the exercise of power, rather than enhancing the Spirit's ministry, they diminished it and restricted it increasingly to the ordained. Although the church gained the benefits of clearer and more effective order, these increased the dangers of the misuse of power, as Origen especially attests, and of the passivity of the laity, as he also attests. It is, therefore, highly questionable whether, as R.E. Brown claims, the evolution of the special priesthood of the ordained to the point we find in Cyprian and the *Didascalia* was 'guided by the Spirit.'[1] The Spirit was understood by the early church to have been poured out on all the faithful, conveying to them gifts for the church's edification. By Cyprian's time these were largely restricted to the clergy who could not be other than a minority of the whole church. Therefore the Spirit could not use just anyone with the appropriate gift(s) to edify the church in such areas as authoritative teaching, discipline of the wayward, presiding at baptism and the eucharist, and administering the church's finances. He had to use the same man, the bishop, for all these, and the bishop had to receive all these gifts through his ordination. The Spirit was thus restricted in whom he could give vital gifts to, and how and when he could give them, and whom he could use in specific, important areas of church life.

We also noted the main reasons for the development of the special priesthood of the ordained as, initially, the need to relate the OT to church life, and the bishop's and clergy's presidency at church worship and in discipline. A little later the necessity of bolstering authority was important. However, the application of priestly ideas to the ordained to the exclusion of other Christians was not a necessary or unavoidable element in the application of the OT to the life of the church. The NT had already indicated the lines along which it was appropriate to relate priesthood to the church, and, in view of the results of the development of the special priesthood which we have noted, such an application was, on the whole, unhelpful. Similarly, it is unnecessary to relate presidency in worship and discipline, or authority, to special priesthood, and the dangers in doing so outweigh the benefits. The apparent reasons why the early church developed an understanding of the clergy's special priesthood are, therefore, not compelling in the light of the NT's teaching and the detrimental results.

7.2 Related matters and further conclusions

One question which remains is what kind of special priesthood of the ordained is appropriate today. The evidence we have examined suggests that where the differences between the general and special priesthoods are stressed, as in Cyprian and the *Didascalia* especially, there the

---

[1] Brown, *Priest and Bishop*, 4.

general priesthood has been seriously undermined. Where, however, the continuity has been stressed, as in Tertullian, there the general priesthood has retained more of its NT value. This points us in the direction of viewing any special priesthood as continuous with, and perhaps a focusing and concentration of, the general priesthood. R.P.C. Hanson is an Anglican who has emphasized this understanding of the relationship between these two priesthoods, stressing that the ordained have no monopoly on access to God or on mediation of the benefits of Christ's salvation, and that their priesthood derives from Christ's in the church's.[2]

However, ecumenical statements tend to preserve the view that the priesthood of the ordained derives from Christ's independently of the church's as well as, or rather than, deriving from the church's priesthood. *Baptism, Eucharist and Ministry* states that their priesthood is related to Christ's priesthood and the church's, but defines the latter relationship in terms of strengthening and building it up, a view accepted by the Anglican-Reformed International Commission.[3] The Anglican-Roman Catholic International Commission stresses that the ordained represent the church in fulfilling its priestly vocation, but that 'their ministry is not an extension of the common Christian priesthood but belongs to another realm of the gifts of the Spirit.'[4] And the Faith and Order Advisory Group of the Church of England holds that 'bishops and presbyters do not participate to a greater degree in the priesthood of Christ; they participate in a different way - not that is as individual believers, but in the exercise of their office. ... Their ministry is an appointed means through which Christ makes his priesthood present and effective to his people.'[5] Whilst it is true that those involved in authority and public ministry in the church exercise their gifts so that, in doing so, they are participating in the mediation of the benefits of Christ's salvation to his people, this is true not only of the ordained but of all who are so involved, whether ordained or not. The NT demonstrates that this need involve only the general priesthood, whereas subsequent Christian history, we have shown, illustrates that the insertion of a third priesthood understood to derive from Christ's in a different way from the general priesthood has resulted in the latter's devaluation. If ecumenism wishes to promote and not diminish the general priesthood,

---

[2] Hanson, R.P.C., *Christian Priesthood Examined*, 100-102.

[3] *BEM*, 23. In section 17 on 'Ordained Ministry and Priesthood' it states that 'ordained ministers are related, as are all Christians, ... to the priesthood of Christ', but, in section 15, it is clear that their authority derives from Christ's through ordination. Cf. ARIC, 50.

[4] ARCIC, 36.

[5] FOAG, 99.

then it must recognize this and respond appropriately.

Related to this is the focus on presidency at the eucharist as that which most clearly expresses the priesthood of the ordained. *Baptism, Eucharist and Ministry*'s explanation of that priesthood is very brief and does not mention this connection, but earlier states that 'it is especially in the eucharistic celebration that the ordained ministry is the visible focus of the deep and all-embracing communion between Christ and the members of his body.' The Anglican-Roman Catholic International Commission goes further than this, stressing that Roman Catholics and Anglicans use priestly terms for the ordained ministry because 'the eucharist is the memorial of the sacrifice of Christ [and so] the action of the presiding minister in reciting again the words of Christ at the last supper and distributing to the assembly the holy gifts is seen to stand in a sacramental relation to what Christ himself did in offering his own sacrifice.' The Anglican-Reformed International Commission is less clear on this, stating that 'from very early times ordination has been connected with the Eucharist', but accepting that the need for the eucharist to normally be presided over by the ordained 'is a matter of the harmonious ordering of the life of the Church. The one who presides does so, not in virtue of a different relationship to the life of the risen Christ from the rest of the body, but because – as a matter of order – he has been so authorized.' While the Anglican Faith and Order Advisory Group views the ordaineds' ministry as priestly because it helps the faithful to realize their priestly character, it states that 'it is in the particular relationship of the eucharist and the ministry of reconciliation to the sacrifice of Christ that the priestly character of the ordained ministry is most evident. This ministry is priestly because through it God makes present to his people the work of Jesus Christ, the mediator who brings humanity to God.'[6]

The Anglican-Reformed International Commission seems closest to the burden of the NT and the lessons we have noted from subsequent Christian history up to AD 300. As a matter of order it is good that the ordained or one generally recognized as a leader should preside at any celebration of the eucharist. In doing so, moreover, that person is representing Christ's priestly self-offering and facilitating God's people's appropriation of its benefits, and representing and facilitating the people's priestly self-offering in response. However, it is only in these ways that this priesthood is different from everyone else's, and there are no grounds in the NT for claiming that such a person has an inherent priesthood different from anyone else's. In other words,

---

[6] *BEM*, 22; ARCIC, 35; ARIC, 51-2.

priesthood goes with the role at the time, it is not permanent. Further, the later attempts to differentiate strongly between the leader's priesthood and the church's resulted in diminution and devaluation of the latter which is clearly taught in the NT. The result is that, as Tertullian holds, it is possible in case of necessity for any Christian to preside at the eucharist, and in some churches today lack of priests or ministers is causing eucharistic malnutrition! In principle, the same is true of any of the tasks, such as ruling, teaching, and exercising discipline, considered to be appropriate normally for the ordained alone to carry out.

Indeed, it seems arguable that it is likely that any understanding of a special priesthood will detract from that of the general priesthood. The only possible exception is where the church's leaders are clearly understood to do no more than focus, represent and express the general priesthood. Even here, human frailty being what it is, the dangers we have found in the third century are bound to be present unless all activities and ministries in the church are open to all Christians on the basis of their common union with Christ and according to the gifts they have received by the Spirit. Hanson's criticism of 'sacerdotal priesthood', that 'it drains believers' priesthood ... all away into the priesthood of the clergy',[7] threatens to be true of his concept of a 'non-sacerdotal' priesthood. The church needs to consider seriously whether it really wants to run this risk to its God-given priesthood by regularly using the term 'priest' for the clergy, although it should remember the kinds of things we have noted concerning the special ways in which the ordained normally focus its priesthood and represent Christ's.

If the foregoing is accepted, it follows that the inherent priestliness of those recognized and accepted as leaders in the church can only ever be the same as that of every Christian. It is derived from the participation of all Christians – the church – in Christ's priesthood by virtue of their baptism into and union with him, as suggested by Origen, and it representatively expresses this general priesthood in various acts of ministry which, in cases of necessity, are open to all Christians in view of their baptism and priestliness, as Tertullian recognized regarding baptizing and offering, and according to their gifting, as Origen realized concerning teaching. Priesthood should, then, play such a role in the understanding of church leaders, a role alongside other images of leadership, in particular that of pastor or shepherd, and above all that of servant.

In fact, recent ecumenical discussions of priesthood are united in

---

[7] Hanson, R.P.C., *Christian Priesthood Examined*, 98.

recognizing that ministry is exercised by and through the whole of the church, although the Anglican-Roman Cathlic International Commission later recognized that it had given insufficient attention to the general priesthood.[8] Even so, their main concern is with the special priesthood of the ordained. Whilst this can be defended by pointing out that these documents were 'primarily concerned with the ordained ministry'[9] because this issue is a major obstacle to reunion, it betrays a continuing emphasis on the special priesthood at the expense of the general. All these documents are concerned to relate to the NT, but, in dealing with ministry in this way, they are not representing the NT's emphasis. On the other hand, *Baptism, Eucharist and Ministry* helpfully stresses the Holy Spirit's bestowal of 'diverse and complementary gifts' which all Christians are to discover and use for the community's upbuilding and the world's service. It also emphasizes that, as the churches seek to overcome their differences 'concerning the place and forms of the ordained ministry', they 'need to work from the perspective of the calling of the whole people of God.'[10] It would be useful to spell out more fully what this calling involves from the perspective of the people's priesthood, and our summary of the early church fathers' teaching on the general priesthood at the end of section 5 provides helpful pointers to how this could be done.

One way in which this is possible is Tertullian's stress on the laity's right to baptize and offer the eucharistic sacrifice in case of necessity. The Anglican-Reformed International Commission report is the only ecumenical document studied to discuss lay presidency at the eucharist. This is because some of the Reformed allow it, whereas those involved in most other discussions do not. This report rightly recognizes that it is a misunderstanding to argue that lay presidency at the eucharist is a necessary witness to the general priesthood, because this implies that only the president is a priest, the very doctrine that the practice would be intended to negate. The report then argues that lay presidency should be allowed where lack of the ordained means that churches can rarely if ever celebrate the eucharist together.[11] This fits well with the emphasis we noted in Justin, Irenaeus, and Hippolytus on the eucharist being the church's offering, connected in Justin and Tertullian with the general priesthood.

All these issues relate to the current questioning of the distinction

---

[8] ARCIC, 40.
[9] Ibid., 41.
[10] *BEM*, 20.
[11] ARIC, 52-3.

between the clergy and the laity and the rediscovery of the laity's role noted in chapter 2. The evidence considered from the third century shows that this distinction opened up a division within the church which institutionalized the distinction between leaders and led, ministers and those ministered to. Whilst the NT and subsequent practice show that leadership and other specialized ministries, such as teaching, based on particular, individual gifts need to be publicly recognized by the church and appropriate respect given, this inflexible division into two contrasting bodies of Christians contributed strongly to the increasing restriction of power and ministry to the ordained. This suggests that it is likely that its removal, together with teaching in theory and practice concerning the general priesthood and the Spirit's gifts to each Christian, would significantly facilitate the participation of all Christians in the church's life and so enhance the church's vitality. To some extent this has been shown in the development of modern basic church communities, house churches, and home groups.

The relevant teaching in these groups has been largely in terms of 'the body of Christ' and/or 'the gifts of the Spirit', much less in terms of the 'royal priesthood'. A reason for this has been the weight which tradition placed on the priesthood of the ordained, and the desire to protect that and maintain its essential difference from the general priesthood. [12] If it were understood that the essential priesthoods in the church are those of Christ and the church itself, and that leaders' priesthood is no more than representative, then, perhaps, the 'royal priesthood' could be released from these bonds and developed to the benefit of the whole.

Further, were these understandings of the church and its members to be adopted, the weight of responsibility on one leader or priest would be greatly lessened, since all Christians could share in the church's leadership and ministry to the extent that they were gifted. In addition, any could perform public ministries when necessary. Moreover, in any community leaders tend to appear. Such can be recognized by that community and then by the wider church, their training following on that recognition. The shortage of leaders is thus lessened. [13] In addition, if it were admitted that ordination or commissioning could be in view of different gifts, such as leadership or teaching or administration or evangelism, then appropriate recognition and training could be devised

---

[12] See, e.g., Congar, *Lay People*, who begins (xxiii) by stating that the laity will always be a subordinate order in the church and explains its priesthood (181-215) largely in contrast with that of the ordained.

[13] The issue of clerical celibacy is not specifically addressed here, but this was clearly not expected in the earliest church and all justifications of its necessity are removed by the kinds of arguments adduced in this conclusion.

and a church could have a number of people commissioned to perform different functions in the church. This would again lessen the pressure on the ordained in many of today's churches in which they are expected to exercise most or all of these functions themselves without always having all the necessary gifts.

Another issue to which our study is relevant is the ordination of women to the priesthood. If the priesthood of the ordained were understood as indicated above, viz., as only one aspect of the understanding of the ordained alongside many others, as no different in essence from the general priesthood, and as consisting in the normal exercise of certain functions in which they represent Christ's and the church's priesthood, and if ordination were understood as recognition, rather than conferment, of appropriate gifts, then many objections to women's ordination disappear.

Finally, this could facilitate the desired reunion of the churches. If it were generally recognized that leadership is a matter of gifts and appropriate recognition and/or commissioning, that all the faithful are eligible to perform all public ministry according to their gifts, and that the only priesthoods which really matter are Christ's and the faithful's, then many of the hindrances to reunion would be removed.

Bibliography

1. REFERENCE WORKS

Bauer, W., Arndt, W.F., and Gingrich, F.W., *A Greek-English Lexicon of the New Testament and Other Early Christian Literature* (Chicago, 1952⁴)

Dekkers, E., *Clavis Patrum Latinorum* (Bruges, 1961²)

Ferguson, E. (ed.), *Encyclopedia of Early Christianity* (New York and London, 1990)

Geerard, M., *Clavis Patrum Graecorum*, vol. 1: *Patres Antenicaeni* (Turnhout, 1983)

Glare, P.G.W. (ed.), *Oxford Latin Dictionary* (Oxford, Combined Edition, 1982)

Kittel, G. and Friedrich, G. (eds.), *Theological Dictionary of the New Testament*, 10 vols.. (Grand Rapids, 1964-1976).

Lampe, G.W.H. (ed.), *A Patristic Greek Lexicon* (Oxford, 1961)

Moulton W.F., Geden, A.S., and Moulton, H.K. (eds.), *A Concordance to the Greek Testament* (Edinburgh, 1963⁴)

Quasten, J., *Patrology*, vol. 1: *The Beginnings of Patristic Literature* (Utrecht-Antwerp, 1950); vol. 2: *The Ante-Nicene Literature after Irenaeus* (Utrecht-Antwerp and Westminster, Maryland, 1953)

2. TEXTS, EDITIONS AND TRANSLATIONS OF ANCIENT WRITERS

a) The New Testament

Aland, K. et al. (eds.), *The Greek New Testament*, (Stuttgart, 1983³)

The Holy Bible containing the Old and New Testaments, Revised Standard Version (London, 1952)

b) The Apostolic Fathers

Camelot, P.T. (ed.), *Ignace d'Antioche, Polycarpe de Smyrne. Lettre, Martyre de Polycarpe* (Paris, 1958)

Grant, R.M. et al. (eds.), *The Apostolic Fathers. A New Translation and Commentary* (Camden, New Jersey and Toronto, 1964-1968): vol. 1, Grant, R.M., *An Introduction* (1964); vol.2, Grant, R.M. and Graham, H.H. (eds.), *First and Second Clement* (1965); vol.3, Kraft, R.A. (ed.), *The Didache and Barnabas* (1965); vol.4, Grant, R.M. (ed.), *Ignatius of Antioch* (1966); and vol.6, Snyder, R.F. (ed.), *The Shepherd of Hermas* (1968)

Lightfoot, J.B., Harmer, J.R. and Holmes, M.W. (eds.), *The Apostolic Fathers: Greek Texts and English Translations of their Writings* (Grand Rapids, 1992²)

Butterworth, R. (ed.), *Contra Noetum* (London, 1977)

Cuming, G.J. (ed.), *Hippolytus: A Text for Students* (Bramcote, 1976)

Dix, G. and Chadwick, H. (eds.), *The Apostolic Tradition of St. Hippolytus* (London, 1968²)

Legge, F. (ed.), *Philosophumena or the Refutation of All Heresies* (London, 1922)

Marcovich, M. (ed.), *Refutatio Omnium Haeresium* (Berlin, 1986)

Irenaeus

Rousseau, A. et al. (eds.), *Irénée de Lyon: Contre Les Hérésies*, 5 vols. (Paris, 1965-1982)

Froidevaux, L.M. (ed.), *Irénée de Lyon: Démonstration de la Prédication Apostolique* (Paris, 1959)

Justin Martyr

Falls, T.B. (ed.), *The Fathers of the Church: A New Translation: Writings of Justin Martyr* (Washington, 1948)

Wartelle, A. (ed.), *Saint Justin: Apologies* (Paris, 1987)

Melito of Sardis

Hall, S.G. (ed.), *Melito of Sardis: 'On Pascha' and fragments* (Oxford, 1979)

Perler, O. (ed.), *Méliton de Sardes: Sur la Pâque et Fragments* (Paris, 1966)

Methodius of Olympus

Musurillo, H. and Debidour, V.-H. (eds.), *Méthode d'Olympe: Le Banquet* (Paris, 1963)

Minucius Felix

Clarke, G.W. (ed.), *The Octavius of Marcus Minucius Felix* (New York, 1974)

Novatian

DeSimone, R.J. (ed.), *Novatian: The Trinity, The Spectacles, Jewish Foods, In Praise of Purity, Letters* (Washington, 1973)

Origen

Barkley, G.W. (ed.), *Origen: Homilies on Leviticus 1-16* (Washington, 1990)

- (ed.), *Origène: Homélies sur Ézéchiel* (Paris, 1989)

Borret, M. (ed.), *Origène: Homélies sur le Lévitique*, 2 vols. (Paris, 1981)

Chadwick, H. (ed.), *Origen: Contra Celsum* (Cambridge, 1965)

Doutreleau, L. (ed.), *Origène: Homélies sur les Nombres I* (Paris, 1996)

Heine, R.E. (ed.), *Origen: Commentary on the Gospel according to John Books 1-10* (Washington, 1989)

- (ed.), *Origen: Commentary on the Gospel according to John Books 13-32*

(Washington, 1993)
- (ed.), *Origen: Homilies on Genesis and Exodus* (Washington, 1982)
Jaubert, A. (ed.), *Origène: Homélies sur Josué* (Paris, 1960)
Klostermann, E. and Benz, E. (eds.), *Origenes Werke,* vol. 10 (Leipzig, 1935)
Méhat, A. (ed.), *Origène: Homélies sur les Nombres* (Paris, 1951)
Messié, P., Neyrand, L. and Borret, M. (eds.), *Origène: Homélies sur les Juges* (Paris, 1993)
Scherer, (ed.), *Origène: Dialogue avec Hèraclide* (Paris, 1960)
Smith, J.C. (ed.), *Origen: Homilies on Jeremiah. Homily on 1 Kings 28* (Washington, 1998)

Tertullian

Arbesmann, R., Daly, E.J. and Quain, E.A. (eds.), *Tertullian: Apologetical Works and Minucius Felix: Octavius* (Washington, 1950)
Dekkers, E. et al. (eds.), *Tertulliani Opera, Pars 1: Opera Catholica; Adversus Marcionem; Pars 2: Opera Montanistica* (Turnhout, 1954)
Evans, E. (ed.), *Tertullian: Adversus Marcionem* (Oxford, 1972)
- (ed.), *Tertullian's Homily on Baptism* (London, 1964)
Le Saint, W.P. (ed.), *Tertullian: Treatises on Marriage and Remarriage* (London, 1951)
- (ed.), *Tertullian: Treatises on Penance* (London, 1959)
Micaelli, C. and Munier, C. (eds.), *Tertullien: La Pudicité* (Paris, 1993)
Moreschini, C. and Fredouille, J.-C. (eds.), *Tertullien: Exhortation à la chasteté* (Paris, 1985)
Refoulé, R.F. and Drouzy, M. (eds.), *Tertullien: Traité du baptême* (Paris, 1952)
Refoulé, R.F. and de Labriolle, P. (eds.), *Tertullien: Traité de la Prescription contre les hérétiques* (Paris, 1957)
Schulz-Flügel, E. and Mattei, P. (eds.), *Tertullien: Le Voile des Vierges* (Paris, 1997)
Souter, A. (ed.), *Tertullian: Concerning the Resurrection of the Flesh* (London, 1922)

Tatian

Whittaker, M. (ed.), *Tatian: 'Oratio ad Graecos' and Fragments* (Oxford, 1982)

Others

Connolly, R.H. (ed.), *Didascalia Apostolorum: The Syriac Version translated and accompanied by the Verona Latin Fragments* (Oxford, 1929)
Edwards, R.A and Wild, R.A. (eds.), *The Sentences of Sextus* (Chico, 1981)
Foerster, W. (ed.), *Gnosis: A Selection of Gnostic Texts,* 2 vols. (Oxford, 1972)
Harris, J.R., (ed.), *The Odes and Psalms of Solomon* (Cambridge, 1909)
Migne, J.-P., (ed.), *Patrologiae cursus completus, series graeca,* vol. 1 (Paris, 1857)
Musurillo, H. (ed.), *The Acts of the Christian Martyrs* (Oxford, 1972)
Nautin, P. (ed.), *Homélies pascales: I Une homélie inspirée du traité sur la Pâque d'Hippolyte* (Paris, 1950)
Robinson, J.M. (ed.), *The Nag Hammadi Library in English* (Leiden, 1977)
Schneemelcher, W. and Wilson R. McL. (eds.), *New Testament Apocrypha,* 2 vols. (Cambridge, 1991),

Tidner, E. (ed.), *Didascaliae Apostolorum, Canonum Ecclesiasticorum, Traditionis Apostolicae, Versiones Latinae* (Berlin, 1963)

Wilson, R. McL. (ed.), *The Gospel of Philip* (London, 1962)

Williamson, G.A. and Louth, A. (eds.), *Eusebius: The History of the Church from Christ to Constantine* (London, 1989²)

3. MODERN LITERATURE

Abbott, W.M. (ed.), *The Documents of Vatican II* (London and Dublin, 1966)

Anglican-Reformed International Commission, *God's Reign and Our Unity* (London, 1984)

Anglican-Roman Catholic International Commission, *The Final Report* (London, 1982)

Ash, J.L., 'The Decline of Ecstatic Prophecy in the Early Church' in *Theological Studies* 37.2 (June 1976), 227-252

Banks, R., *Paul's Idea of Community: The Early House Churches in their Historical Setting* (Exeter, 1980)

Bardy, G., 'Le sacerdoce chrétien d'après Tertullien', *La Vie spirituelle* 58 (1939), 109-124

- *La Théologie de l'Église de saint Irénée au concile de Nicée* (Paris, 1947)

Bârlea, O., *Die Weihe der Bischöfe, Presbyter und Diakone in vornicänischer Zeit* (Munich, 1969)

Barnes, T.D., *Tertullian, A Historical and Literary Study* (Oxford, 1985²)

Barrett, C.K., *The First Epistle to the Corinthians* (London, 1971²)

Beasley-Murray, G.R., *The Book of Revelation* (London, 1974)

Benson, E.W., *Cyprian, His Life, His Times, His Work* (London, 1897)

Best, E., 'Spiritual Sacrifice: General Priesthood in the New Testament' in *Interpretation* 14 (1960), 273-299

- 'I Peter II 4-10 - A Reconsideration' in *Novum Testamentum* 11 (1969), 270-293

- *1 Peter* (London, 1971)

Bévenot, M., 'Tertullian's thoughts about the christian "priesthood"' in de Smedt, A.J., et al. (eds.), *Corona Gratiarum* (Bruges, 1975), 125-137

- '"Sacerdos" as understood by Cyprian' in *Journal of Theological Studies* 30 (1979), 413-429

Bigg, C., *The Christian Platonists of Alexandria* (Oxford, 1913)

Brent, A., *Hippolytus and the Roman Church in the Third Century: Communities in Tension before the Emergence of a Monarch-Bishop* (Leiden, 1995)

Brown, R.E., *The Gospel According To John*, 2 vols. (London, 1966)

- *Priest and Bishop - Biblical Reflections* (London, 1971)

- *The Epistles of John* (London, 1982)

Bruce, F.F., *Commentary on the Book of the Acts* (London, 1954)

- *The Epistle to the Hebrews* (Grand Rapids, 1964)

Buchanan, C. (ed.), *Essays on Eucharistic Sacrifice in the Early Church* (Bramcote, 1984)

Bultmann, R., *The Johannine Epistles* (Philadelphia, 1973)

Caird, G.B., *A Commentary on the Revelation of St. John the Divine* (London, 1966)

Campenhausen, H. von, *Ecclesiastical Authority and Spiritual Power in the Church of the First Three Centuries* (London, 1969)
- 'The Origins of the Idea of the Priesthood in the Early Church' in *Tradition and Life in the Church. Essays and Lectures in Church History* (London, 1968)
Capelle, B., 'L'absolution sacerdotale chez S. Cyprien', *Recherches de théologie ancienne et médiévale* 7 (1935), 221-234
Card, T., *Priesthood and Ministry in Crisis* (London, 1988)
Carey, G., 'Reflections upon the Nature of Ministry and Priesthood in the Light of the Lima Report', *Anvil* 3 (1986), 19-31
Collins, J.N., *Diakonia: Re-interpreting the Ancient Sources* (Oxford, 1990)
Colson, J., *La fonction diaconale aux origines de l'Église* (Bruges, 1960)
- *Ministre de Jésus-Christ ou le sacerdoce de l'évangile: Étude sur la condition sacerdotale des ministres chrétiens dans l'Église primitive* (Paris, 1966)
Congar, Y.M.-J., 'Structure du sacerdoce chrétien', *La Maison-Dieu* 27 (1951), 51-85
- *Lay People in the Church: A Study for a Theology of Laity* (London, 1957)
Cooke, B., *Ministry to Word and Sacraments. History and Theology* (Philadelphia, 1976)
Cranfield, C.E.B., *The First Epistle of Peter* (London, 1950)
- *The Cambridge Greek Testament Commentary: The Gospel according to St Mark* (Cambridge, 1972)
- *A Critical and Exegetical Commentary on the Epistle to the Romans*, 2 vols. (Edinburgh, 1975 & 1979)
Crouzel, H., *Origène et la 'connaissance mystique'* (Paris, 1961)
- *Origène* (Paris, 1985)
Dabin, P., *Le sacerdoce royal dans les livres saints* (Paris, 1941)
- *Le sacerdoce royal des fidéles dans la tradition ancienne et moderne*(Paris, 1950)
D'Alès, A., *La Théologie de Saint Cyprien* (Paris, 1922)
Daly, R.J., 'Sacrifice in Origen' in Cross, F.L., (ed.), *Studia Patristica* 11 (Berlin, 1972), 125-9
- *Christian Sacrifice: The Judaeo - Christian Background Before Origen*(Washington, 1978)
Daniélou, J., *Origen* (London and New York, 1955)
Delorme, J., (ed.), *Le ministère et les ministères selon le Nouveau Testament* (Paris, 1974)
Donfried, K.P., *The Setting of Second Clement in Early Christianity* (Leiden, 1974)
Dunn, J.D.G., *Romans 9-16* (Dallas, 1988)
Eastwood, C., *The Royal Priesthood of the Faithful* (London, 1963)
Elliott, J.H., *The Elect and the Holy. An Exegetical Examination of I Peter 2:4-10 and the Phrase 'basileion hierateuma'* (Leiden, 1966)
- 'Ministry and Church Order in the NT: A Traditio - Historical Analysis (1 Pt 5,1-5 & plls.)', *Catholic Biblical Quarterly* 32 (1970), 367-391
Evans, C.F., *Saint Luke* (London, 1990)
Evans, R.F., *One and Holy. The Church in Latin Patristic Thought* (London, 1972)
Faith and Order Advisory Group of the Board for Mission and Unity of the General Synod of the Church of England, *The Priesthood of the Ordained Ministry* (London, 1986)
Faith and Order Commission of the World Council of Churches, *Baptism, Eucharist and Ministry* (Geneva, 1982)

Faivre, A., *Naissance d'une hiérarchie: les premières étapes du cursus clérical* (Paris, 1977)
- 'Clerc/laïc: histoire d'une frontière', in *Revue des sciences religieuses* 57.3 (1983), 195-220
- 'Aux origines du laïcat', *L'Année canonique* 29 (1985/86), 19-54
- 'The Laity in the First Centuries: Issues Revealed by Historical Research' in *Lumen Vitae* 42 (1987), 129-139
- *The Emergence of the Laity in the Early Church* (New York, 1990)
Fiorenza, E.S., *Priester für Gott: Studien zum Herrschafts- und Priestermotiv in der Apokalypse* (Münster, 1972)
Frend, W.H.C., 'The *seniores laici* and the origins of the church in North Africa' in *Journal of Theological Studies, New Series* 12 (1961), 280-284
- 'The Church of the Roman Empire 313-600' in Neill, S.C. and Weber, H.-R. (eds.), *The Layman in Christian History* (London, 1963), 57-82
- 'Jews and Christians in Third Century Carthage' in *Paganisme, Judaïsme, Christianisme. Influences et affrontements dans le monde antique* (Paris 1978), 185-194
Frickel, J., *Das Dunkel um Hippolyt von Rom: ein Lösungsversuch: die Schriften Elenchos und Contra Noetum* (Graz, 1988)
Fung, R.Y.K., 'Ministry, Community and Spiritual Gifts' in *The Evangelical Quarterly* 56.1 (1984), 3-20
Galot, J., *Theology of the Priesthood* (San Francisco, 1984)
Garrett, J.L., 'The Pre-Cyprianic Doctrine of the Priesthood of All Christians' in Church, F.F. and George, T. (eds.), *Continuity and Discontinuity in Church History* (Leiden, 1979), 45-61
Goetz, K.G., *Das Christentum Cyprians: Eine historisch-kritische Untersuchung* (Giessen, 1896)
Grant, R.M., *Greek Apologists of the Second Century* (London, 1988)
Grollenberg, L. et al., *Minister? Pastor? Prophet? Grass-roots leadership in the churches* (London, 1980)
Gryson, R., 'Les élections ecclésiastiques au IIIe siècle' in *Revue d'histoire ecclésiastique* 68 (1973), 353-404
- 'Review of Vilela, A., *La condition collégiale des prêtres au IIIe siècle, Revue d'histoire ecclésiastique* (1974), 108-114
Guthrie, D., *Hebrews* (Leicester, 1983)
Gy, P.-M., 'Remarques sur le vocabulaire antique du sacerdoce chrétien' in *Études sur le sacrement de l'ordre* (Paris, 1957), 125-145
Hällström, Gunnar af, *'Fides simpliciorum' according to Origen of Alexandria* (Helsinki, 1984)
Hanson, A.T., *The Pioneer Ministry* (London, 1961)
Hanson, A.T. & Hanson, R.P.C., *The Identity of the Church. A Guide to Recognizing the Contemporary Church* (London, 1987)
Hanson, R.P.C., *Groundwork for Unity: Plain Facts about Christian Ministry* (London, 1971)
- *Christian Priesthood Examined* (London, 1979)
- *Studies in Christian Antiquity* (Edinburgh, 1985)
Harvey, A.E., 'Elders', *Journal of Theological Studies, New Series* 25 (1974), 318-332
- *Priest or President?* (London, 1975)

Hein, K., *Eucharist and Excommunication. A study in early Christian doctrine and discipline* (Berne and Frankfurt/M., 1973)

Hinchliff, P., *Cyprian of Carthage and the Unity of the Christian Church* (London, 1974)

Jones, F.S., 'The Pseudo-Clementines: A History of Research', *The Second Century* 2 (1982), 1-33 and 63-96

Kelly, J.N.D., *The Epistles of Peter and of Jude* (London, 1969)

- *Early Christian Doctrines* (London, 1977[5])

Kraemer, H., *A Theology of the Laity* (London, 1958)

Küng, H., *Why Priests?* (London, 1972)

Kydd, R.A.N., *Charismata to 320 AD A Study of the Overt Pneumatic Experience of the Early Church* (unpublished thesis presented to the University of St.Andrews, 1973)

Lanne, E., 'Le laïc dans L'Église ancienne' in *Verbum Caro* 18 (no.71/72, 1964), 105-126

Laurance, J.D., 'Le président de l'eucharistie selon Cyprien de Carthage: un nouvel examen' in *La Maison-Dieu* 154 (1983), 151-165

Lawson, J., *A Theological and Historical Introduction to the Apostolic Fathers* (New York, 1961)

Lécuyer, J., 'Essai sur le sacerdoce des fidèles chez les pères' in *La Maison-Dieu* 27 (1951), 7-50

- 'Sacerdoce des fidèles et sacerdoce ministériel chez Origène', *Vetera Christianorum* 7 (1970), 255-264

Lies, L., *Wort und Eucharistie bei Origenes: Zur Spiritualisierungstendenz des Eucharistieverständnisses* (Innsbruck, Vienna and Munich, 1978)

Lietzmann, H., *Mass and Lord's Supper: A Study in the History of the Liturgy* published with *Introduction and Further Inquiry* by Richardson, R.D. (Leiden, 1979)

Lindars, B., *The Gospel of John* (London, 1972)

Mackey, J.P., 'Another Test Case: Church Ministry (1) A View from Systematic Theology' in Dunn, J.D.G. and Mackey, J.P., *New Testament Theology in Dialogue* (London, 1987), 103-120

Manson, T.W., *Ministry and Priesthood: Christ's and Ours* (London, 1958)

Marshall, I.H., *The Gospel of Luke* (Exeter, 1978)

- *The Epistles of John* (Grand Rapids, 1978)

Martin, R.P., *Philippians* (London, 1976)

Michaels, J.R., *1 Peter* (Waco, 1988)

Moberly, R.C., *Ministerial Priesthood* (London, 1897)

Montefiore, H., *A Commentary on the Epistle to the Hebrews* (London, 1964)

Morris, L., *The Gospel according to John* (London, 1971)

Nautin, P., *Origène: Sa vie et son œuvre* (Paris, 1977)

Neil, W., *The Acts of the Apostles* (London, 1973)

Neymeyr, U., *Die christlichen Lehrer im zweiten Jahrhundert: Ihre Lehrtätigkeit, ihr Selbstverständnis und ihre Geschichte* (Leiden, 1989)

Noll, R.R., 'The Search for a Christian Ministerial Priesthood in I Clement' in *Studia Patristica* 13 (Berlin, 1975), 250-253

- *Christian Ministerial Priesthood: A Search for Its Beginnings In the Primary Documents of the Apostolic Fathers* (San Francisco, 1993)

O'Neill, D.P., *The Priest in Crisis: a study in role change* (London, 1968)

Osborn, E.F., *The Philosophy of Clement of Alexandria* (Cambridge, 1957)

Otranto, G., 'Il sacerdozio comune dei fedeli nei reflessi della 1 Petr. 2,9 (I e II secolo)' in *Vetera Christianorum* 7 (1970), 225-246

- 'Nonne et laici sacerdotes sumus? (Exh. cast. 7,3)' in *Vetera Christianorum* 8 (1971), 27-47

Palmer, P.F., 'The Lay Priesthood: Real or Metaphorical' in *Theological Studies* 8 (1947), 574-613

Powell, D., 'Ordo Presbyterii' in *Journal of Theological Studies, New Series* 26 (1975), 290-328

Quacquarelli, A., 'L'epiteto sacerdote ai cristiani in Giustino Martire (*Dial.* 116,3)', *Vetera Christianorum* 7.1 (1970), 5-19

Quatember, F., *Die christliche Lebenshaltung des Klemens von Alexandrien nach seinem Pädagogus* (Vienna, 1946)

Quispel, G., 'African Christianity before Minucius Felix and Tertullian' in den Boeff, J. and Kessels, A.H.M. (eds.), *Actus* (Utrecht, 1982), 257-335

Rahner, K., 'La doctrine d'Origène sur la pénitence', *Recherches de Science Religieuse* 37 (1950), 47-97, 252-286, 422-456

Robeck, C.M., *The Role and Function of Prophetic Gifts for the Church at Carthage, AD 202-258* (Ann Arbor, 1985)

Ryan, L., 'Patristic Teaching on the Priesthood of the Faithful' in *Irish Theological Quarterly* 29 (1962), 25-51

Sage, M., *Cyprian* (Philadelphia, 1975)

Schäfer, T., *Das Priester-Bild im Leben und Werk des Origenes* (Frankfurt am Main, 1978)

Schillebeeckx, E., *The Church with a Human Face* (London, 1985)

Scholer, J.M., *Proleptic Priests: Priesthood in the Epistle to the Hebrews* (Sheffield, 1991)

Schweizer, E., *Church Order in the New Testament* (London, 1961)

Scott, W.M.F., 'Priesthood in the New Testament', *Scottish Journal of Theology* 10 (1957), 399-415

Stevenson, K.W., *Eucharist and Offering* (New York, 1986)

Strecker, G., *Das Judenchristentum in den Pseudoklementinen* (Berlin, 1981[2])

Taylor, V., *The Gospel According to St. Mark* (London, 1966[2])

Tillard, J.M.R., *What Priesthood has the Ministry?* (Bramcote, 1973)

Torrance, T.F., *Royal Priesthood* (Edinburgh and London, 1955)

Trigg, J.W., 'The Charismatic Intellectual: Origen's Understanding of Religious Leadership', *Church History* 50 (1981), 5-19

- *Origen: The Bible and Philosophy in the Third-century Church* (London, 1985 and Atlanta, 1983)

Vanhoye, A., *Old Testament Priests and the New Priest According to the New Testament* (Petersham, 1986)

Vilela, A., *La condition collégiale des prêtres au IIIe siècle* (Paris, 1971)

Vogt, H.J., *Das Kirchenverständnis des Origenes* (Cologne, 1974)

Völker, W., *Das Vollkommenheitsideal des Origenes* (Tübingen, 1930)

- *Der wahre Gnostiker nach Clemens Alexandrinus* (Berlin, 1952)

Walker, G.S.M., *The Churchmanship of St. Cyprian* (London, 1968)

Walker, J.H., 'Reflections on a new edition of the Didache', *Vigiliae Christianae* 35 (1981), 35-42

Wiles, M.F., 'The Theological Legacy of St. Cyprian', *Journal of Ecclesiastical History*

14 (1963), 139-149

Wilken, R.L., 'Alexandria: A School for Training in Virtue' in Henry, P. (ed.), *Schools of Thought in the Christian Tradition* (Philadelphia, 1984), 15-30

Williams, C.S.C., *The Acts of the Apostles* (London, 1964)

Williams, G.H., 'The Ancient Church, AD 30-313' in Neill, S.C. and Weber, H.-R. (eds.), *The Layman in Christian History* (London, 1963), 28-52

Williams, R., *Eucharistic Sacrifice - The Roots of a Metaphor* (Bramcote, 1982)

Wingren, G., 'Der Begriff "Laie"' in Schröder, H. and Müller, G. (eds.), *Vom Amt des Laien in Kirche und Theologie* (Berlin, 1982), 3-16

Wright, D.F., 'Ministry and Priesthood: Further Reflections', *Anvil* 3 (1986), 195-207

Young, F.M., *The Use of Sacrificial Ideas in Greek Christian Writers from the New Testament to John Chrysostom* (Cambridge, Mass., 1979)

Zell, R.L., 'The Priesthood of Christ in Tertullian and St. Cyprian' in Cross, F.L., (ed.), *Studia Patristica* 11 (1972), 282-8

Paternoster Biblical and Theological Monographs
(All titles uniform with this volume)

Joseph Abraham
Eve: Accused or Acquitted?
A Reconsideration of Feminist Readings of the Creation Narrative Texts in Genesis 1–3
Two contrary views dominate contemporary feminist biblical scholarship. One finds in the Bible an unequivocal equality between the sexes from the very creation of humanity, whilst the other sees the biblical text as irredeemably patriarchal and androcentric. Dr. Abraham enters into dialogue with both camps as well as introducing his own method of approach. An invaluable tool for anyone who is interested in this contemporary debate.
2002 / ISBN 0-85364-971-5 / xxiv + 272pp

Paul Barker
The Triumph of Grace in Deuteronomy
This book is a textual and theological analysis of the interaction between the sin and faithlessness of Israel and the grace of Yahweh in response, looking especially at Deuteronomy chapters 1–3, 8–10 and 29–30. The author argues that the grace of Yahweh is determinative for the ongoing relationship between Yahweh and Israel and that Deuteronomy anticipates and fully expects Israel to be faithless.
2004 / ISBN 1-84227-226-8

Emil Bartos
Deification in Eastern Orthodox Theology
An Evaluation and Critique of the Theology of Dumitru Staniloae
Bartos studies a fundamental yet neglected aspect of Orthodox theology: deification. By examining the doctrines of anthropology, christology, soteriology and ecclesiology as they relate to deification, he provides an important contribution to contemporary dialogue between Eastern and Western theologians.
1999 / ISBN 0-85364-956-1 / xii + 370pp

Jonathan F. Bayes
The Weakness of the Law
God's Law and the Christian in New Testament Perspective
A study of the four New Testament books which refer to the law as weak (Acts, Romans, Galatians, Hebrews) leads to a defence of the third use in the Reformed debate about the law in the life of the believer.
2000 / ISBN 0-85364-957-X / xii + 244pp

Mark Bonnington
The Antioch Episode of Galatians 2:11-14 in Historical and Cultural Context
The Galatians 2 'incident' in Antioch over table-fellowship suggests significant disagreement between the leading apostles. This book analyses the background to the disagreement by locating the incident within the dynamics of social interaction between Jews and Gentiles. It proposes a new way of understanding the relationship between the individuals and issues involved.
2004 / ISBN 1-84227-050-8

Mark Bredin
Jesus, Revolutionary of Peace
A Nonviolent Christology in the Book of Revelation
This book aims to demonstrate that the figure of Jesus in the Book of Revelation can best be understood as an active nonviolent revolutionary.
2003 / ISBN 1-84227-153-9 / xviii + 260pp

James Bruce
Prophecy, Miracles, Angels *and* Heavenly Light?
'De virtutibus': *The Eschatology, Pneumatology and Missiology of Adomnán's* Life of Columba
This book surveys approaches to the marvellous in hagiography, providing the first critique of Plummer's hypothesis of Irish saga origin. It then analyses the uniquely systematized phenomena in the *Life of Columba* from Adomnán's seventh-century theological perspective, identifying the coming of the eschatological Kingdom as the key to understanding.
2004 / ISBN 1-84227-227-6

Colin J. Bulley
The Priesthood of Some Believers
Developments from the General to the Special Priesthood in the Christian Literature of the First Three Centuries
The first in-depth treatment of early Christian texts on the priesthood of all believers shows that the developing priesthood of the ordained related closely to the division between laity and clergy and had deleterious effects on the practice of the general priesthood.
2000 / ISBN 1-84227-034-6 / xii + 336pp

Iain D. Campbell
Fixing the Indemnity
The Life and Work of George Adam Smith
When Old Testament scholar George Adam Smith (1856–1942) delivered the Lyman Beecher lectures at Yale University in 1899 he confidently declared that 'modern criticism has won its war against traditional theories. It only remains to fix the amount of the indemnity.' In this biography, Iain D. Campbell assesses Smith's critical approach to the Old Testament and evaluates its consequences, showing that Smith's life and work still raises questions about the relationship between biblical scholarship and evangelical faith.
2004 / ISBN 1-84227-228-4

Daniel J-S Chae
Paul as Apostle to the Gentiles
His Apostolic Self-awareness and its Influence on the Soteriological Argument in Romans
Opposing 'the post-Holocaust interpretation of Romans', Daniel Chae competently demonstrates that Paul argues for the equality of Jew and Gentile in Romans. Chae's fresh exegetical interpretation is academically outstanding and spiritually encouraging.
1997 / ISBN 0-85364-829-8 / xiv + 378pp

Luke L. Cheung
The Genre, Composition and Hermeneutics of the Epistle of James
The present work examines the employment of the wisdom genre with a certain compositional structure and the interpretation of the law through the Jesus' tradition of the double love command by the author of the Epistle of James to serve his purpose in promoting perfection and warning against doubleness among the eschatologically renewed people of God in the Diaspora.
2003 / ISBN 1-84227-062-1 / xvi + 372pp

Andrew C. Clark
Parallel Lives
The Relation of Paul to the Apostles in the Lucan Perspective
This study of the Peter-Paul parallels in Acts argues that their purpose was to emphasize the themes of continuity in salvation history and the unity of the Jewish and Gentile missions. New light is shed on Luke's literary techniques, partly through a comparison with Plutarch.
2001 / 1-84227-035-4 / xviii + 386pp

Andrew D. Clarke
Secular and Christian Leadership in Corinth
A Socio-Historical and Exegetical Study of 1 Corinthians 1–6
This volume is an investigation into the leadership structures and dynamics
of first-century Roman Corinth. These are compared with the practice of
leadership in the Corinthian Christian community which are reflected in 1
Corinthians 1–6, and contrasted with Paul's own principles of Christian
leadership.

2004 / ISBN 1-84227-229-2 / xii + 188pp

Sylvia I. Collinson
Making Disciples
The Significance of Jesus' Educational Strategy for Today's Church
This study examines the biblical practice of discipling, formulates a defini-
tion, and makes comparisons with modern models of education. A recom-
mendation is made for greater attention to its practice today.

2004 / ISBN 1-84227-116-4

Stephen M. Dunning
The Crisis and the Quest
A Kierkegaardian Reading of Charles Williams
Employing Kierkegaardian categories and analysis, this study investigates
both the central crisis in Charles Williams's authorship between hermetism
and Christianity (Kierkegaard's Religions A and B), and the quest to
resolve this crisis, a quest that ultimately presses the bounds of orthodoxy.

2000 / ISBN 0-85364-985-5 / xxiv + 254pp

Keith Ferdinando
The Triumph of Christ in African Perspective
A Study of Demonology and Redemption in the African Context
The book explores the implications of the gospel for traditional African
fears of occult aggression. It analyses such traditional approaches to
suffering and biblical responses to fears of demonic evil, concluding with
an evaluation of African beliefs from the perspective of the gospel.

1999 / ISBN 0-85364-830-1 / xviii + 450pp

Stephen Finamore
God, Order and Chaos
René Girard and the Apocalypse
Readers are often disturbed by the images of destruction in the book of
Revelation and unsure why they are unleashed after the exaltation of Jesus.
This book examines past approaches to these texts and uses René Girard's
theories to revive some old ideas and propose some new ones.

2004 / ISBN 1-84227-197-0

Andrew Goddard
Living the Word, Resisting the World
The Life and Thought of Jacques Ellul
This work offers a definitive study of both the life and thought of the
French Reformed thinker Jacques Ellul (1912-1994). It will prove an
indispensable resource for those interested in this influential theologian
and sociologist and for Christian ethics and political thought generally.
2002 / ISBN 1-84227-053-2 / xxiv + 378pp

Ruth Gouldbourne
The Flesh and the Feminine
Gender and Theology in the Writings of Caspar Schwenckfeld
Caspar Schwenckfeld and his movement exemplify one of the radical
communities of the sixteenth century. Challenging theological and
liturgical norms, they also found themselves challenging social and
particularly gender assumptions. In this book, the issues of the relationship
between radical theology and the understanding of gender are considered.
2004 / ISBN 1-84227-048-6

Scott J. Hafemann
Suffering and Ministry in the Spirit
Paul's Defence of His Ministry in II Corinthians 2:14–3:3
Shedding new light on the way Paul defended his apostleship, the author
offers a careful, detailed study of 2 Corinthians 2:14–3:3 linked with other
key passages throughout 1 and 2 Corinthians. Demonstrating the unity and
coherence of Paul's argument in this passage, the author shows that Paul's
suffering served as the vehicle for revealing God's power and glory
through the Spirit.
2000 / ISBN 0-85364-967-7 / xiv + 262pp

Roger Hitching
The Church and Deaf People
*A Study of Identity, Communication and Relationships with Special
Reference to the Ecclesiology of Jürgen Moltmann*
In *The Church and Deaf People* Roger Hitching sensitively examines the
history and present experience of deaf people and finds similarities
between aspects of sign language and Moltmann's theological method that
'open up' new ways of understanding theological concepts.
2003 / ISBN 1-84227-222-5 / xxii + 236pp

John G. Kelly
One God, One People
The Differentiated Unity of the People of God
in the Theology of Jürgen Moltmann
The author expounds and critiques Moltmann's doctrine of God and high-lights the systematic connections between it and Moltmann's influential discussion of Israel. He then proposes a fresh approach to Jewish-Christian relations building on Moltmann's work using insights from Habermas and Rawls.
2004 / ISBN 0-85346-969-3

Mark F.W. Lovatt
Confronting the Will-to-Power
A Reconsideration of the Theology of Reinhold Niebuhr
Confronting the Will-to-Power is an analysis of the theology of Reinhold Niebuhr, arguing that his work is an attempt to identify, and provide a practical theological answer to, the existence and nature of human evil.
2001 / ISBN 1-84227-054-0 / xviii + 216pp

Neil B. MacDonald
Karl Barth and the Strange New World within the Bible
Barth, Wittgenstein, and the Metadilemmas of the Enlightenment
Barth's discovery of the strange new world within the Bible is examined in the context of Kant, Hume, Overbeck, and, most importantly, Wittgenstein. MacDonald covers some fundamental issues in theology today: epistemology, the final form of the text and biblical truth-claims.
2000 / ISBN 0-85364-970-7 / xxvi + 374pp

Douglas S. McComisky
Lukan Theology in the Light of the Gospel's Literary Structure
Luke's Gospel was purposefully written with theology embedded in its patterned literary structure. A critical analysis of this cyclical structure provides new windows into Luke's interpretation of the individual pericopes comprising the gospel and illuminates several of his theological interests.
2004 / ISBN 1-84227-148-2

Gillian McCulloch

The Deconstruction of Dualism in Theology

With Reference to Ecofeminist Theology and New Age Spirituality

This book challenges eco-theological anti-dualism in Christian theology, arguing that dualism has a twofold function in Christian religious discourse. Firstly, it enables us to express the discontinuities and divisions that are part of the process of reality. Secondly, dualistic language allows us to express the mysteries of divine transcendence/immanence and the survival of the soul without collapsing into monism and materialism, both of which are problematic for Christian epistemology.

2002 / ISBN 1-84227-044-3 / xii + 282pp

Leslie McCurdy

Attributes and Atonement

The Holy Love of God in the Theology of P.T. Forsyth

Attributes and Atonement is an intriguing full-length study of P.T. Forsyth's doctrine of the cross as it relates particularly to God's holy love. It includes an unparalleled bibliography of both primary and secondary material relating to Forsyth.

1999 / ISBN 0-85364-833-6 / xiv + 328pp

Nozomu Miyahira

Towards a Theology of the Concord of God

A Japanese Perspective on the Trinity

This book introduces a new Japanese theology and a unique Trinitarian formula based on the Japanese intellectual climate: three betweennesses and one concord. It also presents a new interpretation of the Trinity, a co-subordinationism, which is in line with orthodox Trinitarianism; each single person of the Trinity is eternally and equally subordinate (or serviceable) to the other persons, so that they retain the mutual dynamic equality.

2000 / ISBN 0-85364-863-8 / xiv + 256pp

Stephen Motyer

Your Father the Devil?

A New Approach to John and 'The Jews'

Who are 'the Jews' in John's Gospel? Defending John against the charge of anti-semitism, Motyer argues that, far from demonizing the Jews, the Gospel seeks to present Jesus as 'Good News for Jews' in a late first century setting.

1997 / ISBN 0-85364-832-8 / xiv + 260pp

Eddy José Muskus
The Origins and Early Development of Liberation Theology in Latin America
With Particular Reference to Gustavo Gutiérrez
This work challenges the fundamental premise of Liberation Theology, 'opting for the poor', and its claim that Christ is found in them. It also argues that Liberation Theology emerged as a direct result of the failure of the Roman Catholic Church in Latin America.
2002 / ISBN 0-85364-974-X / xiv + 296pp

Esther Ng
Reconstructing Christian Origins?
The Feminist Theology of Elizabeth Schüssler Fiorenza: An Evaluation
In a detailed evaluation, the author challenges Elizabeth Schüssler Fiorenza's reconstruction of early Christian origins and her underlying presuppositions. The author also presents her own views on women's roles both then and now.
2002 / ISBN 1-84227-055-9 / xxiv + 468pp

Robin Parry
Old Testament Story and Christian Ethics
The Rape of Dinah as a Case Study
What is the role of story in ethics and, more particularly, what is the role of Old Testament story in Christian ethics? This book, drawing on the work of contemporary philosophers, argues that narrative is crucial in the ethical shaping of people and, drawing on the work of contemporary Old Testament scholars, that story plays a key role in Old Testament ethics. Parry then argues that when situated in canonical context Old Testament stories can be reappropriated by Christian readers in their own ethical formation. The shocking story of the rape of Dinah and the massacre of the Shechemites provides a fascinating case study for exploring the parameters within which Christian ethical appropriations of Old Testament stories can live.
2004 / ISBN 1-84227-210-1

Ian Paul
Power to See the World Anew
The Value of Paul Ricoeur's Hermeneutic of Metaphor in Interpreting the Symbolism of Revelation 12 and 13
This book is a study of the hermeneutics of metaphor of Paul Ricoeur, one of the most important writers on hermeneutics and metaphor of the last century. It sets out the key points of his theory, important criticisms of his work, and how his approach, modified in the light of these criticisms, offers a methodological framework for reading apocalyptic texts.
2004 / ISBN 1-84227-056-7

David Powys
'Hell': A Hard Look at a Hard Question
The Fate of the Unrighteous in New Testament Thought
This comprehensive treatment seeks to unlock the original meaning of terms and phrases long thought to support the traditional doctrine of hell. It concludes that there is an alternative – one which is more biblical, and which can positively revive the rationale for Christian mission.
1997 / ISBN 0-85364-831-X / xxii + 478pp

Anna Robbins
Methods in the Madness
Diversity in Twentieth-Century Christian Social Ethics
The author compares the ethical methods of Walter Rauschenbusch, Reinhold Niebuhr and others. She argues that unless Christians are clear about the ways that theology and philosophy are expressed practically they may lose the ability to discuss social ethics across contexts, let alone reach effective agreements.
2004 / ISBN 1-84227-211-X

Ed Rybarczyk
Beyond Salvation
Eastern Orthodoxy and Classical Pentecostalism on becoming like Christ
At first glance eastern Orthodoxy and Classical Pentecostalism seem quite distinct. This groundbreaking study shows that they share much in common, especially as it concerns the experiential elements of following Christ. Both traditions assert that authentic Christianity transcends the wooden categories of modernism.
2003 / ISBN 1-84227-144-X / xxiii + 379pp

Signe Sandsmark
Is World View Neutral Education Possible and Desirable?
A Christian Response to Liberal Arguments
(Published jointly with The Stapleford Centre)
This book discusses reasons for belief in world view neutrality, and argues that 'neutral' education will have a hidden, but strong world view influence. It discusses the place for Christian education in the common school.
2000 / ISBN 0-85364-973-1 / xiv + 182pp

Rosalind Selby
The Comical Doctrine
Can a Gospel Convey Truth?
This book argues that the Gospel breaks through postmodernity's critique of truth and the referential possibilities of textuality and its gift of grace. With a rigorous, philosophical challenge to modernist and postmodernist assumptions, it offers an alternative epistemology to all who would still read with faith *and* with academic credibility.
2004 / ISBN 1-84227-212-8

Hazel Sherman
Reading Zechariah
The Allegorical Tradition of Biblical Interpretation through the Commentaries of Didymus the Blind and Theodore of Mopsuestia
A close reading of the commentary on Zechariah by Didymus the Blind alongside that of Theodore of Mopsuestia suggests that popular categorising of Antiochene and Alexandrian biblical exegesis as 'historical' or 'allegorical' is inadequate and misleading.
2004 / ISBN 1-84227-213-6

Andrew Sloane
On Being a Christian in the Academy
Nicholas Wolterstorff and the Practice of Christian Scholarship
An exposition and critical appraisal of Nicholas Wolterstorff's epistemology in the light of the philosophy of science, and an application of his thought to the practice of Christian scholarship.
2003 / ISBN 1-84227-058-3 / xvi + 274pp

Daniel Strange
The Possibility of Salvation Among the Unevangelised
An Analysis of Inclusivism in Recent Evangelical Theology
For evangelical theologians the 'fate of the unevangelised' impinges upon fundamental tenets of evangelical identity. The position known as 'inclusivism', defined by the belief that the unevangelised can be ontologically saved by Christ whilst being epistemologically unaware of him, has been defended most vigorously by the Canadian evangelical Clark H. Pinnock. Through a detailed analysis and critique of Pinnock's work, this book examines a cluster of issues surrounding the unevangelised and its implications for christology, soteriology and the doctrine of revelation.
2002 / ISBN 1-84227-047-8 / xviii + 362pp

G. Michael Thomas
The Extent of the Atonement
A Dilemma for Reformed Theology from Calvin to the Consensus
This is a study of the way Reformed theology addressed the question, 'Did Christ die for all, or for the elect only?', commencing with John Calvin, and including debates with Lutheranism, the Synod of Dort and the teaching of Moïse Amyraut.
1997 / ISBN 0-85364-828-X / x + 278pp

Mark D. Thompson
A Sure Ground on which to Stand
The Relation of Authority and Interpretive Method in
Luther's Approach to Scripture
The best interpreter of Luther is Luther himself. Unfortunately many modern studies have superimposed contemporary agendas upon this sixteenth-century Reformer's writings. This fresh study examines Luther's own words to find an explanation for his robust confidence in the Scriptures, a confidence that generated the famous 'stand' at Worms in 1521.
2003 / ISBN 1-84227-145-8 / xvi + 322pp

Graham Tomlin
The Power of the Cross
Theology and the Death of Christ in Paul, Luther and Pascal
This book explores the theology of the cross in St Paul, Luther and Pascal. It offers new perspectives on the theology of each, and some implications for the nature of power, apologetics, theology and church life in a postmodern context.
1999 / ISBN 0-85364-984-7 / xiv + 344pp

Kevin Walton
Thou Traveller Unknown
The Presence and Absence of God in the Jacob Narrative
The author offers a fresh reading of the story of Jacob in the book of Genesis through the paradox of divine presence and absence. The work also seeks to make a contribution to Pentateuchal studies by bringing together a close reading of the final text with historical critical insights, doing justice to the text's historical depth, final form and canonical status.
2003 / ISBN 1-84227-059-1 / xvi + 238pp

Graham J. Watts
Revelation and the Spirit
A Comparative Study of the Relationship between the Doctrine of Revelation and Pneumatology in the Theology of Eberhard Jüngel and of Wolfhart Pannenberg
The relationship between revelation and pneumatology is relatively unexplored. This approach offers a fresh angle on two important twentieth century theologians and raises pneumatological questions which are theologically crucial and relevant to mission in a post modern culture.
2003 / ISBN 1-84227-104-0 / xxii + 232pp

Alistair Wilson
When Will These Things Happen?
A Study of Jesus as Judge in Matthew 21–25
This study seeks to allow Matthew's carefully constructed presentation of Jesus to be given full weight in the modern evaluation of Jesus' eschatology. Careful analysis of the text of Matthew 21–25 reveals Jesus to be standing firmly in the Jewish prophetic and wisdom traditions as he proclaims and enacts imminent judgement on the Jewish authorities then boldly claims the central role in the final and universal judgement.
2004 / ISBN 1-84227-146-6 / xvi + 292pp

Lindsay Wilson
Joseph Wise and Otherwise
The Intersection of Covenant and Wisdom in Genesis 37–50
This book offers a careful literary reading of Genesis 37–50 that argues that the Joseph story contains both strong covenant themes and many wisdom-like elements. The connections between the two helps to explore how covenant and wisdom might intersect in an integrated biblical theology.
2004 / ISBN 1-84227-140-7

Nigel G. Wright
Disavowing Constantine
Mission, Church and the Social Order in the Theologies of
John Howard Yoder and Jürgen Moltmann
This book is a timely restatement of a radical theology of church and state
in the Anabaptist and Baptist tradition. Dr Wright constructs his argument
in dialogue and debate with Yoder and Moltmann, major contributors to a
free church perspective.
2000 / ISBN 0-85364-978-2 / xvi + 252pp

Stephen I. Wright
The Voice of Jesus
Studies in the Interpretation of Six Gospel Parables
This literary study considers how the 'voice' of Jesus has been heard in
different periods of parable interpretation, and how the categories of figure
and trope may help us towards a sensitive reading of the parables today.
2000 / ISBN 0-85364-975-8 / xiv + 280pp

The Paternoster Press
PO Box 300,
Carlisle,
Cumbria CA3 0QS,
United Kingdom
Web: www.paternoster-publishing.com